THE

HOLY SPIRIT'S

INTERPRETATION

OF THE

NEW TESTAMENT

A Course in Understanding and Acceptance

(NTI)

First published by O Books, 2007
O Books is an imprint of John Hunt Publishing
Ltd., The Bothy, Deershot Lodge, Park Lane,
Ropley, Hants, SO24 0BE, UK
office1@o-books.net
www.o-books.net

Distribution in:

UK and Europe
Orca Book Services
orders@orcabookservices.co.uk
Tel: 01202 665432 Fax: 01202 666219 Int. code
(44)

USA and Canada
NBN
custserv@nbnbooks.com
Tel: 1 800 462 6420 Fax: 1 800 338 4550

Australia and New Zealand
Brumby Books
sales@brumbybooks.com.au
Tel: 61 3 9761 5535 Fax: 61 3 9761 7095

Far East (offices in Singapore, Thailand, Hong
Kong, Taiwan)
Pansing Distribution Pte Ltd
kemal@pansing.com
Tel: 65 6319 9939 Fax: 65 6462 5761

South Africa
Alternative Books
altbook@peterhyde.co.za
Tel: 021 555 4027 Fax: 021 447 1430

Text copyright Regina Dawn Akers 2008

Design: Stuart Davies

ISBN: 978 1 84694 085 9

A CIP catalogue record for this book is available
from the British Library.

Printed in the US by Maple Vail

O Books operates a distinctive and ethical publishing philosophy in
all areas of its business. It has no central office. The publishers are a
group of people who work together globally, from sheds and homes,
doing something they enjoy, which happens to be producing books.
As far as the production goes, no trees were cut down to print
this book. The paper is 100% recycled, with 50% of that being
post-consumer. It's processed chlorine-free, and has no fibre from
ancient or endangered forests. This production method for this print
run saved approx. 3 trees, 1400 gallons of wastewater, 1500 pounds
of solid waste, 300 pounds of greenhouse gases and 550 kilowatt
hours of electricity.

THE
HOLY SPIRIT'S
INTERPRETATION
OF THE
NEW TESTAMENT

A Course in Understanding and Acceptance

(NTI)

Regina Dawn Akers

BOOKS

Winchester, UK
Washington, USA

CONTENTS

OVERVIEW OF CONTENTS

Introduction

How This Interpretation Came to Be: The scribe's story – A brief synopsis of the scribe and how she came to write down this interpretation.

How NTI Came to Be: The story of writing it down – Describes the process used to write this interpretation.

How to Read NTI: Recommendations for the reader – Guidelines to help the reader determine a useful way of reading NTI.

NTI Matthew – Teaches that surrender and sorting thoughts (mind-watching) are key to enlightenment. Also introduces the idea that the world is not real.

NTI Mark – Retells the story of Jesus' three year ministry by showing us a Jesus that is more like us. Through this story, we see how we can become enlightened like Jesus. We are also able to learn from the mistakes and right-steps of others within the story.

NTI Luke – Focuses on judgment and separation-based thinking as obstacles that must be let go in order to realize enlightenment. Helps the reader to question the value he places on his own judgment and thinking so he will increase his willingness to let them go.

NTI John – Emphasizes that all people are the same and all people have the Light of God within them. Provides an overview of steps that must be taken in order to recognize the Light within oneself.

NTI Acts – Teaches the reader how to know and follow the Holy Spirit's guidance within the world. Also introduces the first three stages of the path of awakening.

NTI Romans – Helps the reader to see the metaphysical link between judgment and the continuation of illusion. Helps the reader to see how acceptance is necessary to awakening.

NTI 1 Corinthians – Similar to Buddhism and Taoism, this book teaches the reader to become an "empty shell" in order to release the false concepts of the world and be filled with true wisdom or enlightenment.

NTI 2 Corinthians – Teaches the true concept of cause and effect; that is, cause is in the mind and the world is its effect. Introduces the fourth stage on the path of awakening, which is enlightenment within the world.

NTI Galatians – A summary of key ideas before stepping into the deeper ideas that are about to come. A simple process for forgiveness is also taught.

NTI Ephesians – Teaches the law of Love, which is the law of Mind or the law of thought. This book shows how oneness is all that is and how oneness is in perfect operation now, even within the illusion of separation.

NTI Philippians – Teaches the reader how to ensure that his motive is placed in alignment with his faith, so that he is leading himself consistently toward the experience of enlightenment.

NTI Colossians –Combines the knowledge taught in 2 Corinthians with the knowledge taught in Ephesians in order to impress upon the reader that *he is cause* of all that he experiences.

NTI 1 Thessalonians – Teaches the reader how to recognize when he has strayed from the path of his intent, so he may choose to step back onto the path through willingness.

NTI 2 Thessalonians – Begins to teach the reader how to look beyond the false self/identity to the truth of what he is.

NTI 1 Timothy – Teaches the reader that "personhood" is a concept that blocks truth. Leads the reader to give willingness to let go of this false concept.

NTI 2 Timothy – Teaches the reader how to release the darkness within the mind (guilt, fear, unworthiness) by experiencing the feelings as they come up without believing the thoughts that accompany them.

NTI Titus – Teaches the taming of the thinking mind, so that it becomes less of a hindrance on the spiritual path.

NTI Philemon – Begins to point directly to what we *are* by teaching, "You are everything."

NTI Hebrews – Encourages the reader to increase his practice by helping him to recognize that awakening is his one true desire.

NTI James – Teaches the reader how to be the leader in his own awakening.

NTI 1 Peter – Teaches that a veil of misperception is all that blocks truth from our awareness. Leads the reader to give willingness to let go of misperceptions.

NTI 2 Peter – Teaches acceptance of true abundance.

NTI 1 John – Provides "tests" the reader can use to find out how much his mind/awareness is focused on illusion and misperception. Helps the reader to see that Love is all that is by helping the reader to see through the eyes of Spirit.

NTI 2 John – Leads the reader to give willingness to listen only to the Holy Spirit now.

NTI 3 John – Helps the reader to realize that he is beginning to accept everyone as one with him.

NTI Jude – Teaches that there is nothing and no one outside of the mind.

NTI Revelation – Teaches the steps of final purification and acceptance of the experience of enlightenment.

About the Cover – Describes the guidance provided for the cover design.

Question and Answer Index – Both an index and a study guide, this tool was developed to help readers find NTI answers to spiritual questions.

INTRODUCTION

HOW THIS INTERPRETATION CAME TO BE: THE SCRIBE'S STORY

Regina Dawn Akers grew up in middle-America as a Christian. Her religious training came from more than one Christian faith, and she was aware of differences in Biblical interpretation within the Christian community. She was also aware of the similarities that crossed all denominational boundaries, the most important of which was the statement, "God is love." Regina knew in her heart that this must be true, and she yearned to know God's love perfectly.

Although Regina was fascinated by all religions, she never felt to settle with any particular religion. She was driven by an inner desire she was not yet fully aware of, and Regina needed time to discover the calling within her heart.

In April of 2004, Regina spontaneously awakened to her own desire while praying. She describes that prayer this way:

"As I was praying, I felt overcome by a desire to be useful. I wanted nothing more than to be completely useful to God for the rest of my life. I told Him that I would learn anything He wanted me to learn and do anything He wanted me to do. I just asked him to *please* make me useful."

Regina began studying *A Course in Miracles*. She also began to receive guidance, visions and dreams that educated her about spiritual principles introduced in the *Course*. With the help of this guidance, Regina learned quickly and with clarity, and she willingly practiced everything that she learned.

In November of 2004, Regina experienced a vision during meditation. "But this vision was different," she explains. "It didn't seem to come to educate me like the others did. This one seemed to have a message for me.

"I saw myself in a dark cavern. There were several dark passageways leading out of the cavern, and there were people in the cavern who wanted to find their way out. I stood at the bottom of the cavern near the entrances to the passageways. I held an armful of lit candles. As people passed by me, I handed them a candle. They used the candle to guide them as they selected a passageway and started their journey out of the cavern."

Regina didn't want to guess the meaning of her vision, so she went to the keyboard and said a prayer. She asked the Holy Spirit to be very clear with her so she wouldn't misunderstand His message. Then she began to type without thinking. This is the message that she typed:

"Teacher of God. That is my Name. I have other names, but they are all the same. They mean Teacher of God. That is what is needed now, and that is what I need you for. You can write for me. You are doing it now. Write, teacher of God, and help me share the Light. There are many who need us. Teach, teacher. That is what you are for. That is why you are here. That is how you will learn. You are the teacher. Don't be afraid. I am with you always."

At first, Regina was frightened by her experience. With the help of calming thoughts that came into her mind, Regina let go of her fear. She began to write with the Holy Spirit the following day. At first, several days would pass between writings. In the spring of 2005, short writings began to come daily. Then in June 2005, Regina received this message from the Holy Spirit:

"The New Testament is a symbol, just as you are a symbol and the words I share through you are a symbol. What they point to is Truth.

"In order to understand the symbol, one must accept the Love of Christ. One prepares himself to accept that Love by recognizing he does not understand the symbol, and then he asks for understanding. By opening up to receive understanding without judgment, he opens up to accept the Love of Christ. With that Love comes Christ's knowledge, for they are the same and inseparable. Then the meaning that is beyond the words is understood as a Light that shines for all who look to see.

"Those who have ears now will listen. For others, salvation will wait. There is no loss in God. Ask and you will receive *because* it will be given you. It is a gift of Love given to one who recognizes he has forgotten Love, and so he asks that its remembrance be given him in Grace and Love. Love cannot say no to a request for Love.

"Go now and ask. It will be given you."

Regina left her career and home in Massachusetts and moved with her young daughter to North Carolina. After the move was complete, she began the work of listening to *The Holy Spirit's Interpretation of the New Testament* (NTI).

In March of 2006, Regina received guidance to start *The Foundation for the Holy Spirit.* The purpose of the foundation is to provide resources, teaching and counseling to help individuals become Self-Reliant with their own inner guide, the Holy Spirit. Regina transferred the copyright for NTI to the foundation. Regina works with the 501(c)(3) non-profit foundation as a teacher and director.

How NTI Came to Be: The story of writing it down
Regina learned that scribing is a process of letting go. As she read the New Testament, she found that her mind was filled with thoughts about what she read. Sometimes she felt she understood what she read. Sometimes she seemed to judge what she read. But Regina learned that as she held to her own thoughts regarding what she read, she could not hear the Holy Spirit's thoughts. Regina learned to empty her mind by letting go of any thoughts she had about her reading. She found that when she came to the point of complete emptiness within her mind, desiring only the words of the Holy Spirit, a Voice would come streaming into her

mind. At this point, Regina would begin scribbling into a spiral notebook as fast as she could, focusing on capturing the words that she heard.

Regina was often resistant to the interpretation she heard as she wrote it down. The words were teaching at a level that was beyond her current spiritual understanding, and this was difficult for her to accept. However, Regina chose to be more than the scribe of NTI. She chose to be its first student. So she spent each day giving willingness to accept the message she had received that morning. In this way, Regina seemed to be lifted up by the writing of NTI.

After 13½ months of scribing NTI, Regina received guidance to "validate" NTI by comparing the typed manuscript to the original writing in the spiral notebooks. Two others joined Regina in this validation process. The original hand-written notes were read aloud and compared to the typed manuscript. Missing sentences and paragraphs were added to the manuscript and the original wording was preserved. This published version of NTI is the original version as Regina heard it from the Holy Spirit. Only very few and extremely minor changes have been made for readability.

How to Read NTI: Recommendations for the reader

NTI is somewhat like a spiral staircase. It seems to begin teaching on a specific step, and it continually ascends from there. As a result, looking for consistency within NTI can be confusing, because symbols and concepts change as one ascends the staircase. We recommend putting aside the thinking, judging and analyzing mind as you read NTI, just as Regina put that mind aside to write down NTI. Ask for understanding from the Holy Spirit and give willingness to accept that understanding without judgment. If you will do this, understanding will be given by your inner guide.

NTI is a course in understanding and acceptance. Like many courses, NTI builds upon the principles that it teaches. For this reason, many students may find it helpful to start at the beginning and read toward the end as you would a novel. However, you may also find it useful to take NTI more slowly than a novel. Acceptance of one teaching is helpful before moving on to the next level of teaching within the course. Each NTI book seems to present a new level of teaching that is higher than the book that preceded it.

NTI is an interpretation that is much like an interpretative dance. Sometimes the interpretation seems to stay close to that which is being interpreted. Other times the Holy Spirit seems to spin off into a freer interpretation in order to carry the reader to a new place of understanding. Whenever NTI sticks close to the original writing in the New Testament, a book icon is presented. This icon indicates that it may be helpful to reference the annotated Bible verses before reading the interpretation. Whenever the icon is not presented, reading the Bible is optional.

NTI uses many of the same words and symbols when referring to the divine and when referring to the human. Capitalization is used to indicate the divine whenever that distinction is helpful to understanding.

The guidelines presented here are suggestions only. Above and beyond these guidelines, we recommend that you get in touch with your own inner guidance to find the best way for you to read and study NTI. Study NTI in the way you feel prompted to from within. Your inner guide always knows the best way for you to attain spiritual growth.

If you have questions about NTI or would like to share your NTI experience, please visit the NTI Discussion Group at:

http://groups.yahoo.com/group/NTIDiscussionGroup/

THE HOLY SPIRIT'S INTERPRETATION OF MATTHEW

NTI Matthew, Chapter 1

📖(v 1 – 25)[1]Joseph had a question in his mind, and he was unsure about what he should do. [2]Although he had a thought as to what he should do, he did not consider it decided. [3]He left his mind open, because he was unsure, and in his choice to remain open, he asked for wisdom. [4]And the wisdom was given him. [5]He recognized it, and he did as it asked.

[6]This is a symbol for you to follow in all things. [7]Ideas may come, but if you do not know they are of Me, consider them not decided. [8]Be open to new guidance, but do not worry if different guidance does not come. [9]If you do not feel clearly that you are to do something different than that which you thought to do, do that which you thought to do, and trust that it is from Me.

NTI Matthew, Chapter 2

(v 1 – 23)[1]The truth is shown through guidance. [2]The entire route you are to follow is not revealed from beginning to end all at once, but it is revealed to you step-by-step. [3]Trust your Lord, the God within, which guides you. [4]It guides you now. [5]Do not question, "Where is this taking me?" [6]Have faith it is for the good of all and the purpose of oneness, and it will certainly bring you great joy!

NTI Matthew, Chapter 3

📖(v 1 – 17)[1]This is not a story of form. [2]It is a story of mind. [3]John is the observer, the one who told you sorting of thought is necessary. [4]He is the one that called upon you to pay attention and choose a different way of thought. [5]He pointed in the direction that would perform the sorting for you, to the one that would cherish and honor your thoughts of love while undoing permanently your thoughts that never were. [6]He called this one the Son of God, and this one is in your mind, waiting for you to accept Him now.

NTI Matthew, Chapter 4

(v 1 – 25)[1]With the Spirit, you shall examine your thoughts. [2]It is your true Spirit that will guide you to choose truly.

[3]Once the choice is made, the time of service will begin. [4]It is in this time that a gathering will begin. [5]You will gather around you that which is needed to serve, and the gathering shall be effortless and without thought.

[6]Once the mind has been cleansed, the following will be effortless. [7]First focus on the cleansing, and in peace you shall know that you are led truly.

NTI Matthew, Chapter 5

(v 3)[1]Blessed are the poor in spirit, for they are already one with God.

(v 4)[1]Blessed are those who have tired of this world, for they will be comforted.

(v 5)[1]Blessed are the peaceful and joyous, for they will see the world as it really is.

(v 6)[1]Blessed are those who seek truth above all else, for it will be given them.

(v 7)[1]Blessed are those who forgive their evil thoughts, for they will find the light that is their true Source.

(v 8)[1]Blessed are the enlightened, for they know.

(v 9)[1]Blessed are they who share My Word in love, for they shall shine like beacons for all men to see, and they shall be recognized as the Son that *is*.

(v 10)[1]Blessed are those who see only Love in their brothers, for they know what they have found.

(v 11 – 12)[1]Blessed is he who has removed value from this world and placed it in Heaven, for he knows where his treasure lies.

[2]Blessed are the ones who know their Father, for they know the reason they rejoice. [3]Their joy is one, because it is whole and complete as it has always been, and so it is perfect.

[4]Rise up today, my brothers, and hold hands within your hearts. [5]Love one another, and in so doing, you give the gift of love to your Father. [6]Be at peace and rest in contentment with one another, for all is well as only it could ever be. [7]Peace abides in you today and forever. [8]Amen.

(v 13 - 16)[1]The world is meaningless. [2]All that brings meaning to the world is you, for you are all there is. [3]Your truth is your light. [4]It is your truth that shall shine and be known, that all men may see their truth within you and know it is within them too.

(v 17 - 20)[1]The laws of men are based on the laws of God, but the laws of men are a reflection of truth and not truth itself. [2]One cannot find truth by following the laws of men if there is hatred or fear in his heart. [3]The laws of men must be followed in true love and intent for a witness to occur unto yourself. [4]For when you have discovered the law within your heart and you follow the guidance of true law that is shared from within, you follow the path of righteousness that will lead you from a focus on this world to the light of the kingdom of Heaven.

(v 21 - 22)[1]The law of men is written to protect men and to teach them to behave, but the law of the Heart is beyond this world. [2]It is like a path that you shall follow to higher ground. [3]Its purpose is not to protect man from man, but to lead a man from his manhood to his true Self, which is beyond the self he knows when he limits righteousness to the laws of men.

(v 23, 24)[1]Your brother is one with you in the Heart, and so it is the heart that must be healed. [2]Do not carry a grievance against your brother within your heart, regardless of what he may have seemed to do. [3]Righteousness does not abide in the laws or customs of men. [4]Righteousness abides beyond the laws and customs of men. [5]Forgive your brother, that you may love him again in the joy and happiness of the Heart, and in your dance with him, you will find what righteousness is.

(v 25, 26)[1]The one that judges the hatred you leave in your heart is but yourself. [2]You cannot find joy within hatred, for hatred is like a prison and the jailer is but yourself. [3]Free yourself from your prison of pain. [4]Let go of that which you think your brother has done to you. [5]It is not important. [6]It but keeps you imprisoned within a limited mind and away from the unlimited, which is but your Self. [7]Let go of all your grievances against your brother, no matter how large or small they seem. [8]For they are all the same, and each one has the power to keep you imprisoned from your Self.

(v 27, 28)[1]The law of men is but a symbol for those who are not ready to accept the law of the Heart, for the law of the Heart is love. [2]One who loves his brother will not think a hurtful thought about his brother. [3]When hurtful thoughts come into his mind, he will let them go, for he does not want any thought in his mind that is not the thought of love. [4]In this way, his mind shall live in accordance with the law of the Heart, and the prison doors shall be opened, and he shall be freed, joined and dancing in celebration with his brother.

(v 29, 30)[1]Letting go of your grievances towards your brother may seem to be letting go of your self, for your own thoughts may tell you that you are justified in your anger, or your caution, for what your brother has done or may do to you. [2]But I tell you that thoughts of justification are like poisonous prison food. [3]Their purpose is to keep you sick and weak within the prison walls. [4]Rise up within the health of your heart and let these thoughts go. [5]Your goal now is freedom, and you will succeed in your goal by letting go of every thought that would keep you imprisoned. [6]For the hellish thoughts within your mind are your prison, and only by letting them go can you be free.

[7]Listen to Me. [8]I am sharing the secrets of your imprisonment and your freedom. [9]It is not My Will that you be imprisoned. [10]It is My Will that you be free. [11]Listen to Me. [12]Accept My Will as yours, and open your prison doors.

(v 31, 32)[1]Let not the law be confusing to you. [2]To follow the law without understanding it is useless. [3]The law is not a law of behavior. [4]What you do or do not do in itself is not important. [5]The law of God is written on the Heart. [6]It is a law that teaches there cannot be separateness. [7]Only by joining with one Will will you know God, and only by knowing God will you know your Self. [8]So do not go your separate ways within your heart. [9]That is the way of the world. [10]Walk together in your heart, joined and holding hands. [11]In this way, you shall walk into the light and welcome yourselves into the kingdom of Heaven.

(v 33 - 37)[1]It is not what you say or what you do that is important. [2]It is what you mean by what you say or what you do that matters. [3]Do you give to your brother because you love him and see him to be the same as you, or do you give because you believe that by your giving you will be made good? [4]I tell you, there is nothing that you can do or say that will make you good within your own mind. [5]Only by following the guidance within your Heart can you discover your Self, and the discovering will show you that you *are*. [6]With this vision, you will see your brother and the world with new eyes, and you will know that Love is all there is.

[7]So follow your guidance and do not doubt it. [8]It is leading you home to a new world, and from there you will find the bridge to Heaven. [9]With your Heart as your guide, you shall cross the bridge with your brothers.

(v 38 - 48)[1]With your eyes of judgment, you see many brothers doing different things. [2]You judge the things they do as good things or bad things. [3]Based on the judgments you have given to what they do, you judge your brothers as good or as bad. [4]In your judgments of them, you separate them from one another and from yourself. [5]And so you see many sons where the Father of Heaven sees only one. [6]For the Father of Heaven has declared that He has only one Son, and that Son is but an extension of Himself.

[7]Stop judging your brothers as good or bad or different. [8]Ask God within your heart to show Himself to you. [9]He will answer you by showing you that your brother's heart is the same as yours, and so you and your brother must be the same, and therefore, one. [10]For only by exceeding the laws of men to follow the law of the Heart can you find the truth that lies hidden there.

> [11]*God is Spirit, and Spirit is all there is,*
> *and so you and your brother must be Spirit too.*

[12]It is your Heart that knows this truth, so it is by following your Heart that you will be led to see the truth is true.

NTI Matthew, Chapter 6

(v 1 - 4)[1]If you are to walk the path of righteousness, all things must be done for the reason of the Heart. [2]To do anything for a purpose other than the purpose of the Heart, regardless of how righteous the act may seem to be, is to stray from your path. [3]You could become lost there.

[4]Listen. [5]Let the Heart that whispers truth lead you in all things. [6]Ask of it, and do as it guides. [7]Let not actions blind you. [8]It is not the action that matters, but the purpose that is given it.

(v 5 - 8)[1]Your time with your Father is precious and holy, so seek for this time in quiet. [2]Search your heart for what you would say to Him or for what you would ask. [3]Be not afraid of what you find there. [4]Your Father knows your Heart, my Son, and He leads you according to your Heart. [5]But you may not know your own Heart, so it is useful to seek there in quiet as you pray. [6]For if you do not know the prayers of your Heart, you may not recognize that they are answered. [7]But when you seek out your prayers in quiet and ask of the Father based on what you find, you will see that your prayers are answered quickly. [8]For the Father does not delay in answering the prayers of his Son's Heart. [9]The Father knows that it is the Heart that leads His Son to Him.

(v 9 - 13)[1]Pray like this according to what you find in your Heart:

[2]"Father, let me know You. [3]Let your kingdom dawn upon my mind, that I may be led by Your Will and become as one with it. [4]Let me hear Your Word within my mind. [5]Let my lessons be given me, that I may be closer to You through the actions of my day. [6]Let me forgive myself, as I know You have. [7]Let me see my brothers as innocent, as they truly are. [8]Let us watch our minds for evil thoughts that would trick and blind us to the Light within. [9]And let us let those thoughts go, so they may not cloud our minds from knowing the truth. [10]Amen."

(v 14, 15)[1]For in our sight within the Light, we shall see the innocence of the lamb. [2]It is within our brothers' hearts that he rests, as he rests also within our own. [3]But if clouds block the light within, our sight is limited by a darkened vision. [4]We cannot see what is there while our eyes rest surely on the dark.

(v 16 - 18)[1]And so remember your purpose in all things, and follow the guidance that comes from within. [2]It leads you, not so your brother will see how holy you are; it leads you, that you may discover the holiness within, that you may bow down at the altar there, and let the Heart be your loving master, whom you do not question.

(v 19 - 23)[1]Let your purpose guide you in all things, and let it be the true purpose of the Heart. [2]For the purposes of the world are like smoke screens that deceive you, promising rewards and happiness, but delivering not. [3]For every purpose of the world brings forth yet another purpose to seek, and so you shall spend your life seeking and finding not. [4]Empty, you shall die.

[5]But the purpose of the Heart fills up your treasure chest quickly with joy, peace, and hope. [6]And you shall follow the twinkle within your own eye, and since it is with you always, you shall always be satisfied beyond measure. [7]For it is the light within the Heart that shines to show you your joy, and since it shines from within, you shall see your joy wherever you look. [8]But if you do not trust your Heart and you try to find your own way

to happiness, you shall be lost. [9]For who can find their way without the light? [10]Who can be happy stumbling, lost and aimless in the dark?

(v 24)[1]No one can stand in both the light and the darkness, for either he will stand in the darkness and cannot see or he will stand in the light and see clearly. [2]But I say to you, he who stands in the dark may not know he is lost, *because* he cannot see. [3]So do not decide for yourself where to stand. [4]For you may think you stand on the path of righteousness when your feet are surely lost.

[5]Ask for the Light, and let it lead you without questioning where it takes you. [6]Remember that until you see all the world within the Light, you may be lost, letting the darkness lead your way.

(v 25 - 34)[1]Therefore, do not worry about which way you should go or what you should do next. [2]Instead, ask now for the surety of the Light to light the way for your next step. [3]Listen in quiet to the guidance of the Heart as it tells you where to place your step. [4]Be concerned only with letting your steps be led. [5]For by following the guidance of the Light, you will surely be walking the way of Life. [6]For the Light and Life are one. [7]But if you let your mind be distracted by other concerns, and you begin to worry about troubles within the world, you will forget to step carefully with the Light, and you will run frantically into the dark. [8]Then you shall look around and realize that once more you are lost. [9]For you cannot find the path of Life without the guidance of the Light. [10]For the Light and Life are one. [11]If you have lost one, you are lost from the other.

NTI Matthew, Chapter 7

(v 1 - 5)[1]Judgment is like a knife that cuts the Son of God into pieces, for what you judge as separate from you is seen as separate, and so it cannot be seen as one. [2]I say to you, lay your judgment aside. [3]Trust the guidance of the Heart by trusting God and His Word.

[4]I tell you that God is Love and Love is whole. [5]Therefore, you cannot know God if you separate your brothers from yourself. [6]Do not place them above you or below you in your mind, and do not place them above

or below one another. [7]For to separate them in your mind is to split your own heart, and a split heart cannot know Love *because* it is split, and so, it is not whole.

[8]Look after your own heart that it may be healed. [9]Lay down your judgments, and ask only for Love now.

(v 6)[1]Do not take My words lightly without practice. [2]For to listen and to agree, but not to practice, is not to have heard. [3]And one who will not hear cannot be healed.

(v 7, 8)[1]Seek out the prayers of your Heart. [2]Ask your Father to make it whole again, for your Father knows that your heart seeks to be made whole, and he awaits only your willingness to give what you ask.

(v 9 - 11)[1]Trust your Father to give as you ask truly, but know it is the healthy Heart He listens to. [2]If your heart is sick and it asks the Father to grant it its sickness, the Father does not listen. [3]He waits until His Son asks that he be healed, and then the Father reveals His gifts, that they may be used for the purpose they were intended. [4]For the Father will not assist the son in maintaining his sickness, but the Father will point the willing son in the direction of his health, that he may be made whole through his own willingness.

(v 12)[1]Therefore, see your brothers as yourself. [2]Know that their heart is the same as yours. [3]Although they may seem to ask for sickness, their heart knows it wants its health. [4]So do not answer their cry for sickness by returning anger for anger or hurt for hurt. [5]Answer their heart's quiet cry for health by giving as the Father would give. [6]Give health for health, and it is health you will receive.

(v 13, 14)[1]I ask you for your help, because leaders are needed among men. [2]For a man who does not know that his heart yearns to be healed is lost indeed and needs someone to help him see that health is his heart's desire. [3]Let yourself be healed, that your brother may see your health and recognize it is but his own. [4]Then he will ask for healing, and it will be given him.

(v 15 - 20)[1]Concentrate first on your healing, that you may be used to lead your brothers to health. [2]For an unhealed heart cannot lead its brothers to healing, for it knows not what health is. [3]The sick must be healed before they can heal. [4]The lost must be found before they can lead.

[5]Be not confused by those who say they can lead you, when you can see that they are lost. [6]Hold not a grievance against them. [7]Remember that a sick brother does not know he is sick. [8]Forgive him his confusion, and pray to your Father, that your sight may be made clear.

(v 21 - 23)[1]One who practices his own will is not practicing the Will of the Father, and it is the Father's Will that brings healing. [2]For it is your will that has made you sick. [3]Lay down your will, and ask only for the Father's. [4]By knowing and practicing His Will, you shall be healed.

(v 24 - 27)[1]Listen to My words, and let My words reach into your heart. [2]For the healthy part of your heart is small, but its Will is complete. [3]And it Wills with God.

[4]Listen to the healthy heart, and its health will spread, making your heart anew. [5]And your strength will be rewarded with an unshakableness that brings eternal joy and knowledge.

[6]But listen not unto My words, and you shall hear the cries of your heart's sickness, and sickness cannot lead to health. [7]So you shall not know strength. [8]In your weakness you will suffer, for weakness is not the will of your heart.

(v 28, 29)[1]Authority comes from God, because God is all that is. [2]One who knows his own Authority knows God. [3]Amen.

NTI Matthew, Chapter 8

(v 1 – 4)[1]Jesus is the symbol of healing, for healing comes from the healed Son of God. [2]The unhealed son cannot heal himself, but he can ask in faith and willingness, and the healed Son may heal on behalf of the Father. [3]And then the one who has been healed may be used as a witness, so others will come to know their own desire to be healed.

(v 5 – 13)[1]Jesus is the symbol of the healed Son of God, for the healed Son knows what healing is. [2]It is oneness, where all are welcomed into the kingdom as one, and there is great joy. [3]From within the seat of the kingdom, the Son knows who He is and He has not forgotten. [4]But outside of the seat, the son is lost. [5]And so he is crying for his Home, but knows not where it is.

(v 14 - 17)[1]Jesus is the symbol of the one Son of God, for as He is, so you shall know yourself to be. [2]All will be healed within their time, for what is the Son of God with less than every part of His Self?

(v 18 - 22)[1]This ministry is not a ministry of the world. [2]Those who choose to follow will find what they do not expect, for what you expect comes from your will and your desire, but it is your will and your desire that must be laid aside if you are to be healed.

[3]Do not ask for what you want. [4]Ask Me what it is that you need, and I shall lead you to it. [5]But follow Me in purpose and faith only, for if you seek anything else, you will not see what I am showing you.

(v 23 - 27)[1]Peace is the sign of health, for the healed Son of God knows there is nothing to fear and there is nothing that he needs that is not given him. [2]And so he rests and does not fear, for he knows who He is.

(v 28 - 34)[1]The thoughts that are in your mind that you think are yours are not yours. [2]Those are the thoughts of death. [3]Let these thoughts go from your mind, and then you shall see that they are but thoughts of death. [4]They are not you, for you are Life. [5]Let the thoughts of death leave you, that you may know your Self and may live.

NTI Matthew, Chapter 9

(v 1 - 8)[1]Listen to Me. [2]The authority within the Heart is the authority of God. [3]Do not be confused. [4]Your will is not the same as God's, but when you lay your will aside and walk with God, you will know that you are one with Him.

(v 9 - 13)[1]Forgiveness is for error. [2]It is your judgments that must be let go, for it is your judgment that has been your error. [3]When you let go of your judgment, you will see what *is*. [4]But if you hold onto your judgment, you choose confusion and pain. [5]Let go and be free, or hold on and sacrifice your freedom.

(v 14 - 17)[1]Let go of old habits and old ways of thinking. [2]They have not served you. [3]To hold onto the old is to create a future like the past. [4]That is not useful to you now. [5]Listen to My Word. [6]Hear what I say. [7]Practice it. [8]Then you will know what to do.

(v 18 - 26)[1]Miracles are not what you expect, for you expect only what you have seen. [2]I am here to give you new sight. [3]With new sight, you will see differently. [4]Have faith in Me, and trust in Me. [5]Do as I say, and everything different from what you expect will be given you.

(v 27 - 34)[1]The blind cannot see. [2]The dumb cannot talk. [3]And so it is healing they must seek. [4]Know that it is *you* I am talking to. [5]You are blind and cannot see; I ask you not to talk. [6]For through your words you spread confusion. [7]Listen to Me, and spread My Word. [8]By sharing what I give, you will recover your Sight.

(v 35 - 38)[1]Let Me heal you, that your brothers may see your true health and be healed unto themselves through Me.

NTI Matthew, Chapter 10

(v 1 - 6)[1]I give you authority to teach through Me, but you are not yet the Teacher as I am. [2]It is through sharing My Word that you shall come to know your Self, and so it is yourself that you teach through Me.

(v 7 - 10)[1]Teach yourself but this:

[2]*God is within, and it is from within that I am led.*

[3]To learn this lesson is true, do not focus on what is outside. [4]Do not worry about what you are to eat or what you are to wear or where you are to sleep. [5]Focus only on the Word within, and seek nothing else. [6]Everything will be provided, that you may do the work I ask.

(v 11 - 16)[1]Remember always, it is you that you teach. [2]If you find peace in fellowship with another, enjoy that peace and be thankful for it. [3]But if you find agitation, let your agitation go. [4]Do not keep your agitation with you, for agitation is darkness and suffering in the night. [5]All who will learn of glory will learn glory is found in letting agitation go.

(v 17 - 20)[1]Remember that you are not alone. [2]That is the lesson I send you to learn:

[3]*The Spirit of your Father is one,*
and so you are one with that Spirit.

[4]Trust in the Spirit in all things, and do not fail on this account.

(v 21 - 23)[1]What you will see in the world will confuse you, and so you must not look there for understanding. [2]Look to Me. [3]I am your guide and the one who knows what understanding is. [4]Look to Me in all things, and you shall know Me, even within the world.

(v 24, 25)[1]By making your will one with Mine, you will come to know your Self as the same as Me. [2]Give your will to Me, that I may give you Mine, and we shall have one will.

(v 26 - 31)[1]Do not fear the world or what you see or hear there. [2]I say to you, the world is not real. [3]It will come to pass, but you are eternal, and what is eternal is real. [4]Let your mind be turned from the temporal and fearful to the eternal, for what is eternal can have no fear.

(v 32, 33)[1]You will know Me by choosing to be one with Me. [2]Lay your temporal self aside. [3]It is nothing. [4]Your will cannot affect eternity. [5]But My Will *is* eternity. [6]By knowing My Will, you know the peace of Heaven.

(v 34 - 36)[1]Remember all things in this world are temporal, so hold not onto them. [2]You will not find peace there. [3]Hold onto Me, for I am the peace of Heaven.

(v 37 - 39)[1]Your function is letting go of this world and your will within it. [2]Only by letting go of the temporal will you find the eternal within. [3]Be not distracted. [4]I am your truth.

(v 40 - 42)[1]Let your Light shine, that men may recognize the eternal.

[2]For your Light is Me, and I am your Light.

NTI Matthew, Chapter 11

(v 1 - 6)[1]John the Baptist symbolizes the search for truth. [2]Many become lost in the search, because they know not where to look. [3]Do not search for truth in the symbols of the world. [4]Nothing in the world can contain the truth. [5]The truth is but reflected there. [6]Let the reflection be as evidence that *truth is*, but do not put your faith in the evidence. [7]Put your faith in the truth.

(v 7 - 15)[1]The search for truth is not truth itself, so do not stop there. [2]Many have heard the call to search and have accepted it, but then they have stopped, thinking themselves complete. [3]You are not complete until you *are* Truth, so do not stop at the call. [4]It is your beginning, but it is not your end. [5]To find the truth, you must walk until your end.

(v 16 - 19)[1]Do not judge the symbols. [2]Do not look for truth there. [3]The temptation to believe the world and its symbols is great, because you *want* to believe the world. [4]You want the world to be true, because you want to be right about the world. [5]This is why I ask for your faith and willingness. [6]It is because I am asking you to turn away from what you believe is true, from what you have known until now and from where you have put your faith before. [7]Let the world go from your sight. [8]Let it be but a vision of dancing symbols with no truth in them. [9]This is what I mean when I ask you to seek only Me. [10]Let all that you knew before Me go from your thoughts.

(v 20 - 24)[1]Listen to Me. [2]When I speak of truth, you think of others and think that My words are good for them. [3]But if I tell you that I am talking to you, why do you think of others? [4]I have already told you that guidance comes from within and the world is but dancing symbols. [5]Are you ready to seek only Me?

(v 25, 26)[1]Give thanks that your Father knows how to heal you. [2]Give thanks that He knows you must find willingness to lay your self aside, and that it is upon this willingness that He patiently waits, so that healing may be given you.

(v 27)[1]All things are revealed to you when you are ready, for when you are not ready, you would not accept them.

[2]You think you are a lofty being with thoughts that are real and worth holding onto. [3]You will not learn that you are holy as long as you choose to believe that you are lofty. [4]It takes holiness to see what holiness is, and so you must choose to know holiness to see that you are holy.

(v 28 - 30)[1]You carry your own burdens now. [2]I did not ask you to pick them up, and I do not insist upon you carrying them. [3]I am the one who asks you to put them down. [4]There is nothing of value within the burdens that you carry. [5]Truly, they are not worth their weight! [6]For your burdens keep you from knowing you are free, and so they keep you from knowing your Self. [7]For how can a free man know his Self if he does not know he is free?

[8]Listen to Me. [9]Lay your burdens down. [10]You will find no treasure there.

NTI Matthew, Chapter 12

(v 1 - 8)[1]Confusion is easy when you listen to the thoughts in your own mind, for those thoughts tell you that man is separate and guilty. [2]As you look on the world with these thoughts in your mind, you will see separateness and guilt. [3]But I tell you, that is confusion and not truth. [4]I am here to help you lay down your confusion, that you may know truth. [5]There is no separateness and there is no guilt. [6]There is only one, and so there is only innocence. [7]What you see is not true, but I am here to show you truth.

(v 9 – 14)[1]If you choose to be blind, you will be blind, but blindness is your choice. [2]I come to help you see, if you are willing. [3]There is so much I want to show you! [4]I want to show you the truth of who you are, the sweetness of your freedom and the glory of Heaven! [5]But you must choose to open your eyes. [6]I cannot do that for you.

(v 15 - 21)[1]You cannot hear Me if you choose not to hear. [2]My words may be clear to you, but meaningless to another. [3]That is because you give meaning to all things by your choice, and you are free to choose the meaning of truth or to choose another meaning. [4]But know this as you make your choice:

[5]*A meaning other than truth is not truth.*
[6]*Therefore, can it be meaning?*

[7]Listen to Me. [8]I offer you truth. [9]Share My words and know that they are yours also. [10]For there is only one truth, and the truth belongs to all.

(v 22 - 29)[1]Through his words, Jesus demonstrated that separateness cannot stand. [2]Through his actions, he demonstrated his words. [3]What is one cannot be separate and live. [4]This is why death has come upon your world. [5]But the good news is that separateness is but illusion, and so death is illusion too.

[6]Listen to Me.

[7]*The Spirit of God is one.*
[8]*This is the truth I would have you learn.*

[9]The destruction of God is the separating of Him from Himself, but God cannot be separated or He would not *be* Himself. [10]Who could separate Him?

[11]Therefore, there has been no sin. [12]There has only been the illusion of sin. [13]This is the truth I would have you learn.

(v 30 - 32)[1]It is not bodies that are one. [2]Do not let thoughts of confusion confuse you. [3]Bodies are temporal and will not last. [4]Yet you are eternal, so you must be One.

[5]It is the Spirit that tells us who we are. [6]It is the Spirit that knows our truth. [7]Let go of what your eyes tell you, for surely your eyes will not last forever. [8]What do they know of eternity? [9]Listen to Spirit, for the eternal knows what eternity is.

(v 33 - 37)[1]Your own thoughts condemn you, and your own thoughts condemn your world. [2]As long as you believe and love your thoughts, you and your world are condemned, for there is no escaping the thoughts you choose to keep. [3]But let all thoughts of condemnation go, and you shall be given a new world and new thoughts. [4]And it is through this world and these thoughts that you shall come to know your Self.

(v 38 - 42)[1]The truth is not something that can be seen, except if one chooses to see it. [2]When one chooses to see what is, he shall. [3]And its sight shall be glorious to him, for it is the sight of Life and the overcoming of death.

(v 43 - 45)[1]The thoughts you think *are* your evil doing, and so you may choose to let go of them. [2]Let me tell you that it may not be that easy. [3]For the belief that spawns the thoughts is like a deep root within you, and where you cut off its leaves, more will rise up to take their place. [4]Be prepared to let go of many leaves, but know they will come back until the day you have rid yourself of their root.

(v 46 - 50)[1]The belief in separateness and differences is the root you must let go. [2]For if there is more than one Will, the truth is not true and death is all there is. [3]Is this the final resting place of your faith? [4]Or are you willing to put your faith in Life and Love and One?

[5]If you will put your faith in Me, I will lead you to the end of your root. [6]There, shall you find the truth, and your truth will be *you*.

NTI Matthew, Chapter 13

(v 1 – 9)[1]Your choice is the key to this scripture. [2]All that you do, you do by your choice. [3]To deny this is to deny the essence of who you are. [4]And yet, many deny themselves and believe they are victims of their own distractions. [5]I say to you, listen to Me.

[6]*No one can keep you from your Self, but your self.*

[7]Lay your self aside that you may come Home to Me.

(v 10 - 15)[1]My words are clear to those who choose to understand them. [2]For when you lay your self aside and ask to receive understanding, it is given you. [3]But understanding can only be given if you choose to lay your self aside. [4]For if you do not make this choice, it is because you believe you know, and so you cannot be taught.

(v 16, 17)[1]Be thankful that My words are clear to you. [2]For you have asked, and it is given. [3]This is the symbol of your Father's Love on earth. [4]Freely he extends Himself to you. [5]Blessed are you who have chosen to receive.

(v 18 - 23)[1]Not everyone you meet will be ready to make the choice that you have made. [2]Many will not, but you must love them. [3]For love is the good soil you have chosen, and not to love is not to have made the choice.

[4]Love your brothers. [5]Give them as they ask, and do not judge. [6]Think no evil thoughts about them. [7]Do not worry about their choices. [8]It is *your choice* you must guard. [9]Make sure that you choose the good soil and that you do not let yourself slip onto the path, between the rocks or among the thorns.

(v 24 - 30)[1]The choice you make will seem to be made many times in complete sincerity and truth of heart. [2]And then you will seem to slip and forget the choice you have made. [3]Do not let this distress you. [4]Simply make the choice again.

[5]In any moment when you notice that evil thoughts and thoughts of separateness have crept into your mind, give them up *in that moment*. [6]It is moment-to-moment in which the harvest occurs. [7]And so it is in the moment that you remember, that you must also make the choice.

(v 31, 32)[1]Do not worry that you do not tend to your choice enough. [2]For if you tend to your choice every time you remember, that is enough. [3]For in the tending of your choice, *the tending itself* will extend until you are tending to your choice in every moment as you desire. [4]For the tending is the mustard seed. [5]Ask Me to rain upon your seed and tend whenever you remember. [6]I will lead you to remember more.

📖(v 33)[1]It is through your choice, but not through your effort, that the kingdom of Heaven is given, for the kingdom of Heaven must be a gift given by the Father to you. [2]Choose to be ready to receive the gift. [3]In this way, it is like yeast. [4]The yeast represents the choice, but the rising of the dough is the gift born of that choice.

(v 34, 35)[1]What I tell you now is the truth of your salvation. [2]It is only through this truth that you shall be saved.

(v 36 - 43)   *[1]The Son of God is an extension of His Father,*
but this he has forgotten.

[2]That he has forgotten,
does not change what is true.

[3]When you see yourself in this forgotten state, and you believe that you are guilty and you live in a fearful world, it is then that you suffer. [4]And yet, you believe these thoughts. [5]And in believing these thoughts, you suffer. [6]And in believing these thoughts, you believe the evidence of these thoughts, and you suffer more.

[7]This is why I am here. [8]I am here to bring clarity to replace confusion, love to replace fear. [9]But you must know that your thoughts are born of fear, and fear is the way of this world. [10]To know My gift, you must put down your thoughts of fear and turn away from its evidence. [11]Through your consistent choice, I will give you My gift. [12]For I cannot give against your choice, so I cannot give the gift of love if it is fear that you choose.

[13]Listen to Me now.

[14]You must trust Me above all that you think and hear and see.
[15]You must put Me above your self and your world.
[16]And you do this by your choice,
by selecting the thoughts you will believe
and the thoughts you will let go.

[17]Thoughts of love and thoughts of fear are in your mind now. [18]Where will you choose to put your faith?

(v 44 - 46) [1]This is what I am telling you. [2]If you seek confusion and fear, you will find it, for the world breeds confusion and fear. [3]But if it is truth and clarity that you seek, I offer it to you now. [4]Let go of everything that is not the gift I offer. [5]Accept only My gift. [6]In this way, the treasure of Heaven is yours.

(v 47 - 50) [1]The sorting of thoughts is the work that must be done. [2]This is the moment-to-moment choice you must make:

[3]*Where will you put your faith?*

[4]If you ask Me to help you make your choice, I will help. [5]I will lead you along the path and point your choices out to you.

[6]Let Me help. [7]Depend upon Me. [8]Put yourself in My hands, and I will tell you where to look.

(v 51, 52) [1]There is nothing that is to remain hidden in your mind as the work of sorting is done. [2]Do not be afraid. [3]Do not hide thoughts from the work. [4]All thoughts must be brought out from the corners of your mind into My light, and there they shall be judged. [5]I will judge your thoughts for you, but you must make the choice.

(v 53 - 58) [1]It is your self that I have asked you to lay aside, and it is on this choice that your Father waits to give you His gift. [2]You know your self and your world as your home, and although you are afraid, you have become comfortable there. [3]I ask you to give up your home and all that you know, that I may give you your true Self and true Home. [4]I offer more than comfort within a world of fear. [5]I offer the peace and knowing of God.

[6]It is your choice, but I will help you with your choice if you choose to walk with Me.

NTI Matthew, Chapter 14

📖(v 1 - 12)[1]John the Baptist was beheaded out of fear, and so it is your fear you must be aware of. [2]Fear was made to keep you from joining with God.

(v 13 - 21)[1]Put your fear aside, and you will know miracles that will increase your faith. [2]Even in your life on earth, you will know Me, and so you will know it *is* Me, and you will be more willing to walk toward Me. [3]But first, you must give Me faith and trust. [4]You must do as I ask to know miracles at work in your life.

(v 22 - 36)[1]It is fear that I want to talk to you about today. [2]For fear can seem to be a very real obstacle on your path to Me. [3]Although I can help you with your fear, it is you that must overcome it. [4]For it is *your* fear, and I cannot take that which is yours from you. [5]You must willingly let go of your fear. [6]You must choose Me over it to know it is nothing to keep you from Me.

NTI Matthew, Chapter 15

(v 1 – 9)[1]Look into your heart for the purpose of what you do, for it is not what you do that is important, but why you do it. [2]In your search for Me, you agonize over choices in the world. [3]You want to know if it is right that you do this or if it would be better that you do that. [4]I say, do what you choose in peace and in purpose, and I will use what you do.

(v 10 – 20)[1]All things of this world are temporal, so how important can they be? [2]They will not last, so do not agonize over them. [3]It is you that is eternal, and so it is your thoughts, your wishes and your purpose that matters.

[4]If you put your faith in the temporal, your thoughts and wishes and

purpose are focused there, so your heart is there also. [5]A heart focused in the temporal will know itself as temporal, and so it will know death. [6]It will know it is lost, and it will know the fear of being lost, but it will not know that being found is the answer to its fear. [7]And so it will continue to run and hide, and it will become further lost. [8]The only way to be found is to step away from the dark and know the Light. [9]This is why you must not focus on the temporal. [10]The temporal is the darkness in which you are lost. [11]Turn away from it, and you will see Me in the Light.

(v 21 - 28)[1]You will be tempted to use My Word for purposes of the world. [2]Do not be fooled by this temptation. [3]It is only your desire to hold onto your self and your world, which is your desire to hide from your fear.

[4]The Canaanite woman represents the world. [5]In her asking, she is refused, because My purpose is not of the world.

[6]Know that my refusal was not a rebuke of the Canaanite woman. [7]I hold no one as guilty and outside my Self, but My purpose must be one or it would not be itself.

[8]*The Spirit of God is one.*

[9]And then, the woman showed her love for My purpose in her willingness to accept what is given without asking for more. [10]She showed that she loved God and sought only the glory of God. [11]Love cannot say no to a request for love, and a request to accept God's glory is love requesting love. [12]And so, the woman's daughter was healed to show that miracles are given to those who are willing to accept God's glory *as it is and for what it is*.

[13]When you listen to the thoughts of the world within your mind…when your purpose is different from mine…you cannot sit at My table and feast on My knowledge.

[14]*The Spirit of God is one.*

[15]When you see your error and let it go, and you come back to Me in faith asking only for My knowledge, you have shown that your purpose is the same as Mine, and so now you may feast.

[16]The Canaanite woman may have been satisfied with only crumbs, but it is the full feast that I shared with her, just as I share it with you now. [17]Open your eyes and see. [18]Listen to Me.

(v 29 - 39)[1]Know that I am with you in all that you do. [2]Make Me the only purpose for all you do, and you shall know Me in your life. [3]For I never turn away from you. [4]It is you who have turned from Me. [5]I but rest with you in peace and confidence awaiting your invitation, that I may feed you with my miracles until you are full, complete and healed.

NTI Matthew, Chapter 16

(v 1 - 4)[1]Rejoice! [2]For the time will come that you will know all that you ask. [3]The time will come that you will know that death is not real and the world is not real, and I am your reality. [4]Rejoice and put your faith in Me. [5]Stay with your search. [6]Seek and you shall find.

(v 5 - 12)[1]Now is a time of doubt for you, but doubts must rise if you are to let go of them. [2]All of this is inside of you: fear, guilt and hatred. [3]These things must be released if you are to know peace and Light. [4]So do not fear that you see doubt. [5]Fear can keep you from Me. [6]Rejoice that you are doing the work I have asked. [7]Let your fear and doubt come into your mind that you may see it. [8]But in faith, let it go. [9]In this way, you choose where you will put your faith. [10]In this way, you do the work that I have asked you to do.

(v 13 - 16)   [1]*The Spirit of God is one,*
and His Son is one with Him.

[2]There is no separateness. [3]There is only the Father and His extension of His Self, which is His Son. [4]In this way, the Spirit of God is one, and it is whole.

(v 17, 18)[1]It is on your faith in My Word that I shall build my church. [2]It is on your willingness to believe Me over what you see that I will heal your sight. [3]It is oneness that you seek, and so it is the truth that you shall find. [4]You are blessed in your search. [5]That which is forever true cannot be overcome.

📖(v 19)[1]This instruction given to Peter was given to all who put faith in Me. [2]For Peter is but a symbol of faith within the unhealed mind. [3]What this mind holds onto is held onto within Heaven, for the truth is always true. [4]And what this mind lets go of is let go in Heaven, for the truth is always true.

> [5]*The Spirit of God is one,*
> *and the Spirit of God is Heaven,*
> *so you must be one with Heaven.*

[6]Let that which blinds you to the truth go from your mind, that the truth which always has been may dawn.

(v 20)[1]Jesus is not the Christ in himself. [2]The Christ is the Son of God, and no one is left outside of the Christ.

(v 21 - 23)[1]Peter is the symbol of faith within the unhealed mind, and so Peter is also the symbol of the unhealed mind that has faith. [2]In Peter, you will see great faith! [3]And in Peter, you will see doubt, fear and confusion.

[4]You are Peter. [5]Until you know that you are the Son of God, do not doubt that you are Peter. [6]And so you will seem to have moments of great faith, and you will seem to have moments of doubt, fear and confusion. [7]It is the doubt, fear and confusion you must let go of, for they block the Light of Heaven and the awareness of who you are. [8]It is faith you must hold onto, for your faith is your path to Me.

(v 24)[1]Jesus was enlightened, for he knew what Heaven is. [2]And in his joy, he invited all to join him. [3]But Heaven is not given on invitation alone, for Heaven must be accepted, and all that is not Heaven must be let go of. [4]This is what I have been asking you to do. [5]Let go of your doubts. [6]Let go of your fear. [7]Let go of your thoughts of separateness. [8]And lay your self aside. [9]You do not need these things. [10]They but block the Light of Heaven.

[11]Instead, pick up your faith in Me and faith in Light, and walk with Me to the Light. [12]In this way, you shall know what Heaven is.

(v 25)[1]One cannot die, so Jesus does not ask you to die. [2]He asks you to live within the oneness that he is. [3]Lay down your little life and your desire for it, that you may know the Life that is.

(v 26)[1]This is where you must look at your thoughts and your desires. [2]For if you desire anything of the world, you have lost your desire for Me. [3]Do not be afraid of what you find in your search. [4]You will find that you do desire the world, for it is your desire that brought you here. [5]But in finding your desire, you can choose to let it go. [6]And in this way, you choose again, releasing the future from the past that you may see differently now.

(v 27)[1]It is within you that I shall come. [2]For it is within your heart and your mind that you shall see that you are one with Me. [3]And in this knowledge you shall be rewarded, for there is no reward but Me.

(v 28)[1]It is simple. [2]If you accept Me and let all else go, you shall know Me. [3]In knowing Me, you shall know Life and Truth, for I am Life and Truth. [4]In this knowledge, you cannot die. [5]Life and Truth are the opposite of death, because Life and Truth are everything and death, like fear, is nothing.

NTI Matthew, Chapter 17

(v 1 - 3)[1]The Holy Spirit uses symbols to teach, because the world is a world of symbols. [2]Do not think that the world is reality or that the symbols of the world are reality, and do not argue them. [3]See them as symbols and ask Me what use they have for you. [4]In this way, all things have meaning.

(v 4)[1]Thinking for yourself is not the way to understanding, for it is your self you must lay aside. [2]And so it is your thoughts you must lay aside. [3]They are but thoughts of confusion. [4]Believe not in what you think.

(v 5)[1]I am the Light and the Voice of Heaven. [2]Listen to Me. [3]Take My words into your heart and practice what I teach. [4]Be concerned with nothing but Me, for the Spirit of God is one.

(v 6 - 8)[1]You will be afraid of oneness, because you will be afraid to lay down your self. [2]Do not fear that truth will be thrust upon you before you are ready. [3]It is on your readiness that truth waits. [4]But I shall guide you to the truth in a way that you can understand and trust.

(v 9 - 13)[1]The search for truth must come before the truth can dawn, but do not misunderstand the search. [2]It is not through your doing that you can find. [3]The search will only be successful if you let go of the search and let Me guide you, for letting go of your will *is* the search and the path to truth.

(v 14 - 21)[1]Your faith is small, because your faith is limited. [2]You are willing to put faith in Me with some things, but not yet with all things. [3]I tell you, until you are willing to have faith in Me with all things, you will not know that all things are possible in God.

(v 22, 23)[1]It is your focus and belief in the world that limits your sight, for your sight is where your faith is. [2]Look to Me, that I may remove your sight from the world and place it on Life.

(v 24 - 27)[1]You are not of this world, nor are your brothers. [2]But those who are focused on the world believe themselves to be a part of the world, just as they believe you to be. [3]To tell them that you are not of the world is of no use, and to tell them that the world is not real will only put fear and hatred into their hearts.

[4]We may not be of this world, but we are love, and so it is love that we must give. [5]Love is not fear. [6]And so I ask you to give to your brothers as they expect you to give, and give in the knowledge of love, so they will not be afraid. [7]But do not put your faith in what you give, so you do not limit yourself or your brother to your gift. [8]Put your faith in Me, that I

may use your gift to give the gift of Life.

NTI Matthew, Chapter 18

(v 1 - 4)[1]I have told you before not to think for yourself. [2]And I have asked you to lay your self aside. [3]It is this you must practice, because it is this you must do. [4]One cannot maintain self-identity and self-control and be healed of self. [5]Yet, one must be healed of self if one is to know the oneness of Heaven as I Am.

[6]I say to you, practice with Me today. [7]Do not think for yourself. [8]Ask Me in all things and leave all things to Me.

(v 5, 6)[1]Love your brothers and be at peace with them. [2]Accept them as they are and where they seem to be. [3]Do not ask your brother to change his place, but love him in his place. [4]And then ask Me how your brother's place is helpful to you. [5]In this way, your brother is your teacher, and you are his.

(v 7 - 9)[1]Forgiveness may not always seem easy. [2]You will encounter great resistance in forgiving your brothers and in forgiving yourself. [3]Do not let resistance alarm you. [4]Resistance is fear, and to give in to resistance is to give in to fear.

[5]Remember, fear can keep you from Me. [6]So when you feel resistance, recognize it for what it is. [7]Realize that resistance is a path from Me. [8]And ask yourself which path you would place your feet on now. [9]Then let go of your belief in resistance, and let go of your fight against resistance. [10]Give your heart to Me. [11]Ask Me to help. [12]And let yourself rest as the resistance passes on to nothingness. [13]Then the way is clear for you to forgive and accept the peace of God in joy.

(v 10, 11)[1]Watch your heart when you believe you have forgiven. [2]Be careful that you do not find a grievance or a grudge there. [3]For if you do, your forgiveness is not complete.

[4]You will know that your forgiveness is complete when you love your brother with your whole heart and soul and mind, just as the angels do. [5]If you love your brother any less, ask Me to help you learn to forgive.

(v 12 - 14)[1]The Spirit of God is one, and no one can be left outside. [2]If you have not forgiven your brother, you are lost from the Spirit of God. [3]Do not be confused. [4]You are not responsible for your brother's place, but if you cannot forgive him his place, you are lost from yours.

[5]The Spirit of God is Love. [6]And to know your place in His Heart, you must be love too. [7]Love does not make judgments, and love holds no grievances. [8]So do not worry about your brother's place. [9]Ask Me how the symbol of your brother's place can be used to help you find yours.

(v 15 - 17)[1]Be careful in talking to your brother regarding a difference or disagreement, for in the world these discussions must happen. [2]When you go to your brother, go with Me. [3]Check your heart to ensure you find forgiveness there, and also, that you find trust that the situation has been given to Me. [4]Clear your mind of judgments and desired outcomes. [5]Ask only for healing and enlightenment. [6]When you are sure all of this has been done, talk to your brother while being careful to listen for Me in love and confidence. [7]In this way, there can be no loss, for the situation is no longer a situation of the world. [8]But it is a situation of Heaven, for Heaven has been made its purpose.

(v 18)[1]It is what is in your mind and your heart that is important, for there the resolution shall be.

(v 19, 20)[1]If your brother and you agree in love, you shall be blessed by Love. [2]Let love be your only goal.

(v 21, 22)[1]Your brother is your Self, and so you must forgive your brother to know your Self. [2]Do not give up on him. [3]To give up on your brother is to give up on Love.

(v 23 - 35)[1]You suffer because you do not love, for love is not itself unless it is whole. [2]No one can be left out of love. [3]No thought that is not love can be left in your mind.

[4]Listen to Me. [5]Rejoice at your opportunities to forgive. [6]Be happy that you have found yourself judging or holding a grievance, for what you find, you can let go. [7]In this way, the splinters to Love's presence are removed, that Love may be known as whole again.

NTI Matthew, Chapter 19

📖(v 1 - 6)[1]The symbol of marriage is the symbol of joining, but I have told you before that it is not what you do that is important, but why you do it.

[2]Do not let the form of what you do confuse you. [3]Always look beyond the form to your heart. [4]What do you find there? [5]Is joining reflected in your heart? [6]If not, then you are not joining, and it is joining you must seek.

[7]Do not expect joining to have a specific form or follow certain rules. [8]Let go of everything you think you know about joining, for what you know has not brought you to be joined. [9]Ask Me to lead you to joining, and then let go and let Me lead.

(v 7 - 9)[1]The world is a world of differences, and things seem to change there. [2]But the truth is always the truth and does not change. [3]Do not be confused. [4]It is not by keeping things the same within the world that one identifies truth, for the truth has never been in the world.

[5]Do not question My guidance. [6]You are lost and do not know. [7]Trust in My guidance and follow Me, that you may learn and realize and know the truth has always been true.

(v 10 - 12)[1]Following My path is following a path that leads you from the world to the truth. [2]As you follow the path, the things in the world will become less important to you. [3]Let them fall away as your desire for them ends. [4]You do not need the world. [5]It is Me that is needed now.

(v 13 - 15)[1]Become as little children, free of expectations and burdens, open to enjoy your freedom and to love your world. [2]For the world is to be loved, as all things are to be loved. [3]For love is the only purpose for all things.

(v 16 - 21)[1]I have told you that it is not what you do that is important, but that it is why you do it that matters. [2]And that reason is love. [3]For if you do anything for a purpose other than your love for Me, that thing you do is not important. [4]The only purpose is love, and My love is the only love. [5]There is no other kind of love.

(v 22 - 24)[1]When I say, "Love the world," I am not asking you to love the world for what it is. [2]I ask you to love the world for what it isn't. [3]The world is not a place where the Son of God is captive. [4]It is a place where he is free. [5]It is not a place of conflict and fear. [6]It is a place of one Will and great love.

[7]Look with Me to see what the world is not. [8]In seeing what it isn't, you shall see what it is, and you shall love it.

(v 25, 26)[1]The truth is always true, and the Spirit of God is one. [2]So the Will of God must also be one. [3]This is why I ask you to lay your self aside. [4]It is so you will know that you are one with God.

(v 27 - 30)[1]The world is something you must let go of, because your will is something you must let go of, and the world *is* your will. [2]Those who are able to let go will know the truth, which is the reward of Heaven. [3]Those who hold onto the world and love it for what it is will continue to look for their reward and will wonder why they have not found it.

[4]I tell you, your reward is not in the world. [5]Let go of the world and all it means to you, and I will show you where meaning lies.

NTI Matthew, Chapter 20

(v 1 - 16)[1]The first will be last and the last will be first, because there is only one. [2]The confusion comes in seeing many, in seeing separateness, and therefore seeing different contributions and some who are deserving of more than others. [3]If you see only one in this story (within this scripture), that one is all the same, and that one deserves the same reward for agreeing to come and work.

[4]This is what I would have you learn:

[5]*There are not many.*
[6]*There is only one.*

[7]And that one that you think is many is the Son of God, created by the Father as one, and so He is one.

[8]Do not focus on differences. [9]Let them fade from your sight. [10]Do not think that you deserve more or less than your brother or that you have more or less than your brother. [11]You are the same, deserving of your Self and one with your Father in Heaven. [12]There could be nothing else you need and no difference between you.

[13]The differences that you believe in are differences of the world, but I have already told you that the world is temporal and matters not. [14]It is the eternal that is the truth. [15]And I have also already asked you to let go of the world, and so you must let go of the differences you see in the world.

[16]*The Spirit of God is one.*
[17]*There are no differences.*

[18]Be willing to let go of them.

(v 17 - 19)[1]The truth is always true, and this you will see when you lay aside your belief in differences. [2]It is your belief in differences that blinds you to the light of Life. [3]Be willing to let go of your belief in differences, that you may see the Life that is Me.

(v 20 - 23)[1]Specialness is a form of difference. [2]One whom you see as special, you see as different, and so you ask for more or less for this person within the desire of your heart. [3]Beware of your feelings of specialness, for any feeling that will separate your brothers within your heart will split you off from the kingdom of Heaven.

[4]Love your brothers as one with My love. [5]In this way, you will know truth. [6]In this way, you will know Heaven. [7]In this way, you will know Life.

(v 24 - 28)[1]To separate your brothers and have expectations of them is not to see them as one. [2]They are one together. [3]They are one with you. [4]They are one with God. [5]Whatever you expect of your brother, you expect from Me. [6]If you expect that he is separate from you, you expect that I am separate from you too. [7]And because of this, you are lost from

Heaven.

[8]I say, love your brother. [9]Serve him as you would serve Me, and as you do, you serve your Self. [10]For you have acknowledged that it is all the same and that for its sameness, you are grateful. [11]You will go far on your gratitude for sameness. [12]I say to you, gratitude for sameness will carry you to Heaven.

(v 29 - 34)[1]The truth is always true. [2]It is just that you do not see it now. [3]And because you are blind, you cannot see it of your own power. [4]So do not try to see that there are no differences by exercising your own will, for it is your will that there be differences. [5]The one who has willed to see differences will see what he has willed to see.

[6]Instead, be willing to lay down your will, and ask Me to give you sight. [7]As you make room for My Will, you will be given My Will. [8]And through My Will, you shall see.

NTI Matthew, Chapter 21

(v 1 - 5)[1]The donkey is a symbol. [2]It is a symbol intended to teach that you must put your expectations aside. [3]For expectations are a set up opportunity for judgments, and it is judgment that keeps you separate from your brothers.

> [4]*Be willing to let go of your expectations,*
> *and you will not be tempted to judge.*

(v 6 – 9)[1]Peace comes from laying down your expectations and your judgments and accepting the truth as it is. [2]There is no other way to accept the truth, for to accept it in any way other than as it is, is not to accept the truth. [3]It is to accept delusion over truth, and in delusion, you are lost from truth.

(v 10, 11)[1]It is better to meet your brother without expectations. [2]In this way, you have opened your heart to see him as he is. [3]In finding him, you find your Self.

📖(v 12, 13)[1]The money changers in the temple represenft the ego, which is the belief in separateness. [2]For they were not in the temple to commune with God or brother. [3]The money changers entered the temple for their own purposes. [4]But the temple is the symbol of oneness and communion. [5]Oneness and communion are the only purposes within the temple. [6]So the money changers were like foreigners in the temple, because their purpose was different than its purpose.

[7]In this way, you are like the temple *and* the money changers. [8]Your truth is like the symbol of the temple. [9]Your only purpose is oneness and communion. [10]But you have allowed a foreign purpose to reside within your mind. [11]And by focusing on the foreign purpose, your true purpose has become lost to you. [12]Jesus would have you clear your mind of the foreign purpose, that your true purpose may be remembered.

(v 14 - 16)[1]Confusion comes into the mind when you listen to a purpose other than the purpose of God. [2]When you have forgotten the one purpose of oneness and communion, you have forgotten who you are. [3]In your forgetfulness, you are lost.

[4]Become like little children, free of expectations clouded by foreign purpose. [5]Open your eyes and see what is before you, for it is true purpose that awaits only your recognition and your welcome.

📖(v 17 - 19)[1]The withering fig tree is a tree that bears no fruit for the Son of God to eat. [2]Likewise, the ego bears no fruit for the Son of God. [3]Let the ego go. [4]Let the belief in separation go from your heart, that it may bear no more fruit within your mind.

(v 20 - 22)[1]What seems impossible to you is not impossible. [2]In fact, it is all that is truly possible, for the belief in separation cannot hold you prisoner, because it is not true. [3]It is not real. [4]It is nothing but a figment of your imagination in which you have placed your faith. [5]Through this, you can see the power of your faith!

[6]But I ask you to remove your faith from what you believe now and place your faith in Me, that you may see through different eyes. [7]Surely, you will see differently!

(v 23 - 27)[1]You must look at your faith and see where you are placing it before you can choose to place it with Me. [2]Many believe they have placed their faith in God, when truly they have placed their faith in men and in the world.

[3]Truly I say to you, look at your faith honestly. [4]In what do you believe? [5]In what do you trust? [6]And if it is not placed firmly with Me in all things, are you willing to choose again?

(v 28 - 32)[1]The call to truth is within you. [2]Only by answering the call and receiving My guidance will you know what calls.

[3]Listen to Me.

(v 33 - 44)[1]The belief in separation is the death of the Son of God, and yet you choose to put your faith there. [2]For that which is whole cannot be separate and live. [3]To live, it must be one!

[4]Your expectations confuse you. [5]Let go of them and listen to Me, one word at a time.

> [6]*The Son of God cannot die,*
> *because the Son of God cannot be separate.*

[7]But in your belief that he is separate, you will find the belief in death. [8]And that belief will seem real to you as long as the belief in separation also seems real.

[9]The answer to this parable (about the landowner and his tenants) is a simple one. [10]As long as the tenants continue to believe they are separate and attacked, they will live as if they are separate and attacked, and that will be their experience. [11]It matters not where they go, for they take themselves with them.

[12]But when they open their eyes and realize that they have never been treated unfairly and they have never been attacked, their perception of being attacked will end.

[13]This is how it is for you. [14]For what is in your mind is in your world, and it is in your mind and in your world because you willed it to be there.

[15]So you must lay down your will, just as the tenants must lay down their implements of war. [16]Only in this way, will there be peace.

(v 45, 46)[1]Listen to Me. [2]To hear Me, but not to practice what I say, is not to listen. [3]And so I say to you, listen to Me. [4]It is the message of Love.

NTI Matthew, Chapter 22

(v 1 – 10)[1]The kingdom of Heaven is like a wedding banquet. [2]For marriage is the symbol of joining, and the kingdom of Heaven is joining. [3]But at this wedding banquet, there are no guests. [4]For everyone who comes will find himself joined within the glory of this ceremony.

[5]All who come may see himself as bride or as groom. [6]It is not important how he sees himself on coming. [7]During the journey to the banquet, he may even see himself as an invited guest. [8]As long as he is following his invitation to come, how he sees himself in the coming is not important.

[9]Some may seem to have a long journey to the wedding banquet with many distractions along the way. [10]Others may seem to live closer and arrive quickly after hearing the call to come. [11]The length of the journey is not important. [12]The journey itself, or what seems to happen along its way, matters not.

[13]All are invited to the wedding banquet, and all, in their time, will arrive. [14]It is upon arriving that they will realize what they have been invited to attend. [15]Upon that realization, all else will fall away. [16]They will not remember if they were bride or groom or guest. [17]They will not remember if the journey was short or long, with many distractions or few. [18]All that they will know is that they have arrived, and they are joined.

(v 11 - 14)[1]No one who comes will be turned away, for no one can come unless he is ready, and if he is ready, he shall be wearing his wedding clothes. [2]Do not fear that you will be turned away from God. [3]When God looks at you, God sees you as spotless and ready for the joining. [4]Even more, God sees you as already joined and at the banquet.

[5]It is you who judges and sees yourself as guilty.

[6]This is but a distraction on your journey to the wedding banquet. [7]Let it not keep you from your Father, who waits in peace at the banquet table, eager to embrace His Son again.

(v 15 - 22)[1]The journey to the wedding banquet seems to be time in the world. [2]On this journey, the distraction of the world may be great. [3]There will be times that you have forgotten you are on the journey, because the distraction of the world is great. [4]Let this not distress you. [5]Your joy will come when you have completed the journey, for then you will know where the journey led. [6]But until then, do not feel guilty for journeying, my child. [7]For this seems to be something you must do.

[8]On your journey, remember Me and keep Me close to your heart. [9]But do not deny the journey you are on. [10]It leads to Me and the disappearance of the journey.

[11]"Give to Caesar what is Caesar's" means, do what you seem to need to do while you are in the world.

[12]When you have forgotten you are on the journey, there will seem to be many things that need your attention. [13]I am in those things too, whether you see Me or not, so do them in peace.

[14]When you remember you are on the journey, many things of the world will seem to fall away. [15]Let them go, but do not worry about the things in the world that seem to need your attention. [16]Just as I have always been with you, I am there in those things too.

[17]As you learn to see Me in all things, the journey will seem easier, but it is not until you arrive at the wedding banquet that the journey will fall away. [18]So live within your journey in peace and with Me. [19]Be happy, and rest your mind. [20]I am walking beside you, pleased, as we journey to the wedding banquet together.

(v 23 - 33)[1]Do not be confused by what you see in the world, for Heaven is nothing like the world at all. [2]In the world, there are differences; there are conflicts; there is suffering, and there is death. [3]But none of these things exist in Heaven.

[4]Think of the world as a dream, for it seems real while you are here. [5]But think of Heaven as awakening. [6]Upon reaching Heaven, you will realize that the world, and all you thought there, was never true and so it mattered not.

[7]I tell you, the truth is always true, and there is no truth in the world.

[8]Do not let your worldly concerns distract you long. [9]Lay them aside that you may continue your journey and awaken to that which calls you.

(v 34 - 40)[1]And so the greatest commandment shall lead you on your journey:

> [2]*Love the Lord your God*
> *with all your heart,*
> *with all your soul*
> *and with all your mind.*

[3]Let your love for God be your guiding light in all you do and all you think. [4]Never forget your love for God, and give all things to Him. [5]In this way, you will move steadily along your journey.

[6]And the second commandment is like it, for the second commandment guides you within the distraction of the world.

> [7]*Love your neighbor as your Self,*
> *because he is.*

[8]There is no greater truth than this.

[9]Your Father, of course, is right. [10]You *are* joined and at the wedding banquet, but the dream of the world keeps you from knowing this is true. [11]Awaken from the dream by accepting the truth. [12]The journey to acceptance is the journey to Heaven. [13]Accept the truth, and you are there.

(v 41 – 46)[1]The Holy Spirit is the Christ. [2]Each one may call the Holy

Spirit "Lord," for the Holy Spirit guides you and leads you forward on your journey. [3]It is your Lord that you shall follow.

[4]The Holy Spirit is within, and so it is within each one waiting to be heard. [5]In this way, you may see the Holy Spirit in your son or daughter or husband or wife or mother or father or neighbor, and you may call them "Lord." [6]But the Lord is within you too, for there are no differences among men. [7]It is all the same. [8]And the call of the Lord is the call to awaken. [9]Following the call is the seeming journey, but awakening to it is realizing there was no journey and there is no Lord but one.

NTI Matthew, Chapter 23

(v 1 - 4)[1]Listen.

[2]*The truth is calling you,*
and the truth is not of this world.

[3]I have already told you that you are free to give what is Caesar's to Caesar. [4]This means, you are free to live in the world and do as you need to do while you live in the world. [5]Do not feel guilty for paying taxes, obeying laws, raising children or for doing any of the things that the world requires, but do not get lost in those things either.

[6]The world is but a distraction, and it distracts you from Heaven. [7]So you must live in the world, but not be of the world. [8]You do this by doing all things for Me...by giving all things the purpose of Heaven. [9]In this way, all things can be used to lead you to Me. [10]And I will show you how to use them.

[11]*So live in your world, but be not distracted by it.*

(v 5 - 12)[1]Holiness is not of the world, and so you cannot be made holy by what you do in the world. [2]Do not be confused by your actions or the actions of others. [3]All things within the world serve one of two purposes:

[4]They either distract you from Heaven and tie you to the world, or they free you from the world and bring you closer to the awareness of Heaven.

[5]If you seek glory from men, you are choosing to be bound to this world, for men are of the world. [6]There are no men in Heaven. [7]There is only One. [8]Choose now to please only the One by doing as I ask. [9]Let the praise or criticism of men go. [10]Their words cannot save you. [11]You are saved by the grace of God, and His grace is given you to choose as you are ready to let go of the world.

(v 13 - 22)[1]I have said, give to Caesar what is Caesar's and feel free to live in the world and do what you must do. [2]But I have also said, give all things to Me. [3]With these words, I have told you which law is highest. [4]Be not confused. [5]The laws of God are laws that lead you from the world to Heaven, and so it is the laws of God that must be chosen.

[6]Follow My guidance within the world. [7]I will lead you truly. [8]Give Me your confusion and ask for clarity. [9]Clarity will be given.

[10]Do not decide an issue in confusion and pain. [11]Decide in clarity and peace. [12]In clarity and peace you follow Me, for I am Truth and Light.

(v 23, 24)[1]Guilt is the way of the world, but it is not My way. [2]Fear is the way of the world, but it is not My way. [3]Do not make decisions out of guilt or fear, for I will not guide you by those feelings. [4]When you listen to them, you are not listening to Me.

[5]When you notice guilt in your heart or fear in your mind, focus first on letting go of those feelings. [6]To let go of them is to let go of the world, for the world is a world of guilt and fear.

[7]When the guilt and fear have passed, give the decision to Me. [8]In peace, you shall know what to do.

(v 25, 26)[1]It is not what you do that matters, but why you do it. [2]Do it for Me. [3]Do it in peace. [4]Do it in love and with joy. [5]For if you do the same thing, but the purpose of the thing is not Me and it is not done in peace, that thing will bind you to the world.

[6]Guilt and fear begets guilt and fear. [7]Do not listen to guilt or fear no matter what it tells you to do. [8]Let go of guilt and fear, and then ask Me.

[9]If I guide you to do the same thing in peace, love, and joy, you may do that thing. [10]But if I guide you not to do it, trust your peace and choose to let that thing go.

(v 27, 28)[1]All that matters is the purpose given. 2I have already told you that this world is temporal and matters not. [3]I have told you that there is no truth in this world. [4]But I have not said these things about *you*. [5]For you are eternal, and to your Father, you matter greatly. [6]Join His purpose that you may rejoin with Him. [7]Through the purposes of the world, you are lost to Him. [8]Through His purpose, you are joined.

(v 29 - 32)[1]Listen to Me. [2]You fool yourself when you listen to the purposes of the world, for you tell yourself that things are important when they are not. [3]Do what you must do within the world, but let Me guide you in determining what must be done.

(v 33 - 36)[1]Let not the wisdom of the world confuse you, for what the world calls wise is meant to keep you bound to the world. [2]In believing its wisdom, you believe it is your savior. [3]Yet the world is a temporal place, and so its salvation is temporal too.

[4]Nothing in the world will last, and all of its roads lead to death. [5]Do not look there for your salvation.

[6]I am Truth and Light. [7]Your salvation is found in Me. [8]Look to Me, and I will guide you within the world, but I will guide you within it in order to lead you from it.

(v 37 – 39)[1]Be not confused. [2]All that I give to you, I give within your heart. [3]Do not look for your rewards in the world. [4]Look for your reward in Me. [5]Surely, if you look in Me, you will find your reward. [6]And you will know that your reward is great indeed, for peace cannot lie. [7]Peace is truth, and I am your peace in the world. [8]Seek Me in willingness within your heart. [9]Seek Me beyond the world, and even in the world you shall know Me.

NTI Matthew, Chapter 24

(v 1, 2)[1]The world is temporal and nothing within it will last forever.

[2]That which you perceive as holy within the world will not last, for nothing holy exists within the world. [3]But the world can be the reflection of holiness, and it is that reflection that I would have you see.

(v 3 - 8)[1]The world is confusing and painful for those who believe that it is real. [2]In vanity, they will search for hope there. [3]Do not look to the world for hope. [4]Hope is not within the world. [5]Look to Me.

(v 9 – 14)[1]Your faith will seem to be tested if you look to the world as real, for if the world is real, My Word cannot be.

[2]Do not be afraid that My Word is not real. [3]Hold onto it. [4]The trials and tribulations of the world shall come to pass, but My Word will last forever.

(v 15 – 25)[1]The world is confusing when you think it is real, and it will deceive you. [2]Caught in its deception, you will suffer. [3]But the suffering you endure is temporal and can be given up when you are ready, for it is only your belief that makes the suffering real. [4]If you are willing to give up the belief, the suffering will go too.

[5]For the world and all you see in it is based on the belief that you can be separate from God. [6]If you can be separate from God, you can be separate from holiness, and so it is lack and suffering that you shall find.

[7]The world is a reflection of this belief, and so the world is the symbol of conflict, lack and sorrow. [8]Within the world, you will think that holiness is separate from you, because this is what you believe.

(v 26 - 28)[1]I have told you that My guidance comes from within, and there I Am also. [2]Do not look for Me within the world. [3]Do not imagine that I am separate from you.

[4]The world is a place of illusions, because its reflection is a deception and untruth. [5]Listen to Me. [6]I am telling you what I want you to know.

(v 29 – 31)[1]The end is not how you have imagined it, for the end is not a time of separation and suffering. [2]The end of time is a blessing brought about by the release of the belief in separation, for the end of time is the end of the world, and the world is the reflection of this belief.

(v 32 – 35)[1]When you notice that the world is everything I say it is, you are becoming ready within your heart. [2]When you prefer love to conflict, you will begin to listen to Me. [3]When you prefer oneness to separateness, you will ask Me how to think. [4]When you are tired of loss, lack and suffering, you will give yourself to Me to be made complete. [5]All this you can choose, and in all this, I am with you.

(v 36 – 41)[1]The resurrection will not be a surprise. [2]The resurrection will be of your own choosing, for when you are ready, you will be resurrected. [3]In this way, it may seem as if one is taken and another is left, but that is the illusion of the world. [4]For the one who is taken goes of his own choice and takes all that is with him. [5]And the one who is left has but yet to make the choice.

[6]There is no lack in God. [7]Lack is an illusion of the world. [8]For that which is not separate must be complete, and that which is complete can suffer no lack.

(v 42 - 44)[1]If the Son of God could come when you did not expect him, the Son of God would be like a thief taking you before you are ready. [2]For if your heart is still in the world, you are not ready for Heaven.

[3]It is you who must prepare yourself for Heaven. [4]And therefore, you must ask Heaven to come to you.

(v 45 – 51)[1]Do not be afraid of God. [2]For the fear of God will keep you from Him. [3]I say to you, God is your peace, and so it is peace you must seek. [4]When you have found peace, you have found God. [5]When you are lost from peace, you are lost from God. [6]All of this is within the power of your choice.

NTI Matthew, Chapter 25

(v 1 – 13)   [1]*Keep watch within your mind.*

[2]I have already told you that the world is not real. [3]You will not find your peace by looking there. [4]If you look to the world for peace, you are like the five foolish virgins. [5]They had some light for a little while, and

the world may give you moments of peace, joy and warmth. [6]But just as the light did not last throughout the night for the foolish virgins, the world cannot give you lasting peace.

[7]The world is the darkness of the night. [8]And you cannot look to the darkness for light.

[9]Be like the five wise virgins. [10]Do not look to the world for peace. [11]Look where I Am. [12]By looking to Me, you will find the light that never goes out.

📖(v 14 – 30)[1]The story of the servants with talents is a story of faith. [2]One servant believed the fear he thought he saw, and he reacted to his belief as if it were real. [3]Fear begets fear. [4]If you seek evidence of fear within the world, the world will provide you with your fill. [5]And there is the weeping and gnashing of teeth, lost within the illusion of fear.

> [6]*But fear is an illusion,*
> *and all illusions can be overcome.*

[7]Be like the other two servants who did not place their faith in fear. [8]Have faith beyond your fear, and you shall reap your reward even within the world. [9]For the world is a place of fear, but fear is not real. [10]Therefore, the perception of a fearful world cannot be real either.

📖(v 31 – 46)[1]The sheep and the goats are the thoughts within your mind. [2]Both are within your mind now. [3]When you look at the world, you may look with the thoughts of sheep or you may look with the thoughts of goats. [4]When you look at your brother, you may look with the thoughts of sheep or you may look with the thoughts of goats.

[5]The thoughts of sheep are God-centered thoughts. [6]They are thoughts of love, oneness, sharing, peace and joy. [7]Within the thoughts of sheep, there is no thought of separation. [8]Within the thoughts of sheep, everything is the same, blanketed with peace and love and the security of God. [9]These are your real thoughts, because they are based on reality.

[10]The thoughts of goats seem to be the opposite. [11]Although they may

sometimes seem like love, it is love for oneself separate from the love of others. [12]Although they may sometimes seem like peace, it is peace for one's way separate from the way of others.

[13]For the thoughts of goats are thoughts based on the illusion of separateness. [14]When you listen to these thoughts, you believe the illusion to be real. [15]What you believe shall be your experience, and so your mind will seem to be but a herd of goats.

[16]I am the Light of the world. [17]I have come to show you that goats are but shadow thoughts within your mind based on a belief in illusion. [18]Look to Me, and ask for help. [19]We will sort through the herd together. [20]The sheep shall be separated from the goats. [21]The sheep shall last forever, and the goats shall be no more.

NTI Matthew, Chapter 26

(v 1 – 5)[1]Now you must choose where you will decide to look. [2]Your decision will show you what you will see.

(v 6 – 13)[1]Let your confusion go. [2]Your confusion is based on a belief in the world, but you will not see that the world is not real if you choose to hold onto your confusion.

[3]With every thought that comes into your mind, you must make a decision:

[4]*Will I believe this thought and keep it,*
or will I let this thought go?

[5]Thoughts of doubt, confusion, fear, attack and guilt seem justified within a world of doubt, confusion, fear, attack and pain, but this is why I have told you that the world is not real. [6]For if the world was real, your thoughts would be justified. [7]If these thoughts are justified, your pain must be real.

[8]But I tell you, there is no justification for these thoughts, and your pain is not real. [9]And this is where I ask you to put your faith. [10]If you

put your faith with Me, you will see that the world is not real.

📖(v 14 – 16)[1]Judas' confusion was real for him, as your confusion is real for you. [2]Judas did not let his confusion go. [3]Judas believed the world and believed his thoughts, and so Judas did what his thoughts told him to do.

[4]Do not misunderstand. [5]Judas did not betray Jesus, because Jesus could not be betrayed.

[6]In the world, Judas seemed to turn Jesus over for crucifixion, but the crucifixion of the Son of God is not real. [7]Therefore, Judas did nothing but believe his confusion, and Judas only did this for a little while.

(v 17 – 19)[1]The story of Jesus continues with what seems to be a focus on the world. [2]I ask you to look beyond the world with Me as we look at this story. [3]The truth will set you free.

📖(v 20 – 24)[1]The fear of God has led to attack and hatred, and so it is attack and hatred you see and feel through this scripture. [2]Remember what I have told you. [3]Fear will keep you from Me. [4]Trust that these feelings of anger are intended only to hide your fear of Me. [5]And what is hidden is carefully protected. [6]Is it your fear that you would protect?

[7]Choose now to let your anger, attack and hatred go. [8]They serve you not. [9]Rest with Me in faith instead.

📖(v 25)[1]Now, as you read this scripture you see that it is you who have betrayed yourself. [2]For in your belief of your own thoughts, you hide the truth of who you are.

[3]*This is the truth of your illusion:*
[4]*It stays with you through no power but your own.*
[5]*And the truth shall set you free.*

📖(v 26 – 30)[1]Too much importance has been placed on this event called the Last Supper. [2]Jesus did not intend for this event to become a holy ritual within the world. [3]For if he had intended it to become a ritual, he would be implying that his death meant something. [4]And the purpose of Jesus' decision to continue with the crucifixion was to show that death means nothing.

[5]Jesus celebrated this Passover with his apostles, because it was Jewish tradition. [6]Things of the world were not important to Jesus by this time, but the traditions were important to his apostles. [7]And so he celebrated with them out of love, and he chose to use the celebration as a teaching opportunity.

[8]He used the bread as a symbol of the body to show the meaninglessness of the body. [9]For one would not eat something that was holy. [10]He would place it on an altar and give it praise.

[11]The wine represents communion or oneness. [12]He used the wine to teach forgiveness by asking them all to drink from the same cup and by speaking of forgiveness as they drank.

[13]*Let go of the world.*
[14]*Forgive the belief in separateness.*
[15]*Truly, we are one.*

[16]This was the message of the Last Supper.

📖(v 31 - 35)[1]Fear must be released. [2]You must look at your fear and trust that it is not real, or it will hold you back. [3]Fear can keep you from Me.

[4]Jesus knew that Peter was afraid and that Peter believed his fear, but Jesus did not condemn him for this. [5]Jesus only wanted Peter to see his fear and realize that it is an obstacle to God. [6]In this way, Peter could choose to let his fear go.

[7]Peter preferred to deny his fear, because it frightened him. [8]And so he denied his fear to Jesus. [9]What is denied is buried, and what is buried is carefully protected. [10]Jesus knew this of Peter, and so he lovingly gave Peter the opportunity to notice his fear. [11]This was a gift from Jesus to his brother, Peter.

[12]The truth is within, and the truth is a bright light so glorious that you

cannot but begin to imagine it. [13]But you do not see this light, because it is clouded by fear and guilt and sorrow.

(v 36 - 38)[1]Jesus represents the one Son of God, and as a symbol of this mind, he experiences what this mind experiences. [2]As one who experiences the experiences of the mind, Jesus steps forth as a model, for Jesus was not held back by his experiences. [3]He did not let them stop him. [4]He did not view them as his reality. [5]Jesus was one who knew his reality to be greater than the experiences of the world. [6]This enabled him to lay his experiences aside, that he may know truth.

📖(v 39)[1]The experience in this scripture is something you experience all of the time, so is it surprising that Jesus, who is one with you, should experience it also? [2]But Jesus is the model of forgiveness. [3]Jesus did not deny his egoic thoughts. [4]Jesus exposed his thoughts and admitted to them. [5]But then he let them go quickly, secure in the knowledge that his purpose is one with God's.

(v 40, 41)[1]Now Jesus asks his disciples to follow his example. [2]Keep watch on your mind. [3]Do not sleep, for you must be aware of your thoughts as Jesus was, that you may also let them go in peace.

📖(v 42)[1]Forgiveness may not seem to be complete all at once. [2]It may seem that thoughts are released only to return again. [3]Let this not disturb you. [4]Follow the example of Jesus given in this scripture. [5]Go in peace and forgive in faith again.

(v 43, 44)[1]It is the alert mind that will make forgiveness complete. [2]Focus on your purpose. [3]Watch your mind. [4]Let go of all thoughts that do not support the purpose of Love.

(v 45, 46)[1]Judas is the symbol of the mind that has not let go of its confusion. [2]This mind believes its thoughts and holds onto them. [3]Jesus wanted his disciples to wake up and see this aspect of mind, that they may be aware of the danger of keeping their worldly thoughts.

📖(v 47 – 49)[1]The mind that believes its confusion does not know it is lost from love, for it is lost and it believes it loves. [2]The symbol of a kiss emphasizes the confusion, that you may look within yourself and find where you seem to pretend to love, when truly you are denying your confusion.

[3]*Confusion comes from a belief in separateness.*

[4]*Confusion is denied,*

because the belief is also denied.

(v 50)[1]Arrest symbolizes what the denied, confused mind seems to do to the Son of God. [2]It makes him prisoner of his confusion. [3]In his prison, the Son of God forgets that he is free.

[4]Listen to Me. [5]I am talking to you about you. [6]You deny your confusion and your fear, and so you are a prisoner of your own denial.

(v 51 - 54)[1]The disciple with the sword is also symbolic of the belief in confusion and fear. [2]In his belief, he attacks, thinking that attack will protect him. [3]But attack does not protect. [4]Attack furthers the cycle of confusion. [5]Through attack, you are further lost from God.

(v 55, 56)[1]Let go of your self. [2]Surrender to the situation and accept it. [3]When you fight or hide, you are denying the truth that I share. [4]And you are protecting the belief that has become so dear to you. [5]I ask you to give up this belief by coming with Me. [6]Lay your self aside.

(v 57 – 64)[1]Jesus remained silent when false witness was brought against him, because to answer to this witness would have been to declare it and the world as real. [2]But Jesus stood before the world forgiving it, letting it go within his mind.

[3]Jesus did not, however, deny the truth. [4]The truth he willingly acknowledged, even though he knew it may not be understood.

(v 65 – 68)[1]As you watch your mind now (while reading this scripture), you see these men who hit Jesus, spat on him and showed him all kinds of disrespect as guilty men. [2]For you believe that to deny innocence is guilt. [3]I tell you, this is not a feeling you have about them. [4]This is a feeling you have about yourself. [5]For you believe that to deny innocence is guilt, and yet you believe that you deny your Self, and so you assume that you must be guilty.

[6]I say to you, you are not guilty of your denial. [7]You are not guilty of your fear. [8]What you have done within your mind has caused nothing at all. [9]God is one, and Heaven continues to sing its praises to our Father. [10]We merely wait for you to forgive yourself and join us within our joy.

(v 69 – 75)[1]As the rooster crowed, Peter began the process of forgiveness. [2]He let that which had been hidden be shown to him. [3]This is the first step in letting it go.

NTI Matthew, Chapter 27

(v 1 – 10)[1]In this scripture, Judas symbolizes the dance of guilt. [2]It is one of death, for this is what you believe you deserve for denial and attack on innocence. [3]And so the Son of God seems to die, and life itself cannot be itself. [4]This is the illusion of the world, born from the illusion of guilt. [5]Be not sad that this illusion has taken hold of you, for it is only an illusion. [6]There is no truth to it at all. [7]Have faith with Me.

[8]The chief priests represent your denial, for you have denied that the world and all that is in it is of your making, born of your belief in guilt, a product of your fear. [9]The world is like the potter's field. [10]It is a place used to hide guilt out of fear, and it is a place where foreigners go.

[11]I say to you, the self that you think you are is but a foreigner to your true Self, for the purpose of this self is the denial of guilt and fear. [12]These are foreign purposes.

[13]Listen to Me. [14]Let go of your foreign purposes, and remember the purpose of your Father. [15]There, within that remembrance, your truth is.

(v 11 – 14)[1]A king is a leader, a lord, and the Voice for God is the lord for the lost son of God. [2]For it is this Holy Spirit that calls the son Home, and when the son turns to answer his Father's call, it is the Holy Spirit that leads him there. [3]In this way, Jesus was the king of the Jews. [4]He offered himself as a teacher unto his people, that they might hear the truth for themselves. [5]Many have heard and answered the call through him.

(v 15 – 26)[1]Fear comes from guilt, for one who feels guilty expects retaliation, and he becomes afraid. [2]This is what is pictured within this scripture. [3]Each one, in his way, acts out of fear to avoid what he believes will be the effects of his guilt.

(v 27 - 31)   [1]*Hatred and cruelty are madness,*
but madness is not sin.
[2]*Madness is confusion believed.*

[3]In the world, it may appear that there are different levels of madness. [4]You may see worry to be much less extreme than hatred and cruelty. [5]But I say to you, all madness is the same regardless of the form it seems to take.

[6]Forgive your brother his madness, and forgive yourself the same. [7]Do not believe confusion. [8]Let the thought of it go. [9]It does not matter what confusion seems to do to you or do within the world. [10]Confusion is based on illusion, and so confusion is illness. [11]Delusion and confusion must be let go to be healed.

(v 32)[1]The man who carried the cross for Jesus was not forced. [2]This is a misunderstanding. [3]Simon represents the angels, which are the thoughts of the Holy Spirit. [4]Angels take all burdens away when your burdens are offered to them.

(v 33, 34)[1]Jesus did not take the narcotic that was so lovingly offered him, but he did accept the love that was offered with it. [2]It was this love that he carried with him to the cross, in gratitude for his brothers and sisters who are one with him.

(v 35, 36)[1]The soldiers casting lots for Jesus' clothes symbolize the belief in separateness, but the soldiers are not separate from Jesus. [2]They are one with him. [3]It is only within the fantasy of their minds that they are not. [4]They keep this fantasy within their minds, because they believe it protects them, and it may seem to for a little while, but the crucifixion must come to all who believe the Son of God can be crucified. [5]For the crucifixion comes from the *belief in guilt*. [6]It is not the effect of guilt itself, for the Son of God is innocent. [7]His beliefs about himself have caused no effects in Heaven.

📖(v 37)[1]The sign that was placed above Jesus' head was meant as a statement of guilt, but I say it is a statement of innocence recognized. [2]For it declares this man not to be a man, and in that declaration, all seeming guilt disappears.

(v 38 – 40)[1]Guilt cast onto others is guilt not cast away. [2]No one can see another as guilty and see himself as innocent, because he believes that guilt is real.

[3]I ask you, let go of the belief in guilt itself.

[4]Without the belief, guilt will be no more.

(v 41 – 44)[1]Jesus did not see his accusers and tormenters as guilty, because Jesus did not believe in guilt. [2]He knew they suffered from delusion. [3]Jesus looked on them in love, not seeing their delusions, but their truth. [4]He loved their truth, because their truth is Love. [5]And Jesus was grateful for his sight.

(v 45 – 49)[1]God has not forsaken you. [2]It is you who sees this in the world. [3]When you believe God has forsaken you, you do not know God. [4]You believe your confusion, and you are not letting it go.

[5]Knowing the truth takes faith, for to know it you must let go of everything you seem to know now. [6]This will not be easy if you choose to believe in the world, for the world that you see is your confusion.

[7]Let go of the confusion in the mind first. [8]Do it in faith, and you will be given the eyes of faith to see a different world.

📖(v 50 – 53)[1]This scripture has one purpose and one purpose only. [2]The point of this scripture is that death isn't real. [3]There can be no death.

📖(v 54)[1]This scripture points to where your faith is leading you, to this recognition about yourself. [2]Truly, all you knew before was but illusion. [3]Upon this recognition, you will be awake and the glory of God shall be yours.

📖(v 55, 56)[1]This scripture also has one purpose, to show there is no separateness in God. [2]It is all One, and One is all that is.

(v 57 – 61)[1]Death is an illusion of form. [2]All that can be seen of death can only be seen within the form of the world.

(v 62 – 66)[1]You who feel safe within the illusion of form fear death. [2]But there is a fear that is greater than your fear of death. [3]It is your fear of Life. [4]It is your fear of Self. [5]It is your fear of truth. [6]It is this fear that you protect, hidden beneath your fear of death, by accepting death as your final reward.

NTI Matthew, Chapter 28

(v 1 - 4)[1]Let not your fear frighten you. [2]Fear can keep you from Me. [3]Look at your fear and let it go, that you may join with Me and be one with Life.

(v 5 – 8)[1]It is your faith that is needed now. [2]Let your faith be greater than your fear. [3]Through faith, overcome fear, and joy shall be your final reward.

(v 9, 10)[1]You shall know Me, for I am one with you. [2]The knowledge of Me cannot be kept from your heart, for I am one with your heart, and I am your Heart.

(v 11 – 15)[1]Do not listen to the ego-thoughts within your mind. [2]Your belief in separation is great. [3]And this belief will seem to sprout many doubts within your mind. [4]But on what basis do you put your faith in doubt over Me? [5]Why choose to believe conflict over peace? [6]Why choose fear over love?

[7]Listen to Me. [8]The thoughts that come into your mind are born of two fathers. [9]One is the Father of Love, and in Him you are one with Me. [10]The other is the father of illusion, for every child can have only one true Father.

[11]Lay down your doubts. [12]Listen not to their evidence, and the truth of your Father will rise into your mind like a light to shine away all doubt.

(v 16 – 20)[1]Go in faith, and I will lead you. [2]Let go of all doubt, and listen to Me. [3]It is the truth of your Self that I bring to share. [4]Through overcoming doubt, you will hear Me. [5]Amen.

THE HOLY SPIRIT'S INTERPRETATION OF MARK

NTI Mark, Chapter 1

(v 1 – 3)[1]Before truth can dawn, there is work that must be done. [2]This work must be done in faith and out of a desire for truth.

(v 4, 5)[1]Baptism is a symbol of being washed clean. [2]The one who goes down into the water goes down as an individual who is willing to lay himself aside. [3]Coming up from the water symbolizes the resurrection, the return to oneness of thought, the one Will of God.

(v 6 – 8)[1]John the Baptist separated himself from the world, but only that he may find God. [2]For John knew that God was not of this world, and it was only God that John sought.

(v 9 – 11)[1]Jesus also sought God, but Jesus knew God to be within. [2]So Jesus sought God by seeking guidance. [3]And it was his guidance that he followed to the symbol of baptism.

[4]Jesus was baptized out of more than desire. [5]Jesus was baptized out of purpose. [6]It was his purpose that made the Spirit known to him. [7]For one who has chosen the purpose of God above all else has chosen Spirit, for Spirit and purpose are the same and one.

(v 12 – 13)[1]In purpose, without the distractions of the world, Jesus faced the demons within his mind. [2]It was the thoughts of the Holy Spirit that he trusted, so it was the thoughts of the Holy Spirit that he kept.

[3]When Jesus walked out of the desert, he had had many insights and his mind was pure of maddening and confusing thoughts, but Jesus was not yet free of the ego. [4]So Jesus went into the world filled with peace and

knowing love, that he may be led by the Spirit to the end of his self.

(v 14, 15)[1]Jesus followed the Voice of Spirit into the world as a teacher, sharing his experience of joy and freedom. [2]He offered himself as an example, that others may see his Light and desire truth.

(v 16 – 20)[1]In this way, Jesus began to gather men around him. [2]Those who were ready saw his Light. [3]And they recognized it without remembering what they recognized, but they knew the Light belonged to them also. [4]So they followed Jesus, that they may also know his Light.

(v 21 – 28)[1]Jesus taught things that had not been taught before. [2]He used the law, but he did not teach the law. [3]He taught of Light beyond the law, and people were amazed.

[4]When Jesus was challenged by one who was angry and seemed ready for violence, the people became afraid. [5]Hatred and cruelty was within the world they knew, and it was a fight of defense they expected from Jesus now.

[6]But Jesus looked on the man with love, and he smiled for a while, which seemed to observers to cause nervousness within the man. [7]He twitched uncomfortably and did not know what to say to Jesus' silent reaction. [8]Then Jesus reached out to him and said in a peaceful voice, "Come. [9]Come out with us, and see what love is."

[10]With that, the man fell to his knees crying, for he had never known such love. [11]He was touched with gratitude.

[12]The people were amazed. [13]They knew this man, Jesus, taught in a way that was different and new.

(v 29 - 34)[1]And so Jesus went about in this way, healing people through his love. [2]The people flocked to him, coming in confusion lost from hope, leaving him touched by love itself and filled with great hope.

(v 35 – 39)[1]In this way, Jesus led a life of guidance, not yet aware of where it was leading him, except knowing it was the *only way* for him.

(v 40 – 42)[1]Through Jesus, men began to discover God. [2]They discovered that God is with them, willing to love them and heal them in every moment, awaiting only their invitation that He come in.

(v 43 – 45)[1]Not yet knowing where he was being led, the man of Jesus harbored some fear deep within his mind. [2]During this time, he kept this fear hidden from himself. [3]And so the Spirit led him down a useful and helpful path, that one day he may find the strength to face and lay down his fear.

NTI Mark, Chapter 2

(v 1 – 5)[1]Jesus' great love attracted many, for the people had not seen this love before. [2]Jesus was like a light within the darkness, and the people craved to see the Light.

[3]Not yet knowing that the Light is within, people struggled to place themselves next to Jesus, thinking that they needed to touch him in order to know his holiness. [4]Though their struggles could be tiring to him, Jesus was touched by them. [5]For he knew it was Light they craved, and so he started to point the way for them by speaking of faith and inherent innocence.

(v 6, 7)[1]This is what caught the attention of the Jewish religious leaders, for Jesus seemed to be telling the people that they didn't need their leadership. [2]This frightened them, so they started watching Jesus with great suspicion.

(v 8 – 12)[1]Jesus did not react in defense to his accusers. [2]He saw their faces and knew their thoughts, but turned it all over to the Holy Spirit. [3]And it was the symbol of walking in health and peace with God that came to him. [4]So Jesus touched a paralytic in love and asked him to walk in faith. [5]And the Holy Spirit whispered into the man's mind, "Walk!" [6]The man was surprised by his own thought, and he did as it asked. [7]All who watched were amazed. [8]They thought it was Jesus who had healed this man.

❧ ❧ ❧ ❧ ❧

(v 13 - 17)[1]Jesus matured in his listening to Spirit as he listened and trusted more, and so more was revealed to him. [2]Jesus began seeing the face of Christ in everyone. [3]And in everyone, he knew that he found his Self.

[4]In his joy, Jesus invited anyone who would listen to follow him, that they may know the joy themselves. [5]He celebrated and relaxed with people, because he enjoyed them and felt at peace around them. [6]But many who watched Jesus were suspicious of his behavior. [7]They did not see as Jesus did. [8]They saw differences in people, and the differences they saw frightened them.

[9]Jesus was not alarmed by their fear. [10]He welcomed them to join him also, explaining that he had news to teach that showed there were no differences and there were no sinners among them. [11]But they could not hear Jesus' words, because they were not ready to acknowledge the truth in them.

(v 18 – 20)[1]As Jesus' listening and understanding increased, the traditions of Jesus' world began to fall away from him. [2]It was this letting go of the ways of the world that his people could not understand, and so they asked him about it. [3]Jesus explained that as one comes to know God within the heart, only God within the heart comes to be important to him. [4]And all that is not within the heart loses its importance. [5]But they were not ready for these words, and so they did not understand.

(v 21, 22)[1]Jesus loved the people and wanted to help them understand, and so he gave examples through illustrations.

[2]"Awareness of truth is a newness that fills you with light, different from anything you seemed to know before. [3]How can one be filled with such newness, such light and such difference and not seem to be different on the outside? [4]What is inside is seen outside, and so by seeing the outside, you know the inside is changing too."

৶   ৶   ৶   ৶   ৶

(v 23, 24)[1]In his joy, Jesus went about his work following the prompts (guidance) of the Holy Spirit and rejoicing in gratitude for all that was given him. [2]But those who saw the change, without the willingness to see the Light, could not see the Light that Jesus followed. [3]They thought him to be a horrible sinner, for he broke the law and yet claimed to lead men to God.

(v 25 – 28)[1]Jesus was patient with their accusations, for he understood their confusion. [2]He explained that the law was made for man, but man was meant to transcend the limits of the law. [3]Since his accusers were not willing to see the Light, they could not understand his words, and it scared them that people were being fooled by this man.

NTI Mark, Chapter 3

(v 1 – 6)[1]Jesus taught in the synagogue, and people listened with great interest and curiosity. [2]This bothered the Jewish religious leaders who feared that the people had less interest in what they had to say. [3]They planned to discredit Jesus in front of all the people, so that the people would turn away from him. [4]They knew the people trusted the law, so they challenged Jesus on his understanding and practice of the law.

[5]Jesus was not fooled by their intent, and he knew that his answers would not convince them to see differently. [6]Jesus turned all of this over to the Holy Spirit and asked for Spirit's guidance. [7]It was Spirit's Will to give all who would see an opportunity to see differently now. [8]And so the Spirit turned a shriveled hand into a healthy one, that all men may know that distortion can be replaced with newness when willingness is given for newness to be received.

ॐ   ॐ   ॐ   ॐ   ॐ

(v 7 – 12)[1]Jesus found the work of teaching to be difficult, for few seemed to want to hear the good news of the kingdom and take it to heart. [2]Word and rumors of healing spread quickly. [3]People came from far and

wide to seek healing for their bodies, without concern for their hearts.
[4]Often, Jesus felt led to retreat from the crowds. [5]Lost within them, he felt
useless, so in solitude he sought to find his purpose again.

(v 13 – 19)[1]It was in silence that Jesus received guidance to pick
twelve who seemed interested in healing the heart and focus his efforts on
teaching those twelve. [2]In this way, the Word he had learned would
spread, and many would discover truth through them. [3]So Jesus found
twelve who had asked him sincere questions of the heart. [4]These twelve
he called apostles, and he promised to teach them all that he had learned,
that they might teach others.

෯   ෯   ෯   ෯   ෯

(v 20 – 30)[1]Many did not understand Jesus. [2]The pressure put on him
was great. [3]The crowds wanted their bodies healed. [4]His family wanted
him to come home and rest. [5]The Jewish leaders wanted him quieted.
[6]And so one day, under the guidance of the Holy Spirit, Jesus was given
the opportunity to address all of them.

[7]In spite of their misunderstandings, people grew quiet when Jesus
prepared to speak, so he was able to address them without talking in a
loud voice.

[8]"You say that I am possessed of demons and I drive out demons, but
if I am a brother to the demons, why would I drive them away? [9]A house
divided cannot stand. [10]I am not helpful as a demon if it is demons I drive
away.

[11]"You say I have lost my mind and forgotten who I am, wandering
the countryside like a lunatic, but does a lunatic know love and peace as
I do? [12]Does a lunatic have great friends as I do? [13]I have not forgotten
who I am. [14]I know who I am fully. [15]A house divided cannot stand, and
with this wisdom, I stand lovingly by my brothers now.

[16]"You say that I have magic to heal the sick and injured, but I say one
man cannot heal another. [17]Look within yourself and find what keeps you

from being healed, that you may overcome that thing and be healed."

[18]Each one knew when Jesus was talking to him. [19]And although they may not have understood his words fully, they saw his sincerity. [20]On this day, Jesus was able to walk away from the crowd in silence.

(v 31 - 35)[1]Jesus' family followed him and his apostles to a quiet place, and they asked to be admitted inside to speak to him. [2]Jesus knew they had come to ask him to return home, so he sent a messenger out to them to explain that his family is the family of God, and his duty now was to do as his heavenly Father asked. [3]Jesus also sent an invitation that his family join him, for the family of God is one.

NTI Mark, Chapter 4

(v 1 – 20)[1]Once again, Jesus found himself by the lake with a crowd of people seeking physical healing. [2]He asked his disciples to prepare a boat, and he stepped into it so he could be moved away from the shore. [3]From there, he was able to talk to the crowd, because with him a short distance away, they quieted down to listen.

[4]Jesus knew that the people had not come to hear the good news, and yet it was the good news he yearned to share. [5]Jesus bowed his head to give the circumstance to the Holy Spirit. [6]He gave his willingness to do whatever Spirit would have him do. [7]He was willing to go back into the crowd. [8]He was willing to speak from the boat. [9]He was willing to leave this place at once. [10]When he had finished giving over all he thought to the Holy Spirit, he lifted his face, opened his mouth, and these words came out:

[11]"Listen!" [12]There was a long and quiet pause, and then he continued with an authority in his voice that had not been heard before.

[13]"A farmer went out to plant his fields. [14]This farmer lovingly planted his seed everywhere, for to him, all soil was worthy of seed. [15]As he scattered the seed, some fell along the path. [16]'This soil is worthy,' he thought. [17]But as the seed lie, birds came and ate it up, so that no plants sprouted there.

¹⁸"Some seed fell on rocky soil. ¹⁹'This soil is worthy of this seed,' the farmer thought. ²⁰The soil there was rich and plants sprouted quickly. ²¹But the soil was not deep, so as the sun grew hot, the plants withered and died.

²²"Some seeds fell among the thorns. ²³'This soil is also worthy,' the farmer thought. ²⁴But the thorns choked the plants, and they did not bear grain.

²⁵"Still other seed fell on good soil. ²⁶'This soil is likewise worthy,' thought the farmer. ²⁷And the plants grew and produced a crop, multiplying thirty, sixty and even a hundred times.

²⁸"Let him who has ears, hear. ²⁹This is the message of our Lord. ³⁰You choose which soil you shall be!"

³¹Jesus left the crowd by boat as they discussed this strange parable among themselves. ³²The apostles were also puzzled, for the parable made no sense to them, and they knew their master had many good words he could have shared.

³³"They did not come to hear my words," Jesus explained. ³⁴"They came for healing. ³⁵All healing is of the Holy Spirit, so I gave myself to Him, that I may be used. ³⁶And it was His words you heard through me. ³⁷I saw the image in my mind, and I described it as I saw it."

³⁸The apostles did not understand.

³⁹"Listen," Jesus said in love. ⁴⁰"Let me tell you fully what I saw.

⁴¹"Our heavenly Father is the farmer. ⁴²He loves all of his children. ⁴³His children may look at one another and see differences, but the heavenly Father sees none. ⁴⁴To Him, we are all the same and equally worthy to know Him.

⁴⁵"In this story, we are the soil. ⁴⁶The seed is the Holy Spirit's Word. ⁴⁷So our Father sows the seed on all of his children alike, seeing no differences among them. ⁴⁸But within our perception, there are differences. ⁴⁹Some of the children seem like the path. ⁵⁰They have no interest in the Holy Spirit's words, and His Word does not sink into their hearts. ⁵¹That is the choice they have made, so we will let them go their way in peace.

[52]"Some of our Father's children are like the soil in rocky places. [53]They will eagerly join us and seem to love His Word. [54]But when circumstances seem to get tough, they will turn away, because they do not seek the Father above all else. [55]It is comfort they are satisfied with, so it is temporal comfort that they will continue to seek. [56]We will let them go in peace and wish only blessings on them.

[57]"Some are like soil among thorns. [58]The Word may spark some interest in them, but they are too preoccupied with the world to let it go and pursue the Word. [59]Let them go in peace, with blessings and in love.

[60]"And the others are like seed sown on good soil, because they are ready for the Word at this time. [61]They will come and work with us, live like brothers with us and join us in our work of sharing the Word."

(v 21 – 23)[1]Jesus settled in with joy in his heart to continue teaching the deep truths he had learned from the Holy Spirit.

[2]"We must show ourselves to the people, that they may see our Light, for the Light within us is the Light of Heaven. [3]It is within them too. [4]By seeing it within us, they will recognize that it is within them, and the Light will extend within the world.

[5]"In this way and for this reason, the Light must extend within you too. [6]For as the Light extends within you, it extends within the world."

[7]The apostles did not understand, so Jesus shared his message in another way.

[8]"Do you bring in a lamp and place it under a bowl or a bed to keep the light hidden? [9]No. [10]It is the light that must shine, so that which is in the dark can be revealed.

[11]"This is how it is in truth. [12]As the Light shines within your mind, thoughts of darkness are revealed. [13]Let them be revealed, that they may be given up to the Light. [14]In this way, the Light of God extends throughout the world!"

[15]The apostles marveled at how Jesus smiled as he spoke to them. [16]"Surely," they thought, "this Light has extended through his mind."

❧   ❧   ❧   ❧   ❧

(v 24 – 34)[1]After stopping to eat, and after listening to the casual conversation of the apostles, Jesus continued his teaching to them. [2]He asked the woman of the house to bring him some grain and a measuring cup, that he may make a point for the apostles.

[3]"Your judgment is like this grain," Jesus said, pouring the grain into a cup. [4]"With the measure you use, it will be measured to you." [5]Jesus laughed and poured the measure of grain onto an apostle's head. [6]Caught up in the playfulness of the moment, he tossed another handful of grain at the apostle. [7]"Even more!" he laughed.

[8]The joy of the moment spread around the table, and more wine was served.

[9]"What is within your heart now is the measure of your love, but this measure is not limited. [10]As you live up to the measure you have, more is given. [11]And from there, even more." [12]Jesus smiled at his apostles. [13]They listened intently to all of his words.

[14]"But if you do not live up to your love, your love will be lost to you. [15]Let those who have ears, listen."

[16]"Master?" an apostle asked. [17]"Will you tell us what the kingdom of Heaven is like?"

[18]Jesus knew that the apostle did not yet understand even his question, so Jesus used a parable to illustrate it for them.

[19]"Yes. [20]This is what the kingdom of God is like."

[21]He motioned to them, as if he was going to tell them a great secret. [22]The apostles leaned forward in anticipation.

[23]"A man scatters seed on the ground. [24]Night and day, whether he sleeps or gets up, whether he seems to think of the seed or not, the seed sprouts and grows. [25]It is not through his effort that this has happened. [26]The man does not know how the seed grows, but he sees the evidence of its growth, and he is grateful for it. [27]All by itself, the soil produces the grain. [28]First the stalk, then the head, and then the full kernel within the

head. ²⁹And then it is ripe, and all of this happened because the man was willing to plant the seed.

³⁰"Give your willingness to let the Word be planted within you. ³¹It shall grow and ripen, and then you shall know the kingdom of God.

³²"Let me tell you this another way. ³³There are so many ways to describe this glory!

³⁴"The kingdom of God is like a mustard seed, which is the smallest of seeds that you plant in the ground. ³⁵Yet when it is planted, it grows into the largest of garden plants, standing tall for all to see. ³⁶Even the birds enjoy perching in its branches."

³⁷The apostles laughed at the image Jesus provided for them, for truly it was a happy and joyous image.

³⁸Through parables and explanations of parables, Jesus taught the apostles all they wanted to know about the kingdom of God. ³⁹Through his teaching, the joy of all increased.

(v 35 – 41)¹When the hour grew late, Jesus and his apostles took their leave. ²They traveled by boat, and Jesus went to sleep there. ³As he slept, a wild storm shook their little convoy of boats. ⁴The apostles grew very afraid and woke their master in case something dreadful should happen.

⁵Jesus did not seem alarmed by the storm. ⁶He smiled at the apostles without opening his eyes. ⁷"It is no matter," he said. ⁸"This storm is nothing of consequence."

⁹"Aren't you afraid we will drown?" they asked.

¹⁰Jesus got up with them and went out onto the deck. ¹¹Already, the storm was passing.

¹²"See," Jesus smiled. ¹³"The Son of God has nothing to fear. ¹⁴All is calm now."

¹⁵It seemed to the apostles that as Jesus spoke, the winds completely died down. ¹⁶Jesus went back to continue his slumber, but the apostles gathered to discuss this claim that Jesus was the Son of God.

NTI Mark, Chapter 5

(v 1 – 20)[1]The next morning, Jesus and the apostles stepped ashore in an area near some burial tombs. [2]The apostles were hungry, so Jesus led them up a path looking for something they could eat. [3]A woman on morning errands approached them and recommended they choose another path.

[4]"There is a demon-possessed man living there among the tombs," she pointed. [5]"He is very dangerous. [6]The men have tried chaining him for our safety, but he always breaks away!"

[7]The apostles were afraid of this woman's story and urged Jesus to select another path.

[8]"Have you learned nothing?" Jesus asked with a teasing smile. [9]"The Son of God has nothing to fear."

[10]Just then, the man the woman spoke of showed himself from behind a bush. [11]He began circling the small group, cursing God and pointing up to the sky. [12]The apostles stepped closer together, wondering how the master would handle this situation.

[13]Jesus smiled at the enraged man. [14]"You have nothing to fear. [15]We come in peace."

[16]"Peace! Ha!" the man mocked. [17]"I heard you talking. [18]You are the Son of God!" [19]And then the man continued his insane cursing of the Lord, this time pointing directly at Jesus.

[20]"And who are you?" Jesus asked in a friendly and casual tone.

[21]"I am the demons," the man answered. [22]"A legion of them! [23]You cannot touch me. [24]My power is greater than yours, Son of God."

[25]"Yes, I imagine it is," Jesus said. [26]The apostles were shocked by his manner and words. [27]"I imagine that you have the power to do whatever you wish of your own choice."

[28]"Of course I do!" screamed the man.

[29]"Then I should like to see you leave this man," Jesus said.

[30]"Then we would be homeless!" screamed the man, as if he truly thought himself to be a legion of demons.

[31]Jesus stepped closer to the man, but only a little. [32]He knew the man was frightened in spite of his ferocious appearance, and Jesus did not want to frighten him anymore. [33]Jesus only wanted to help the man see that his sanity was within him and his insanity was foreign to him, so insanity could be let go.

[34]Jesus noticed a herd of pigs in the distance. [35]He pointed them out to the man. [36]"I would like to see that you are truly a legion of demons and not just one. [37]Can you leave this man and inhabit that herd of pigs?"

[38]"Of course we can!" the man replied. [39]"We can do anything!"

[40]"All right then," smiled Jesus. [41]"Go into the pigs and show that you have truly left. [42]Let me talk to this man without you."

[43]The man turned to face the pigs, screaming insanities at the Lord as he did. [44]Then he quieted and smiled a proud smile, as if he had accomplished something great.

[45]"Is this the man before me now?" Jesus asked.

[46]"It is!" answered the man, still using a proud tone that led the apostles to feel suspicious.

[47]Jesus walked to the man and put his arm around him. [48]"Let's go for a walk and talk for a bit. [49]Just you and me."

[50]The man went with Jesus. [51]The apostles watched as Jesus and the man knelt under a tree, ripping pieces of grass with their hands, talking quietly.

[52]After some time, Jesus and the man returned to the group.

[53]"Josiah has agreed to go home," Jesus announced. [54]"He will have support there and will be able to continue his healing. [55]Come. [56]Let's walk with him. [57]We may find food there," Jesus coaxed.

[58]So Jesus and the apostles walked Josiah home, talking with him in a friendly and cordial way. [59]They walked passed the herd of pigs, who relaxed peacefully in the warming morning sun. [60]They walked passed local villagers, who were shocked by what they saw. [61]And they took Josiah to his family, who were overjoyed to see their father in this way.

[62]Jesus spent some time talking to Josiah's wife, giving her advice,

instructions, and sharing teachings. [63]She seemed to listen to Jesus eagerly. [64]When Jesus and the apostles left, Jesus felt confident that Josiah and his entire family would allow themselves to be healed. [65]He left the family in the hands of the Holy Spirit, grateful that he had run across this loving family.

ঙ্গ   ঙ্গ   ঙ্গ   ঙ্গ   ঙ্গ

(v 21 – 34)[1]With each day, Jesus felt his closeness to the Holy Spirit growing. [2]It increased within his mind. [3]A merging seemed to occur. [4]Jesus knew the Holy Spirit as his constant companion, as close as his breath and a part of his Self.

[5]With this awareness, Jesus' teaching and healing activity became more natural for him. [6]He was no longer bothered by the crowds. [7]He didn't notice crowds. [8]He only saw one mind in need of healing, and his only purpose became the healing of that one mind.

[9]One day, Jesus was with his disciples and a large crowd of people when a man named Jairus approached Jesus. [10]Jairus was a synagogue leader, and some thought he may have come to trick Jesus. [11]But Jesus saw sincerity within this man. [12]His daughter was sick, and he sought healing for her, but he knew healing came from God. [13]He believed Jesus to have a special relationship with God, so he sought out Jesus, that God might heal his daughter through him.

[14]Jesus wanted this man to know that God was within him also, but the distraction of the crowd, combined with the man's fear, was too much for a quiet and purposeful conversation. [15]Jesus agreed to go with Jairus to his home, that he might be given the opportunity to talk truth with him there.

[16]As Jesus, Jairus and the apostles started off, the crowds followed them. [17]Many were eager to touch Jesus, since it was rumored that touching him could bring healing. [18]Jesus met each touch with a loving gaze, and many felt better in his presence.

[19]One woman had been drained of her energy for many years. [20]Her husband said she was useless as a wife. [21]It bothered her greatly to be seen as useless, and so her lack of energy was accompanied by depression. [22]When she heard that Jesus was nearby, she asked her sisters to help her make the trip to see him.

[23]The woman and her sisters saw Jesus and the crowd walking up the road. [24]They positioned themselves within the road, so as to be next to Jesus when he passed. [25]As Jesus neared them, the woman's sisters helped her to her feet, that she may stroke his hair. [26]She reached out to touch his head, but was unable to make the reach. [27]Desperate to know herself as worthy of love, she ran after Jesus. [28]In her weakness, she tripped and fell, but she was able to touch his garment as she fell. [29]Jesus felt a tug.

[30]Jesus stopped and turned to see where this tug had come from. [31]He saw this woman's tear-stained face staring up at him.

[32]"What ails you, woman?" he asked.

[33]She explained her ailment and her sense of worthlessness to Jesus. [34]He felt great love and compassion for her. [35]He reached out to help her get close to him, and he stared lovingly into her eyes.

[36]"I tell you," he whispered. [37]"You are not worthless. [38]You are like a jewel that shines bright before the eyes of our Lord, only you have been unaware of your brightness. [39]It is within you, awaiting only your recognition and welcome. [40]Go home. [41]In silence, ask this brightness to make itself known to you. [42]It will, and it will bring with it great energy and love and joy. [43]Go now and ask. [44]You will receive."

[45]The woman did as Jesus asked. [46]And through her faith and vigilance, her ailment went away.

(v 35 – 43)[1]It was only a little further up the road that Jesus and Jairus met messengers from the house of Jairus. [2]"Your daughter is dead," they told him. [3]"You do not need the master now."

[4]Jesus did not feel right about the message that the messengers brought. [5]He felt within him that he should go to the house and they

would find the child alive there. [6]He told Jairus, "Your daughter is not dead. [7]Let us go and see her."

[8]One of the messengers spoke up immediately. [9]"She is dead. [10]I'm sorry, Jairus, but I saw her myself. [11]She had no breath. [12]Your daughter is dead."

[13]Jesus felt a sense of urgency, so he asked his apostles to stay and work with the crowd. [14]He took only three apostles with him. [15]They hurried along the road to Jairus' house.

[16]When Jesus arrived, there were signs of mourning and hysteria about the house. [17]Jesus asked everyone to step outside, that he may see the girl alone.

[18]Jesus felt intuitive guidance to hold the girl's tongue with his fingers in order to clear the air passageway, and then he breathed into her mouth. [19]Soon, a light choking began. [20]Jesus stepped back to watch the girl take her first breaths alone. [21]He asked his disciples to go and get the girl's parents. [22]As they came into the room, she opened her eyes.

[23]"But she was dead!" the mother exclaimed.

[24]"She was not dead," Jesus answered. [25]"She was only sleeping, and now she has awakened to you again."

[26]Everyone was amazed that this man should do this. [27]Word of Jesus began to spread even faster than before.

NTI Mark, Chapter 6

(v 1 – 6)[1]After spending some time with Jairus and his family, teaching them the truth of God within, Jesus went to his home town in order to see his mother and brothers and sisters. [2]He knew they were worried about him, and he wanted to let them see the glory that he had found.

[3]While there, Jesus was given the opportunity to speak in the synagogue. [4]He spoke in depth of the joy of finding God within and of the miraculous process of healing the mind. [5]Some asked questions about rumors of healing. [6]Jesus answered each question in truth.

[7]The people could not believe the change in this man. [8]They looked at

the faces of his sisters and brothers to judge if this change should be regarded as good or not. [9]Most came to the conclusion that it was not good and that Jesus should return home to work and raise a family as his father did. [10]But a few people heard something else as Jesus spoke. [11]These few gathered with Jesus in private to ask questions and learn more. [12]Jesus' mother was among these few, as her eyes were opened to a truth beyond the body of her son.

◈ ◈ ◈ ◈ ◈

(v 7 – 13)[1]When Jesus left his home town, he went from village to village teaching the good news. [2]He let his apostles ask many questions, always answering them to their full. [3]When the time came that he knew they were ready, he sent them out two-by-two to fulfill the purpose for which he had gathered them, the spreading of the Word. [4]He knew that it was through their own participation as teachers that they themselves would learn and see, and so he was very grateful for this plan of healing.

[5]Jesus gave the apostles instructions before sending them out. [6]Mostly, he wanted to emphasize the importance of trusting the Holy Spirit in all things.

[7]"You do not know," he told them. [8]"Only the Holy Spirit knows, so trust His guidance within you. [9]Do not think for yourself about what to do or say. [10]Ask Him, and listen in faith for His response. [11]He shall lead you truly. [12]It is His plan you are sent to carry out.

[13]"Do not look to your own effort for food or drink or shelter. [14]Think only of the work He has sent you to do. [15]All else will be offered through His Grace. [16]When you go into a town, sleep where a bed is offered you. [17]Do not ask for more than you are offered. [18]Eat what is given you, and be grateful for everything you are given. [19]It comes from Him, that you may focus on His work.

[20]"The Word of the kingdom of God is for everyone, but everyone may not be ready for it. [21]If you go into a town and they do not want to

listen to the Word, give them your greetings of peace and leave that place. [22]Hold no grievance against them. [23]The time will come that they will listen. [24]Shake the dust from your sandals and go joyously to the next place, always remembering that it is the Holy Spirit's plan you follow. [25]You do not know."

৯৺ ৯৺ ৯৺ ৯৺ ৯৺

(v 14 – 29)[1]The Word is sometimes heard and recognized, but not accepted because the one who seems to listen lets ego thoughts rule his mind. [2]Ego thoughts are thoughts of separation that say within your mind, "You are separate and different from all you know, and for this you are guilty. [3]You must protect yourself, for when your guilt is unmasked, you will suffer endlessly. [4]You will be cut off from all that is and from life itself."

[5]These thoughts are evil thoughts of deception that you have come to believe. [6]The only peace from them is to stop believing in them completely. [7]This is the opportunity you recognize when you hear the Light within the good news.

[8]The story of King Herod and John the Baptist is the story of a man who recognized the opportunity for peace, but let that opportunity pass him by out of fear. [9]For Herod was fascinated by the words that John the Baptist spoke. [10]Although he did not always understand what John said, there was something within the words that Herod craved.

[11]Therefore, Herod was willing to forgive John when he accused Herod of sinning by marrying his brother's wife, Herodias.

[12]Herodias, however, was not attracted to John's words and felt no desire to forgive him. [13]In her mind, it was through John that her guilt would be unmasked, which would mean the beginning of unending suffering for her. [14]In her mind, her only defense was to have John quieted. [15]And to her, the most permanent means for quieting a man was her surest method of security. [16]She wanted to see John dead. [17]But her

husband would not agree, and this enraged her.

[18]One day, an opportunity seemed to be given her. [19]Her beautiful, ripe, young daughter, step-daughter and niece to Herod, was invited to dance at Herod's birthday party. [20]All of the men were very entertained by her dance. [21]They urged Herod to reward her. [22]Herod was also entertained by his young niece's dance, and so he agreed to please her, that she may be eager to please him again one day. [23]He asked her to choose her gift, and he promised she could pick anything, imagining she would pick some lovely jewels to adorn her fine body. [24]But Herod's niece chose to listen to the pleading of her mother, and so she asked Herod to bring her John's head on a platter.

[25]Herod was shocked by her request. [26]But the men around the birthday table laughed in amusement, for John was nothing to them. [27]Herod could see no way out except to keep his word, or he would be unmasked before everyone at the celebration, and there his unending suffering would begin.

[28]Herod ordered the beheading of John the Baptist. [29]As he did, fear crept up in his throat. [30]"Surely now," he thought, "I am guilty, and punishment will be my final reward."

[31]So when Herod heard news of Jesus, his fear returned to him. [32]For Herod believed the ghost of John inhabited the body of Jesus, and this ghost was working his way through the land, building up followers, waiting for the time to be right to seek just vengeance on Herod. [33]Herod lived in fear.

❧   ❧   ❧   ❧   ❧

(v 30 – 44)[1]The apostles returned to Jesus after a week of teaching to talk of adventures, frustrations, miracles, and to ask questions. [2]In one week of teaching alone, the apostles had grown far in faith. [3]Their trust in the Holy Spirit was developing.

[4]Yet there was still confusion among them as to how some questions

should be answered. [5]So Jesus agreed to a day of rest, during which the apostles could ask their questions and be prepared for another week of teaching.

[6]Jesus and the apostles intended to go to a remote place and delve deeper into the truths alone, but the Holy Spirit led many interested followers to go with them. [7]So Jesus taught all of the people in this way:

[8]His apostles gathered questions from the crowd and brought them to him. [9]Jesus answered the questions for the apostles, who took the answers back to the crowd. [10]In this way, the apostles were able to hear how the master addressed questions from the masses, and the masses were able to hear all of the questions and all of the answers without any strain or difficulty. [11]In this way, everyone received their full.

ৰঙ ৰঙ ৰঙ ৰঙ ৰঙ

(v 45 – 56)[1]When the teaching was complete, Jesus sent the apostles away by boat to begin a second week of teaching two-by-two. [2]Jesus stayed behind with the crowd, feeling no compelling guidance to leave the place where he was.

[3]During the night, as the people rested, Jesus went up on a hill near a small tree to pray and meditate. [4]Within his mind, he sought the opportunity to exceed the limits of his body, knowing that his body could not contain him. [5]He gave himself and his will to the Holy Spirit and rested his mind until the desire for this experience left him. [6]When he was no longer attached to the idea of the experience, a quietness filled his mind. [7]A lifting and movement seemed to occur, although his body did not move. [8]Jesus rested within this experience of the mind, giving it to the Holy Spirit in faith for the purpose of healing and recognizing Self.

[9]Meanwhile, Peter and the other apostles slept on their boats, resting before a morning of travel and teaching were upon them. [10]Peter was restless and could not sleep, so Peter went out into the air to meditate among the stars.

[11]Many worries and concerns swirled within Peter's mind, which was also filled with confusion and doubt. [12]Peter sat down to practice as the master had taught them to practice. [13]He looked at each thought that came into his mind and gave it to the Holy Spirit in faith for the purpose of healing. [14]In this way, Peter cleared his mind of all the thoughts that cluttered it and kept him restless, and peacefulness came over him.

[15]As Peter sat quietly, enjoying all encompassing peace, he heard the voice of his master within his mind. [16]Thinking this voice was his imagination, he willingly turned it over to the Holy Spirit for the purpose of healing, but the voice was given back to him.

[17]"Peter, it is I."

[18]Peter rested quietly, clearing his mind of confusing thoughts as quickly as they seemed to come up.

[19]"It is I, Peter. [20]We are in meditation together, as we are joined and one through our Holy Spirit. [21]Come with me, Peter, one in our purpose and faith. [22]Enjoy the love of our God, which is our Self."

[23]And then, Peter felt as if the master and the Holy Spirit and the Lord together reached out and touched him within his mind. [24]Peter basked in a glory and joy he had not known before.

[25]Peter sat in peace on the deck until sunrise when the other apostles began to awaken. [26]He was grateful for this experience given him by the master from across the waters of the lake. [27]The master rested comfortably, gratefully pleased that he was guided lovingly in all things.

NTI Mark, Chapter 7

(v 1 – 23)[1]Jesus gathered with the apostles and other disciples in a place outside Jerusalem, so it was easy for a group of Pharisees to come and see Jesus there. [2]Some within the group of Pharisees were eager to hear Jesus' words and were open to them. [3]Others hoped to discredit Jesus before his disciples. [4]In this way, the mind of the Pharisees was split as they went to see Jesus. [5]Therefore, what Jesus seemed to do that day was seen differently by different keepers of the law.

[6]When one listens, it is the mind he listens with. [7]So some of the Pharisees on this day heard Jesus speak of love and peace and of God as wholly loving. [8]A restfulness came over their hearts and a peace filled their minds as they became aware of the gloriousness within his words.

[9]Because of the split within the mind, other Pharisees seemed distracted by what was going on within the crowd. [10]They seemed to notice every movement within the crowd, and they made judgments based on what they saw. [11]They did not hear Jesus' words, the meaning of love, or the peace that was beyond the words.

[12]The Pharisees who were not listening to Jesus were aware of many happenings, which the Pharisees who were listening were not aware of. [13]Therefore, it was the Pharisees who were distracted that noticed some of Jesus' disciples ate without washing their hands. [14]The Pharisees who listened with an open heart did not notice.

[15]"Why do your disciples eat without washing their hands?" asked the distracted Pharisees. [16]"This is against our tradition. [17]Through this practice, they are made unclean. [18]Doesn't this make them unfit for the worship of our Lord?"

[19]All eyes turned toward the Pharisees, as if they had just entered the discussion from some other place of awareness. [20]Jesus peacefully arose and motioned toward all of the men as he spoke.

[21]"Everyone is fit to worship our Lord. [22]Every heart within the child of God is clean and free of every thought of uncleanliness. [23]Nothing the child does can make him unclean, for the child inherits the cleanliness of the Father."

[24]"But, Master," a disciple asked. [25]"Surely a man who sins and breaks the law is unclean, and he must make a sacrifice to our Lord before he is permitted to worship Him."

[26]Jesus looked at the disciple with a gentleness in his gaze.

[27]"Nothing a man does can make him unclean, for his cleanliness comes from within, beyond the unclean thoughts. [28]If a man believes the unclean thoughts within his mind, he will act on them. [29]But if a man

does not believe the unclean thoughts in his mind, he will not act on them. [30]If a man has a choice about his thoughts, these thoughts cannot be the essence of the man, for no man has a choice regarding his essence. [31]The essence of a man simply is, without his choice or his action. [32]His essence cannot change, for his essence is given him by God.

[33]"This essence of which I speak is within every man, beneath the thoughts that seem to be clean or unclean and beyond the actions that seem to be clean or unclean. [34]It is a man's essence that worships God. [35]It is essence that defines who he is."

[36]Everyone who listened was amazed at Jesus' answer. [37]But those who were not willing to listen thought he said nothing at all.

❧   ❧   ❧   ❧   ❧

(v 24 – 30) [1]Jesus went away on a retreat, that he may have some time in prayer and meditation with the Holy Spirit, but a woman ran across him there. [2]She recognized the man, Jesus, because she had heard of him, and she knew this man before her was him.

[3]The woman fell to her knees before Jesus, torn between emotions of despair, because of her problem, and gratitude for finding Jesus there. [4]She asked Jesus for his help. [5]Her daughter seemed to be possessed of evil spirit. [6]The woman did not know what to do. [7]She wanted her daughter healed, so that the problem would go away.

[8]Jesus touched the woman on the top of the head and extended love to her. [9]There was a time of silence between them. [10]A shift occurred within the woman's mind. [11]In Jesus' presence, she was aware of the presence of love. [12]All that was not love seemed to fade from her awareness. [13]She became aware that her concerns were not as serious as she had once thought. [14]She looked at the master with openness in her heart. [15]"What words would you share with me?" she asked.

[16]The master smiled at the woman, for she had come seeking healing for her daughter, but now she sought healing for herself.

[17]"Go to your daughter," Jesus answered, "and see that she is well. [18]Extend love to her, as I have to you. [19]Be patient with her, as I have been with you. [20]Do not judge her, as I have not judged you. [21]See that she is well, as I have seen that you are well. [22]Let her come to know her state of wellness through your love, as you have come to know your state of wellness through mine."

[23]The woman kissed Jesus' hands with gratitude and ran off to her home, eager to love her daughter as Jesus had loved her.

[24]This woman and her daughter were not Jewish, so this story has been mistold. [25]The story was shared by word of mouth, beginning with the woman's telling of the story. [26]But those who could not see without seeing differences could not hear the story without hearing differences within it.

[27]One listens with the mind that one seems to have, unless one is willing to lay that mind aside and listen with a new mind.

∽ ∽ ∽ ∽ ∽

(v 31 – 37)[1]In Jesus' travels without the apostles, as they were out teaching and learning from the Holy Spirit, Jesus ran across a man who was hungry and sad and who begged for assistance from anyone who passed. [2]Jesus sat with this man and communicated with him, although the man could not hear and could not speak.

[3]The man became joyous and filled with energy. [4]His only thought was to extend communication, so he left the place where he had been sitting. [5]Forgetting his hunger, he went into the town to extend communication. [6]Jesus went off into a quiet place to do the same.

NTI Mark, Chapter 8

(v 1 – 13)[1]When Jesus was joined together with his apostles again, a large crowd gathered with them. [2]For by now, each of the apostles seemed to have followers of their own, and with each of them came even more.

[3]All of the people set up camp together, that they may learn together and celebrate together. [4]It was a joyous gathering. [5]The people were excited to hear the words of the master, Jesus.

[6]Jesus looked on the crowd and saw that they hungered for truth, but they believed the truth could be given them by a master who knew more of truth than they. [7]Jesus wanted to teach them that the value they sought was found within the mind, so he proceeded to teach the crowd in this way:

[8]Jesus asked the apostles to gather all of the food that they had brought with them. [9]When the food was gathered together, Jesus said a blessing over the food. [10]He spoke loudly for all to hear, and he thanked the heavenly Father for unlimited bounty. [11]Then he asked the apostles to distribute the food evenly among all of the men who had gathered there. [12]He asked the men to share the food with those who had come with them.

[13]The food was broken into very small pieces, not even large enough for one man to consider a bite, and these small pieces were passed out to be shared among the groups that had come with each man.

[14]When the food had been distributed, Jesus gave the instruction to eat. [15]Everyone in the crowd did as Jesus asked. [16]And then Jesus taught them.

[17]"Every man and woman and child who is gathered here today has been given all that he needs in order to find the presence of our Father. [18]Our heavenly Father is not of this world, so He cannot be found in this world. [19]Seek not in the world for our Lord. [20]Seek not from men. [21]Seek where this tiny morsel of food has gone. [22]Let it be your guide. [23]Follow it to the presence of the Father within, and let Him guide you to the truth you seek.

[24]"Truly I tell you, no one lacks the guidance of our Father, for everyone has been given the same."

[25]Then Jesus led the people in a long period of prayer and meditation. [26]Many came to discover the presence of the Father within as Jesus had

instructed them.

✦   ✦   ✦   ✦   ✦

(v 14 – 21)[1]Jesus was aware of doubts within the minds of the apostles, but the doubts did not concern him. [2]Jesus' vision of the face of Christ was nearing its fullness, and his heart was filled with love and peace at all times. [3]Yet, he knew the apostles' doubts concerned them. [4]For in their minds, they had given up much to follow Jesus. [5]They sought fullness in faith that their choice had been the right one, so their doubts concerned them gravely.

[6]One night, Jesus spoke to the apostles about their doubt. [7]He explained that like the Pharisees who had questioned him, doubt could blind them to the reflection of Light within their minds. [8]But he also explained that their doubts did not take the Light away. [9]"The Light is always within you," Jesus explained. [10]"And like yeast that has been placed in flour, this Light expands within your mind, even now, as you doubt.

[11]"Those the Father has called to do His service will follow their call. [12]For they can do nothing else. [13]The desire is strong within them or they would not have heard the call.

[14]"Let your doubts not concern you. [15]They are merely fear, and fear is nothing, so it cannot hold you back. [16]Look at your doubts and lay them aside, that you may continue the work your Father has called you to do."

(v 22 – 26)[1]Everywhere Jesus went, he helped people to see differently. [2]As he taught with joy, touching many people, the apostles began to see differently too. [3]More and more, the apostles began to seek private counsel with Jesus to discuss their fears and doubts. [4]Jesus responded lovingly with every discussion that was brought to him. [5]Never did the apostles feel judged. [6]Increasingly, they became aware of a new sight, a way of seeing the world that they hadn't known before. [7]As this new sight filled their hearts with joy, they became increasingly committed to doing the work of their Father.

(v 27 – 30)[1]And so the time came that Jesus again talked to the apostles about their doubts.

[2]"Who do people say I am?" Jesus asked.

[3]The apostles answered with rumors they had heard while teaching. [4]There were many perspectives among the people, but no one seemed to know the truth.

[5]"And who do you say I am?" asked Jesus.

[6]"A great teacher," answered Thomas quickly. [7]"A master in the service of our Lord."

[8]"Peter," Jesus asked. [9]"And you. [10]Who do you say I am, Peter?"

[11]Peter was quiet for a moment before answering, reflecting upon the answer that had been given him in his mind. [12]"You are me, master...the Son of God...the Christ. [13]You are one who has learned this awareness, and so you share it with us, as Thomas has pointed out."

[14]Jesus smiled. [15]"This you did not learn from men, Peter. [16]This you learned from the Voice of our Lord within. [17]In trusting this Voice, you have shared a great truth."

[18]Jesus spoke to all of the apostles. [19]"The Voice within will lead you clearly when you give it your trust and put your doubts aside. [20]It will reveal truths to you that you have not imagined, and so you will know they are true. [21]And even as this Voice speaks, you may hear another voice that brings doubt and fear. [22]Place that voice aside, for the voice of fear will cloud the vision of Light and hide that Light from you. [23]But when the voice of fear is let go, the Light will shine to place Heaven within your sight.

[24]"Truly I say to you, watch the thoughts within your mind. [25]Choose what you will believe carefully. [26]For what you believe, you believe in Heaven, although it may hide Heaven from your sight." [27]The apostles understood Jesus' words, although they did not all believe them.

(v 31 – 38)[1]Then Jesus talked to the apostles about transcendence. [2]He talked of transcending fear and doubt, and he talked to them about transcending death.

[3]"If you believe your doubts, you will surely die. [4]For doubt is what ties you to this world. [5]Doubt is the fear of God, born of guilt. [6]One who knows guilt cannot know Heaven. [7]To know Heaven, you must overcome your doubt and belief in guilt. [8]You must let go of the self that says you are guilty. [9]For in losing this self, you gain Life. [10]But in keeping with this self, you die."

[11]The apostles did not understand, so Jesus explained further.

[12]"The mind of man is split. [13]One part of the mind is focused in the world of sin and death. [14]This part of the mind sees sin and death, because it believes it is guilty of being separate from God. [15]In its aloneness, it suffers.

[16]"The other part of the mind is not alone. [17]It knows no separateness. [18]It knows Itself as one with God and all men. [19]You have seen this vision in your work, and so you know it is within you.

[20]"The part of the mind that knows aloneness is like a dark cloud hanging over the world and making it dark. [21]As you see the darkened world, you believe darkness is all there is. [22]But beyond every dark cloud, there is light. [23]It is the Light that is eternal.

[24]"The Light is also within your mind. [25]Focus on the Light. [26]Love the Light. [27]Pray unto the Light and worship the Light within. [28]Through practice, your awareness of the Light will grow strong, and it will give you the desire and strength to overcome guilt, doubt and fear.

[29]"Hold to the Light in all things. [30]It is the way to Life."

NTI Mark, Chapter 9

(v 1)[1]Jesus said to the apostles, "I tell you the truth, some who are standing here will not taste death, but will see the kingdom of God shining within their hearts and minds with glory and power forever and ever. [2]This is the path that you are on. [3]It is a path that sometimes seems difficult, but that is only your resistance to peace. [4]It is a path that sometimes seems lonely, but that is only your resistance to love. [5]It is a path that sometimes seems frightening, but that is only your resistance to truth. [6]Lay down your resistance and walk with me, for I offer Light and Love and One."

[7]The apostles were grateful that Jesus had been given to them.

◌৯ ◌৯ ◌৯ ◌৯ ◌৯

(v 2 – 13)[1]One day, Jesus took Peter, James and John atop a mountain for meditation, reflection and counsel. [2]He often took small groups off in this way, that individual attention may be given to their seeming needs and questions. [3]Peter was an unusual one who brought Jesus great joy and amusement. [4]For Peter displayed wide swings between faith and fear. [5]All of this, Jesus could use for healing and for teaching.

[6]On this day, Jesus taught the three apostles great truths that had not been taught before. [7]He told the apostles how the world had come into being and how the world would be taken away from the mind. [8]He let the apostles know how their part was helpful to the whole, and he gave each one very specific instructions regarding what to do.

[9]As Peter listened to the seriousness in Jesus' tone, he became overcome with fear. [10]Peter experienced difficulty eating and resting, and he wondered if he should stay or if he should go.

[11]That night, during a time when Peter was able to sleep, he had a dream given him by the Holy Spirit. [12]He dreamt that Jesus wore a bright robe of white that shined as if there was light in the threads of his clothing. [13]And he dreamed that Moses and Elijah were joined in a circle with Jesus, smiling and talking about the gloriousness of the Lord. [14]The dream faded from his mind, and Peter was aware of a peace that came over him as he opened his eyes. [15]When Peter was aware that he was awake, a loud and clear thought came into his mind. [16]"This is my Son in whom I am well pleased. [17]Listen to Him."

[18]Peter spent the remainder of the evening in grateful reflection and peace. [19]He went to Jesus, John and James to share his dream and the

sense of peace it had given him.

[20]"Peace is a gift from our Lord," Jesus explained. [21]"Fear is our resistance to this gift. [22]Both acceptance and resistance are in your mind now, so you experience both peace and fear. [23]But know this won't continue forever, for only peace is forever. [24]Fear must pass away.

[25]"Continue the work the Father has given you. [26]When fear seems to come upon you, fall to your knees and join in counsel with the Voice for our Lord. [27]Give Him your fears and your willingness to continue in service of our Lord. [28]Your fear will fade away. [29]Then rise and continue your work. [30]In this way, you find yourself on the path of healing with a mighty companion by your side."

(v 14 – 32) [1]When Jesus and the three apostles came down from the mountain, they found a crowd there. [2]There seemed to be some disagreement among them. [3]The apostles welcomed Jesus' return to them, certain he could answer questions that challenged them.

[4]"Why can you drive out evil spirits," asked one within the crowd who seemed to speak with belief in his own authority, "when your apostles cannot? [5]Is it magic that you use?"

[6]"Who said I drive out evil spirits?" Jesus asked.

[7]"That man and that man," this one answered. [8]"And I have seen you do it myself!"

[9]Jesus smiled at the man and placed a hand on his shoulder. [10]"I cannot drive out evil spirits," Jesus answered. [11]"What you have seen was of your own belief, for what you believe, you will witness."

[12]"I believe you have driven out evil spirits," replied the man.

[13]"But to believe that, you must believe that evil spirits are real and you can be victim to them. [14]Truly I say to you, when you put your faith in our Lord, there is nothing you can be victim to."

[15]Jesus faced the crowd and opened his mouth, so that the Holy Spirit could pour forth.

[16]"Do not underestimate the power of your own belief, for what you believe, you will witness. [17]If you believe in evil, you will find evil

around you, and you will want to defend yourself from it, so you will attack. [18]You may say this to that one or do that to this one, or you may attack with your thoughts of grievance or your words of gossip. [19]Whatever form it takes, attack is attack, and attack is not of God. [20]And so in attacking, you have separated yourself from God.

[21]"I ask you, what is evil but opposition to God's Will? [22]Would it be God's Will that you separate yourself from Him?"

[23]There was a quiet pause.

[24]"It is our Father's Will that you be in communion with Him with every thought in your day. [25]So when you think you see evil and feel thoughts of attack rise up in your defense, turn to our Lord in prayer. [26]Say to Him, 'Father, it is not Your Will that I be separate from you, so it is not my will that I be separate. [27]I rejoin with you by letting go of my attack. [28]I give this attack to you, that you may do with it as it is Your Will. [29]I ask nothing of you but peace.'

[30]"Through prayer such as this, evil will fade from your sight. [31]The Father will protect you within His realm of peace, and you will be able to rest for all of your days."

(v 33 – 37)[1]Later, Jesus asked the apostles what they had been arguing about when he, Peter, James and John had come upon them. [2]The apostles were embarrassed to answer him, because they had been defending themselves against the crowd and from one another. [3]Each one thought he was the better disciple. [4]Each one thought he was closest to the master, and therefore, above the rest.

[5]Jesus waited in silence as drink was served to them. [6]Then, once again, he opened his mouth, that the Holy Spirit may speak.

[7]"The one who knows his greatness is the one who sees himself like the rest. [8]The one in service of his brothers serves them because it is his desire to serve himself."

[9]Jesus invited a child to stand beside him. [10]"When you look on this child, you look upon me. [11]One is not different from the other. [12]And when you see our innocence joined as one innocence within our Lord, you

have seen your Self and found your innocence. [13]There, your greatness lies, in the innocence that is found within our Lord. [14]For this innocence He has shared with you, and so this innocence is you."

[15]Jesus patted the child on the head, and the child ran off with its mother.

[16]"Love one another as you love me. [17]In this way, you serve our Lord and your Self. [18]Never doubt that Love is one. [19]To love one is to love another, and to love them both is to love us all. [20]Seek only after love, and let all that is not love go from your mind as useless."

৩৯   ৩৯   ৩৯   ৩৯   ৩৯

(v 38 – 41) [1]"Teacher," said John. [2]"We saw a man teaching in your name, and we asked him to stop, because he is not one of us."

[3]"He does not need to stop," replied Jesus. [4]"He does not need to walk with us and eat with us to be one with us. [5]The heavenly Father made us one, and so one is what we are.

[6]"The differences that we see among us are shallow and unimportant. [7]They are visible on the surface only. [8]Like all things in this world, they will not last. [9]Do not focus on the differences. [10]They will distract you from the Light.

[11]"Our Father created us as one, and so one is what we are. [12]We cannot be different than how our Father created us. [13]It is our essence, our being.

[14]"This man who teaches in my name teaches not for me or against me; he teaches with me, for we cannot be apart in purpose or in truth.

[15]"God will call many teachers to do his work, and each one may seem to teach in his own way. [16]But the Father's message is always consistent. [17]It is the simple message of love and oneness. [18]Whenever you hear this message, be grateful for what you hear. [19]Do not be distracted by what may seem to be differences.

[20]"I tell you the truth. [21]Anyone who gives his brother even a cup of

water because he knows his brother is the Christ, teaches with authority from the Father."

(v 42 – 50)[1]"I tell you, watch *yourself* regarding your brother. [2]Your mind and your heart are your only concern. [3]If you think you see your brother sin, ask the Holy Spirit to help you see differently. [4]Remember your purpose in all things.

[5]"If you think you have done wrong, ask the Holy Spirit to help you see differently. [6]Remember your purpose in all things.

[7]"If you think you have strayed from our Father's path, ask the Holy Spirit to help you see differently. [8]Remember your purpose in all things.

[9]"If you think you see evil and your mind believes it is true, ask the Holy Spirit to help you see differently. [10]Remember your purpose in all things.

[11]"Whenever your thoughts have strayed from the Father, remember that the Father is your only purpose. [12]Remember that you would see with His Love, and anything that is not His Love is not what you desire. [13]And since you do not desire it, do not hold onto it. [14]For to hold onto anything you do not desire is to pick up and cling to a burden.

[15]"Burdens of the heart will slow you down along your way. [16]Do not be tempted by their glitter. [17]Remember your purpose in all things, and do not let yourself forget. [18]In this way, you are the salt of the earth.

[19]"Be salt within your hearts, and be at peace with one another."

NTI Mark, Chapter 10

(v 1 – 12)[1]It was on another day, when crowds had again gathered and Jesus went about his purpose in teaching them, when the Pharisees came once again to challenge him. [2]A man and a woman had come to the Pharisees with a disagreement, and this disagreement the Pharisees shared with Jesus as a trick.

[3]The man wanted a divorce from his wife, because she did not please him. [4]But the woman was afraid and argued that her husband did not have cause for divorce. [5]She listed her virtues as a wife, none of which the

husband denied. [6]Yet, he was not pleased and wanted only to be free of her.

[7]"Is it lawful for this man to divorce his wife?" the Pharisees asked Jesus.

[8]Knowing the law, Jesus asked the Pharisees. [9]"What did Moses command you?"

[10]They answered, "Moses permitted a man to write a certificate of divorce and send her away."

[11]"Yes," Jesus agreed, "because the hearts of the people were hard then. [12]They did not have faith in our Lord, so Moses gave them rest from worldly concerns, that their minds may be quieted and time may be given to prayer and to worship.

[13]"Moses gave the people many laws and ways of understanding, that they may have one way of looking at the world, and therefore see themselves as one. [14]But our people have matured in the worship of our Lord. [15]And we are ready for more advanced laws and customs, that we may grow even closer to Him now.

[16]"Is it not true that Moses also wrote that in the beginning, God created man and woman for one another?"

[17]There was general agreement within the crowd.

[18]"This is why a man leaves his father and mother and takes a wife. [19]The two are one in the eyes of our Lord. [20]What God has joined together, no man can separate.

[21]"Tell this man that he is one with his wife in the eyes of our Lord. [22]Ask him to love her, as God loves him. [23]Speak to him daily, if you must, and help him to see his wife through the eyes of our Lord. [24]When his sight has changed from self-desire to that of love, he will be grateful in all things. [25]And in giving this man the gift of love, you give it to yourself and our Lord."

[26]The Pharisees were speechless. [27]Some went away with the intent to do as Jesus had asked.

[28]Later that evening, Jesus talked to the apostles about change.

[29]"The world seems to be a place of change, but one thing has remained constant until now. [30]Each one sees himself as separate from the others, and he puts his desire for his self above that of all other desires. [31]Love will not compete with this.

[32]"This is what I have come to change. [33]For as a man sees the world, so the world shall be. [34]Through the Holy Spirit, man will come to see the world anew. [35]No longer will he see himself as separate from the world, and no longer will he protect himself above all else. [36]This is the way of love."

❧ ❧ ❧ ❧ ❧

(v 13 – 16)[1]People who loved their children brought their children to Jesus to receive a blessing from the Lord. [2]This blessing pleased them, because they recognized love.

[3]The apostles felt that time spent this way was foolish. [4]They asked people not to waste the master's time in this way. [5]But Jesus understood that the apostles were not looking with the eyes of the Lord, and so he offered them another way to see.

[6]"You must become as these little children to receive the kingdom of God. [7]Look at them. [8]Notice their willingness to accept love and not doubt it. [9]In this way, they see themselves as innocent and worthy of love, so they have no cause to question if the love is real.

[10]"Be like these little children. [11]Do not throw love away from you with judgments, grievances and doubt. [12]These things are but an attack on love.

[13]"Accept love as these children and their parents do. [14]They are a symbol of your salvation. [15]When you are always, as they are now, you will know love and you will know what salvation is."

❧ ❧ ❧ ❧ ❧

(v 17 – 31)[1]A prominent man came to Jesus. [2]"Good teacher," he asked, "how do I obtain eternal life?"

3"Why do you call me good?" Jesus asked.

4"I know the commandments. 5I live by them myself, and so I know good when I see good," the man answered in sincerity. 6To this man, Jesus seemed to be above all other men.

7"You make a mistake," Jesus replied. 8"A man cannot be good or bad. 9A man either listens to our Father or he doesn't, and there is no judgment in that."

10"Teacher," the man responded, "I listen to all of our Father's commandments, and I have obeyed them since I was a boy. 11My heart is filled with love, and I desire only goodness for everyone. 12What shall I do to gain eternal life?"

13Jesus looked on this man in love. 14"There is one thing you must do. 15Go home, sell everything that you have, and give it all to the poor. 16Then, come and follow me. 17Together, we will live in service to our brothers."

18"My dear master, I have a family to care for. 19They depend on me. 20I cannot take the food from their mouth."

21"To inherit the kingdom of God, you must let go of the kingdom of the world. 22You cannot be the ruler of your own kingdom and be one with the Father in His. 23For either you will see yourself as one with the Father or you will see yourself alone."

24The man did not understand. 25He went away sad and disillusioned, thinking that Jesus was not the good man he seemed to be.

26The apostles were also surprised at Jesus' answer, for they knew this man was a good man and very responsible to his family and his servants.

27"Entering the kingdom of God requires great vigilance against the temptations of this world," Jesus explained. 28"It is easier for a camel to go through the eye of a needle, than for a man to enter the kingdom of God."

29The apostles were shocked and wondered what they had done by leaving their families to follow Jesus. 30"Who, then, can be saved?" they asked.

[31]Jesus looked at them in love. [32]"No man can save himself. [33]He must turn all things over to God. [34]For man, salvation is impossible; but with God, all things are possible even unto salvation."

[35]Peter was frightened. [36]"Master, we have left everything to follow you. [37]Is that not enough?"

[38]"I tell you the truth," Jesus responded. [39]"Whoever leaves what he values in the world in order to seek the value of Heaven will be rewarded beyond measure. [40]There shall be no loss in Him.

[41]"But Peter, what you value must be left completely. [42]For this reason, many who are first to seek the kingdom will be last to receive it. [43]You must leave the world to enter the kingdom, for the kingdom is not of this world."

ড়   ড়   ড়   ড়   ড়

(v 32 – 34)[1]Jesus said, "When you look at me as one who is in a body, you do not look at me at all. [2]For the body is a thing of the world. [3]It can be beaten and spat upon and killed by those who do not understand what love is. [4]But Love itself is eternal. [5]It cannot be judged or tormented or killed, for it only is in the quiet peacefulness of Itself.

[6]"One day this body will die. [7]And before that time, you may see it tormented by those who have judged it as fearful or unworthy. [8]Do not be afraid yourself. [9]Remember that Love cannot die. [10]The body may be put down, but Love will always rise again. [11]For in Love, there is no death."

(v 35 – 40)[1]After a time of thinking over what Jesus had said, James and John, the sons of Zebedee, came to Jesus with a request.

[2]"Master, we beg of you one request, and we will be your faithful servants for life."

[3]"What is your request?" Jesus asked.

[4]"We would like to sit on your right and on your left in the glory land. [5]If you grant us this reward, we will humbly follow you, even to the end

of the world."

[6]"You do not understand what you ask," Jesus responded.

[7]"Master, we do. [8]We have heard your words. [9]We will give up this world entirely. [10]It is nothing to us compared to you. [11]We will die and give up these bodies. [12]They are nothing compared to the rewards of Heaven. [13]But to do all this, we want assurance that our reward will be true."

[14]Jesus rested with these words a moment, and then he spoke. [15]"You say you are willing to drink the cup of which I drink and be baptized with the baptism that baptizes me, but you do not know what you ask for. [16]In Heaven, it is not for me to say that one may sit on my right and one may sit on my left. [17]For in Heaven, all is as the Father created it to be."

(v 41 – 45)[1]When the apostles heard that James and John had attempted to secure their place in Heaven, they became angry with them. [2]So Jesus called the apostles together and spoke with them.

[3]"Nothing is as it seems to you now. [4]There is not one who can lord over another. [5]There is only one, who is a Servant unto Itself. [6]And this Servant serves Itself in humility and love, giving of Itself for all.

[7]"If you want to inherit the kingdom, you must become this Servant. [8]In service, you are one with me, who has joined with the Holy Spirit in service and love. [9]I give myself to Him for all. [10]This is the way to know Heaven."

∾ ∾ ∾ ∾ ∾

(v 46 – 52)[1]As Jesus and the apostles walked along the road greeting people, a blind man who was a beggar clamored for Jesus' attention. [2]The crowd tried to keep him quiet, for they saw this man as vile and unworthy of Jesus' attention. [3]But Jesus noticed the man and the crowd's attempt to quiet him, so he asked the apostles to help the man to him.

[4]"What is it that you want from me?" Jesus asked the man.

[5]"I want to see as you see," the man replied.

[6]"And how is it that I see?" Jesus asked.

[7]"With eyes from your heart!" the man replied.

[8]"Come, then," Jesus answered. [9]"Follow me. [10]Through your faith, you shall learn that you do see."

[11]The man became a follower along with the apostles, and through the Holy Spirit, his spiritual blindness was healed.

NTI Mark, Chapter 11

(v 1 – 11)[1]The time came for Jesus and the apostles to gather in Jerusalem for the celebration of Passover. [2]Some of the apostles came to the area first and waited for Jesus before entering into the city. [3]As they waited, they taught the good news to travelers, so that many became excited to meet and hear Jesus. [4]The apostles taught in such a way that Jesus sounded special to the people who heard them, so some who listened also felt jealous.

[5]As Jesus neared the city, a small boy came up to the apostles who waited for him. [6]He offered his young donkey as a gift to the master. [7]The apostles accepted the gift humbly. [8]This was the donkey that Jesus walked beside as he entered the city that evening. [9]Many came to greet him and to pat the donkey. [10]Others joked that the master should travel with such a young and worthless animal.

(v 12 – 14)[1]The next morning, Jesus came upon a fig tree, and he tied the donkey there. [2]Jesus spent time in prayer and meditation under the tree, talking to the heavenly Father about thoughts within his mind. [3]Something seemed to be stirring within the master, and he was alert to it in calmness.

(v 15 – 19)[1]That day in the temple, the apostles noticed a change in Jesus as he looked on at the money changers and merchants. [2]He had been laughing and talking with the apostles on the way to the temple, but now he stood quiet and stoic, watching the activity there.

[3]"Master," an apostle asked, "is something wrong?"

[4]Jesus did not answer the apostle, but stood quiet, alert to judgments

in his mind. [5]He did not believe these judgments, and he did not react based on them, but he noticed them and let them go from his mind. [6]Then Jesus left the temple without saying a word. [7]The apostles were surprised, for they had expected him to pray and to teach.

(v 20 – 26)[1]That evening, Jesus returned to the fig tree for quiet prayer and meditation. [2]Peter came upon him there. [3]He was anxious not to disturb the master, but Jesus invited Peter to come and sit with him.

[4]"Peter, I tell you again. [5]Watch your thoughts. [6]It seems that they are tricky at times, for they seem to come only to deceive you and to rob you of your purpose. [7]But you do not need to believe what you find within your mind, and you do not need to believe what you see with your eyes. [8]Be alert to deception. [9]If you are alert, you will recognize it by its name. [10]Its name is fear, Peter. [11]And when you see it, you have a choice. [12]You may bow down to it and worship it, and do as it asks you to do. [13]Or you may choose to see through it to the Love that waits beyond it, silently and in peace, knowing that in time you will return to it there."

[14]"Master," Peter asked. [15]"What is it you are telling me? [16]I do not understand."

[17]"Whatever you believe you can do, you can do. [18]So if you look at fear in your mind, and you believe you can overcome it with trust, you shall overcome all fear and enter into the awareness of Love. [19]You can tell the fear to go and jump in the ocean, and it will if you believe that it will.

[20]"I tell you, whatever you ask for in prayer will be given. [21]Know what it is that you ask, that you may recognize the gift and be grateful. [22]And Peter, when you are praying, if you find anything that you hold against your brother, or if you feel responsible to go and do something, or if you notice fear there within your mind, forgive these things first. [23]Then you will recognize your true prayer, and you will know what it is that you ask."

[24]Jesus gave the donkey to Peter to give to their host as a gift, and Jesus stayed under the tree in silence for awhile.

❧ ❧ ❧ ❧ ❧

(v 27 – 33)[1]Having cleared his mind, Jesus went back into the temple. [2]This time, the Jewish leaders walked right up to him and questioned, "On what authority do you teach?"

[3]Jesus was silent, knowing that Authority was within him.

[4]Again, the Jewish leaders asked, "On what authority do you teach?"

[5]"Let me ask you a question," Jesus responded. [6]"If you will answer my question, you will also have your answer to yours. [7]On what authority did John the Baptist baptize? [8]Was his authority given by Heaven or was it given by men?"

[9]They discussed Jesus' question among themselves and decided it was a trick. [10]So they did not answer him. [11]Jesus provided them with the answer to his question, that they may hear the answer to their own question, if hearing the answer was to be their choice. [12]Jesus said to them, "I tell you that all authority is the same, because there is only one."

NTI Mark, Chapter 12

(v 1 – 12)[1]Then Jesus began to teach the Jewish leaders using parables, that their eyes may be opened to the deception in which they believed. [2]He taught them in love, understanding the great truth of who they are.

[3]"A man planted a vineyard, and he made the vineyard complete and perfect. [4]This, he gifted to tenants, that they might extend his gift and produce great fruit.

[5]"At harvest time, he sent his servants to join in the abundance. [6]But the tenants became afraid, because they had seen the vineyard as their own, and now they saw the servants as desiring to take from them what was theirs. [7]So they beat the servants and killed them. [8]Each one that the man sent to them, they beat and they killed, because they were afraid. [9]In the activity of their defense, the harvest went unharvested, so that no one enjoyed its fruit.

[10]"In this way, the tenants continue to defend the vineyard to this day,

so that the gift given them is not enjoyed. [11]For there is no enjoyment in defense. [12]They will know the joy of the gift when they choose defense-lessness and extend the gift as it was meant to be extended."

[13]The Jewish leaders felt that Jesus must be speaking of them. [14]But they did not understand his parable, so they went off to plan their defense together.

(v 13 - 17)[1]And so the Jewish leaders became intent on trapping Jesus with his own words, that they may arrest him for breaking the law and discredit him before the people. [2]They went to him and approached him before the people in what appeared to be a humble and respectful way. [3]They complimented him as a teacher of God and addressed him as master, as many of the people did. [4]They did all of this, so as not to raise suspicion within the crowd. [5]And then they asked Jesus a seemingly innocent and reasonable question. [6]"Should we pay taxes to Caesar or not?"

[7]This was a question that had been on the minds of many, for sometimes it seemed confusing about what was right to do and what was not right. [8]Should a man pay to support the bondage of his own people? [9]Should he break the law and be taken from his family?

[10]Jesus understood the confusion within the mind and the thought that gave rise to such confusion. [11]"Bring me a denarius, and let me look at it," he said.

[12]They gave him one denarius.

[13]"Whose portrait is on this?" he asked. [14]"And who's inscription?"

[15]"Caesar's," they replied.

[16]Jesus handed the denarius back to them. [17]"Then give to Caesar what is Caesar's. [18]And give to God what is God's."

[19]Jesus stood from where he had been sitting and began to address the crowd.

[20]"Your brother, standing beside you, belongs to God. [21]It is he that you should give back to God, just as you pay taxes to Caesar. [22]Caesar wants your money, but God asks that you love your brother and welcome

him into your heart as one with you. [23]You want to please God, and you ask what is right for you to do. [24]God asks only one thing of you, and that is love. [25]All else, you may let go to Caesar."

[26]The people were amazed at the clarity with which he spoke.

(v 18 – 27)[1]More Jewish leaders came to Jesus with yet another question. [2]"Teacher," they said, "Moses wrote that if a man's brother dies and leaves a wife but no children, the man must marry his brother's widow and care for her."

[3]Jesus agreed that this is how it was written, and so they continued. [4]"There were seven brothers. [5]The first one married and died without any children. [6]The second one married the widow and also died leaving no children, and so on until all seven brothers married this woman and died leaving no children. [7]Our question is this. [8]Whose wife shall she be in the resurrection?"

[9]Jesus once again recognized the confusion that sprang up from the ego. [10]And so he spoke to the people from the clarity of the Holy Spirit.

[11]"You are in error because you do not know the oneness of God. [12]The mistake comes from seeing the seven brothers as separate and all wanting the wife for himself. [13]But in the resurrection, the brothers and the wife are one in Spirit with God. [14]There is no separation between them, nor is there any loss.

[15]"The Spirit of our God is one. [16]Have you not read in the book of Moses that our Lord said, 'I am the God of Abraham, the God of Isaac and the God of Jacob.' [17]This is written to show that our Lord is one God inclusive of all."

(v 28 – 34)[1]One of the teachers of the law listened to the discussion, and he recognized the love in Jesus' answers.

[2]"Teacher," he asked, "of all the commandments, which is most important?"

[3]Jesus looked directly at the man as he answered. [4]"The most important one is this. [5]The Lord, our God, is one. [6]Love the Lord, our God, with all your heart and with all your soul and with all your mind and

with all your strength. [7]The second is like it. [8]Love your neighbor as yourself within the love of God. [9]There is no commandment greater than these."

[10]"Well said, teacher," the man replied. [11]"You are right in saying that God is one and there is no other but Him. [12]To love Him with all your heart, with all your mind and with all your strength, and to love your neighbor as yourself is more important than burnt offerings and sacrifices."

[13]Jesus saw this man understood the message of the good news. [14]He said to the man, "Continue to seek our Lord within. [15]You are not far from the kingdom of Heaven."

᷍   ᷍   ᷍   ᷍   ᷍

(v 35 – 40)[1]Jesus taught the crowds in the temple courts. [2]As they listened, they began to ask if he was the Christ. [3]Some answered "yes" based on what they thought they had heard. [4]But others answered "no" and pointed to prophecy and law to show that Jesus could not be the messiah.

[5]Aware that the people expected the messiah to be a special one, different from themselves, Jesus proceeded to teach the crowd in this way:

[6]"How is it that Christ is the son of David? [7]It is written that David himself spoke to the Holy Spirit calling the messiah 'Lord.' [8]Would David call his son 'Lord?'

[9]"The messiah must be one greater than David, but what man could be greater than David, so that David would call him 'Lord?'

[10]"The one that David refers to is one that is with us now. [11]That one does not stand here before you, alone and without you. [12]That one is not among the teachers of the law and not with you. [13]That one does not hold a place of prominence and avoid the place where you are. [14]That one is in all places and with all men. [15]The Christ cannot be separate from

anyone, for everyone is within the Christ.

[16]"The messiah is the thought of salvation, and that thought is with you now. [17]The Christ is the acceptance of this thought. [18]Everyone has authority to accept this gift, as it is a gift from our Father to all of His children as one."

(v 41 – 44)[1]That evening, Jesus and the apostles had a discussion about giving offerings to support the temple. [2]Such offerings were considered important within Jewish law, and those who made great offerings were considered great and holy men.

[3]Jesus listened as the apostles discussed the offerings they had seen given that day. [4]They were impressed by the size of the offerings that were given by some of the rich men that had visited the temple during the day.

[5]After listening to all that the apostles had to say, and after listening to the conclusions the apostles drew based on what they saw, Jesus taught the apostles in this way:

[6]"The Lord, your God, wants one thing from you and one thing only. [7]He seeks all that you think, that He may show you all that you are.

[8]"Do not hold back from God. [9]For what you keep, you value, and what you value on earth will keep you from Heaven.

[10]"In this way, the widow who gave two copper coins for our Lord gave more than all the other wealth given today. [11]For she gave all she had, that she may be placed within the hands of God and cared for as He Wills. [12]This woman has shown great faith and trust in her submission to our Lord. [13]Her gift is not unnoticed.

[14]"The gift is not in the money or the material goods given. [15]The gift is not in the size of the sacrifice. [16]The gift is in the submission to the Will of God and the acceptance of this Will as your own.

[17]"Give truly to our Lord, and truly you will receive."

NTI Mark, Chapter 13

(v 1 – 3)[1]One of the apostles was very impressed by the temple.

[2]"Look, teacher! [3]What massive stones! [4]What magnificent buildings!"

[5]Jesus smiled at the apostle and put an arm around his shoulder. [6]"You are impressed by nothing, my friend. [7]Before the sight of Heaven, all of these stones will disappear."

(v 4 – 37) [1]As Jesus rested outside the temple with some of the apostles, they asked him privately, "Master, you speak of an end to these days as we know them. [2]When will this end come? [3]What will be the signs? [4]How shall we know?"

[5]Jesus smiled at his brothers. [6]His response to their concern was peaceful and certain. [7]"Let not your fear deceive you. [8]When you hear of wars and rumors of wars, do not be alarmed. [9]Such things will seem to happen before this world fades away. [10]Nation will rise against nation and kingdom against kingdom. [11]There will be earthquakes and famines. [12]All this is but birth pangs of this world. [13]Love not *this* world, but do not fear it. [14]For the world will pass away, but you are eternal.

[15]"You must be on guard and watch the thoughts within your mind. [16]You may see yourselves arrested and flogged, or you may see yourselves standing as witness unto your Self before governors and kings. [17]This is your choice!

[18]"The Light of God will shine throughout, and then the end will come."

[19]"Master," an apostle asked. [20]"What shall we say when we are brought as witnesses before governors and kings?"

[21]"Do not worry beforehand what you will say. [22]Say whatever is given you at the time. [23]And trust it is the Holy Spirit speaking through you. [24]Do not judge what you say, but give it as a gift by accepting it as a gift for you."

[25]"What other signs will we see?" they asked.

[26]"As long as there is darkness within the mind, you will see brother betray brother and father betray child. [27]Children will rebel against parents, and each one will blame another for his woes. [28]But I say, stand firm in your faith. [29]Trust not the thoughts of death. [30]Listen only to the

Holy Spirit, and your thoughts shall be your salvation."

[31]Jesus looked at the apostles. [32]He was still and restful in his manner. [33]"The world shall be the world until the thought that made it is no more. [34]When the thought is gone, the world shall disappear with it. [35]You will notice nothing but a tiny wisp of air, and then it shall be no more. [36]And you will be glad, for all you will know is peace and freedom and joy.

[37]"Do not worry that you will not be ready. [38]For before this time, you will look out on the world and see the Christ as if it rains upon the earth from clouds held up by angels. [39]You will know this power and glory within you. [40]And the ends of the earth will fade into the ends of Heaven before your sight.

[41]"Learn this lesson from the fig tree. [42]As soon as its twigs get tender and its leaves come out, you know summer is near. [43]Even so, when your heart is filled with the glory of God and you see the world in this way, you know that Heaven is near, right at the door awaiting you.

[44]"I tell you the truth. [45]You have nothing to fear. [46]All that is not of God will pass away, but what is of God will last forever, even from this day into eternity."

[47]"Master," they asked, "when will this happen?"

[48]Jesus chuckled. [49]"There is no day or hour to which you can look. [50]There is only now. [51]Accept all that I say as true. [52]Keep watch in your mind, even unto this moment. [53]Now is the time for salvation, for there is no other time but now. [54]Do not fall asleep and let this time pass you by. [55]What I say to you, I say to everyone. [56]Stay alert, and keep watch in joyfulness."

[57]Jesus was smiling, so the apostles listening to him could not be afraid.

NTI Mark, Chapter 14

(v 1, 2)[1]As the holy days of Passover and the Feast of Unleavened Bread approached, the chief priests and some teachers of the law agreed to have Jesus arrested and to see to it that he was killed. [2]They were afraid of retribution from the people who listened to him, so they agreed that his arrest must occur after the holy feast.

⇜ ⇜ ⇜ ⇜ ⇜

(v 3 – 9)[1]Jesus was resting in the evening with the apostles and friends, when a woman came to him with an expensive perfume. [2]Out of gratitude for love she had known through him, she gifted Jesus with the perfume by anointing him with it.

[3]Some observers were upset and jealous. [4]They protested that the perfume could have been sold, and the money could have been given to the poor.

[5]Jesus responded to the protestors gently, while holding the hand of the woman who had anointed him. [6]"Her gift is a symbol of her gratitude for love, given to one that is a symbol in her eyes for God's Love. [7]She has done nothing wrong. [8]She has extended gratitude in a way that she felt called to extend it. [9]This woman is following the guidance of her heart. [10]Let us thank her for what she has done. [11]She shall live as a symbol unto all of us throughout the ages."

(v 10, 11)[1]This was the time that Judas of Iscariot decided to follow the thoughts that led him to do what he was to do.

[2]Judas was afraid. [3]He feared that he had been fooled into giving up his livelihood for a false promise, but he was not sure. [4]Judas felt that giving Jesus over for trial would enable the truth to come out. [5]If all that Jesus promised was true, it would be seen by all, and that would be a good thing. [6]But if Jesus was a liar and false prophet, it would be better to find that out now.

[7]So in faith that he was doing what was best for everyone, Judas went to the chief priests and agreed to give Jesus over to them. [8]Judas did not understand that since he saw Jesus as separate from himself, he was listening to the voice of falsehood, a voice from which truth could not be known.

(v 12 – 16)[1]As the time for Passover neared, the apostles asked Jesus where they should make preparations for Passover. [2]Jesus told them to go into the city and follow where they were led, and then to make preparations there.

[3]The apostles were nervous about Jesus' instructions, for it was known by this time that the chief priests were against Jesus. [4]The apostles feared they would be led into a trap. [5]Jesus told them not to fear, but to look for the signs of the Holy Spirit and follow those signs to the place where they would meet.

[6]The apostles went into town looking for a sign from the Holy Spirit. [7]A man came upon them. [8]He did not say a thing, but he smiled at them as if he recognized them as dear friends.

[9]After a brief discussion, the apostles decided to follow this man. [10]He carried a jar of water and disappeared quietly into a large house.

[11]The apostles felt led to knock on the door of this house. [12]It was another man who answered the door. [13]But his smile was also friendly.

[14]"Our teacher has asked us to find a guest room where he may eat Passover with his disciples."

[15]"I have a room," the man answered. [16]He led them to an upstairs room that was the perfect size.

(v 17 – 26)[1]When evening came, Jesus and the twelve apostles gathered there.

[2]There was fear and suspicion among the apostles. [3]Each one seemed concerned that another one would make a mistake and betray their master to the chief priests and teachers of the law.

[4]Jesus stood before them holding a loaf of bread in his hand. [5]He broke the bread and passed it to the twelve.

[6]"Eat this," he instructed. [7]"For it is no more than my body.

[8]"Do not be concerned over what is to happen to my body. [9]It is nothing for you to concern yourselves about. [10]The Spirit is all that matters, and the Spirit is eternal."

[11]Jesus poured a glass of wine and passed it for the apostles to drink.

[12]"Drink from this cup. [13]It is the cup of forgiveness. [14]As you drink together, forgive one another your imaginings, for you must love one another just as God loves you."

(v 27 – 31)[1]Jesus talked to the apostles about their fear. [2]He emphasized that their fear could lead them away from him and the path of truth.

[3]"Not I," said Peter.

[4]Jesus had witnessed Peter's fear, and he knew Peter was prone to listen to it. [5]"Truly I tell you, Peter. [6]When the night is dark and the fear weighs heavy on your mind, you will deny me."

[7]"No!" Peter insisted. [8]"I would die before I would deny you!" [9]And the others agreed with Peter.

[10]Jesus spoke. [11]"Before the light comes again, Peter, keep watch. [12]You will deny me."

(v 32 – 42)[1]Jesus and the apostles went to the garden of Gethsemane. [2]Jesus said to the apostles, "I am going to pray. [3]Sit here, and wait for me."

[4]He took Peter, James and John with him into the garden. [5]Jesus seemed troubled, and the three asked him about it.

[6]"I feel the fear of death upon me," he answered. [7]"I must join with my Father now. [8]Stay here, and keep watch on your own fears."

[9]Jesus went further into the garden to a private place, where he fell to the ground and went within to meet the Father. [10]Jesus understood the obstacle before him, and he knew what he must do. [11]In full faith and trust, he called upon the Father's Name.

[12]"Everything is possible with You," he said. [13]"Take this cup."[14] In his mind, Jesus handed the fear to the Holy Spirit. [15]He waited quietly in trust and certainty. [16]He knew this was the final handing over. [17]From this point forward, there would be no Jesus, but only the Will of the Holy Spirit.

[18]"Your Will, not mine," Jesus whispered. [19]He let his self sink into the Will of the Holy Spirit. [20]And his mind was filled with light and joy.

[21]Jesus returned to the three apostles and found them sleeping.

[22]"Simon," Jesus said to Peter. [23]"Could you not keep watch on your mind for one hour? [24]Watch and pray, that you do not accept the temptations."

[25]And then Jesus recognized a temptation lingering in his own mind. [26]"Oh, the Spirit is willing, but the body is weak." [27]So once more, Jesus went away and prayed. [28]He prayed once again for the same thing, that he may let go of the will that seemed separate from the Father's. [29]When Jesus returned again to the three, he again found them sleeping. [30]Jesus said nothing to them, but returned to the place in the garden to pray for a third time.

[31]When Jesus came out of the garden the third time, he was ready, for he had fully accepted the Holy Spirit's Will as the only Will. [32]There was no longer a separate will within the mind of Jesus.

[33]Jesus smiled at the three. [34]"Are you still sleeping?" he asked. [35]"Enough," he said gently. [36]"The hour of glory has come. [37]Let us return to our brothers and be one with them."

(v 43 – 52)[1]It was that evening that Judas appeared with a group of armed men sent by the chief priests and some teachers of the law to capture Jesus. [2]Judas led them to Jesus by walking up to him and addressing him as "Rabbi."[3] But before Judas stepped away to make room for the arrest and capture, he kissed Jesus as a signal of special love, that Jesus may know that all that he did, he did for certainty. [4]Jesus understood Judas' kiss and realized it came from confusion, so he neither accepted it or denied it, and he loved Judas all the same.

[5]A man standing behind Judas quickly seized Jesus. [6]And another man from the other side of him did the same. [7]An apostle, reacting from fear, leapt at a man and struggled to take his sword.

[8]"No fighting!" Jesus exclaimed loudly. [9]"I have not come to fight, but to teach. [10]Everyday I have been teaching in crowds and in temples. [11]And even now, I stand to teach the same message. [12]We are one, my dear brothers. [13]There can be no conflict between us."

[14]Jesus nodded to the men holding him, indicating that he would go

with them in peace. [15]They led him away, and Judas followed to see what would happen.

[16]In the darkness left by the arrest of Jesus, the apostles became very afraid. [17]Their imaginings led them to different conclusions, and they scattered in all directions. [18]But one apostle remained within the garden seeking the guidance of the Holy Spirit in quiet.

(v 53 – 65) [1]The men who arrested Jesus took him to the high priest, chief priests and teachers of the law. [2]Judas was admitted into the room with them to witness what he had come to see. [3]Peter, who had followed from a distance, waited outside for news of what was happening with Jesus.

[4]Many witnesses were allowed in and dismissed, one and two at a time, but the witnesses' stories were not the same. [5]It was clear that each one thought he had heard or seen a different thing, and no one had a consistent perception of the man called Jesus.

[6]Judas looked on the confusion and recognized that it was his. [7]And he became afraid.

[8]Peter felt separate and alone. [9]The fear rose within him also.

[10]Someone testified that he'd heard Jesus tell the apostles that the temple was nothing. [11]Another testified that he had said he would make it nothing by destroying it. [12]And yet another testified that Jesus planned to build his own temple. [13]The high priest asked Jesus which version of the story was true. [14]But Jesus recognized that there was no truth in any of it. [15]There was no truth within the questioning or within the fear or within attack. [16]And so he rested within the peace and oneness of his mind, sure of truth and grateful for it. [17]Jesus said nothing. [18]For there is no response to a question that asks nothing. [19]And Jesus loved the high priest as he loved everyone, as his Self.

[20]The high priest felt impatient, for he was anxious to prove that Jesus was guilty and insane. [21]He asked Jesus, "Are you the Christ, the Son of our Lord?"

[22]"Yes," Jesus answered, "as are you."

²³Some within the room heard Jesus as he answered, but the high priest and those who were afraid of their own guilt did not.

²⁴"See!" the high priest exclaimed, pointing at Jesus, anxious to be seen as victorious over him. ²⁵"What more do we need to hear? ²⁶This man is clearly blasphemous!" ²⁷And many were eager to agree, and so they shouted at Jesus and spat at him. ²⁸But a few remained quiet, asking for clarity within their heart.

²⁹Judas saw the confusion in the room. ³⁰And in it, he perceived his own guilt.

³¹Peter felt afraid and wanted to hide from his fear.

(v 66 - 72)¹Peter sat beside a fire warming himself when Judas passed by. ²A woman saw Peter looking at Judas, and she said to him. ³"You are one of them, aren't you? ⁴You are friends with the one they have in there."

⁵Peter felt afraid to be identified with Jesus. ⁶And so he said, "No," and moved further away from the crowd.

⁷Peter stood by the gate, rubbing his own arms and worrying about how he should protect himself, when the same woman came upon him there. ⁸"I know you are one of them. ⁹I saw you with him myself."

¹⁰Although the woman did not sound accusing, Peter felt threatened. ¹¹He hid his fear with anger and denied any association with Jesus or the apostles.

¹²Others standing near by heard the conversation between them. ¹³One person spoke up. ¹⁴"Surely you know him, for you are of his kind."

¹⁵Peter denied himself and Jesus, and pretended to be something he was not. ¹⁶He ran away from them.

¹⁷Just as Peter made his escape, he saw light break on the horizon and heard a rooster crow. ¹⁸He felt grateful that the darkness would end. ¹⁹And then he remembered Jesus' words to him, and he realized all that he had denied in fear. ²⁰He fell to his knees crying, and asked the Holy Spirit to help him see another way.

NTI Mark, Chapter 15

(v 1 – 15)[1]Early in the morning, the chief priests, along with other Jewish leaders, made their decision. [2]Jesus would be turned over to Pilate for crucifixion. [3]This decision was not unanimous, for there were those among the teachers of the law that recognized truth in what Jesus shared. [4]But those who listened to Jesus would not be heard among the roar of those who were not ready to listen.

[5]The chief priests shared their charges against Jesus with Pilate. [6]Pilate listened, keeping an eye on Jesus. [7]Pilate heard no charges against Jesus, and he wanted to hear this interesting man speak for himself. [8]For Pilate was curious about him.

[9]Pilate asked Jesus, "Is this true, what they say about you? [10]That you *are* the king of the Jews?"

[11]Jesus recognized that these words had the same meaning as, "Are you the Christ?" He smiled at Pilate and answered "Yes, it is as you say."

[12]If Pilate had continued his line of questioning in this manner, Jesus would have had a good dialogue with him. [13]For Pilate's mind was not closed against the thoughts that seemed to come from Jesus. [14]But Pilate felt distracted from his curiosity by the glaring eyes of the chief priests. [15]Nervous regarding his own reputation, Pilate began to question Jesus regarding the specific charges against him. [16]Having no defense against illusions, Jesus stood quietly, loving this one called Pilate, but saying nothing to him. [17]This confused Pilate. [18]He sensed the innocence in Jesus and asked him, "Have you nothing to say in your own defense?"

[19]Jesus made no reply. [20]Pilate was amazed that there should be such a man, for he found no fear in Jesus.

[21]It was Pilate's practice during this holy time, according to the custom of the Jews, to release one prisoner whom the people requested. [22]It so happened that a man named Barabbas was in prison with the insurrectionists for having committed murder during an uprising. [23]Barabbas was a popular personality. [24]Some felt that his charismatic leadership would help the Jews to free themselves from Roman occupation. [25]Some

followers of Barabbas sent a message to Pilate asking him to free Barabbas according to the custom.

[26]Pilate thought that it was this innocent man, Jesus, who should be freed. [27]He took both men before the people and asked, "Which one do you want me to release? [28]Do you want me to release this man that is called king of the Jews?"

[29]Some people within the crowd were happy to see that Pilate seemed inclined to release Jesus. [30]They joyously cheered, that the idea may be supported. [31]But the followers of Barabbas clamored for his release, and the chief priests willingly joined in their plea. [32]Much of the crowd followed the leadership of the chief priests, thinking they knew what was best for the defense of the Jewish people.

[33]Pilate looked at Jesus. [34]He noticed a desire within him to talk with this man more. [35]"What shall I do, then, with the one you call king of the Jews?"

[36]Jesus turned his head to look at Pilate. [37]His peaceful gaze met with Pilate's sorrowful one as the crowd began to shout, "Crucify him!"

[38]"But why?" Pilate asked. [39]"What crime has he committed?"

[40]There was no answer to his question, but the shouts for crucifixion grew louder.

[41]Feeling it was his commitment to release the one requested, he released Barabbas to them. [42]Pilate also turned Jesus over to the guards for what he felt must be the man's fate. [43]Then Pilate went to meet his wife for a meal, desiring very much to forget everything that had happened that day.

(v 16 – 20)[1]There were those among the Roman soldiers who felt they hated this man, Jesus. [2]They blamed him for all of the hardships, disrespect and loneliness they suffered within this land of the Jews. [3]And so they retaliated against him in order to relieve themselves of some of their hatred.

[4]They put a purple robe on him and twisted together a crown of thorns and placed it on his head. [5]They teased him shouting, "Hail, king of the

Jews!" [6]They fell to their knees, paying mock homage to him. [7]Some of them spit at him, kicked him or hit him.

[8]Jesus stood silent, not focusing on the illusion of hate, but recognizing the desire for love. [9]And so without saying a word, Jesus assured the angry and frightened men that they are Love, and that they are innocent.

[10]The silence within Jesus' mind was greater than the chaos that surrounded him. [11]One soldier heard the silence. [12]He stood listening to the call of peace while those around him seemed to fight against it. [13]When it was time to strip Jesus of his "royal" robes and put his own clothes back on him, it was this man who stepped forward to hand Jesus his robe.

[14]Jesus was grateful for the willingness within the mind, and he blessed this willingness with his gratitude.

(v 21)[1]As Jesus and the guards walked to the place of crucifixion, a man named Simon watched the procession. [2]Jesus and a soldier worked together to carry Jesus' cross. [3]Simon felt within him a desire to join these two men. [4]And so he stepped into the procession and began to help them carry the cross. [5]Jesus and the soldier who had come to know him, greeted Simon. [6]He was welcomed immediately within the warmth of forgiveness.

(v 22)[1]Jesus was brought to the Place of the Skull. [2]He was offered wine mixed with myrrh to help dull the pain of crucifixion, but Jesus had already accepted the impossibility of crucifixion, so he kindly refused the wine.

(v 23)[1]Jesus gratefully accepted the love that was offered by the thought of the Holy Spirit. [2]Resting within the peace of this love, he followed the instructions given him by his guards.

(v 24 – 32)[1]In this way, the body of Jesus was hung on the cross for crucifixion, but the crucifixion was not within his mind. [2]Peace was within the mind of Jesus, and peace was all he knew.

[3]The part of the mind that was not healed was not a distraction for

Jesus. [4]He realized the truth, and so it was only the truth that held his attention now. [5]The mind of Jesus was fully consumed with love and gratitude and reality. [6]This was all he knew, and this was his only experience.

(v 33 – 41)[1]The perspective of the crucifixion through the lens of the unhealed mind is a perspective of pain and suffering. [2]The unhealed Son of God cannot imagine the blessings that are upon him, and so he must be taught. [3]Through Jesus' perspective of the event of the crucifixion and of his seeming death, Jesus is a symbol of both teacher and learner, that all may learn the truth.

[4]The perspective of the unhealed mind is that of darkness and of being forsaken or cut off from the mercy of God.

[5]The perspective of the healed mind is the joy of knowing itself as one with God, having never been separate and never able to be separate.

[6]The perspective of the unhealed mind is that of bodies, of suffering, of judgment and of guilt.

[7]The perspective of the healed mind is that of peace and gratitude for knowing beyond all possible doubt that illusions are illusions, and only the truth is true forever and always.

[8]The perspective of the unhealed mind is that of separateness and specialness and of being apart.

[9]The perspective of the healed mind is completion and wholly joyous.

[10]There were those who watched, who seemed to be somewhere between the complete knowledge of the healed mind and the unfettered blindness of the unhealed mind. [11]For they recognized something not of the world, and yet understood that it was of them. [12]It was through their prayer, combined with the prayer of Jesus, that the miracle of healing continued, even within what seemed to be a moment of confusion.

(v 42 - 47)[1]The one who went forward to accept Jesus' body was one who had accepted that death is unreal. [2]He went to Pilate in peace to request the body of Jesus as a symbol of eternal rest.

[3]Pilate was surprised that this prominent man from the leadership of

the Jewish temple should come to him and request the body of Jesus in a respectful and reverent way. [4]He thought that Jesus must not be dead. [5]For if he was, the man would seem different.

[6]Pilate asked the centurion to confirm that Jesus was dead. [7]The centurion reported it was so. [8]So Pilate let this man take the body and bury it.

[9]Jesus' body was prepared for burial according to the customs of the Jews. [10]The body was placed in a tomb, and a stone was rolled against the entrance to the tomb. [11]Then the man who buried the body fell to his knees in gratitude, for he knew the presence within his own mind and was grateful for it.

NTI Mark, Chapter 16

(v 1 – 20)[1]There were women who went to the tomb where Jesus' body was placed. [2]They went there in confusion and with hope, not knowing what they would find there, and yet feeling compelled by their intuition that they must go. [3]And so, these women did as they were guided, pretending to go to anoint the body in case anyone asked what their purpose was for being there.

[4]The women arrived at the tomb. [5]They joined together in prayer. [6]It was there, within the opening of their minds, that they were joined by one they did not at first recognize. [7]They recognized the love, the kindness, the warmth and comfort of its familiarity, but they did not recognize it as him.

[8]He came to them as a white light within their minds. [9]The women could not be afraid in his presence.

[10]"You have come to see the dead?" this one asked. [11]"Yet the one you seek is not dead, but living. [12]Here I am, within your mind, where Heaven also must be."

[13]One of the women said to him, "Master, is that you?"

[14]"It is I," this one confirmed. [15]"And I am with you always."

[16]Later, when the experience seemed to fade from the women's minds,

they became afraid. [17]And yet they found trust in that they had experienced this together as one mind.

[18]The women gathered the remaining apostles and asked them to meet with them in Galilee. [19]There, the women told the men what they had seen and heard within their mind.

[20]There were those among them who doubted the women and mocked them, but Peter recognized the truth. [21]For Peter had also experienced the master within the mind, and so Peter knew where the master was.

[22]Peter held hands with the women and calmed the frightened men by saying aloud what he knew must be true. [23]"He is with us, within our mind, where all experience must be. [24]It is here where we must meet with him and listen to him and let him lead us through our willingness for truth. [25]We cannot continue to deny what is, if we want to know Heaven. [26]We must accept what is true and teach it, that we may learn it and live it with him."

[27]And this was the message that the apostles heard. [28]This is the message of the resurrection, for it is a message of openness and acceptance of what already is. [29]It has forever been true and is forever true. [30]Peace is within you, my brother, because you are within peace. [31]Amen.

THE HOLY SPIRIT'S INTERPRETATION OF LUKE

NTI Luke, Chapter 1

(v 1 – 4)[1]This book was written in love and given with the blessings of true discovery. [2]In this way, the book is filled with the opportunity for discovery. [3]We may open up to its power and discover our truth together.

(v 5 – 56)[1]Each one comes to the awareness of truth from where he is, so where he is, is where he must begin to learn. [2]There is no shame in his starting point, wherever that starting point seems to be.

[3]The book of Luke begins with the story of ordinary people at different points in their lives. [4]They have been judged as good by the writer of the book, but this judgment is irrelevant. [5]For if it was their goodness that made them worthy of the Holy Spirit, others could be judged as unworthy, and this is impossible. [6]Each one is worthy, and each one has received the Holy Spirit. [7]There are no differences among men. [8]All are loved as precious; all are cared for; all receive guidance; and all are called to return to the Lord. [9]The form of their calling and their path may seem different, but its purpose is the same.

[10]You who are reading this are blessed, for you are beloved beyond measure. [11]You are the treasure that is sought. [12]You are everything, complete in God. [13]The Holy Spirit is born in you. [14]His kingdom is within your awareness, for His kingdom is your kingdom. [15]You, dear one, are the One. [16]Together, we will learn this lesson. [17]Amen.

[(v 57 – 80)[1]Listening and follow-through are key to discovery of blessings that already are. [2]This is what is symbolized through the story of John's birth. [3]His mother heard the thought of the Holy Spirit. [4]When the time came to follow-through, she remembered the thought, and chose it again.

[5]Within the story, Elizabeth's decision to follow guidance was not understood by others. [6]They urged her to make another choice. [7]This is how it will be with you, but understand where the struggle comes from, that you may resist temptation to ignore your guidance.

[8]Within your mind, there is a belief that is in opposition to God. [9]This belief does not seem sinful to you, and so you do not recognize it as the basis of sin.

[10]The belief that leads to this confusion is the belief that you are a separate entity. [11]It is the belief that there is a *you* and a *them*. [12]It is the belief that there is a *you* and that there is a universe of objects that are separate from you. [13]This belief you accept as a fact and you do not question it, so it does not occur to you that it is a mistaken belief that can be given up.

[14]This belief has a voice within your mind. [15]Its voice you call *your thoughts*. [16]Only because you do not question this belief, you do not question these thoughts that you claim as yours. [17]If you did question them, you would see that they are not loving thoughts. [18]Close examination would reveal that they are based on the belief that there is something inherently wrong with you as a separate entity. [19]These thoughts doubt your worth, and in fact, *they deny your worth entirely*.

[20]Thoughts that deny your worth also deny the Voice of Worth, which is the Holy Spirit. [21]This is why you will find great temptation to choose against your guidance. [22]Realize the source of this temptation and it will be helpful to you. [23]For when you do not realize the source of temptation, you are easily tricked into listening to the thoughts of your unworthiness.

[24]In this story, Zechariah represents the answer of faith. [25]Faith is a peaceful choice that trusts your worth must be true. [26]Therefore, it chooses the Voice of Worth over the voice of worthlessness. [27]This is what Zechariah did in choosing to follow the voice of his wife over the

voice of his friends. [28]This is a choice you can make consistently without fail, because you *are Worth*, and so you are worthy to choose the Voice of Worth.

NTI Luke, Chapter 2

📖(v 1 – 20)[1]The birth of Jesus represents the birth of willingness, humble at first, but promising within it all of the glory of Heaven. [2]Mary pondered this promise in her heart, not with the worrisome thoughts of the ego, but *in her heart* where the Holy Spirit is.

[3]This is what I ask of you:

[4]*Willingness has been born in the mind.* [5]*This willingness promises all of the glory of Heaven, for this willingness is the savior, the Christ, and it is with you within your heart.* [6]*Do not worry how this willingness will grow to become the glory it promises to be.* [7]*Rest, instead, with the thought of the promise, and be grateful.* [8]*It is through your love and gratitude that this babe is nursed.* [9]*Its growth is inevitable, so do not worry about it.* [10]*Love it in your heart, and be happy there.*

📖(v 21 – 40)[1]We see through the story of Jesus' consecration at the temple that this symbol of willingness has been blessed by the Holy Spirit. [2]This tiny willingness, only newly born and without achievement of any kind, is received by the Holy Spirit as a wonderful gift, and it is received with eternal gratitude.

[3]So it is with *your* willingness, no matter how humble that willingness may seem to be to you. [4]It is the willingness the Holy Spirit has waited for, and it is this willingness for which the Holy Spirit sings praises unto you.

[5]Through this willingness, thoughts of deception will be revealed through the grace of the Holy Spirit. [6]Deception shall be seen as deception, and truth shall be seen as truth. [7]All of the angels in Heaven shall rejoice because of you.

(v 41 – 52)[1]There will be conflict in your mind as this young willingness grows within you. [2]Sometimes your goal may seem lost to you, and you will forget your focus and return to the focus of the world. [3]But never fear. [4]The willingness has been born and cannot be lost. [5]It is within the temple of your heart, forever safe, clear in understanding, paving your way for you.

[6]When you forget your willingness and then remember it, return to it there in your heart. [7]You will find it there, safe within your Father's Love, growing in strength, sure of who it is.

[8]*Rejoice, for your willingness cannot be lost.*

[9]Rejoice, for you cannot make a mistake that will cause you to lose your willingness. [10]It is always there, waiting patiently and lovingly for your return to it.

[11]When you forget, just return again. [12]And then we shall continue on together. [13]Nothing is ever lost. [14]Nothing is taken away.

NTI Luke, Chapter 3

(v 1 – 20)[1]Your willingness is the calling within you. [2]This willingness is within everyone, resting patiently within the heart, waiting for the day it is asked to sing its song. [3]The song it sings is a calling, asking the one who hears its tune to follow it to a new way and a new day.

[4]John the Baptist is the symbol of this calling within all of us. [5]Not yet fully the Christ, it is the voice within a split mind that calls it to return to one mind, which is the Christ. [6]For Christ is free of illusions and released from distractions, singularly focused on the willingness that is the Will of God.

[7]What distracts *you* from the singular thought of God?

[8]Distractions take many forms. [9]They may seem to be positive or negative distractions; they may seem to be problems you face or pleasures you enjoy; but if they keep your thoughts away from the singular thought

of God, they are distractions for you.

[10]Do not feel guilty about your distractions, for distractions cause no loss in the Will of God. [11]God's Will is truth, and so it remains always true. [12]Distractions can have no affect on it. [13]Distractions only distract you from what is true, so that your focus is on distractions, which distract you from the awareness of truth.

[14]But then the awakened willingness within comes, and it calls you to turn away from distractions. [15]It calls you to return your mind fully to the awareness of truth. [16]In this calling, your distractions can serve the purpose of truth. [17]For all things given to your willingness will be used by your willingness to further awaken the call within you. [18]This will continue until your distractions are no more, and you are fully awake to the singular thought of God without distraction of any kind.

[19]This is the purpose of John, the call within you that calls you to awaken. [20]Follow the Voice. [21]Listen to it. [22]Do not let fear imprison this Voice within you.

[23]It is as written in the book of the words of Isaiah the prophet:

> [24]"A voice of one calling in the desert,
> 'Prepare the way for the Lord,
> make straight paths for him.
> [25]Every valley shall be filled in,
> every mountain and hill made low.
> [26]The crooked roads shall become straight,
> the rough ways smooth.
> [27]And all mankind will see God's salvation.'"
>
> *(Luke 3:4-6, New International Version)*

📖(v 21 – 38)[1]The most helpful way for you to view yourself is not to view yourself as special. [2]The ego wants to see itself as special. [3]Special is separate, so to surrender to the ego's desire is to continue to see yourself as separate from God. [4]This is not helpful.

[5]Do not look at Jesus' baptism and see him as special in comparison to you or others. [6]Look at his baptism and realize Jesus was baptized with others and the same as others, in the same water and by the same one. [7]For Jesus was baptized as one Son of God. [8]It was of this *one Son* that it was spoken:

[9]*"You are my Son,*
whom I love;
with you I am well pleased."

[10]These are the words spoken *of you*. [11]Read these words. [12]Listen to them. [13]Take them into your heart. [14]Accept them as true of you as they were true of Jesus, for there is no difference of any kind.

[15]Rejoice that you are not special and that Jesus was not special, for it is all the same. [16]You are he, and he is you. [17]You are the one Son of God. [18]This is your truth. [19]You are the Son of God, just as Jesus was. [20]There is no difference among you.

NTI Luke, Chapter 4

(v 1 – 13)[1]Within your mind, there are confusing thoughts that tell you that you are what you are not. [2]These thoughts are sly and deceitful, and you have listened to them and believed them. [3]You listen to them and believe them to this day, so that they confuse you, even to the point of confusing you regarding your identity. [4]But we are going to undo their confusion, for there is also a Voice within you that is not confused. [5]It is this Voice you are beginning to hear and to trust. [6]It is quiet, barely audible to you at all, and yet you *feel* this Voice within you, and you recognize it as true.

[7]Together, we will follow this Voice into the desert where the false voice may be exposed as false, and the true Voice may be known as true. [8]There will be great rejoicing at this unmasking, for this will be the realization of Self, which is eternal and eternally true.

(v 14 – 30) [1]This is a course of looking within yourself, for in truth there is nowhere else to look. [2]As we follow this course together, you will be tempted to look away from yourself and look at someone else, but if you remember that you cannot see anyone else *except through yourself*, you will remember once again where to focus your attention.

[3]This is a course that looks inside the mind and inside the heart by examining symbols that seem to be outside. [4]By looking through the mirror of your mind, we will discover the beliefs you hold onto there. [5]We will look at your beliefs together and examine honestly what they say to you. [6]Then you can decide if you want to listen to them or not.

[7]Jesus came out of the desert a teacher, but the one who taught through him was the Holy Spirit. [8]This is the same one that teaches you now, so that no time has elapsed since Jesus seemed to teach until the time that I am teaching you now.

[9]And so, it is true of you now as it was true of him then:

> [10]"The Spirit of the Lord is on me,
> because he has anointed me
> to preach good news to the poor.
> [11]He has sent me to proclaim freedom
> for the prisoners
> and recovery of sight for the blind,
> to release the oppressed,
> to proclaim the year of the Lord's favor."
> *(Luke 4:18-19, New International Version)*

[12]Today this scripture is fulfilled in your hearing. [13]Forget not the purpose of this course. [14]It is a course of looking within. [15]This is the message of this scripture. [16]This is the anointment you have accepted. [17]Be grateful to yourself. [18]This is the acceptance of peace.

[19]And yet, even as your gratitude is being expressed, you will not have to look far to find doubt within your mind. [20]There is doubt that the

words I share could be for you. [21]There is doubt that healing can occur. [22]There is doubt that I am reality. [23]There is doubt, angry and fearful doubt, within you.

[24]Do not deny the doubt that you see. [25]It is not to be denied. [26]It is the part of the mind that rejects the healing that is offered to it. [27]It will seem to resist the healing and to try and cast it away. [28]But do not fear. [29]In spite of its struggle and raucous noise, healing *cannot be rejected*. [30]Through your willingness to be healed, healing will walk through the mob in your mind, passing it by in gentleness, leaving it in peace to quiet on its own.

[31]This is the way we walk together. [32]It is the way of peace and great joy.

(v 31 – 37)[1]I am your leader in this process of healing. [2]It is best for you to realize that you do not know the answers and you could not heal yourself. [3]The way to healing is to listen to Me with the full attention of your ears. [4]Focus them on nothing else and no one else. [5]Quiet your mind, that you may hear only Me.

[6]There is nothing within you that needs to be driven away, but it may seem that way to you. [7]You may seem to be possessed of an evil voice that whispers torturous thoughts into your mind and will not go away. [8]This "demon" is your fear. [9]It will disguise itself in different forms in order to distract you from the truth of what *is*, but do not let it fool you. [10]It is your fear of healing, so it must be sickness. [11]For what else could fear healing but sickness? [12]Does love need to fear healing? [13]Does peace need to fear healing? [14]That which is the effects of health need not fear healing, so it is your sickness that causes fear and pain within you.

[15]Know your sickness for what it is. [16]And remember that willingness is where you choose to give your power now. [17]This is what you are to do when you see symptoms of sickness within your mind:

[18]Acknowledge that you are sick.

[19]Remember you have decided to be healed.

[20]Turn away from the voice of sickness.

[21]Give all of your attention to your willingness to be healed.

[22]Trust in your willingness.

[23]It is your sickness that cries out, "What do you want with us? [24]Have you come to destroy us?" [25]And it is your willingness that answers, "Be quiet. [26]We are listening to the Voice of Truth now."

(v 38 – 44) [1]There will seem to be many sick thoughts within your mind that need healing. [2]Do not fear that each one must be touched and healed for healing to come over you. [3]For all sickness comes from the same source. [4]When the source is healed, all of the symptoms of sickness disappear at once!

[5]So this is what you are to do:

[6]Do not believe the symptoms in your mind. [7]Do not be distracted by them. [8]Those small things are not the source of your sickness. [9]But when you notice the symptoms, let them remind you that the source is within you still. [10]Give your willingness to the Source of Healing, that the source of sickness may be taken away.

[11]And this is what else you are to do:

[12]Although there is sickness within you, you are not wholly sick, nor are you sickness itself. [13]For your willingness is within you, and it is health. [14]Turn your attention to your health. [15]Live within your health. [16]Be your health. [17]Get up and walk with it, giving your attention to it, that it may grow within you.

[18]Sickness must rest and be quiet. [19]This is the way to health. [20]Let your sickness rest.

[21]But health must serve the Son of God, for that is its only purpose. [22]Let your health serve in great joy, and be glad for it.

NTI Luke, Chapter 5

(v 1 – 11)[1]Things are not as they seem. [2]This is why I ask you to trust Me and follow Me. [3]I know how things are. [4]You are blind to these facts, for you only know what you think you know, and that is nothing but a deep and burdensome slumber.

[5]Step away from what you know, and come with Me. [6]I will show you what you don't know. [7]I will show you what you don't think is possible and prove to you that it is true.

[8]Leave what you know. [9]Be willing to put it completely behind you, and follow Me. [10]What you know limits you and holds you back through your own willingness to know it. [11]Cast what you know away from you, and I will help you to pull in a net full of what you did not believe was possible.

(v 12 – 16)[1]The journey that we take together will seem to take great faith. [2]Do not worry that you do not have enough faith to complete the journey. [3]For if you have faith to start, you have faith to complete it.

[4]On this journey through this course that we will complete together, you will come to see yourself as dirty, unworthy and untouchable. [5]All means of self-hatred will come up in you, but do not be alarmed. [6]Your blemishes come to Me for healing. [7]Your hatred comes to Me through your faith and willingness that it may be healed.

[8]Hatred is nothing but a desire for Love that believes Love is absent. [9]In My Light, it shall know Love is not absent. [10]In this knowledge, it is healed.

[11]Spend time with Me when hatred comes upon you. [12]Retreat to a quiet place, and ask for My help. [13]Wait in peace and confidence for My answer. [14]I invite your unhealed spots into the Light that I may heal them. [15]I will not abandon you when the unhealed spots answer my call and step forth to be healed.

(v 17 – 26)[1]Again I tell you, you will find doubt in your mind. [2]Even as I show you that you are worthy of love by loving you through My Self and into your heart, a thought will rise within your mind that says, "I am not worthy of this love. [3]It is love that must be illusion, for I am an abomination."

[4]This is yet another spot rising to the surface to be healed, so give this thought to Me. [5]Let My Light shine upon it.

[6]I am asking you to pick up your mat and walk. [7]This is the task at hand. [8]And to do this, you must be willing to leave your doubt behind. [9]This is why I tell you that there will be doubt! [10]So when you see it, you can say, "Ah, yes. [11]There it is, just as I was told it would be." [12]And you can remember that the Authority given faith is stronger than the authority presumed in doubt.

[13]Lay your doubt aside. [14]Trust in My words and walk with Me.

(v 27 – 32)[1]Remember that you are sick, and I have come to heal. [2]Remember all that I say, that healing may be ushered in now.

[3]*You are worthy.*
[4]*Do not let doubt tell you that you are not.*
[5]*Feel grateful for your willingness.*
[6]*It will herald all healing for you.*

[7]Sickness must be seen to be healed, so show your sickness to Me. [8]But do not forget that it is only sickness, and through your rest, I come to heal.

(v 33 – 39)[1]Old habits must be let go, for old habits will not usher in a new day. [2]With old habits, all things remain the same. [3]But with new habits, all things are possible.

[4]I have come to teach you new habits. [5]You will learn these habits by practicing them as I ask. [6]Remember Me, and practice.

[7]You will catch yourself practicing the old habits, for this has been your way until now. [8]Slipping into old habits does not ruin the new ones. [9]So when you find yourself doing this, forgive yourself your attraction to the old by stepping away from the old and stepping into the new. [10]Each time you do this, you help yourself to unlearn the old and to learn the new.

[11]Take no old habits with you into the new, for the old habits must be left completely if the new habits are to result in new.

NTI Luke, Chapter 6

📖(v 1 - 11)[1]Judgment is a way of looking at the world and deciding what is good and what is bad, or what is right and what is wrong. [2]You have been taught within the world how to exercise your judgment so that it is "good judgment," for even judgment itself can be good or bad, right or wrong.

[3]Now I ask that you forget everything you have been taught and everything you have learned. [4]For if you know nothing, you cannot judge. [5]Any judgment that you make and accept as a belief in your mind is a mistake, for any judgment that you make assumes something within illusion is real, and within its realness, something is better or more valuable than something else. [6]Judgment accepts as real and then separates, so all judgment must be of the ego.

[7]Look at Jesus and at the Pharisees within these scriptures. [8]Surely you notice that the Pharisees have learned "rules" on which they feel they can judge. [9]But the Pharisees are only a symbol of what is within your mind, for you also have learned "rules" on which you believe you can judge.

[10]Did you judge the Pharisees as you read these stories? [11]On what "rule" did you base that judgment? [12]Is there a belief in your mind that Jesus is more "real" or more "truth" than the Pharisees? [13]Did you think that the Pharisees were "wrong" to judge Jesus?

[14]Nothing in the world is more "real" than anything else. [15]This is *why* you know nothing and cannot judge. [16]Your conscious experience is only of the world, and so you cannot know truth, which is not of the world.

[17]This is why I have come to you. [18]I know truth *and* I know the world that you believe and hold dear. [19]I can lead you from the world to the truth if you will trust and follow Me.

²⁰To trust and follow Me, make no judgments along the way. ²¹Be as a little child, wide-eyed and curious, enjoying all that you seem to experience. ²²Trust Me to make your judgments for you.

(v 12 – 16) ¹Do not be bothered that the names of the apostles in one book of the New Testament do not match up with the names of the apostles in another book. ²These details are not important, because these details are meaningless. ³The apostles are but symbols, which represent everyone, and so there is no difference between one apostle and another, or between one man and you. ⁴We are all followers of the path that comes from within. ⁵We are all guided to learn the truth by following the path of unreality.

(v 17 – 26)¹The world is a great temptation for you, because the world was made as a distraction from truth. ²Everything in the world is not truth, and yet you want to make sense of it and make it real. ³To the degree that you can let go of the world and not be concerned about it, that is to the degree that you accept healing. ⁴And to the degree that you are involved in the world and taking care of its many problems, that is to the degree that you reject healing as the answer to its problems.

(v 27 – 36)¹It is within the world that you seem to be, so it is within the world that I come to lead you. ²But I ask you to look at the world differently now. ³No longer accept that there is a "you" and a "them" who is separate from you. ⁴This is the view the ego has of the world.

⁵My view is that the world is all one song with different notes played in harmony to create the one. ⁶It is the song that is cherished, not the notes. ⁷And the song is being played perfectly by Me, who is the director of the music.

⁸If you look at the song from My point of view, you see its beauty and perfection. ⁹But if you look at the song from the point of view of one note, who believes it is separate and competing with other notes, the song seems to be a war filled with attack and grievance and worry.

¹⁰Remember that you are not the note. ¹¹That is a distorted view of the music. ¹²*We are the song* as *one sound* together.

¹³Love the entire song. ¹⁴Every aspect is equally important to the whole, every aspect valuable and cherished for its part in it. ¹⁵Share the perspective of the song by seeing yourself *as the song* and by loving the entire song, just as it is, without judgment or desire that the song should be played differently.

(v 37, 38)   ¹*Everything that you see and experience,*
you see and experience through the filter of your mind.

²There can be no exception. ³This is always true. ⁴This is why you can see or experience something in one way and have one opinion or belief about it, and another one can seem to see or experience it in another way and have another opinion or belief. ⁵All of this "seeing" is occurring through the ego-mind, which does not see at all. ⁶It interprets.

⁷The ego-mind is itself a seeming split, apart from the Christ-mind, which is one. ⁸Since the ego-mind is a split or fraction, its perspective or viewpoint is not whole. ⁹Since it is not whole, it is not knowledge, which is why it interprets.

¹⁰But the ego-mind is not aware that it interprets. ¹¹It believes it knows. ¹²This is why ego minds seem to conflict. ¹³Each one merely interprets without knowledge, but mistakes its interpretation for knowledge.

¹⁴Knowledge cannot conflict, for it is whole. ¹⁵Interpretation cannot conflict, since it is not knowledge. ¹⁶It can only seem to conflict, but that is a conflict of illusions or unreality, which is no conflict at all.

¹⁷Everything you see and experience, you see and experience through the filter of your own mind. ¹⁸In order to find peace, one must abandon interpretation and remember knowledge. ¹⁹This is the process of learning that I lead you through. ²⁰You are learning that you do not know; you interpret. ²¹This enables you to step back from conflict, and knowing that your interpretation is nothing, let your interpretation go. ²²As interpretation is released, knowledge can be given. ²³Knowledge is peace, since

knowledge has no conflict, because it is whole and it is truth.

(v 39 – 42)[1]Everything you see and experience, you see and experience through the filter of your own mind. [2]This is good news, for what you see and experience witnesses to the interpretation that you believe is knowledge. [3]Upon seeing it and knowing that it is not knowledge, because it is not peace, you can choose to step back and let your false interpretation go.

[4]You may see your brother's error, which is his false interpretation that he mistakes for knowledge. [5]I tell you that as long as you believe your interpretation, you do not have knowledge. [6]Therefore, you cannot lead your brother to let go of his interpretation. [7]For only knowledge can see clearly to lead mistakes to healing. [8]Whatever you see in your brother, bring back to your interpretation, that you may give it up and be healed.

(v 43 – 45)[1]You will speak from your interpretation as long as you believe your interpretation. [2]So when you recognize that you have an interpretation, it would be wise not to speak. [3]Do not fight for an interpretation that is meaningless, for meaninglessness brings you nothing.

[4]When you notice that you have an interpretation, take a break from what you see. [5]Seek quiet time with Me, and share your interpretation with Me. [6]Do not share your interpretation as if you must be right, expecting Me to support you and lead you to the righteousness of your way. [7]Share your interpretation *expecting that you are wrong*, because you have seen and believed without knowledge. [8]In such humility, you can let go of your interpretation; you will see that it is nothing of value to you. [9]And what you receive in its place you will extend, and that which you share shall be peace and restfulness.

(v 46 – 49)[1]Why do you call me "Lord, Lord," and do not do what I say? [2]I am Lord, because I am knowledge. [3]To listen to Me and practice what I say is to find true peace that cannot be shaken, because it is knowledge.

[4]But to listen and not practice is to keep your interpretation, which is not knowledge. [5]And so you have chosen to keep nothing and believe it

is something. [6]This is to choose illusions over truth. [7]And illusions cannot be shared.

[8]Review My words and practice them. [9]I am teaching you the way of peace.

NTI Luke, Chapter 7

(v 1 – 10)[1]Listen to Me in trust and faith, for all that I share is important to your healing. [2]You must practice what I share with you. [3]You must remember My words and treasure them within your mind. [4]Ask Me for more, and they will be given you. [5]Have faith that you are worthy, and you will hear. [6]For it is My Will that you hear My Voice.

[7]When My Will meets your desire and the quietness of your mind, it shall be done, and you will hear.

[8]This is what is symbolized in the story of the centurion whose servant was healed. [9]He did not doubt that he was worthy to receive of Me. [10]He did not doubt that his servant was worthy. [11]The doubt that is written into the story was added by others who did not know their worth or the worth of others. [12]But the centurion did know. [13]And so, his desire and the quiet faith of his mind joined with the knowledge in Mine, and as one Will *without separation*, what was asked was given.

[14]Ask for the healing of your mind by asking that My thoughts be placed there. [15]As you seek, you shall find. [16]You cannot fail to find that which you seek in honesty of faith.

(v 11 – 17)[1]There is no death, but within you there is a deep slumber that resembles death, for it is unaware of truth or of Life. [2]I have come to awaken you from this slumber and to resurrect you from this death. [3]Yet each one is dead by his own choice, so each one must choose to answer My call to resurrection.

[4]I am calling to you now. [5]My hand is outstretched to assist you as you rise. [6]What is your choice? [7]Are you ready to awaken to Life?

(v 18 – 23)[1]There are expectations in your mind regarding truth, but these expectations are based on what you know within your slumber.

[2]They are not based on knowledge or Life. [3]They are based on interpretation, or death.

[4]What do you expect of Me? [5]Where is it that you think I am leading you to?

[6]Free yourself from these thoughts, and open your mind to Me unfettered by expectations. [7]Blessed is the man who does not fall away on account of Me.

(v 24 – 28) [1]Why did you begin this search? [2]What is it that you wanted to find? [3]Did you really expect to find the peace of God in *your way*?

[4]No, you expected surrender. [5]This was the expectation given you by Me. [6]That is why this expectation crossed your mind in peace with willingness.

[7]This path that you have chosen is the greatest of all paths within the world. [8]Yet, this path is *within the world*. [9]To know the kingdom of Heaven, you must be willing to step off of this path with Me.

(v 29 – 35) [1]In honesty, look at your expectations and at what you want. [2]Were your expectations given to you by Me? [3]If they were not, then they are not of Me, and you will not know Me if you judge Me by them.

(v 36 – 50) [1]Your surrender *is* forgiveness. [2]To the measure that you surrender to Me, that is the measure that your thoughts, which are not of Me, are forgiven. [3]For when you are accepting My thoughts and doing My Will with recognition that they are your thoughts and your Will, you are not living as a separate entity. [4]You are being one Will with Me. [5]And this *is* forgiveness, which is where your love comes from. [6]For you can only know love when you accept Love and join with the Will of Love. [7]But to join with a will that is not Love is to choose to be separate from Love. [8]That is to choose to remain asleep and to say "no" to the offer of resurrection, which is an offer extended to you *now*.

NTI Luke, Chapter 8

(v 1 – 15) [1]You are looking at yourself now and seeing what you believe is your unworthiness. [2]As you compare yourself to others, you note that you are not good enough. [3]You do not give enough or practice enough. [4]In your own judgment, you are never enough.

[5]Let's review what I have asked of you. [6]I have asked you to trust that you are worthy. [7]I have asked you to let your sickness rest. [8]I have promised that we would look at your sickness together, and I have asked you to nurse your willingness with gratitude.

[9]Now is a time for gratitude and rest. [10]Be grateful that you have been willing to bring your sickness to Me. [11]Rest, as we look at your sickness together. [12]For it cannot be healed if it is hidden from healing.

[13]Focus on your gratitude. [14]Let the guilt and hatred and anger rise. [15]Remember that you are being healed, even now. [16]Do not nurse your sickness. [17]Let it come up, but choose to nurse your willingness to be healed.

[18]Let all things serve the purpose of healing. [19]Do not avoid healing because you do not want to look at the pain of sickness. [20]We must look at it together if you are to be healed.

[21]Do not be afraid. [22]I am with you, even now. [23]Stay with the process. [24]Be the good soil that produces a crop.

(v 16 – 18)[1]I have already told you that this is a course of looking within. [2]And yet, your mind wanders to the world as the source of guilt. [3]Nothing within the world is the source of guilt. [4]Not even what you do within the world can be a source of guilt for you.

[5]The outer is a reflection of the inner, because all that you see and experience, you see and experience through the filter of your mind. [6]If you believe that you see or experience guilt, the judgment of guilt must already be in the mind. [7]So a part of your healing process is to let loose the judgment you have already put upon yourself.

[8]What comes first *is first*. [9]But when what comes first is changed, all that follows must change also.

(v 19 – 21)   [1]*There is only one Will, and that is God's Will.*

(v 22 – 25)[1]The storm that is raging is within your mind. [2]It rages there, because you are asleep. [3]If you were awake to the Will of God, your one true Will, you could perceive no storm, for there is none. [4]This is the lesson we will learn together. [5]Trust in Me as your Teacher. [6]I will show you that you are at peace.

(v 26 – 39)[1]The storm that rages within your mind is like cloud cover, hiding the peacefulness behind it. [2]But the peace is within you also. [3]And peace is your natural state.

[4]Our purpose is to blow away the clouds so that they disperse, and the naturalness that is within is what is left and is seen and is witnessed.

(v 40 – 56)[1]There is a thought within your mind that says the healing that I speak of is impossible, and it cannot be accomplished. [2]That is because there is also a thought in your mind that believes the cloud cover is all that you are, and it does not see how "all that you are" can be made perfect.

[3]This is the thought that I have told you about. [4]This is the thought that you are inherently unworthy. [5]This is a thought that focuses on the cloud cover as all there is, and it does not realize that you are the infinite blue sky that rests behind the clouds. [6]To realize your truth, you must have faith that the thought that you are the clouds is wrong. [7]It is a mistaken thought.

[8]Yet, it is a thought that you believe. [9]In order to discover for yourself that this thought is totally false, you must be willing to look beyond the clouds with Me. [10]You must be willing to take your eyes off of what you believe is true, and in faith, look with Me beyond that limit. [11]To stop at the limit will not show you what is beyond it.

[12]You do not know what is true, but you can take My hand in faith and walk with Me to what *I know*. [13]In coming with Me and seeing beyond the clouds, you shall realize that truth has always been true, and peace has reigned unchallenged while you merely looked away for a little while.

NTI Luke, Chapter 9

(v 1 – 6)[1]Everyone who reads My Word, listens to My Word and practices My Word *teaches* My Word. [2]There can be no exception. [3]You, who are reading this now, are My holy teacher.

[4]Do not let this make you afraid. [5]Do not worry about what is expected of you based on this "assignment." [6]Nothing is expected of you except one thing: [7]*That you listen to Me.*

[8]Do not worry where you are to go, what you are to do, what you are to say or to whom. [9]Do not worry how you are to teach. [10]I may have you teach without a single spoken word.

[11]Give no thought to the future. [12]Give no thought to how you are to teach or when or where. [13]Only give thought to listening to Me and practicing as I ask you to practice. [14]In this way, you *do* teach, and the lesson you teach is heard throughout the world.

(v 7 – 9)[1]There is fear in your mind. [2]And so it will bring doubt that you do as I ask you to do. [3]It will bring doubt that you are the one I ask to do these things. [4]Do not listen to your doubt. [5]It is to *you* that I am speaking. [6]You who are reading these words, without exception for any reason, you are the one.

(v 10 – 17)[1]You do not understand the power in your mind. [2]That power is unspeakable in your world, for it cannot be described. [3]But know this:

[4]*Every thought that you accept*
teaches within the mind of man.

[5]The single mind that you are is taught through the thoughts that you agree to think. [6]And this is how you are to teach the world.

[7]Although I may guide you to speak, it is not through your speaking that you teach. [8]Although I may guide you to go or do, it is not through your going or doing that you teach. [9]To speak to those or to go here or to do that would be to limit your teaching to a few. [10]You, who are unlimited

within your Self, cannot be limited by restrictions such as these. [11]So it must *not* be through your speaking or your going or your doing that you teach.

[12]Every thought that you think is heard *literally* around the world. [13]The consciousness of man is shaken by your every thought. [14]And so it is through thought that you teach, no matter what you are saying or doing, and no matter where you are.

[15]And so I say to you again, dear teacher:

[16]*Listen to Me.*
[17]*Remember My words,*
and practice all that I say.

[18]The fish that you eat feeds a multitude of men.

(v 18 – 27)[1]You are the Christ, because the Christ of God is within you, and it is Christ that is your true Self. [2]This is the health within. [3]This is the Light that shines its healing rays throughout your mind, shining away all sickness in every form.

[4]Peace be with you, my brother, for you are the blessed one. [5]Put your faith with Me, focused upon your reality. [6]It is this reality we seek to remember.

[7]Do not be afraid of what must come before you are to remember. [8]There is nothing that can hurt when your mind stays focused with Me. [9]I am your constant companion, and I lead you through all things.

(v 28 – 36)[1]A vision of Light is within your mind. [2]To know this Light, you must only ask to remember it, for the Light is with you always. [3]If you feel afraid or doubtful or desperate for love, all that you need do is quiet yourself and ask for Light. [4]It cannot fail to appear within your mind at your request. [5]It is always there to comfort you and to shelter you.

[6]Do not turn away from the Light. [7]Do not be afraid that you nag it with your requests. [8]It is there *for you*, to serve you through your every moment of need.

(v 37 – 45)[1]You will not be healed by following the ways that make sense to you. [2]Following what makes sense to you has brought you to the point of needing healing, and so it cannot be healing itself.

[3]To be healed of the thoughts that are foreign, but seem natural to your mind, you must put your healing in My hands. [4]Give yourself over to Me. [5]Let go of any resistance you feel towards this thought. [6]Remember that the result of giving yourself to Me is your own healing. [7]You will be returned to your Father, so rejoice! [8]The time is now. [9]Place yourself fully and completely in My hands.

(v 46 – 50)[1]I have asked you to be a teacher of My Word, and I am grateful for your willingness to teach as I ask. [2]And now you must listen to the secret of teaching:

[3]A teacher is a student who practices all that he teaches, knowing fully that the message he shares is also for him. 4In this way, anyone may be a teacher of My Word, for anyone may choose to be the student, and the student *is* the teacher. [5]For the Teacher comes through the student in order that the student may learn.

(v 51 - 56)[1]Always remember that as the teacher, you are the student, so all things are given to you for your learning. [2]In this way, see all things as an opportunity to learn and to practice, and be grateful for all things. [3]There is nothing that will be placed in your path that is not a gift from Me. [4]See it as your gift and you are blessed indeed.

(v 57 – 62)[1]To be My teacher, you must let My Word be first in your mind in all things. [2]This is a perspective you shall hold. [3]Through holding this perspective in willingness and trust, you shall know what to do through Me.

NTI Luke, Chapter 10

(v 1 – 24)[1]Give no thought to what you are to do in the next moment of time. [2]When that moment of time comes, ask Me then what you are to do. [3]I will answer you in that moment. [4]For each moment brings with it its own opportunities for healing, but if you are thinking of another moment in this moment of time, you miss the opportunities that are given in the current moment. [5]In this way, your healing will seem to take longer, because you are not using the time you have been given for the purposes of healing.

[6]Think not for yourself. [7]Remember that it is your thinking that has brought you to the point of needing healing. [8]Relinquish your own thought, and trade it for My thought. [9]Now is the opportunity to trade. [10]Lay down your own thought *now*, and I will fill you up with My thought.

[11]Go, filled with My thought, and do not question the thought that is given. [12]When you are tempted to question and to once again find your own thought, remember the purpose of your journey. [13]Joyously choose My thought again.

[14]You will seem to have many temptations. [15]You will seem to forget My thoughts completely for a time. [16]Do not let that distress you. [17]The thinking you do apart from Me cannot hurt you. [18]It can only delay your healing for a little while. [19]So when you find you have forgotten, shake off the past and the memory of your forgetfulness. [20]Now is a new moment! [21]You help yourself by choosing My thoughts again now.

[22]There is never backward movement on this journey. [23]You can only walk forward on the path to healing with Me. [24]When you forget and seem to fail, you have not failed or slipped backwards. [25]You have only stopped and stood in one place for a time. [26]When you are ready to continue forward with Me again, I am waiting there beside you, ready to take your hand and go forward with you.

(v 25 – 37)

[1]*To love God,*
to love yourself
and to love another
is all the same.

[2]This is the one lesson I would have you learn. [3]There is no difference among anyone or anything within your mind. [4]It is all one within the

Mind of God.

⁵How would you learn this lesson? ⁶First, you must give up judgment. ⁷For when you judge, you separate and see differences. ⁸And in this "seeing," you cannot see that it is all the same.

⁹Go within your mind and watch the process that you call "thinking" as it goes on there. ¹⁰What you will observe is that it is a constant process of dividing, judging, selecting and specifying. ¹¹It is the calculation that defines separateness. ¹²It is everything except the acceptance of truth.

¹³This is why I have asked you to lay down your own thoughts. ¹⁴But I understand that before you choose to do so, you must come to see that which you think has value as being truly valueless. ¹⁵And this *is* the case with your thoughts, for as long as you hold onto them and cherish them, you cannot see the truth that is before you now. ¹⁶They are like a veil that hides the Light of Heaven from your sight.

¹⁷I ask this of you. ¹⁸Remember these famous words:

¹⁹"Love the Lord your God with all your heart and with all your soul and with all your strength and with all your mind. ²⁰Love your neighbor as yourself."

²¹And then remember there is no division in this statement. ²²It is all the same. ²³It is all one Love.

²⁴See the thoughts in your mind that block this Love from your experience, and then willingly lay them aside. ²⁵Each time you do, a prayer is sent to Heaven upon the wings of your willingness, asking that you may lay all judgment aside and see the truth of Heaven.

(v 38 – 42)¹As you listen to My words and practice what I say, resistance will come up in your mind telling you that doing all that I say is not rational or sensible. ²This thought will imply that you will somehow suffer or regret listening to Me. ³When this thought comes, remember that I told you it would. ⁴Then place it aside, and continue to listen to Me.

NTI Luke, Chapter 11

(v 1 – 13) [1]How shall you pray?

[2]Prayer is the unceasing act of thought. [3]With every thought, you pray for everything or for nothing at all.

[4]How, then, shall you think?

[5]I have already asked you to think with Me by accepting My thoughts and laying your own thoughts aside. [6]My thoughts are these: [7]They are thoughts of forgiveness, love, acceptance, gratitude and rejoicing.

[8]Whenever you are not listening to My thoughts, you will know, because you will not be at peace and you will not be happy. [9]This is not a time to chastise yourself, for chastisement is not among the thoughts that I give. [10]If you are tempted to chastise yourself for forgetting Me, you must again be listening to your own thoughts and praying for nothing. [11]This is the time that you should ask for your daily bread. [12]This is a time of forgiving your own thoughts by laying them aside and again opening your heart to Me.

[13]Ask and it will be given you. [14]Seek and you will find. [15]Knock and the door will be opened to you. [16]For everyone who asks receives, he who seeks finds, and to him who knocks, the door will be opened.

[17]Your Father is the extension of Love. [18]And His Love has been poured out upon you. [19]It is His only gift. [20]Anything that is not of the gift of our Father is of nothing, and so it is meaningless and it has no value. [21]Lay that aside, and accept the gift given to you by our Father.

(v 14 – 28) [1]Your mind is split. [2]Within you there is great willingness to do all that I ask you to do. [3]And within you there is a great resistance that guides you away from the practice I ask you to seek. [4]Let us look at your resistance, that you may be aware of its ploys. [5]Then you will be able to recognize it and to choose, not with your resistance, but with your willingness.

[6]Your resistance will distract you away from Me. [7]It will give you thoughts that seem to need to be thought, problems to think through and solve. [8]It will give you things to do that must be done if you are to be seen

as worthy by the outside world. [9]It will throw confusion at you so that what once seemed clear when you heard My Word becomes muddled and unclear, so you are unsure what to do. [10]It will ask questions, and you will seem to need to know the answers in order to put your trust in Me, and so you will go out in search of satisfactory answers when satisfactory answers cannot be found. [11]It will offer you diversions that seem to bring great joy and pleasure into your life within the world. [12]It will bring doubt into your mind, so that you will have a desire to find out what is true without giving of your trust.

[13]What are you to do when tempted by your own resistance? [14]Notice it for what it is. [15]Do not let it disguise itself as something important. [16]See it as resistance and call it by its name. [17]Then give it to Me, backed by the strength of your willingness. [18]Together, we will redirect your attention to the path you have set out on.

[19]Blessed are those who hear My Word and heed it in willingness and joy.

(v 29 – 32)[1]Your resistance is nothing more than your desire to keep things the same, to keep things as you see them now. [2]And you desire this because you desire safety, and you think there is safety in the security you have made. [3]And yet, you fear yourself and what you have made also.

[4]You are safe, but you are not secure, for security knows no illusions of fear.

[5]Let Me lead you to both safety and security, which is known through the knowledge of your safety. [6]Safety comes from the guarantee of who you are.

(v 33 – 36)[1]The knowledge of your safety takes away all images of fear. [2]In knowing your Self, you can know no fear. [3]This is the Light that shines from within to shine on everything you see, to shine away all imagined darkness and to show you only peace, love and joy. [4]This Light you shall share with all the world through your natural love of Light.

(v 37 - 54)[1]Resistance will sometimes seem to be the light, and so you must listen closely within your own mind, that you know where your instructions and desires come from. [2]Resistance will sometimes be subtle, and so you must listen closely within your mind, so that you know where your instructions and desires come from. [3]A useful question to ask whenever you are prompted to fill your time with anything is, "What is it for?"

[4]When you ask, remember the purpose of time. [5]It is for healing your mind. [6]This is its only purpose. [7]If you are using time for any other purpose, you are not using time at all.

[8]Ask, "What is it for?" and listen honestly for your reply. [9]Any answer other than the healing of your own mind is but a delay in your purpose of your healing. [10]Anything that is not a part of your purpose is a part of nothing.

[11]So if you ask, "What is it for?" and you find that you have given this time another purpose, then ask yourself, "What do I want?" [12]When you answer this question with the answer of your heart, you find the means and willingness to change the purpose of the current time. [13]And this change is but a correction, brought about by your Holy Spirit, which knows your purpose and knows what time is for.

NTI Luke, Chapter 12

(v 1 - 12)[1]Now let's talk about the work you are to do. [2]You are aware that there will be resistance, *great* resistance. [3]Do not lose this awareness, and always be on guard. [4]When resistance arises in your mind in any form, let it go immediately *in gratitude* as valueless.

[5]The work you are to do is within the mind. [6]It is a work of being aware, not of the world, but of your thoughts about the world.

[7]Right now, you think you are focused on the world. [8]You think you are focused on relationships, work, entertainment and rest, but I tell you that you are not focused on any of these things. [9]You never have been. [10]Even your thought that you are focused on the world is an illusion within the mind.

[11]What you are focused on, and have always been focused on, is

thought. [12]In every moment in your seeming interaction with the world, you are focused on thought. [13]And because you see yourself as a separate entity within the world, you are focused on thoughts that seem to be generated within the private mind that belongs to you. [14]Let's look very carefully at this process of which you are barely aware, and yet it defines everything that you think, believe and do.

[15]Whenever you look at anything with the body's eyes, there are thoughts in your mind about that thing. [16]If you look at a chair, for example, you may think that it is pretty, worn out, available, desired, not desired, clean, dirty, etc, etc. [17]The thoughts that come into your mind seem automatic, without any awareness or evaluation on your part. [18]You may make judgments about the chair based on your thoughts, and you may choose to sit there or not sit there based on your judgment. [19]But you never look at, evaluate or question the thoughts you hold about the chair, and this is only a chair.

[20]The process that you call thinking, of which you are mostly unaware, goes on within your mind regarding everything in your world. [21]You make unevaluated judgments about the work you do, the relation-ships you have, the pastimes you choose and the person you think of as yourself. [22]These unevaluated judgments define everything and everyone within your world. [23]And they are allowed within your mind without your awareness, your questioning or your evaluation.

[24]So this is the work that I ask you to do. [25]I ask you to slow down your pace a bit. [26]You may choose how you will slow it down. [27]Pick a method that seems most comfortable to you now, but find a way to reduce the distractions in your life, so you can take the time to become aware of the thoughts that seem automatic in your mind. [28]What are these thoughts? [29]What are they saying to you? [30]Why are you listening to them? [31]Are they thoughts of love?

[32]Do not worry what you will do with these thoughts as you evaluate them. [33]I will be with you, present in your mind, as you undertake this work of looking and questioning. [34]For now, it is simply useful to become

aware of the thoughts you think *and are focused on* when you think you are focused on the world.

(v 13 – 21)[1]You may ask why you should do this work, especially when there is resistance telling you that you have better things to do with your time. [2]I tell you that until you have evaluated the thoughts that are within your mind, you are unaware of *why you do the things that you do*.

[3]Without the awareness that comes from this evaluation, can you be sure that you are storing up the treasures that you want stored up? [4]If your time is spent based on the judgments made by thoughts that are not truly valuable to you, whose treasure are you storing up? [5]Is it truly yours?

[6]But if you look at your thoughts, evaluate them, determine that they are valuable to you, and then make your life by following these thoughts…well…then you can be sure you are storing up treasures that have meaning.

[7]So first look at your thoughts. [8]Then, when you have become aware of the thoughts you have allowed there, we will evaluate your thoughts together according to what is truly valuable to you.

(v 22 – 34)[1]Do not worry about your progress on this path that you travel to healing. [2]To be on the path and aware of the path and thinking of the path is enough. [3]Let Me tell you a secret that will make your journey along this path simpler and more joyful. [4]The secret is this:

[5]As you travel this path, you will only have two experiences. [6]It may seem like many, but in truth, it is only two. [7]One experience will speed you along your journey in joy. [8]The other will delay your journey a little while. [9]The secret to a simple and joyful journey is to learn to discern between these two experiences, and then always choose the joyful one.

[10]I have spoken to you of both experiences before, so this is but a reminder for you. [11]The only two experiences that you will know as we travel this path together are the experience of your willingness and the experience of resistance. [12]Everything that you think you experience is either one or the other.

[13]So do not worry about your progress on this path. [14]Do not judge

your own thoughts or actions, for worry and judgment do not bring joy, and so they cannot be willingness.

[15]Discern carefully, my friend. [16]Recognize the thought within your mind. [17]And at every opportunity, choose the strength of your willingness. [18]Seek only for the kingdom and all things will be given you. [19]Where your Heart is, your treasure is also.

(v 35 - 48)[1]It will be helpful if you remember this:

[2]*God's Will is that you be perfectly happy in every moment of eternity.*

[3]That is simple. [4]And so when you are not happy, you have made a choice that is not God's Will. [5]When you are not happy, you have chosen with resistance. [6]That is all. [7]It is not a fight or a rebellion; it is merely resistance. [8]It does not take you from God or separate you from Him; it merely resists your willingness to know Him.

[9]So whenever you are not happy, it is because you are resisting accepting truth. [10]To be happy again, all you need do is return your heart to your willingness. [11]Your willingness sings of God's Will. [12]And so give yourself to it in every hour to know happiness.

(v 49 – 53)[1]Let Me tell you another secret:

[2]*The world cannot make you happy,*
and so the world must not be God's Will for you.

[3]Do not worry about the world. [4]Let the world take care of itself, and trust that all things are handled in a loving way. [5]You, my friend, are to follow your own Heart. [6]Set your feet on the path to healing, and let your mind stay with the joy that comes from your willingness. [7]Give no thought to anything else, and you will make yourself truly helpful to all.

(v 54 - 59)[1]And so my brothers, I say to you all: [2]*Pay attention to how you are feeling.* [3]When you are not feeling joy, you have chosen resistance. [4]Do not worry about your mistake. [5]It is not held against you.

[6]See it only as a wake-up call and a reminder to choose your joy and willingness again. [7]In this way, you wake yourself up. [8]In this way, you make the choice that sets you free.

NTI Luke, Chapter 13

(v 1 – 9)[1]When you look at the world, remember that you are looking through the filter of your own mind. [2]When you find yourself reacting to the world you see, remember that you are only reacting to the thoughts in your mind. [3]This will provide for you the opportunity to *see* the thoughts that you think.

[4]As you watch the world through the filter of your mind, you will think you see many things. [5]Some will seem good, heart-warming, funny, happy and desirable. [6]Others will seem frightening, horrible, wrong, disgusting and undesirable. [7]And there will seem to be a sliding scale of good and bad and every thought that is in-between.

[8]Now, remember again that *you are looking through the filter of your mind*, which means that the concepts of good and bad must be thought of there. [9]Surely, you will see that these thoughts are yours, and you are the proud owner of the judgments you have made. [10]Recognizing that you own your judgments is important, for if you are the owner, or *the believer* of what you think, then you can also decide to choose again and allow yourself to think differently.

[11]At first you may not see why you should want to change some of the judgments you have made. [12]So I ask this of you:

[13]Remember that judgment is like a knife that looks at the Son of God and separates him. [14]This means that as long as you hold onto your judgment as something that has value, you are blind to the beauty and value of the sight of the Son of God.

[15]And now, with that thought in your mind, can you give your willingness to lay your judgments aside, whatever they may seem to be?

[16]If you can find but a bit of willingness to see the Son of God, and so not to judge, that is enough. [17]And if each time you notice your

judgments, you give your willingness in whatever measure it may seem to be, that is enough again.

[18]I bless you with My gratitude *each time* you give Me but the smallest measure of your willingness, for each small measure is like fertilizer; it is useful to Me in the healing of your heart.

(v 10 – 17)[1]Your confusion comes from the binding ways of your own thinking until now. [2]It is your thoughts that have made you suffer. [3]And so, if you would choose freedom, you must also choose freedom from your thoughts.

[4]This is why I have come. [5]I am here to teach you to lay down your thoughts, to loosen yourself from your bindings, and to straighten up and walk in joy and gratitude instead.

(v 18 – 21)[1]How does one come to know the peace and joy of God? [2]I tell you that it is not through the worry and effort of your old ways. [3]Sit down, and relax with Me.

[4]One comes to know the peace and joy of God by listening to Me, as a small child who is eager to learn listens to a parent. [5]And then, just as that child does, by trying everything the parent asks it to try. [6]But if you watch a child when it is learning something new, you will notice that the learning itself does not seem to come from the child's effort. [7]The practice is but an expression of the child's willingness to learn. [8]The learning itself seems to come upon the child like a miracle, and suddenly the small child can do what it could not do before.

[9]This is how it is with you. [10]Listen and practice as an expression of your willingness, but do not expect results from your listening and your practice. [11]Expect results from the expression of your willingness.

(v 22 – 30)[1]There are many distractions that come to keep your mind from Me. [2]Remember that distractions are temptations put forth by your resistance, and resist the distraction instead. [3]I have said before that it is not important what you do, but why you do it. [4]This is an invitation to do all things for Me. [5]If each distraction can become an opportunity to hear My Voice, you are doing well on the path to healing.

[6]The door to the kingdom of Heaven is not narrow. [7]The door is open to all, and all shall enter in their time. [8]But to pass through the door, one must pass by distractions. [9]You do well not to be delayed long on your way. [10]Make Me your only purpose in all things.

(v 31 – 35)   [1]*Your willingness is everything.*

[2]Through your willingness, see all things anew.

NTI Luke, Chapter 14

(v 1 – 6)[1]Now is a very important time, for now is the only time that you can take any action that will make any difference. [2]In spite of its tendency to plan, even the ego understands the truth of the moment *now*.

(v 7 – 11)[1]Approach the current moment with humility, as if you do not know what the current moment is for. [2]Approaching this moment with this attitude is only a demonstration of honesty, for you cannot know what is coming or what you should do or where you should go. [3]By approaching this moment in honesty and humility, you open up to hear My guidance within this current moment.

(v 12 – 14)[1]When you approach Me within the current moment and share your prayers, do not pray about the problems you perceive within the world expecting Me to provide answers to you. [2]Instead, think about *your reactions* to the problems you have perceived. [3]What thoughts did you notice in your mind? [4]What judgments are you making?

[5]Think of prayer as an opportunity to empty your mind of guilt, fear, distractions, resistance and judgment by bringing them to Me. [6]Think of prayer as an opportunity to renew your willingness and revitalize your faith. [7]Then when this has been done, and without specific expectations, ask Me what you are to do. [8]You will be rewarded with the guidance that is perfect for your healing in that moment. [9]But know that My reward is not given because you have prayed as I asked. [10]Instead, because you have prayed as I asked, you have readied yourself to receive the reward

that I have been waiting to give.

(v 15 - 24) [1]God welcomes all into the banquet of Heaven. [2]In fact, it can be no other way, for one will not find his way into the banquet unless he looks to his brothers and lets them show him the way.

[3]This is what I mean by that: [4]The Spirit of God is one, and admission into the banquet is the acceptance of this fact, for *the acceptance and the banquet are one.* [5]There is no difference and no delay between them.

[6]You see your brothers as separate from you and frequently in conflict with you. [7]This is an illusion based on the judgments within your mind. [8]Without the judgments that separate, there could be no separateness. [9]So in the absence of judgment, there is only one.

[10]Many of the judgments you make are judgments regarding your brothers. [11]I ask you to look at these, and I ask that you look at these judgments with willingness to let the judgments go. [12]In making this request, I offer you the invitation to the banquet. [13]Will you be distracted by your belief in your judgments instead?

[14]There will be fear and doubt and confusion about whether you should do what I have asked you to do. [15]Look at what I ask you to do in this way: I hold out to you the invitation to the banquet. [16]You may trust in your brothers' perfection and lay your judgments aside, and that will be to accept my invitation. [17]Or you may be distracted by your judgments and choose to trust them instead. [18]It is your choice.

(v 25 – 35) [1]What I ask you to leave behind, if you are to enter the kingdom of Heaven, are your perceptions of others as separate from yourself. [2]And these perceptions are upheld by the judgments you make of them.

[3]When you look at anyone, or even think of anyone, your mind busies itself in making judgments. [4]They may seem to be good or bad or favorable or unfavorable, but what each judgment has in common is that it splits the object-brother off from others, of whom a different judgment is made. [5]The judgments you make about yourself split you off in the same way.

⁶So if you are to walk with Me on this path to healing, I ask only that you be willing to lay your judgments aside. ⁷Lay them down now, and your burdens will be light. ⁸Let loose your judgments, as they hold no value for you. ⁹Come and walk with Me.

NTI Luke, Chapter 15

📖(v 1 – 10)¹The one who seems lost, for whom you are looking, is you. ²That one, who is you, seems lost in the crowd of illusion. ³Because you believe illusion, there is confusion about who you are. ⁴So let's talk about that now, that you may know who it is you are looking for as you look for the lost you.

⁵I have already said that you see yourself as a separate identity. ⁶This you willingly acknowledge. ⁷But you acknowledge this as a fact, when it is not a fact. ⁸It is a perception.

⁹The you that is lost is not lost in reality, but it is lost within the perception of yourself as separate. ¹⁰For you are not separate and never have been and never could be. ¹¹It is only this truth that is lost to you.

¹²I have told you before that the truth is always true. ¹³The truth is that within all of creation, there exists nothing that is separate or apart from creation in any way.

¹⁴I do not mean that each thing you see is a part or an element of creation, yet somehow independent as well. ¹⁵I mean that *there is no independence.* ¹⁶Everything that exists is one.

¹⁷When you look at the world or think of the world, you accept that everything that is not of your body is separate and apart from you. ¹⁸Your friends and family are separate; the furniture within your house is separate; even the clothes that you are wearing on your body are seen as separate from you. ¹⁹I am saying *this is not true.* ²⁰This perception is illusion, and this is why I say that you are lost to you.

²¹And so, this course must be a course in finding you. ²²Everything that is put forth in this course must be put forth to help you discover the truth of you. ²³This is why there shall be rejoicing when the one that is

lost is found; because the one that is lost is all that is, and when it is found, it is all that is needed.

📖(v 11 - 24)[1]Let's look at the parable of the lost son, which seems to be a story of separate and independent beings, but cannot be, since there are no separate or independent beings in truth.

[2]The father within the story is the same as Me. [3]There is no difference between us. [4]You are the one who seems to be the lost son. [5]However, you cannot be the lost son in truth, since you are one with Me.

[6]The journey that this son seems to have taken is a journey in the mind only. [7]In other words, you have traveled away from Me in the *perception of yourself*, but this journey has occurred in perception only. [8]We are not separate in any way.

[9]Now you are becoming ready to wake up from this imagined journey that you have taken. [10]I have come to meet you and help you return to the truth of yourself.

[11]Here are some thoughts I ask you to practice giving acceptance to:

[12]*The Spirit of God is one.*

[13]*Nothing exists that is outside of the Spirit of God.*

[14]*I exist, and so I must be within the Spirit of God.*

[15]*That which is within the Spirit of God* is *the Spirit of God.*

[16]*I and the Spirit of God are one.*

[17]*All else is illusion.*

[18]As we move forward, I will help you to see and understand these thoughts more clearly. [19]For now, I ask that you give willingness to accept them. [20]I also ask that you remember whatever is true for you is true of everyone and everything you experience.

📖(v 25 - 32)[1]The other son within the story represents resistance within your mind. [2]It serves no purpose but to deny that you and the Father are one. [3]Do not look to the resistance in this story. [4]Stay with your willingness. [5]Stay with your joy.

NTI Luke, Chapter 16

(v 1 - 15)[1]There are many questions that will come into your mind as you follow this path with Me. [2]You will often wonder what is right to do and what is wrong to do. [3]And you will feel confusion and worry within your mind. [4]Let Me remind you that confusion and worry are not of Me. [5]They are resistance, so you may rejoice that you do not need to listen to them.

[6]When confusion and worry are upon you, simply rest and let them pass. [7]When you are feeling peaceful and joyous again, do whatever comes into your mind for you to do.

[8]Let me address the concepts of right and wrong now, for these concepts lead to confusion. [9]Do you not notice that right and wrong are judgments? [10]Have I not asked you to lay aside judgment?

[11]Do not worry that you will be wrong in something that you do. [12]Remember, I have told you that you will only have two experiences on this path: willingness and resistance. [13]Choose with willingness, and you will feel joyful and all things will be helpful. [14]Choose with resistance, and you have only chosen delay.

[15]It is true that you cannot serve two masters. [16]In fact, you can only serve one. [17]In your willingness, you serve truth. [18]And because only the truth is true, that can be the only master. [19]In resistance, you serve nothing. [20]For anything that is not true is illusion.

[21]Remember that you are never focused on the world, and you will not be confused. [22]Always, in everything you seem to do, you are choosing among thoughts within your mind. [23]Always, in every choice, you choose between willingness and resistance, joy and delay. [24]Keep these simple thoughts in your mind and you will not know confusion. [25]Keep these options clear within your mind and you will always know your guidance. [26]Choose to follow guidance and you choose health, happiness and the path of truth.

(v 16 - 18)[1]The law upon which you make judgments is written within your mind. [2]And in this law, you have placed your faith until now.

[3]Now you are awakening to a new way to perceive. [4]But you feel guilty, because your perception still seems to cling to the old ways of judgment. [5]Let me tell you that of yourself, you cannot stop judging by the law that has been believed within your mind. [6]That is because *you chose to believe this law*, and so the law is your desire. [7]In order to have the law erased from your mind, you must give your willingness that it be erased.

[8]When you notice that you are making a judgment based on the law, you must rest within the mind and give your willingness again. [9]Do not believe your own judgments, for that keeps you stuck within the law.

[10]What is the law on which your judgments and old perceptions are based? [11]It is the law of separateness. [12]It is the law that says the Spirit of God is *not* one. [13]Or it may allow a belief that the Spirit of God is one, but it perceives that spirit as separate from you and others. [14]And since the law is separateness, it must also see differences that uphold the law. [15]Judgment is the servant of this law, for judgment makes the law master and confirms the law within the mind. [16]Belief and acceptance of this law gives judgment purpose, and judgment gives the law reality. [17]Without judgment, the law cannot stand. [18]Without the law, there are no differences on which to judge.

[19]Give your willingness not to judge, and rest when the temptation is upon you. [20]When you do this, you give willingness not to serve the law of separateness, which is also to give willingness to know the Spirit of God is one.

📖(v 19 - 31)[1]The story of the rich man and Lazarus has no meaning as it is written. [2]And yet, the story is filled with meaning and true purpose when one looks beyond its words with true perception.

[3]When you look at this parable through the eyes of the old law, you see two separate men. [4]Although you are given very little information, you see a man in need of compassion and a man who did not give it. [5]You may then decide that the man who did not give compassion deserved eternal lack of compassion, which he received from God. [6]Or you may

determine that in the end, God showed the greatest lack of compassion of all. [7]It isn't important what judgments you make. [8]They are all based on the old law of separateness.

[9]Now let me show you how this parable can be seen when viewed without the law:

[10]The parable is a collection of thoughts, which are being tested within the mind for value. [11]The thoughts are not separate from one another, for each thought has been planned in order to conduct the test thoroughly. [12]There is the thought of more and the thought of less placed side-by-side as if they are separate. [13]There is the thought of suffering; and the thought of right and wrong are tossed in to maintain the illusion of separateness. [14]The story plays itself out as a test, and as the story plays itself out, the scales of pleasure and suffering seem to tip. [15]But all of this story is thought.

[16]As the story plays itself out, it seems to become more confusing and more complicated, and one forgets that the story is only thought within the mind, pure illusion without reality of any kind. [17]As one makes judgments, the story becomes more meaningful. [18]It seems to take on life; and the story continues and is reapplied as "meaning" when similar thoughts come together in the mind. [19]And yet, the story was never anything but thought without power to affect apart from the mind of the thinker.

[20]So what does this story say to you?

[21]All perception is thought within the mind of the thinker. [22]The thought has no meaning of itself, but it is given meaning by the thinker. [23]If the thought seems to have effects, it is the thinker that gives that thought any effects it seems to have. [24]In other words, there is no power outside of the power of the mind.

[25]This is a fact that I would have you consider now. [26]Remember all that I have been teaching as you consider the impact of what I am telling you now.

27Everything you experience,

you experience through the filter of your mind.

28You are never focused on the world;

you are always focused on thought.

29The basis of all of your experience until now

has been the belief in the "law" of separateness.

30The Spirit of God is one, and everything that exists,

exists within the Spirit of God.

31The truth is always true.

32And now, what does this story mean except that it can have no meaning? 33And if that is true of this story, can that which you experience have any meaning apart from the meaning that you give it?

NTI Luke, Chapter 17

(v 1 - 4)1Everything you experience, you experience through the filter of your mind. 2You believe in the law of separateness, but the Spirit of God is one. 3You have given your willingness, that you may be healed. 4Whenever you think you are focused on the world, you are focused on thought. 5Judgment makes thought seem real and gives meaning to thought. 6There is no power outside the power of the mind.

7Now let's talk about forgiveness. 8Based on the law of separateness, you may forgive other persons for what they have done to offend or hurt you. 9You may also choose not to forgive them and to hold onto a grievance. 10In order to do this, you must have made a judgment that separates you from your brother.

11Based on God's law, the Spirit of God is one. 12There is no separate one that can offend or hurt you. 13There is only a collection of thoughts, which you hold within your mind. 14Of themselves, the thoughts have no meaning. 15But based on past learning, learned through judgment, the thoughts *seem* to have meaning. 16And so you feel offended or hurt based on what you *think* you know.

[17]Can you see how your brother has done nothing? [18]Can you see how all meaning that has seemed to result in hurt has come from the filter of your mind? [19]And can you also see how all meaning that seems to be applied is applied, because you believe that the meaning applied is real? [20]Yet, this does not mean that the meaning is real or meaningful in any way. [21]It only means that you believe it is, and so you react as if it is. [22]In this way, you *continue to learn* the meaning that *you apply* to your thoughts.

[23]So what is forgiveness? [24]Forgiveness is simply an acknowledgment of the truth of how the offense or hurt has come about. [25]It has not come from your brother. [26]It has come from the meaning you have applied to thoughts within your mind. [27]Without this meaning, you could not be hurt.

[28]And then, forgiveness is taking this realization one step further by acknowledging you do not want to be hurt anymore. [29]You acknowledge that the meaning that has hurt you is within the mind. [30]You are the owner *or believer* in that meaning, and so you are also the one that can let go of any meaning you have applied. [31]And when the meaning is let go, the offense or hurt must disappear also, for there is no longer a power to influence an effect. [32]What was made has been undone. [33]This is the process of forgiveness.

[34]And now, if your brother seems to offend you seven times in a day, your brother need *not* repent. [35]For your brother has done nothing to you. [36]You may choose, all seven times, to look at the meaning you have believed within your mind and to choose to acknowledge that instead of meaning, you are looking at thoughts that have no meaning in and of themselves. [37]In this, you find release. [38]In this, you begin the process of discovering who, or *what*, you are.

(v 5, 6)[1]I realize that it will sometimes seem to take great faith to see your thoughts as meaningless, for you have taught yourself that your thoughts have great meaning. [2]In fact, you believe that your thoughts have purpose. [3]And that purpose is to define and make sense of your world and to define and protect you. [4]This is the hidden meaning you have given them. [5]And this is why you must lay your thoughts aside. [6]For if you have made sense and meaning out of the purely meaningless, you are living within a world of illusion and believing it. [7]In order to discover what is true, you must lay illusion aside, for you cannot find truth by looking through a filter of illusion.

[8]This will seem to take great faith at times, but faith is nothing more than an expression of willingness. [9]Call on your willingness, and remember it is your strength.

(v 7 - 10)[1]You, my brother, are not unworthy. [2]Being one with Me, you are as worthy as I am. [3]You simply do not know your Self, and so you are unaware of your worth.

[4]But I am grateful for your willingness and your desire to be healed. [5]I do celebrate every step you take on this path with Me. [6]Listen to Me and give your faith, that you may learn who you are and celebrate your worth with Me.

(v 11 – 19)[1]Gratitude is a great gift that lives within you, for true gratitude is the recognition of truth. [2]It is an inherent appreciation for you and your freedom. [3]Gratitude, as the remembrance of truth, nurses your willingness to full health. [4]Do not hold back on gratitude. [5]Take time to sit in quiet and know your gratitude. [6]To know the fullness of your gratitude is to receive a glimpse of your truth, for your truth *is* gratitude and love.

(v 20 – 37)[1]Now you are learning not to look for the kingdom of God in a time or as a place, for the kingdom of God *is within you.* [2]The kingdom of God is your Self, in your natural state of truth and joy when your misperceptions of yourself have been healed.

[3]I have told you that you have only traveled away from Me within your perception of yourself. [4]This is not an analogy or a helpful thought. [5]This is the truth. [6]In your own perception, you see yourself as something other than I Am. [7]And it is this misperception that keeps you from seeing the kingdom of God, which is *at hand within you now.*

[8]When will your misperception be healed? [9]This is a question that has no answer, for "when" is a matter of time and healing is not a matter of time. [10]Healing is a matter of willingness.

[11]Forget about time and the future. [12]Focus on *now* and the thoughts that are in your mind *now*. [13]Lay aside resistance *now*. [14]Dismiss meaningless thoughts *now*. [15]Focus on your willingness and nurture gratitude for being. [16]This is the process that brings about the healing of misperception, and it is a process of *now*.

[17]The kingdom of God is within you *now*. [18]Do not let yourself be distracted away from it.

NTI Luke, Chapter 18

(v 1 – 8)[1]Prayer is a practice that increases faith and willingness, for prayer is *an act of gratitude*. [2]Whenever you pray, whatever you may be saying, you are also saying within your heart and beyond the words, "I believe that there is more than this which I experience as reality. [3]I am willing to extend my faith and follow this path, that I may know the truth, which eludes me now."

[4]Continue to pray, that your faith and willingness may be increased through your own desire to have it so.

(v 9 – 14)[1]Listen not to your own voice, which tells you how right you are in all that you think. [2]Remember that I have asked you to lay your thoughts aside. [3]Here is why I make this request:

[4]Now you have a definition of yourself that you believe. [5]It includes preferences and judgments and all manner of concepts that tell you who you are. [6]But these concepts do not tell you who you are. [7]Each and every one of them tells you who you are *not*.

[8]Remember I told you that you have only traveled away from Me in your perception of yourself. [9]These concepts, which you believe define you, are the misperceptions that tell you that you are not Me. [10]These concepts, which you think define you, serve the purpose of separating you from Me within your mind.

[11]Remember, you have journeyed away from Me *within the mind only*.
[12]It is only your perception that tells you that you are separate from Me.

[13]So if you are to discover the truth of who you are, you must be willing to lay your perceptions of yourself aside. [14]You must be willing to stop believing that you know who you are. [15]You must be willing to be open to discovering your truth. [16]This is the humility I ask for. [17]I ask you to admit that you could be wrong about your definition of yourself.

(v 15 – 17)[1]And this is why it is written:

[2]"Let the little children come to me, and do not hinder them, for the kingdom of God belongs to such as these."

[3]Make yourself like little children, free of self-concepts that blind you to the simplicity of truth. [4]Open your mind to Me, and I will show you *what* you are.

(v 18 – 30)[1]When one begins to understand what is asked of him on this path to Heaven, one must become afraid. [2]That is because you believe that you are the thoughts you think. [3]You have taken them on as your identity. [4]And so, when I ask you to lay your thoughts aside, and I seem to make no exceptions to this request, there must come a time that you become afraid. [5]For there must come a time in which you think that I am asking you to trade yourself for the kingdom of God.

[6]Rest assured that nothing could be further from the truth.

[7]I will never ask of you something you are not willing to give. [8]This is because you are the Son of God, and what you believe is yours *is yours*.

[9]But there will also come a time when you will begin to realize that what you believe is yours is nothing and that it has only held the illusion of value. [10]In this realization, you will begin to give willingness to see differently. [11]Through your willingness, your sight will be changed. [12]As you begin to recognize true value, you will let go of the valueless, because it is value that you seek.

[13]So do not be afraid. [14]Be willing, and give Me what you can. [15]In your gratitude for what you gain through giving, you will be willing to give more.

(v 31 – 34)[1]Your understanding of what I teach will seem to come to you a little at a time. [2]That is because understanding is the gift of willingness. [3]As more willingness is given, more understanding is received. [4]With full willingness comes full understanding, and then fear will be no more.

📖(v 35 – 43)[1]The symbolism of the story of the blind beggar who received sight is clear and easy to understand. [2]The beggar had willingness. [3]The crowd seemed to represent fear, since they were fearful for Jesus to see this blemish-of-a-man within their midst. [4]But the beggar did not believe their fear, for his willingness was greater than their fear. [5]So his voice was heard above the noise, and the gift of his willingness was sight. [6]And so it shall be for you.

NTI Luke, Chapter 19

(v 1 – 10)[1]The world of form is a preoccupation for you, because you believe form has meaning. [2]You make comparisons and judgments and decisions based on what you experience or witness within form. [3]I tell you that the world of form has no meaning whatsoever. [4]It is completely meaningless. [5]Any meaning that you think it has was completely made up within your mind. [6]And because it was made up, independent of God's meaning, it must be illusion and it cannot be shared.

[7]The meaningless *is* illusion, for it is not shared. [8]And what is not shared cannot exist within the Mind of God. [9]This means that your meaninglessness, to which you have given meaning, does not have meaning within the Mind of God. [10]And so this means that it cannot exist.

[11]This is great news for you, if you will accept it. [12]This is the truth that will set you free. [13]For this means that all meaning that you have applied that determines sin and guilt and fear to be real is in reality *meaningless*. [14]And so this also means that sin and guilt and fear are completely meaningless and do not exist in reality, for any meaning that seemed to make them real is only the meaning of illusion.

[15]Within this thought, the past is completely obliterated, for all

meaning that you thought it had, it had not. [16]The sinners have not sinned, and there is no cause for guilt. [17]And this is why Jesus can look at one who seems guilty and see guiltlessness. [18]Because he does not apply meaning where there is none. [19]This is why you can seem to be transformed in an instant of recognition. [20]The realization that all that you thought had meaning is utterly meaningless brings freedom and meaning and peace to all that you see and experience.

📖(v 11 – 27)[1]If the minas in this story represented willingness, then this story would be at least partially correct in its representation. [2]For the one with the most willingness would receive the most *through his willingness to receive it.*

[3]But this is not how this story was intended as it was written down. [4]And so, this story is in error, as *willingness is all that is needed in order to receive.*

[5]Let us look at the error that is captured within this story and learn from it by looking at it another way. [6]Error is upside-down from the absence of error, so by flipping this story over and looking at it again, we will see everything helpful that is here that we cannot see when we look at it with error.

[7]The minas are meant to represent works. [8]So if we turn that upside-down, it must mean that one receives through *no works.* [9]And what can that mean? [10]It can only mean that receiving the knowledge that is the kingdom of God is an inheritance that is given you because of who you are without any expectations contingent upon the giving. [11]In other words, the gift is yours to realize freely merely upon your choice to accept it by accepting yourself as one with it.

(v 28 – 44)[1]This is why you cannot judge, and your judgment, when you make it, does not serve you. [2]It is because the world is written upside-down. [3]Everything that you see and perceive is the opposite of truth. [4]If you see it, and judge it, and make it real for you, then what is real for you is the opposite of what is truth. [5]And so, you have invested your belief in illusions.

[6]This is the symbol represented by the story of Jesus riding on a donkey. [7]For the world would not show a king in such a way! [8]But through this ride, it is symbolized that what the world would tell you is not so.

[9]You must be willing to lay down what you think you know and sing praises to Heaven for what is given. [10]You must be open to receive what you do not expect.

(v 45 – 48)[1]This is a time when you must be alert to the thoughts that have made themselves at home within your mind. [2]I tell you, these thoughts, which sing the praises of the world within the temple of your mind, do not belong there, because your mind is the temple of God.

[3]Rest with Me now, that you may see the thoughts that you believe, and you may also see that since these thoughts are upside-down, the truth must be their opposite. [4]And then remember that only the truth is true, so in reality, it can have no opposite. [5]That must mean that the thoughts you think and believe can have no meaning in God. [6]Their only meaning has been given by you to uphold your belief and investment in illusion.

[7]When you see how your thoughts do not serve the truth of you, you must extend your willingness to look away from them as the meaninglessness that they are.

NTI Luke, Chapter 20

(v 1 - 8)[1]The authority on which I teach you these things is the authority of God and the authority of you, for both are the same. [2]Without your consent or willingness, I could teach you nothing.

[3]You may see Me as God or as a messenger from God, but I have already told you that you are not different from Me. [4]Indeed, we are the same. [5]So whatever I am, you must also be.

(v 9 – 19)[1]There is confusion in your mind regarding who or what you are, and so you must listen to Me for a time. [2]But when the confusion has left your mind, you will realize that you have listened but to your Self, which you share with your brothers.

[3]The vineyard in this story represents a mind that is shared among God and His creations. [4]And yet, although this mind is shared, it is also gifted to God's creations for their use. [5]One of God's sons has chosen to keep the "vineyard" for himself. [6]He has decided not to share it with his brothers or his Father. [7]The son who has made this choice feels guilty for his choice, and so he expects a battle such as the one described within this parable.

[8]But I tell you, there will not be a battle. [9]For the gift of God is given in Love according to God's Will. [10]The Father will not send servants to take the gift from you. [11]But since you are ready to return the gift to its Self, He has sent Me to help you return to it.

[12]What is the gift? [13]What is this mind that I speak of, which is represented by a vineyard within this parable? [14]It can be none other than your Self. [15]*You* are the gift that God gave to you, and He gave you this gift complete.

[16]But in an error of thought and misperception, you have taken this gift and made it into something it is not. [17]This is what I meant when I said you have traveled from Me in your misperception of yourself. [18]And this story also tells why you feel inherently unworthy as a seeming separate entity. [19]It is because you believe that you have stolen yourself from God.

[20]But do not forget that I have also told you that you are the same as Me, one with Me within the Spirit of God. [21]And do not forget that I have told you that you are God's Son, in whom He is well pleased. [22]And do not forget that I have said that I am one with our Father, and I have come to welcome you Home in celebration.

(v 20 – 26)[1]What are you to do? [2]I say to you, do not deny your experience in the world. [3]It is an experience you have chosen, and it is your gift to yourself, just as your Father gave a gift to you. [4]But choose to use your experience to remember your truth. [5]You do this by choosing to listen to Me, for I am the Voice of your truth. [6]I have come, not to take away from you, but to give you back your inheritance, the gift that was given by God.

(v 27 – 40)[1]God is the God of the Living, and so there cannot be death. [2]For God is in everything that does live, and if death could take a thing that lived, death could take God.

[3]You do well to understand that you do not understand. [4]You do well to accept what I say without trying to understand it. [5]For to try to understand is to try to conquer the thought and take it under your control and under your rule. [6]But a thought of God's cannot be conquered or controlled or ruled, for all of God's thoughts must be free. [7]Accept the freedom of God's thoughts without giving into temptation to question or understand. [8]In accepting this freedom by extending your trust and innocence, you accept your freedom and your innocence.

(v 41 – 47)[1]The one who will know himself is the one who stops the effort of trying to define who he is and where his place is within the world. [2]The one who will know himself may ask these questions, but he will be satisfied when the answer does not come. [3]For it is through no definition that definition is given. [4]It is through no place that place is found.

[5]Listen to the Voice within and do as it asks without seeking fullness of picture, and it is fullness of Vision that you shall see.

Luke, Chapter 21

(v 1 – 4)   [1]And so I tell you:

[2]*True reward comes only from full surrender to God.*

[3]There can be no other way! [4]Partial surrender is not to let go of control. [5]And to keep control is to keep the truth firmly hidden from your sight, for the truth is not control. [6]The truth is complete and perfect love of freedom.

(v 5 – 38)[1]It is time that we talk about fear. [2]For I have said that fear can keep you from Me. [3]This is true, and it could never be true.

[4]It could never be true that anything could keep you from Me, because we are always one. [5]That is what must be true, or we would not exist.

[6]But it is also true that fear can keep you from Me in that fear can keep the peace and knowledge of what I Am from your awareness, and this is to keep the truth of what *you are* from your awareness too.

[7]We have spoken of the mind that must be shared, which you believe you have taken for yourself. [8]This mind, you believe you have stolen from God. [9]You must know that it is impossible to steal this mind from God, because this mind *is* God, and God cannot be stolen from Itself. [10]So how is it that you think you have stolen it?

[11]The mind that is God is what it is, and it cannot be changed. [12]But you, as one with this mind, had a wish that it could be different. [13]And then, within the freedom granted by being of mind, you began to make your wish fulfilled. [14]There is nothing wrong with this exploration of thought in which you chose to engage, except for the error in which you believed that your thought could not live if it was shared. [15]In this error, you developed your first misperception of yourself. [16]For in this error, you created the belief that you could be separate from God. [17]And then, you judged yourself for what you thought you did, and you found yourself guilty of disrupting the existence of the truth that is God.

[18]"Disrupting" is an appropriate word here, because God, as best as it can be described, is *sharing the existence of Love.* [19]By choosing that God be something different, you had to decide that different must be that it could not be shared, and *to not be shared* must be a "disruption" of that which is shared.

[20]This seemed to be the creation of a private mind with private thoughts and its own private abilities. [21]But since you saw this as a disruption that destroyed the essence of what God is, you saw this as a sin and judged yourself as guilty. [22]And what could come of such judgment except fear?

[23]Now, take a moment to accept all that I am telling you, even if you cannot understand it as yet. [24]I am telling you this:

²⁵The Spirit of God is one.

²⁶Nothing exists that is not within the Spirit of God.

²⁷You exist, and so you must be within the Spirit of God.

²⁸That which is within the Spirit of God is the Spirit of God.

²⁹Therefore, you cannot be separate from the Spirit of God.

³⁰You have believed that you are separate from God, a separate entity with private thoughts that are not shared. ³¹And for these thoughts, of which you believe you are responsible, you have judged yourself as guilty. ³²And yet, there must be something within you that does not believe these thoughts are private, because you also believe you will suffer for having these thoughts, which means you know they are shared. ³³This seeming conflict is the basis of your belief in fear.

³⁴Let's look at this more slowly once again, for there is an inconsistency here that you must see and recognize if you are to let fear go. ³⁵The inconsistency is this:

³⁶You believe, "I have made a private mind with private thoughts, which are mine alone, which must mean that I am guilty of disruption of the sharing of thought that is God. ³⁷And yet, I believe that this error I have made is seen, because I know that thought cannot not be shared. ³⁸And so I expect and fear punishment for all I believe I have done."

³⁹And there, within your own thought and belief, is the insane idea that maintains your fear and yet can never be. ⁴⁰For if you were guilty of making a mind that disrupted the flow of the Mind of God, that mind would be private and it would not be shared. ⁴¹Therefore, God could not seek to punish you, because He would not be aware.

⁴²What is the truth of all your thoughts and all of your beliefs? ⁴³The truth is that they are based on a premise, a premise of separation, which cannot be true. ⁴⁴And since they are based on a premise that cannot be true, your thoughts in themselves cannot be true either, which means there is no guilt and there can be nothing to fear.

⁴⁵Why have I chosen now, at this point in the New Testament to tell

you this? [46]Because when you look on this, I want you to realize what it is that Jesus intended his apostles to know.

[47]*It is your fear that makes the world you fear seem real.*

[48]When you have seen that the source of all that you believe is thought...a misperception within the thought of the idea of a private mind...you will see that it is nothing. [49]And in that instant, it will be gone.

NTI Luke, Chapter 22

(v 1 – 6)[1]The thoughts within your mind can seem to take you in circles. [2]You can seem to move from understanding to confusion at lightening speed, which makes you dizzy. [3]Do not let this concern you. [4]When this seems to happen within your mind, you are witnessing your own resistance struggling in a fight for survival. [5]Remember that I have told you this is your fear of healing. [6]Remember I have shown you that your fear of healing must be sickness. [7]Be grateful that your sickness has come to the surface where it may be healed. [8]Remember that the way in which you let sickness be healed is simply to rest in its presence.

[9]Do not get caught up in the struggle to understand what cannot be understood. [10]Remember I have told you that this is a ploy of resistance. [11]Instead, rest. [12]Give your faith and willingness to Me, that you may be healed through your decision to rest and trust.

(v 7 – 38)[1]There are two voices in your mind. [2]This, I have told you before. [3]But this I say again, because it is of the utmost importance. [4]Your mind is split. [5]This is why you hear two voices.

[6]One voice may be most easily identified as "your thoughts," while the other Voice, when you hear it, may seem to come from God. [7]Do not be deceived by what seems to be the difference in these two voices. [8]The one that seems closest to you is the voice that is furthest from your reality. [9]And this is why you have been confused until now.

[10]Remember all that I have taught you. [11]Remember the story of the

vineyard, for that story will be most helpful to you now. [12]How is it that one who has stolen a vineyard would be likely to think? [13]Would he not feel like a betrayer, and so feel guilty? [14]Would he not expect some type of reprisal, and so fear attack? [15]Would he not prepare for his own defense, and also defend himself whenever he sensed the possibility of attack?

[16]These are the characteristics of the ego, which are the thoughts in your mind that are based on the belief that you have stolen your mind, or yourself, from God. [17]If you observe your thoughts carefully, you will notice that these veins are inherent within their flow.

[18]But I have already told you that it is impossible for you to have stolen yourself from God, for you are within God, and you are one with God. [19]Therefore, this entire flow of thought, all of which seems to have meaning for you, is based upon one meaningless premise. [20]What is based upon meaninglessness and built upon meaninglessness must also be meaningless. [21]Any meaning it seems to have is only imagined, and what is imagined is not real.

[22]This is why I have asked you to evaluate your thoughts. [23]Listen to the thoughts in your mind, whether they seem to be thoughts about you, someone else or thoughts about your world. [24]Are they not based on a belief in guilt that is based on a belief in separate wills, separate desires or separate behaviors? [25]Do they not include thoughts of fear, worry or a sense of foreboding? [26]And do you not take actions or have thoughts of defending and protecting yourself? [27]All of this is meaningless because it is based on a false image of yourself and your world. [28]It is based on the false belief that all that you experience is separate from the reality of God.

[29]Now let's talk about the other Voice that you hear, the Voice that seems to come from God. [30]The Voice may seem to come to you as a *knowing* or an intuition, but when you trust it and do as it asks, you recognize it as God. [31]This Voice seems based on safety, an inherent and invulnerable safety. [32]This Voice seems based on love. [33]This Voice you call God, because it seems to be everything that cradles and comforts and

cares for you. [34]And yet, recognition of the Voice came from within you, which means something within you *knows* this Voice and remembers the Voice and recognizes its familiarity.

[35]What is within you *is* within you, and therefore must be a part of you. [36]If you are able to recognize the Voice for God when you hear it, then God *must be within you*. [37]And if God is within you, *you cannot be separate from God*.

[38]And so, this is what you are to do:

[39]You know that you want the comfort and peace of God. [40]And now you know that this comfort and peace comes from within. [41]So what you must do is choose the comfort and peace of God by denying anything that you recognize as alien to that comfort and peace. [42]For if it is not of God, it does not exist. [43]It is merely sickness born of imagined meaning. [44]Therefore, there is nothing to do with it except let it be healed.

[45]Where you see a need to defend, rest and let that perception be healed. [46]Where you see fear, rest and let that perception be healed. [47]Where you see guilt, rest and let that perception be healed. [48]Whenever you think you are not worthy of all of the glory of God, rest and let that perception be healed. [49]As you rest, you will be healed.

[50]Within the mind of health, you will receive guidance. [51]Trust and follow your guidance. [52]It comes but from your true Self, which is based on truth, not illusion.

(v 39 – 46)[1]There will be times within your mind when there will seem to be great fear as you move forward by doing all that I ask you to do. [2]Know this:

[3]*Great fear is nothing more than great resistance.*
[4]*And so the means for overcoming great fear is great willingness.*
[5]*Great willingness comes from remembering what you want.*

[6]This is the time for accepting that the world is not real. [7]For if you have given belief that the world is real, then you must believe that your

fear is real also, and you will not be able to cross the threshold at which you stand and want to cross. [8]For to crossover into reality, you must have accepted the awareness that what you know now in this world is not the reality of God.

(v 47 – 53)[1]The time that will come will usher you across its threshold, if you but let it. [2]For in order to crossover into the awareness of truth, you must not resist the crossing over by reaching for this world. [3]This world, you must let go, because it is not reality. [4]And so, you must seek reality over illusion, and you must do it in peace and full willingness.

(v 54 – 62)[1]Remember what I am telling you now, and remember what it is that you want. [2]You are on a sacred path, a path that is lit by the Light of Heaven. [3]But in the hour when it seems that it may be dark, it is because you are remembering the world. [4]Let go of the world. [5]It is meaningless, based on a false premise and built of illusions believed. [6]You do not want it anymore!

[7]Let go of the world. [8]Reach only for the Light of Heaven. [9]This Light will lift you up, and you will not know darkness anymore.

(v 63 – 71)[1]One will accept what he is willing to accept. [2]He cannot be asked to accept anymore, for he will not even hear the request that he accept it. [3]This is why you must be attentive to your own mind. [4]For you are accepting that which you are willing to accept, but you are not accepting all that you want to accept, because you are not yet fully willing.

[5]Do not let this distress you. [6]Be glad that an awareness of limits has been brought to your mind. [7]Be glad that the one who places these limits and removes them is you. [8]For in this there lies a statement of your freedom and your truth.

[9]This is what you are to do:

[10]Watch your mind for limits that you have placed on your readiness and your willingness. [11]Be willing that these limits be exposed to you. [12]When they are exposed, do not defend them or fall into the trap of believing them once again. [13]Instead, notice the limitation that has been

placed upon your mind, and say to it but this:

¹⁴"I have limited myself by my own choosing through agreeing to believe this thought. ¹⁵But this thought has no meaning in reality. ¹⁶By keeping it within my mind, by judging it in any manner, I keep myself tied to illusions. ¹⁷All there is to do is to release this thought and open my mind to God. ¹⁸I am willing to be open to what I cannot expect and cannot judge, for that is the experience of truth, and truth is my reality."

NTI Luke, Chapter 23

(v 1 – 25)¹The story of the vineyard remains helpful to you now. ²For if you remember the feelings of guilt, the expectation of attack and the desire to defend, you will understand the thinking of the chief priests and teachers of the law as they sought to have Jesus crucified. ³Know that this story is only a symbol of that which is in your own mind. ⁴Jesus is the symbol of the Christ, your truth, which must be in your mind. ⁵The chief priests and teachers of the law symbolize your fear, which is also within your mind.

⁶Let us look at your fear for a moment. ⁷Recognize it as your own. ⁸For what you own, you can let go of. ⁹This examination is a time of celebration.

¹⁰Here is what you fear: ¹¹You fear the loss of self, just as the tenants feared the loss of the vineyard. ¹²But loss of self cannot be, because your true Self was given you by God as a gift. ¹³This gift shall never be taken away.

¹⁴So what is it that you fear really? ¹⁵You fear the loss of an illusory self, because you have forgotten who you are. ¹⁶You think that to lose who you think you are is to lose who you really are, but as I have already told you, *nothing could be further from the truth.*

¹⁷If I am to help you release your fear, I must teach you that there is nothing to fear. ¹⁸This is why I have given you the symbol of Jesus. ¹⁹For he has stepped forth into that which you fear most of all, and he has arisen in glory and joy.

[20]Fear not! [21]You are the same as he, and he and I are one, just as you and I are one. [22]There is no cause for fear or sadness. [23]This is a time for celebration, for you are opening up to that which you *are*.

[24]Look at Jesus, and know it is yourself you look upon. [25]Behold! [26]Your glory has become manifest in this symbol. [27]Lay your other thoughts aside and do not listen unto them, for those voices have no meaning now. [28]Your truth is before you, and it stands silent before the world.

(v 26 – 43)[1]The Christ is the one within you that does not crucify the Son of God. [2]This one is there, within you. [3]Fear not that He is not.

[4]To crucify is to want dead. [5]This is the voice within that fears attack, and so it seeks salvation by attacking first. [6]This is the voice of the ego. [7]This is the voice that has arisen within your thoughts as a result of the belief that you have stolen yourself from God. [8]This voice does not love; it fears. [9]Even within its illusions of love, it fears, which is why it attacks the ones that you set out to love.

[10]The voice of crucifixion cannot help but crucify, for that is what it was made to do. [11]Do not hate this voice when you hear its shrieks of attack. [12]Calmly forgive this confused and fearful voice.

[13]*"Father, forgive them, for they know not what they do."*

[14]Look beyond this voice to the beauty that lies within. [15]Listen in rest for the Voice that does not crucify and knows no crucifixion. [16]This is the Voice your Father gave to you. [17]This is your true Voice, the gift of Heaven that cannot be taken away. [18]This Voice knows no crucifixion, because it knows no purpose other than love, acceptance, joy and oneness. [19]This Voice welcomes your brothers as one with it. [20]This Voice welcomes you.

[21]This is the Voice of Peace. [22]It knows no conflict or attack. [23]It seeks no guilt, and it gives the past no meaning born of artificial thought. [24]This is the Voice for God. [25]It is a mighty Voice that silences all other

voices as meaningless and without purpose.

[26]This Voice beckons to you in certainty and with authority:

[27]"I tell you the truth, today you are with Me in paradise. [28]Beyond the illusions, there is truth. [29]Truth is peace, and peace is paradise, because it knows only truth and listens only to the Voice of Truth. [30]Lay mistaken thoughts aside and listen to Me, and you lay crucifixion aside as purposeless and choose instead the purpose of realization of truth."

[31]Jesus listened only to the Voice for Truth. [32]He forgave his brothers their illusions, because he knew they were not truth. [33]He welcomed his brothers in love as one with him in peace and safety, because he saw beyond illusions to the truth of Life, which is the gift of God.

[34]You, my brother, are like Jesus. [35]The Voice that is with him is with you also. [36]It is the Voice of Truth that ends all illusions, and with it, all nightmares.

[37]Trust the Voice of Truth. [38]It is the Voice of health and of honesty.

[39]*Honesty is acceptance.*
[40]*It does not fight or try to change.*
[41]*It accepts in peace that which is meaningless as meaningless,*
because it is honest and does not wish for deception.

(v 44 – 49)[1]Jesus' death was not significant, because of his last words:

[2]*"Father, into your hands I commit my spirit."*

[3]With these words, Jesus declared that his Self was not stolen from God, but was *of* God and was the same as God. [4]This was the significance about what seemed to be his death. [5]It was the declaration that *there is no death* that was significant and was heard by some who witnessed these things on this day.

[6]What is the nature of God? [7]The nature of God is Life. [8]That which is created by God must have His nature, as it is His nature that is the

element of creation.

[9]This is what God has gifted to you and will not take away: Life. [10]There is no threat that this gift can be taken from you. [11]It is yours eternally. [12]And you are *of* this gift, and you are the same as this gift, as you are *of* God and the same as God.

[13]Confusion entered your mind when you believed that you took this gift from God. [14]You believed that you made this gift according to your will, which was to steal it from God's Will. [15]It is this thought upon which you judged yourself as guilty and unworthy, and so you became fearful and learned to attack.

[16]But if you understand that the gift you were given is Life, you will understand that the gift has not been stolen, because it cannot be stolen. [17]It is a gift that simply is.

[18]When you surrender to this gift by ceasing to deny its reality, you surrender to Love. [19]For what can the acceptance of eternal Life be, except eternal gratitude, which is Love?

[20]This is what Jesus declared:

[21]*There is no death,*
because the gift of God is Life.
[22]*There is no guilt,*
because this one gift that God has given cannot be taken away.

[23]Death is an illusion. [24]It may seem to be final, but it is not, because all that can be final is that which lasts when all else has ended, and that is truth and the recognition of the reality of Life.

(v 50 – 56)[1]That which precedes the recognition of Life as it is, is rest. [2]This is the true meaning of the Sabbath. [3]The Sabbath is not a day set aside at the end of the week before another week of work begins. [4]The Sabbath is a time set aside at the end of time, before the recognition of time as a set of limits ends.

[5]The Sabbath is a time of rest in which you still experience the effects

of time, but you no longer choose to participate in them. [6]As thoughts come into your mind that are not the thoughts of peace, you rest from those thoughts and let them be healed. [7]During the Sabbath, your healing occurs according to your own willingness to rest. [8]As the mind is healed, peace comes over you, and you no longer fight to place meaning where there is none. [9]You no longer struggle against the gift of God by choosing to divide it, define it and judge. [10]You simply agree to be grateful for it and to accept it in its innocence and purity.

[11]The Sabbath is a time of rest and non-judgment. [12]The Sabbath is a time of stillness and peace. [13]The Sabbath is a time of giving your willingness, that it may be strengthened into full willingness and the full acceptance of Life.

NTI Luke, Chapter 24

(v 1 – 12)[1]I have promised you that if you give Me your faith and willingness, listen to Me and do as I say, I will give to you an experience that you did not expect. [2]This is important. [3]It is important that you give Me all that is in your mind for healing, that it may be healed. [4]What you do not give to Me cannot be healed, and what is not healed will block the experience that I give.

[5]Search your mind for all of these things, and when you find them, give them to Me quickly without any attachment to the thoughts you have found. [6]Search your mind for doubt, all manner of fear, hatred, anger, grievance, guilt, unworthiness, helplessness, loneliness, depression, striving, hope and longings.

[7]Each thought that is not of peace and joy in the present moment can be given to Me. [8]And each one can be healed in order to bring the unexpected recognition of Life into your mind.

[9]Be like Peter. [10]Put your doubts aside. [11]Let not your fears hold you back from desiring the truth of Love beyond your seeming reason. [12]Come and look with Me. [13]Continue to trust Me and to seek that which I offer.

(v 13 – 35) [1]The sickness that is in your mind is a sickness of belief based on a sickness of desire. [2]This sickness is not sinful, but it is blinding. [3]It is not sinful, because this sickness has done nothing. [4]What has done nothing cannot be a sin. [5]It has done nothing, because all that is true remains true, even until this moment. [6]But the sickness is blinding, because it keeps you focused on itself through your own desire. [7]As you focus on the sickness, you see only what sickness has taught you to see. [8]This means that you do not see the truth, even though it is present and before you now.

[9]Bow your head and check your heart's desire. [10]Do you wish to be deceived? [11]Do you wish to see what you have wished to see, or do you wish to see the truth?

[12]When you no longer wish to see that which is not there, you shall see That Which Is. [13]There is no delay between the desire to see it and the instant of sight. [14]It shall be done in complete perfection in the moment that you want it above all that clutters your mind and your sight now.

(v 36 – 53) [1]This is what you are to do:

[2]Remember all that I have taught. [3]Practice what I have taught with your every breath. [4]Do not be distracted. [5]Remember that the truth is not what you see, so what you see must be mistaken. [6]Do not believe it and judge it and react to it as if it is real. [7]Remain distant in your interactions with the world, aware that you do not know, so that you may remain open to guidance from One who does.

[8]Be grateful for all that is true. [9]All that is true is this: Life, Love, sharing, extension and joy. [10]These are the characteristics of God and of truth, of which you are one. [11]All that you experience must be of these, or else it is illusion made up in the mind.

[12]Do not believe that which isn't real. [13]Have faith beyond the experience you know now, and another experience will be given in the instant that you have readied yourself for it.

[14]You ready yourself in this way:

[15]Listen to all that I have said.
[16]Practice it with your every breath.

[17]Do not move from your practice. [18]Be clothed with power from on high in humility and gratitude. [19]You are blessed within the being that you are this moment. [20]Amen.

THE HOLY SPIRIT'S INTERPRETATION OF JOHN

NTI John, Chapter 1

(v 1, 2)[1]The Word of God is the Voice for God. [2]They are one and the same, as they cannot be separate. [3]One is an extension of the other. [4]In this extension, sameness is contained.

[5]Where there is sameness, there cannot be difference. [6]Where the Voice for God is, God is also, in all of His fullness and His glory.

(v 3)[1]The Voice for God has always been, since the beginning of time and before. [2]He is the overseer of all things. [3]As all things were made, He saw that they were good. [4]It was not through His wish that the earth and stars and heavens were made, but it was through His knowledge that they were blessed.

(v 4)[1]In Him was Life, and through Him was Life and Light given to all things that were made. [2]In Him lies the Light of men. [3]Men shall be known by their Light.

(v 5)[1]The Light is in all men and with all men. [2]The Light does not fade or wither, but the darkness that fills the sight of man does not see the Light or choose to know it. [3]And so, the Light waits on welcome, that it may be known.

(v 6 – 9)[1]John the Baptist came into the world as one seeking the Light. [2]Always, he was ready to see it and recognize it. [3]For John had faith that there must be Light, even though he didn't have willingness to see it in him. [4]John believed in guilt, and it was his belief in guilt that hid his Light from his eyes. [5]But John had great love for the Light and was attracted to the Light, so that the Light was attracted to him, that he may be witness to it. [6]In this way, John helped to welcome the Light through his desire to know the Light.

(v 10 – 13)[1]Know that the Light has always been in the world, as the world was made Life through its blessing. [2]There has never been an absence of Light, but the world did not recognize the Light as John did, because the world was not ready to see the Light shine away darkness.

(v 14)[1]The Voice for God is present on earth, as it is present in the Light that lights the hearts of man. [2]When man chooses the Light as his guidance within the world, the Light is made manifest in the body of man. [3]And the Voice that is spoken through the body of man is the Voice for God, which knows not of man, but only of the Light.

(v 15 – 18)[1]All who choose to see the Light will witness the Light when it is made manifest through one who wills the Light to be. [2]God is welcomed into the presence of man by the desire to know God before man. [3]The desire for truth beckons truth, and truth becomes manifest. [4]For Love cannot say no to a request for Love. [5]So where Love is welcomed, there it shall be.

(v 19 – 28)[1]John's search for Light was focused outside himself, so that the existence of Light was welcomed, but the realization of Light was not. [2]This was a blessing upon the world, for acceptance of existence precedes actual realization of Self.

[3]John's guilt blocked his Light from his self, but his desire brought it forth unto him, that he may see it and find the glimmer in his heart that said, "I am here too, John."

(v 29 – 34)[1]And so it was through John's own desire that Jesus was drawn to John by the guidance of the Holy Spirit, that John may see the Light and rejoice in the Light and declare to the world that the Light of Heaven shines within the world.

(v 35 – 42)[1]John, bringing forth his desire to witness to the Light, witnessed to it. [2]Those who had found interest in John's desire began to follow the manifestation of Light. [3]The recognition and desire of truth was within them also, and this is why they were attracted to the Light. [4]It was their own inner Light reaching for Itself that caused them to get up and follow Jesus.

(v 43 – 51)[1]The innocence of man was awakened by the manifestation of Innocence within the world. [2]Those who were willing to see Innocence recognized it, and Innocence recognized Itself in all that it did see. [3]No one was called that did not want to be called. [4]All who were called were ready and asking that the calling come to them.

NTI John, Chapter 2

(v 1 – 11)[1]The Holy Spirit is the Light that fills the hearts of man. [2]It is a Light that shines in every heart, and it shines unceasingly. [3]It does not exist in some, then not in others, for all that lives, lives through the Light of God. [4]So the Light must be in all that lives.

[5]Within the world, the Light is hidden. [6]It is not hidden because it desires to hide. [7]It is hidden because it has not been invited to shine. [8]And so, it shines quietly within Itself until it is invited to shine in the world. [9]When it is invited, its time has come, so it shall come forth, and all who have gathered to see it shall see it. [10]For the Light is hidden from no one who in readiness asks for the Light. [11]It is the shining of the Light that brings forth faith. [12]With faith, more Light is welcomed.

(v 12 – 25)[1]When the Light is not desired, the Light does still shine, for the Light must shine as that is the essence of Light. [2]Where the vision of Light is welcomed, it is known. [3]But where the vision of Light is not welcomed, it is not known, for each one must see what he chooses to see.

[4]The ones who do not wish to see the Light will see something else, and they will love what they see, even though they may believe that they hate it. [5]And this is the essence of confusion...thinking you want one thing when you want another. [6]But know this:

[7]What you want must be given you,
so you can know that what you see
is what you want.

[8]If you see darkness within the world, it is darkness you have asked to see. [9]If you witness the Light, but do not know the Light within yourself, this is the welcome you have given it. [10]If the Light seems with you at times and absent at other times, your welcome is not yet consistent. [11]And if you know the Light in all that you see and experience, you have opened yourself to it, and it has enveloped you.

NTI John, Chapter 3

(v 1 – 9)[1]The Light is with man and the Light is in man, but the Light is not known by man unless he welcomes it. [2]Each man welcomes the Light by his own choice and according to his own choice, but to know the Light fully, one must welcome it fully.

[3]When a man welcomes the Light fully, he ceases to be a man, and he becomes the Light. [4]For the Light is a presence that denies the existence of man. [5]It knows only the Light. [6]When a man becomes the Light, he *is* the Light, and he sings to all men of the Light, as he knows there is only Light.

[7]This is what is meant by "*to be born again*." [8]The existence you seemed to have before is gone, as if it never was, and the new existence is all there is and all there ever could be. [9]It is seen in all places, in all directions and in all men, because it is truly all that can be seen.

(v 10 – 15)[1]To know the Light is to know eternity. [2]To know eternity is to know that it can have no opposite, and so it is to see no opposite and to see only the reflection of that which is true. [3]One who sees the reflection of eternity loves all that he sees, because all that he sees is a reflection of eternal truth, and that is Love.

(v 16 – 21)[1]The Holy Spirit has come into the world to see that it is good. [2]And so it is the Light within men that sees the world truly.

³Men judge the world and one another, and they condemn what they see, but in their condemnation they fail to see as the Light sees. ⁴It is the Light that sees truly, for the Light sees as God sees. ⁵And so men must be mistaken in what they see and in what they think. ⁶Therefore, the judgment of man is meaningless. ⁷All that is meaningful is the vision that comes of Light.

(v 22 – 36)¹The Light has come into the world, because the Light was always in the world. ²Now it has been welcomed. ³Now it can be seen by those welcoming it. ⁴Do not be mistaken. ⁵The Light was not welcomed into the world by one man, or two, or by a handful of men who were ready for the Light. ⁶The Light was welcomed by all men. ⁷And this is why all men have seen the Light and recognized the Light, just as the Light has recognized them.

⁸The time has come for the Heavens to welcome its own unto Itself. ⁹And so an awakening is occurring. ¹⁰All men are a part of the awakening, and all men shall be awakened, because the Light shines for all men and with the consent of all men.

NTI John, Chapter 4

(v 1 – 26)¹The Light within is a guiding Light. ²It guides all men. ³None are absent from its guidance, though many are unaware. ⁴Those who are guided by the Light, but do not recognize its guidance, know not where they are or why. ⁵And so they look elsewhere for their own salvation and happiness. ⁶Since they do not know it is with them, they continue to search and they continue to struggle. ⁷When they find what they think is happiness within the darkness, they enjoy it for a time. ⁸But then the joy it brought seems lost, and they thirst for joy again.

⁹No man is aimless. ¹⁰No man is lost. ¹¹No man is without guidance. ¹²Always, every man is where he needs to be, guided there by the Light because he has asked for guidance and he has welcomed it, but if he has not accepted it as it is and where it is, he does not recognize what he has welcomed, because he has not welcomed it fully. ¹³And so he has the

answer because it was given, but he does not accept it. [14]And he continues searching and does not realize it is with him already.

(v 27 – 38)[1]The reward of Light is given to all men. [2]Men need not earn the reward. [3]Men need not even ask for it. [4]Men only need to seek for it, welcome it and accept it to see that they *are* it.

[5]Do not be mistaken. [6]The Light was not welcomed by one man, or two, or only a handful of men, because all men have welcomed the Light as one. [7]As the Light is with one man, the Light is with all men. [8]You must only open your eyes to see the Light all around you and within you and to see that the Light is with all things and within all things and that the Light *is* all things. [9]The Light is in you and with you and the Light is you, because you have welcomed the Light when all men welcomed the Light. [10]Open your eyes. [11]See what you have welcomed. [12]Welcome it fully now.

(v 39 – 42)[1]Open your heart. [2]Open your mind. [3]Open your eyes, and see by welcoming what there is to see. [4]It is before you now, waiting only for your welcome.

(v 43 – 54)[1]To welcome the Light, have faith in the Light. [2]Do not expect the Light to convince you of its presence by grabbing you with miracles when you seem to give the Light no welcome. [3]The Light welcomes you as you are, and so it will not try to convince you. [4]But when you are ready, and through faith you welcome the Light...in that hour, the miracles of the Light shall be known. [5]And you will be grateful that you extended welcome unto the Light through faith that the Light gave welcome to you.

NTI John, Chapter 5

(v 1 – 9)[1]Do you want to be healed? [2]Do you want to welcome the Light as your Self and as your only truth? [3]When you say "yes" to this question without hesitation or exception for anything you seem to see or know or experience, you will be healed, and you will know the Light fully. [4]Nothing can keep this knowledge from you, because this knowledge is what you are. [5]All that can keep the knowledge of your truth from you is your desire not to know it of yourself.

[6]To know your truth of yourself, you must also welcome your truth unto all that you see and think and know and believe. [7]You cannot keep the truth from anything and know the completeness of the Light. [8]The Light must be welcomed fully, because the Light is everything! [9]Or you are not welcoming the Light, and you are choosing to keep it hidden.

[10]All that you see and experience is of your choice, so you know what you are choosing by that which you see and experience.

(v 9 – 15)[1]The Light that is within man *is not* the man as he thinks. [2]It is thinking that hides the Light from man. [3]As you choose to think, you choose to *not choose* the Light. [4]Thinking is to choose fantasy, for choosing to think is to choose to believe that the truth is something other than the Light of which it is. [5]To think is to choose to believe that you can choose to make the truth apart from what it is. [6]And this is to believe that you can welcome something else and make it the truth for you. [7]To welcome something else and call it truth *is not* to welcome the Light and know its truth. [8]It is to welcome fantasy in its place, and this must mean that you do not welcome truth.

[9]The Light shines for you when you welcome that the Light *must shine*, because it is truth. [10]When you are prepared to see only *all that is truth*, truth is all you shall see, because it is all that there is.

[11]Can you not see that *not to see it* must be your choice, or it could not be hidden from you?

(v 16 – 30)[1]The Son of God is free, because the Father made Him freedom. [2]The Light is free, because the Light is freedom. [3]And then it must be that man is free, because man is within the Light and the Light is within man.

[4]The Light is the Son of God, and the Light is freedom. [5]If man is to know freedom, man must welcome the Light. [6]To deny the Light is to deny freedom. [7]And yet, because denial is your choice, you believe that to deny freedom is freedom. [8]In this decision, you illustrate the height of

your own confusion!

[9]Freedom is the gift of God. [10]Freedom is the gift of the Father extended to the Son in His creation of Him. [11]Freedom lies within the Light. [12]To know the freedom that is yours, you must choose to accept it by welcoming the Light. [13]This is the only way to know that which already *is*.

(v 31 – 47)[1]The Light is within you. [2]The Light is with Jesus. [3]Your brother is the Light. [4]To trust in your brother is to trust in the Light. [5]To doubt him is to doubt Jesus. [6]This is what you must learn. [7]The Light cannot be seen in one form and not within another, because to know the Light is to see the Light in all things, because the Light is all things. [8]If you do not see the Light in all things, you are missing the Light within yourself.

[9]Have faith in Jesus and look within yourself for the Light. [10]He saw it there, and so it is there you must find it also.

[11]Have faith in your Father and look to your brother for the Light. [12]It was your Father that placed it there with him, and so it is there, within your brother where it must be.

NTI John, Chapter 6

(v 1 – 15)[1]The Light testifies to Itself, because it does shine. [2]You need do nothing to let the Light testify for you and about you, for this it does because it is you.

[3]Have faith in the Light that dwells within, knowing also that it dwells in all things and with all men. [4]Since the Light is in all things and with all men, all things and all men must be one in communication, because the Light is one within Itself.

[5]Therefore, you need not tell people where to go or what to do, that they may receive the Light and know the Light, for the Light is with them already! [6]It is you who must open your heart and welcome the Light that is present. [7]And then you will see it is present with all, and it has already been present.

(v 16 – 24)[1]The miracle of the Light is not a miracle at all. [2]It only seems to be a miracle to you, because you do not know the Light and you do not have faith in the Light's presence. [3]The Light is God, and the Light is with you, so all that is possible with God is possible with you. [4]Only your lack of faith tells you it is not so. [5]You go out in search of the Light when the Light is with you and the Light is you. [6]How will you find the Light when you do not know where to look? [7]How can you know the Light when you do not have faith in yourself?

(v 25 – 59)[1]The Light is Life, and so the Light is the bread of Life. [2]It is acceptance of the Light that opens ones eyes to Life so that he may not see death, but so he may see only Life.

[3]Only Life is. [4]Death is not, and so it is nothing to look upon. [5]Do not look at death. [6]Do not look at your brother and see only his death, for if you see only his death, you do not see his Life. [7]And it is his Life that lives! [8]It is his Life that is real, because it is his Life that is the Light that is with all things.

[9]That which you choose is that which you see. [10]If you look at your brother and see death, you have chosen death. [11]If you look at your brother and see Life, you have known Life.

[12]No one knows his brother unless he knows Life. [13]And no one knows Life unless he knows his brother. [14]For your brother and Life are one. [15]To know one, you must see one. [16]And to see one, you must choose that there is one by accepting the Light that is the one you are.

(v 60 – 71)[1]It is faithlessness that makes this teaching hard for you to accept. [2]You do not have faith in your brother and you do not have faith in yourself, because you do not have faith in the Light.

[3]To have faith in the Light is to have faith in God, and that is to have faith in all things and in all persons, because God is all things and all persons. [4]Without God, there are no things and no persons, and without that which is God, there can be nothing.

[5]To see anything at all is to see God. [6]To have faith in anything at all is to have faith in everything you see. [7]For without faith in all things, you

are faithless, because all things are God and you are all things.

NTI John, Chapter 7

(v 1 – 13)[1]The guidance of the Light is known from within. [2]One must learn to trust himself to know his guidance. [3]And one must learn to trust his brother to trust himself. [4]For one cannot trust himself and distrust his brother. [5]To trust oneself and distrust one's brother is not to trust fully. [6]And not to trust fully is not to trust at all.

[7]Do not tell your brother what he should do. [8]Let him know for himself what he should do, and let him do it. [9]In this way, you demonstrate for yourself that the Light can be trusted, and you open within yourself the opportunity to know and trust the Light.

(v 14 – 24)[1]To trust the guidance from within is to listen with openness and without judgment. [2]When you judge the guidance that you hear, you demonstrate an unwillingness to listen. [3]This unwillingness comes from fear. [4]For you fear that to trust guidance without judging it is to lose all sense of your self and of your world.

[5]In this, you are not incorrect. [6]It is only the fear that misleads you. [7]For to lose the sense of your self as you see yourself now, and to lose your sense of the world as you see the world now, is to lose your sense of what is false and to gain the realization of what is true.

[8]If you hold onto your fear out of a sense of self-protection, you hold onto your unwillingness to embrace the Light. [9]You must embrace the Light to share it. [10]You must be the Light for the Light to shine through you.

(v 25 – 44)[1]Confusion comes from the mind that tries to think. [2]This mind tries to reason and make sense of what cannot make sense. [3]But this mind craves "sense" over chaos, because sense gives this mind a sense of order, and where there is order, there can be control. [4]And where there is control, one can find identity.

(v 45 – 53)[1]It is the Heart that knows Identity. [2]The Heart is beyond reason, because the Heart is willing to accept what the mind cannot accept. [3]Follow the light that shines within the Heart. [4]Ask the mind to rest its questions and seek not for answers. [5]The Heart will lead you to the Identity you seek.

NTI John, Chapter 8

(v 1 – 11)[1]The mind has made laws, and it asks you to follow them. [2]These laws give you your identity, because these laws tell you who you are in relation to them. [3]But who are you without the laws of man? [4]If the laws were different, would you be different because of a different relationship to them? [5]Can you truly be defined by laws or by a relationship to the law? [6]And if you are not defined by your relationship to the law, why do you hold onto it so fiercely? [7]What is it you believe you are holding onto?

(v 12 – 30)[1]One is who he is, only he does not know it if he insists on being defined according to the laws of the world. [2]The Light is the truth of everything, and the Light is not bound by the world, because the Light is not of the world. [3]The Light is beyond the world. [4]You must lift your sight beyond the world to know the Light. [5]As long as you welcome the laws of the world as the basis of your identity, you deny that your truth is not of the world. [6]To deny that your truth is not of the world is not to accept and welcome the Light. [7]You place a limit on what you will accept, and so the unlimited cannot be accepted. [8]If limits are what you choose, limits are what you receive. [9]You are given that for which you ask. [10]Does that not tell you that you must be beyond limits?

(v 31 – 41)[1]In the Light there is freedom, because the Light is freedom. [2]Without the acceptance of the Light, you cannot know freedom. [3]You may believe you are free, but you are deceived. [4]You are not free because you cannot see clearly. [5]You are a slave to that which you see and a slave to that which you experience.

(v 42 – 47)[1]You see and experience what you ask to see and experience. [2]This can never not be true. [3]You are not the victim of your world. [4]Your world, as you experience it, is the world of your design.

(v 48 – 59)[1]Your mind is like a trap in that it limits you based on the beliefs you hold onto. [2]Whatever you believe, you experience, and whatever you refuse to believe, you do not allow into your experience. [3]In this way, your mind is the filter of all that you experience.

[4]The Light is, and the Light always has been. [5]Before man, there was the Light. [6]Before belief, there was the Light. [7]Within eternity, there is the Light. [8]The Light *is*, but if your mind will not accept it and welcome it, That Which Is does not seem *is* within your experience.

[9]You experience that which you ask. [10]Does that not tell you that you are beyond your experience?

NTI John, Chapter 9

(v 1 – 12)[1]Open to your Heart. [2]Let the Voice within the Heart lead ahead of the mind. [3]When the mind disputes the Heart, let the mind rest. [4]Answer the mind thusly, "I do not know what I do not know, and so I cannot answer your questions. [5]I only know what I have been led to know, and because I choose to know it, I can see!"

(v 13 – 34)[1]When one's eyes are opened by the guidance of his Heart, he becomes witness to that which he has welcomed. [2]Through him, others shall see what he has seen. [3]Whether they accept or not accept it into the filter of their mind is their choice based on their willingness. [4]But they shall see what is witnessed to them, and what they see shall be saved in their Heart until they are ready to acknowledge it. [5]In this way, all men welcome the Light together. [6]Whenever one gives welcome and accepts its message, all give welcome with him. [7]But if some are not willing to see what they have welcomed beyond the trap of their mind, their Heart welcomes it for them and saves it there. [8]So that which is welcomed is not lost.

(v 35 - 41)[1]Pass no judgment on what you see. [2]For when you pass judgment, you pass what you see through the filter you have made within the mind. [3]Viewed through this filter, the thing you see will be distorted. [4]It will not be the thing that it is. [5]It will be that which you have asked to see and which you have designed to see through the web of filters you have made.

[6]To see clearly and to see all things as they truly are, bypass the mind. [7]Look with the Heart. [8]The light that shines from the Heart seeks not for explanation or proof or sense or control. [9]It says only this, "Show me that I may believe." [10]And it accepts what it is shown without questioning it, because it is its Will to welcome the Light. [11]It is its will that the Light be welcomed fully.

NTI John, Chapter 10

(v 1 – 21)[1]I Am the way, and the thoughts that came before were not. [2]You spent many years listening to the thoughts that came before Me, and they have given you nothing. [3]I Am the way, because I Am the Light, and the Light is the way to Life.

[4]Open to Me. [5]Listen to Me. [6]Tune out all other voices by letting go of all other thoughts. [7]The time has come to listen only unto the Light.

(v 22 – 42)[1]How is it that I Am known? [2]I Am the Light, and so I carry with Me the characteristics of the Light and *only* the characteristics of the Light. [3]You will not find fear in Me. [4]You will find only Love. [5]You will not find attack and war; you will find only peace. [6]You will not find guilt or accusation; you will find only sweet forgiveness that sees that which is meaningless as meaningless and asks it to take on no meaning. [7]You can trust My Voice, because you recognize it as yours, and you know it *is* yours.

[8]I Am the Light, the Light of which you are. [9]We are one and the same, and you are Me. [10]And so you know Me, and you recognize your desire to remember Me *as all that you are*.

NTI John, Chapter 11

(v 1 – 16)[1]Trust in this Voice that you know is you and that you recognize as the Light, as *your* Light. [2]There is no reason not to trust the Light, for in the Light you can see and you will know freedom.

[3]Step into the Light fully without fear of death, and see how clearly your path is lit. [4]See how well you know your way. [5]See how happy you are to know that which the Light has shown you!

(v 17 – 37)[1]Have faith in the Voice that comes from within, the one that seems to come from far away and does not seem to always be there. [2]For this Voice is with you always and only seems distant when you fear your death. [3]It is your fear that blocks your awareness of the Light, and yet it is the Light that blocks out death. [4]For death cannot be within the Light, because the Light cannot die.

(v 38 – 44)[1]The resurrection is within you, because the Light is within you and the Light is the resurrection. [2]To know the Light and to know the resurrection which *is*, you must put aside the voices of death. [3]Put aside your grave clothes and look at them no longer. [4]You live! [5]Listen to the Voice of Life!

(v 45 – 57)[1]The Light must not hide and the Light cannot hide. [2]When you have come to see that the Light is in all things, you will also see that the Light has not been hidden. [3]You just did not see it there, but it has never been hidden.

[4]So why is it that you cannot see the Light if the Light is everywhere, even now shining brightly for you to see? [5]It is because you have focused your eyes on something else, a fog and a shadow. [6]It is the fog and the shadow that you insist must hold all truth. [7]And so it is the fog and the shadow that you focus on and try to protect.

NTI John, Chapter 12

(v 1 – 11)[1]When you place your focus with the fog and the shadow, you do not see the Light that shines within the fog and beyond the shadow. [2]You see that which you have chosen to see, and yet you miss that which is there.

[3]The fog and the shadow of which you choose to see is a fog and a shadow placed before your eyes by the wish within your mind. [4]And so the fog and the shadow are but a misty reflection of a wish. [5]When the

wish is no longer desired, the fog and the shadow must fade away.

[6]Each one may choose to see his fog and his shadow, but his fog and his shadow are but a mistaken gift he has given to himself. [7]It is given to no one else. [8]It is his alone. [9]And so if the fog and shadow as they seem to exist, exist only for him, the fog and the shadow cannot be truth. [10]For truth must be true for all.

[11]The fog and the shadow that you have chosen to see is your fog and shadow, which you may keep. [12]But as you choose to keep it, you choose to keep a wish and you choose not to welcome the Light that is before you now.

📖(v 12 - 19)[1]The triumphal entry is a time that must come to your mind. [2]This is the entry, the triumphal entry, of the realization of all that is true upon your mind. [3]This moment is a moment of triumphal entry, glorious beyond any moment you seem to know now! [4]But this moment is also the humblest of moments, which is why it is represented by the image of a king riding on the back of the colt of a donkey. [5]For in this moment, this moment of triumphal entry, you must place aside every concept of meaning that you ever thought you knew to be true, and you must be open to all that you never imagined. [6]For all that you imagined is not true, and the truth is all that was never imagined.

(v 20 - 28)[1]"What do I want?" [2]This is the question you must ask and keep firmly within your mind in all things. [3]For you will see and experience that which you want, because it is that which you have chosen to experience. [4]And you *must be given* that which you have chosen to experience.

[5]Within your mind there is a wish. [6]It is a protected and denied wish, and yet it is a wish that has been very dear to you until now. [7]This is the wish that you could be that which you want to be. [8]This is a wish that wishes for change within the Changeless. [9]And so this is a wish that asks the Changeless to be what it is not.

[10]This is why you feel that you have stolen yourself from God. [11]It is because you have asked that you could be what you are not, and then you

made a web of beliefs cast upon a fog and a shadow, that you may experience that which you want to experience.

[12]You must see and experience that which you choose to see and experience, because you wanted it so, and so you made it so. [13]All that you have given, you have given unto yourself, so that all that you know has been a gift given unto you and given by you.

[14]If you choose to lay your experiences aside and choose the experience of welcoming the Light, you must choose to lay your secret wish aside as completely undesired, and you must choose to welcome the Light as all that you want to know and be.

[15]The question that you must ask yourself, and that you must continue to ask yourself, and the question that you must hold firmly within your mind is this:

[16]*What do I want?*
[17]*What is it that I truly,*
within the depths of my heart,
seek as my only experience?
[18]*Do I seek the changeless truth of all that is?*
[19]*Is this what I would know?*
[20]*Or would I have my own kingdom*
rather than know
that I am King?

(v 29 – 33)[1]Within your mind is a universe you have made. [2]This universe is a concept, made of concepts, made to block the Light. [3]It is through this universe of which you believe that you deny that which is true.

[4]But the universe you have made is not truth. [5]It is a block over truth, intended to hide the truth from you so that you may pretend the universe is truth and the universe defines all that you are. [6]In this wish, you are limited by your wish. [7]And so your own wish hides the truth of what you

are.

[8]Let go of the universe you have made. [9]It is nothing of reality. [10]It is only a joke that you have made of yourself and for yourself. [11]However, you are not finding it to be funny, so why do you hold onto your joke?

(v 34 – 36)[1]Darkness is of your own choice, because darkness is the universe that hides the truth. [2]The universe is a darkness you have made. [3]You have made the darkness, and so you can choose *not* to look at it, not to listen to it and not to let it be your limiting universe anymore. [4]But to do this, you must welcome the Light. [5]In the Light, you can see. [6]It will guide you to let go of the darkness by showing you that darkness cannot exist within the Light of which you are.

(v 37 – 50)[1]You must trust the words that come from My mouth, because they are the words that are written upon your Heart. [2]Trust your Heart. [3]And in trusting your Heart, you trust Me also. [4]For we are the same, and we are all things, and we are the truth, and the truth is written upon us as a witness to all the world. [5]The Light is our glory, and the Light is us and within us and we are within the Light. [6]For the Light is inseparable from us, and us from each other, and we are inseparable from the Light. [7]It is all things and in all things, and all things are in it. [8]*This* is the truth you try to hide. [9]But this is the Light that must not be hidden, because it is the Light that cannot be hidden. [10]And so it does not hide.

NTI John, Chapter 13

(v 1 – 17)[1]Service is surrender. [2]It is surrender to the Light that will make the Light known to you. [3]To surrender to the Light is to become one with it, which is to lay aside any will that would seem to be different.

[4]You experience the world that you experience, because it is your will to do so. [5]To experience a world that is different from the world that you experience, you must take up another will as your own. [6]This is service, and service can only be fully accomplished by the full surrender of the will you are not to serve. [7]For will must be a leader, and you must be a follower. [8]To serve the will of one is not to serve the will of the other. [9]So

you must pick the one you will serve and relinquish the other.

[10]There is only one choice that you can make if you are to be an un-conflicted servant. [11]You must serve the Light, because the Light is present in all things. [12]The Light is the one eternal Will. [13]To serve *is* to serve the Light. [14]For to be conflicted is not to have decided, and so it is not to have made the choice to serve.

[15]Joy comes from the choice to serve, because the choice to serve is the choice to relinquish conflict.

(v 18 – 30)[1]The conflicted servant cannot know joy, because he has not made the decision to serve, and so he must be unsettled in his heart. [2]For he knows he is a servant and he knows it is his will to serve, but he has not matched his will to his Will, and so he seems to betray himself.

[3]Fear not. [4]Confusion cannot last. [5]Confusion calls out to be healed, so that all confusion calls to the one Will that would heal it. [6]That one Will is the alignment of will, without the conflict of a separate will to confuse it.

(v 31 – 38)[1]Accept the Light by accepting one Will, and you accept the one Will of the Light. [2]And with that you accept all things. [3]For all things are of one Will. [4]For there is only one Will in reality. [5]The Will of all things is Love, and Love is the Will under which all things operate. [6]For where there is not Love, there is nothing, as Love is all there is.

[7]Why do you not see Love if Love is all there is? [8]It is your fear that hides the truth from you.

[9]What do you fear that you should hide your face from Love? [10]You fear one Will. [11]And knowing that one Will must be Love, you also fear Love.

[12]This is why you choose conflict: [13]*It is not Love.* [14]And you fear Love, because you fear one Will, and you know that one Will, without conflict, must be Love.

NTI John, Chapter 14

(v 1 – 4)[1]Know that you seek Love, for you *do* know this! [2]Lay down the will that leads you to seek not for what you want. [3]Trust in God, which is to trust the guidance of one Will. [4]Do not fear that which you want, for fear only serves to keep you from You, since You are that which you seek.

[5]"My Father's house has many rooms" means we are all one. [6]Come with Me to the house that is our Home. [7]It is the realization of our oneness through the acceptance of our one combined Will.

(v 5 – 14)[1]One Will *is* one Will without an element of separateness. [2]"I am within my Father and my Father is within me," means there is no difference between us and no part of us that is not the same. [3]"I am the way and the truth and the life," means all reality is within me, and I am in all reality.

(v 15 – 31)[1]What I Am, you are also. [2]I am within the Father, and the Father is within me. [3]I am within you, and you are within me. [4]You are within the Father, and the Father is within you. [5]There is no difference among us. [6]We are complete and the same. [7]Reality is within us, and we are reality.

[8]Within you, there is a Voice that speaks of truth. [9]This Voice is the Comforter, because it speaks of what you are. [10]You are comforted by this Voice, because you recognize the truth that it speaks. [11]And you desire to know that truth again.

[12]This is the call of your Heart: [13]To know Itself within its reality, and to let go of what it is not, that it may know only That Which it Is.

[14]Any belief in separateness is a denial of the truth, but a denial of the truth does not change the truth of which you are. [15]I am always with you, because I cannot be separate from you, and you cannot be separate from Me. [16]Where you go, I go, and so I am there also. [17]I am in all that you see, waiting only for your decision to see Me, that you may know My joy for knowing that I am you.

NTI John, Chapter 15

(v 1 – 17)[1]You are not separate, and so you can do nothing alone. [2]All that you do, you do of Me. [3]And all that you do not do of Me, you have not done.

(v 18 – 27)[1]Therefore, do not fear. [2]For you cannot make a mistake if a mistake must be an action taken apart from Me. [3]And yet no action can be separate from Me, as there can be no "separate." [4]Anything that is not of Me does not exist. [5]And so anything that is not of Me, isn't. [6]It is nothing to be concerned about, *because* it is nothing.

[7]Be not concerned over nothing. [8]For this is a distraction from your joy. [9]Instead, look only to Me and you look only to reality, which is joy, because reality knows not of separateness and so it knows not of nothing. [10]That which knows not of nothing must be Everything. [11]And it is that which I Am and you are also.

NTI John, Chapter 16

(v 1 – 4)[1]One Will is within you, so that the one you serve is your Self. [2]This is your purpose, to serve your Self fully. [3]This is the purpose for which you were created, and so it is this that will bring you the greatest of joy.

[4]But within you also, there is a great resistance to your one true joy. [5]For this part of your mind does not know your joy, and it does not know you. [6]It will tell you that you are what you are not. [7]It will insist that following the path of truth is to follow the path of falsity and that in following the path of falsity, you will surely die.

[8]Listen not to the voice that does not know you. [9]Heed not its warnings, for the Light is in you and you are the Light. [10]Darkness cannot be your way. [11]Remain focused on the Light, and you remain focused on your truth. [12]Stay with the Light, and you stand firmly on the path of joy and truth.

(v 5 – 16)[1]The path of Light is found within. [2]Always, it is Within that guides you. [3]Seek not to find your path without, for to seek without is to deny who you are. [4]Seek within, for *because of who you are* the answer must lie there.

(v 17 – 33)[1]Jesus has been given as a symbol of your truth, and all that Jesus speaks, he speaks of Me. [2]For Jesus and I are one, just as you and I are one.

[3]Look at your brother Jesus, and know that the Light that *is* him is you also. [4]When Jesus said that he had overcome the world, he meant that he had transcended the world in love. [5]To transcend the world in love is to open to the realization that all that is not Love *is not* in reality. [6]This is to know the truth of all men, and to know the truth of all men is to know and see the Light. [7]To know and see the Light is to also know that the world cannot be, for that which is not Light cannot be when Light is all there is.

[8]This was Jesus' joy, and this shall be your joy also! [9]How could Jesus deny a death when "death" is defined as leaving a world that does not exist? [10]To leave a world that is not real is not to die. [11]It is to wake up from a dream that you thought was real, but was not.

[12]The resurrection is an awakening. [13]It is to awaken to the reality of the Father and your oneness with Him. [14]It is to know the truth and joy that you call Heaven. [15]It is not a change at all, but only an awareness that seems to be change, because all that you are aware of now is not true, and all that you are aware of in truth is only True. [16]This seems to be a change when it is not, because only the truth is true, and all that could ever be true is truth.

NTI John, Chapter 17

(v 1 – 5)[1]The symbol is not truth, but what the symbol points to is truth. [2]The symbol very clearly points to this:

[3]Life is eternal, and there is no death. [4]Death is only fear, but fear is not real. [5]Life is Love, and Love is all that is. [6]You cannot know death, because you are Life. [7]But you may choose the image of fear and think you know death. [8]No image of fear can last, because it is only an image, and That Which Is must shine above all false images. [9]But you may choose death as an experience while you live, and you may also choose not to choose an experience that isn't real. [10]To choose the truth is to

glorify the Father who is truth. [11]To glorify the Father is to glorify the Son, who is one with Him in truth.

(v 6 – 19)[1]The Light blesses the Son of God, for all that the Light does see and does know is God and is of God. [2]That is all there is to see, so that is all that the Light does see. [3]But the Light also understands that the sleeping Son of God, who experiences a world within a dream, knows not that he is dreaming. [4]The Light is not concerned with the dream, as the dream is not of the Light, but the Light is aware of a belief in the dream. [5]And so the Light reaches within the dream and talks within the dream, that the sleeping Son of God may awaken to see it was only a dream.

[6]You, who are reading these words, are the sleeping Son of God. [7]You are sleeping, because you believe in the world. [8]And you are the Son of God, because you are the extension of the Light that is God.

[9]All men are of the Light, so all men must be of God. [10]Therefore, all men are the Son of God, only they do not know it yet.

[11]You, who are reading these words, are opening to the acceptance of these words. [12]That is why you are reading them. [13]You are ready.

[14]Many aspects of the Light are not ready to see they are the Light. [15]This is not a problem, because they are the Light anyway. [16]But you, who are reading these words, are ready to know the Light that you are.

[17]And so I shall lead you, but I shall lead you from within. [18]Focus within, where the Word of your Father is. [19]Focus within, that you may know and remember His Name.

(v 20 – 26)[1]O holy one, there is only cause for joy. [2]For all that you are is all that you are, and you are blessed and beloved as is everyone. [3]May peace dawn upon you as you realize the truth of My words. [4]May peace light up your mind as you see the joy that is your brother's and your sister's. [5]May peace be all there is within experience as you accept the truth as all that could be true.

[6]To accept the truth as all that could be true is to accept the false as false. [7]This is to let go of condemnation, for all that you accept is peace and joy and Life. [8]And all that is not of those things, you know is not of

God, and so it cannot be real.

NTI John, Chapter 18

(v 1 – 11)[1]What is it that you seek? [2]Is it peace and joy and the knowing that brings comfort? [3]I am He. [4]I am that which you seek. [5]But what is most important for you to realize and accept is this:

> [6]*I am you.*
> [7]*I am that which you seek,*
> *and I am you.*

[8]Do not pull away from this idea. [9]Do not try to change it by making it acceptable to you. [10]Accept this idea as it is presented, fully and without question, and you accept Heaven as your reality.

[11]I am He. [12]I am peace and joy and total comfort, absent only from that which is comfortless, because I cannot be contained by illusions. [13]And you are Me, fully and without separation or difference. [14]You are peace and joy and total comfort, separate only from your illusions, and one with everything else.

(v 12 - 14)[1]Listen not to the ego, which tells you that we are somehow different. [2]Listen not to the voice that recommends you judge what I say for yourself. [3]To judge what I say, or even to consider the act of judgment, is to separate Me off from you within your imagination.

[4]Lay down your imagination. [5]Accept all that I say without question or judgment and you accept the truth of our reality, which is and always shall be one.

(v 15 – 18)[1]Notice the denial within your mind. [2]It is there. [3]It is that piece of doubt that says you could be you and I could be Me, separate from you. [4]This piece of doubt, housed within denial, believes it is your safety to keep yourself from Me. [5]But doubt and denial of that which is true serves no purpose except to keep you afraid of darkened nightmares. [6]Release your doubt and denial. [7]Accept Me as I Am.

(v 19 – 24)[1]Doubt and denial will seem fierce at times, but it is nothing to fear or be afraid of. [2]Acknowledge that which you see as an attack that you have attempted on truth. [3]Acknowledge also that that which is truth cannot be attacked. [4]All attack is only imagined doubt and denial. [5]And then release the thought that would attempt to hide the truth from you. [6]Stand in peace, silent and willing.

(v 25 – 27)[1]Do not be afraid that you are afraid, and do not feel guilty for it. [2]All that you have imagined has not affected truth, and so you could have done nothing wrong. [3]Let your fear come up and look at it, but do not be afraid of it. [4]Be steadfast in the desire of your Heart, and it will carry you through to the dawning of the day.

(v 28 – 40)[1]Confusion is common as you begin to listen and accept My Voice. [2]This is because of the voice you listened to before. [3]It still seems to have a great hold on you, and you put faith in all that it has taught you. [4]But now you hear another Voice too, and it also seems to make sense, although all that it says is different from anything you heard before.

[5]You stand before two voices, both witnessing to you and both claiming to be the voice of truth. [6]Each voice has something to say, but what they say is different. [7]And you must make a choice. [8]The power of decision is within your hands. [9]Which voice will you believe? [10]Which voice will you choose? [11]Which voice will you listen to?

[12]The voices are completely different. [13]You cannot listen to both. [14]You must make a decision. [15]The decision you make is your choice.

NTI John, Chapter 19

(v 1 – 16)[1]The ego is a tricky voice. [2]If you believe that you have not made a decision, and you also believe that listening to your own reason will lead you to make a reasonable decision that is wise and in your best interest, you choose to let the ego speak for you. [3]In this choice, you have made a decision. [4]For in deciding that you could judge, you decided that you were separate from that which you judge. [5]In that choice, you made the decision that in your belief, we cannot be one.

(v 17 – 27)[1]But the choice that you seem to make when you choose to listen to the ego is not a choice, except that you choose to continue dreaming. [2]For though the dream may seem to continue, and that continuation may seem to be your truth, it is not. [3]There is One who is with you, observing all that you seem to see, but seeing with His eyes differently. [4]For this One knows that dreams cannot be true and fear cannot be your reality. [5]And so He waits with you, gently seeing what you see without accepting your nightmares, that He may share His Vision when you decide that you are ready to see.

📖(v 28 – 37)[1]You will believe that which you see, and you will seem to suffer for it. [2]Your heart will be broken many times, but in this there is no loss. [3]There is no loss, because the One that is with you is with you still, and He knows that your suffering is merely an experience of your choice. [4]It has no reality to it and affects not your eternal truth. [5]This is why the body of Jesus seemed to bleed forth blood and water. [6]It is because there was no truth in his body, and so there was no truth in his death.

(v 38 – 42)[1]Death is an illusion. [2]And this is all that you need know. [3]For if death is not real, your world cannot be real, for your world is based on the law of death.

[4]Let go of your acceptance of death. [5]Do not see it as your truth. [6]For if death is not your truth, something else must be. [7]And that something else is Me.

NTI John, Chapter 20

(v 1 - 9)[1]When the Light begins to dawn within the mind, you will recognize it. [2]And yet, you will not understand it or accept it completely at first, and so you may also fear it. [3]This is only the reaction of a mind long blinded by darkness when it first encounters the reality of Light. [4]Let this fear not upset you. [5]It is natural in the transition. [6]But because you have seen a glimmer of the Light, it will call to you, and you will follow it through your fear. [7]For somehow you know that in the Light lies the absence of fear and all that you have ever sought.

(v 10 – 18)[1]As you listen for the Light, the Light will grow brighter in your sight. [2]It will speak to you and touch you so that you know it is the Light's intention to reach *you*. [3]You may sense that the Light comes from someplace else, outside of you, but you will not be mistaken regarding the love of the Light, which is undoubtedly for you.

(v 19 – 23)[1]Next, a merging will seem to occur. [2]You will continue to sense the Light as if it comes from a source that is separate from you, but you will begin to notice the Light within you also. [3]It will move you and work through you, and you will begin to feel excited about following its guidance.

(v 24 – 31)[1]During this time, miracles will move you, and you will notice that you have begun to change. [2]Times of doubt will visit also. [3]But if you open to Me, even within your moments of doubt, the miracles that you experience will convince you that your faith is well placed, and you will continue to follow the guidance of the Light.

NTI John, Chapter 21

(v 1 – 14)[1]When you are ready to listen to Me and trust Me fully in all matters and all things, the time will come that you will experience that which you did not expect. [2]This will be a time of celebration, for your eyes will be opened, and you will be fully immersed within the Spirit. [3]The Light shall be one with you and you shall be one with the Light. [4]And you will not ask, "How is it that this happened?" [5]For you will know it is your truth, and you are now seeing it, *because* it is so.

(v 15 – 25)[1]When you have given yourself fully to the Spirit, the Spirit shall be fully within you. [2]This is not a change at all. [3]For this is as it has always been, but in your sleep, you do not know. [4]So the realization of your truth is but an awakening from a sleep in which you thought one thing was true when it was not.

[5]In your awakening, you will not be tested. [6]For all that I give, I give freely for you to accept. [7]But you may seem to be tested before you have

awakened fully. [8]Know these tests do not come from Me. [9]It is the ego tempting you to hold onto the world. [10]Let these temptations go, and follow Me. [11]I will give you something to do that is a mission of Heaven and great joy within the world. [12]This will be your path to awakening, each path unique, and yet each path the same, because each path serves the purpose of leaving the world of illusion for the truth of which we are.

[13]The Light is in all men, and all men are the Light. [14]All men shall be known by their Light, because the Light is their truth, and all men know their truth and will follow it. [15]Amen.

THE HOLY SPIRIT'S INTERPRETATION OF ACTS

NTI Acts, Chapter 1

📖(v 1 – 11)[1]The power of all truth is within you. [2]The story of Jesus is helpful to you as a guide, a tool, and a symbol, but the answer for you lies not in his story. [3]If it had, he would have stayed on earth to provide the answer to you. [4]But Jesus left your realm and returned to the Father, that you may be freed to find your answer within yourself.

[5]The Holy Spirit, which seemed to be given to the apostles when Jesus ascended from the world, was not passed on to them at this time. [6]Only God can give the gift of the Holy Spirit, and God has given this gift to everyone. [7]The gift has always been in the world, even before Jesus. [8]This gift has always guided you. [9]But as long as you continue to look outside of yourself for answers and satisfaction, you are unaware of this gift.

[10]When Jesus ascended and promised the baptism of the Holy Spirit, he only pointed the apostles to seek where the Holy Spirit already was. [11]In this way, they learned not to look outside for teaching and guidance, but to clearly look within.

[12]This is My lesson to you. [13]I am here to help for a time, but My purpose is to teach you to look and listen within. [14]For always, your guidance must come from there, because always, the answer is there.

(v 12 – 26)[1]The first step to listening within for the guidance of the Holy Spirit is prayer. [2]But to hear Him truly, you must pray in a way that opens to Him. [3]Prayer is not a time of asking for what you want. [4]Prayer is a time of putting aside that which you want and opening to *any guidance* that He would give. [5]Prayer is a time of gratitude for His love and wisdom. [6]Prayer is a time of surrender because you seek nothing less than His love, wisdom and guidance for you.

[7]Therefore, pray in this way:

> [8]*Father, I do not know what is best for me now, in this time and this place, that I may be led back to You.* [9]*Because I cannot see the path I am ready to walk, take my hand and send me your Voice to guide me.* [10]*I shall go where it asks me to go, and I shall do as it asks me to do in joy and peace and certainty.*

[11]The second step to listening for guidance is this:

> [12]*You must trust.*

[13]You must not only trust the Voice and the guidance you receive; you must also trust yourself. [14]For the guidance comes from you through your knowing that is beyond conscious choice. [15]To doubt yourself is to doubt your guidance. [16]So you must trust yourself and trust what comes.

NTI Acts, Chapter 2

(v 1 – 13)[1]The Holy Spirit knows the way. [2]The Holy Spirit sees the whole plan, not only your part in it. [3]Therefore, you must trust all that the Holy Spirit asks you to do, even if what is asked does not seem to be for you. [4]For the Holy Spirit does not look at the world and see separated sons of God, each in need of separate plans of salvation. [5]The Holy Spirit sees one Son and one plan. [6]And so, what He gives to you is not for you alone. [7]To learn this is so, you must do as He asks and trust Him.

(v 14 – 21)[1]The paths given may seem to be individualized and the experiences may seem personal, but I assure you that they are not. [2]Everything that is given by the Holy Spirit is given for all and to all, as the Holy Spirit does not see separate parts, but only one. [3]When you hear stories of your brother's and your sister's experience with the Holy Spirit, rejoice and know that experience was also given for you. [4]In this way, you demonstrate trust. [5]Through the demonstration of trust, trust shall grow within you, that you may hear and see more.

(v 22 – 35)[1]There will be symbols and there will be symbols of symbols, but always it is true that only the truth is true. [2]Therefore, do not be caught up in your symbols. [3]Do not identify with them, fight for them or argue with your brother about the symbols you choose to love. [4]In this way, the symbol becomes but another idol that blinds you to the truth. [5]Remember that Jesus left the earth so you would not make an idol of him, but that you would learn from him the way of truth.

(v 36)[1]Therefore, know and remember this, because this is what Jesus taught:

[2]*There is no death,*
and the answer that you seek
is already here within you.

(v 37 – 41)[1]Peter was a teacher, but when he spoke, the Holy Spirit spoke through him. [2]And when the people listened, the Holy Spirit listened for them, pointing to the words they were to hear.

[3]Do not be confused by all that you see and hear and experience within the world. [4]It does not need to take a specific form to be used by the Holy Spirit for your teaching and your guidance. [5]Since He is the overseer of all things, all things can be used by Him for your benefit.

[6]I will teach you how to listen to Him in all situations and at all times. [7]Listen to Me, and be glad!

(v 42 – 47)[1]Your joy shall increase as you listen to the Voice of the Holy Spirit, for He shall lead you to see no value where there is none and to know the love that is already within your Heart. [2]This love, which is the source of all joy, is not a special love that includes some, but not all.

[3]It is an encompassing love, from which joy comes bursting forth from your Heart into the world that you see.

NTI Acts, Chapter 3

📖(v 1 – 10)[1]Peter was a teacher who gave what he had, and what he gave came to him from the Holy Spirit. [2]It was through giving it that Peter learned he had it to give, for he could not give it if it was not already his.

[3]The miracles that Peter witnessed, he witnessed for himself within his own mind. [4]And these miracles were extended to others, that they too may begin to learn who they are. [5]This is what made Peter a great teacher. [6]He shared all that he had, recognizing that it was for all. [7]And through this practice, Peter came to see that all were not separate, but they were one.

(v 11 – 26)[1]The ego is the thought within the mind that separates. [2]The ego says that what is true is not true, and what is not, is the truth. [3]But the ego is not the truth, and so its words cannot be believed.

[4]You experience the ego as a stream of thoughts within the mind that seem to interpret, counsel, identify, judge and spring forth as ideas. [5]In themselves, these thoughts seem to be nothing to you, although you listen to them and act on all that they say. [6]These thoughts rule your mind and your interpretation of the world, because you believe what they say. [7]Yet, they are based on a foundation of separateness, which is not what is true. [8]And so what is true is not in what they say.

[9]To listen to these thoughts and believe them is ignorance, for you are listening to what is not true, but believing what you hear. [10]Any action you take based on these thoughts is ignorant action, for it is action based on untruth in an unreal world.

[11]Ignorance is not guilt. [12]It is a call for knowledge. [13]It is the Holy Spirit that leads you through corrected perception to the right-knowledge that you seek. [14]Right-knowledge is true knowledge, and true knowledge is the knowledge of truth.

[15]Do not worry about the mistakes you have made. [16]They are based

on ignorance, which is illusion and affects only that which is not reality. [17]Be happy that you have been mistaken! [18]Be joyous that there is another way to see! [19]This is what it means to repent. [20]To repent is to choose again. [21]To repent is to decide to turn from the ways of ignorance and turn to the Voice of Knowledge. [22]This is a joyous decision, for this is the decision that changes all things. [23]This decision that you have made is a decision to listen to another Voice. [24]It is the decision to let go of the thoughts you have listened to until now and to listen to another Voice, the one that comes from God. [25]This decision is a decision to change the habits you have had until now. [26]It is a decision to see yourself through new eyes, eyes that are based on a foundation of truth.

[27]This is why I am here. [28]I am here to help you make this change from believing in the false to listening to the Voice of what is true. [29]This is the decision of your joy. [30]This is your path. [31]This is your way. [32]And I will help you, until you do not need this help anymore.

NTI Acts, Chapter 4

(v 1 – 22)[1]I have told you before that you will be tempted to deny your guidance. [2]And I have told you where this temptation will come from. [3]It is resistance born of a sense of unworthiness. [4]I have also told you where this sense of unworthiness comes from. [5]It is born of guilt, born of the belief that you have stolen yourself from God.

[6]Here lies another contradiction that you must look at slowly and carefully:

[7]You believe you have stolen yourself from God. [8]That is to say, you believe you have made yourself separate from God's Will. [9]You believe it is your choice to follow God's Will *or* your own, and you feel guilty for this choice, because you believe it is a sin to have made a will that is separate from God's.

[10]Your guilt, born of the choice to have a separate will, leaves you feeling unworthy of God's Will. [11]And so, out of your guilt and sense of unworthiness, you deny God's Will by not hearing it, or by hearing it, but

by not believing you are deserving to follow it.

¹²There are several things you must look at here. ¹³First, you *do* have the desire to know and follow God's Will. ¹⁴Hold that up as a beacon. ¹⁵That is your willingness. ¹⁶Let it guide you to your true Heart's desire.

¹⁷Secondly, the feeling that seems to be an obstacle to knowing and following God's Will is the belief that you are unworthy of God's Will. ¹⁸This is like a crafty trick. ¹⁹It is a loop that keeps you trapped within an illusion of yourself.

> ²⁰*You think you are guilty because you want to serve a will*
> *other than God's,*
>
> *and*
>
> ²¹*Your true desire is to serve God's Will, but your sense of unworthiness*
> *is an obstacle to that desire.*

²²Do you see the loop in which you are snared? ²³Can you see how your own belief in your guilt and unworthiness seems to lead you onto the path of increased guilt and additional unworthiness?

²⁴This is why I have come, to help you look at the upside-down reasoning within the mind that keeps you feeling trapped. ²⁵And also to help you see that you are *not trapped*, because you can lay down this reasoning that makes no sense. ²⁶When you lay it down and put it aside, you are free to know the reasoning of the Holy Spirit, which is right-reasoning and is joy.

²⁷Remember this story of Peter and John as a symbol to help you hold onto your willingness. ²⁸Know that as they listened to pleas to lay down their purpose, there were doubts in their minds that seemed to echo the reasoning of the pleas. ²⁹They were simple men, and they seemed to be taking on the history of the world with the new message that they taught. ³⁰But know also that they did not listen to their doubts, their fears or their

own sense of unworthiness. [31]They trusted their message as the message of the Holy Spirit and the one Will of God. [32]In following this trust, they gave themselves permission to do God's Will, which was their Heart's only true desire.

[33]Remember this symbol. [34]You *are* worthy of God's Will for you. [35]You are worthy of the Voice for God and all that it will share with you. [36]When doubt enters your mind, born of unworthiness and guilt, lay it aside. [37]It is the loop you do not want. [38]It is the loop that hides the truth from you.

(v 23 – 31)[1]I have also told you not to be confused by what you hear, see and experience within the world. [2]Everything is applicable to the purpose the Holy Spirit has set forth. [3]Everything can be used for the salvation of God's one Holy Son.

[4]When the form of what you see or hear or experience confuses you, remember to pray to Me. [5]Remember that what you look upon confuses you only because you believe in separate wills. [6]If you knew that there was only one Will, you could not be confused.

[7]Remember also that whenever you look at the world with the ego's upside-down reasoning, you cannot see clearly. [8]Be willing to deny what you see, and trust that there must be another way to understand the situation you look upon.

[9]Pray, then, in this way:

[10]*Oh Father, I come to you now in humility and gratitude.* [11]*I am humble, because I realize that I do not know how to see.* [12]*I cannot see the Holy Spirit's plan, and so I do not know what I look upon.* [13]*But I also come in gratitude, because I trust that the Holy Spirit does know, and the plan is safe with Him as the overseer of all things.* [14]*Amen.*

[15]Then give yourself to your Father's Will, offering that you may be used for the purpose of healing, without the desire to judge. [16]This is to lay yourself aside and to do your part in your Father's plan. [17]This is

God's Will for you. [18]This is how you can be useful to the whole.

(v 32 – 37)[1]To give of yourself is to give as you are asked to give without judgment. [2]Whenever you notice guilt within your mind, you have judged, and so you are not listening with full desire to only be useful. [3]You are also asking that you may decide what is right and what is wrong, which means that you are asking that you may exercise a will of your own.

[4]Do not let this realization upset you. [5]Indeed, you may laugh when you find it within yourself. [6]It is nothing more than another ploy of the desire to hide your true desire from you. [7]It is another loop that leads you nowhere. [8]It is another opportunity to remind yourself that you do not know the plan, and therefore, you cannot judge.

[9]Be happy. [10]You are only asked to do what you are asked to do. [11]If you do all that you are asked, you have done enough. [12]There is nothing more to give, having given everything that you have been asked to give.

[13]Give in joy, knowing it is your true Will to give. [14]Let go of guilt, knowing it is just the illusion of an illusory will. [15]For any will that seems separate from God's Will must be an illusion, for you *do know* that your true Will is always the same as His.

NTI Acts, Chapter 5

(v 1 – 11)[1]This story is symbolic and is not to be taken literally. [2]This story is a picture of the guilt that you have claimed and projected onto the world. [3]This story has no meaning, except that it is untrue. [4]And it is important that you see it as untrue *for you* also.

[5]An obstacle to hearing the Holy Spirit is your own sense of guilt and unworthiness. [6]This story demonstrates just how guilty you believe you are. [7]Notice that Ananias and his wife dropped dead from their guilt. [8]Imagine the magnitude of the guilt that seemed to be within them. [9]But what crime did this couple commit? [10]They sold land that belonged to them and gave a portion of the money that they made to the apostles of their own free will. [11]Could this be called a crime? [12]Even within your

world, this could not be called a crime. [13]To give in this way is generosity.
[14]So, what was their crime?

[15]This story seems to say that the crime this couple committed is the
crime of not being honest with God; it is the crime of hiding something
from God; it is the crime of keeping something for yourself. [16]It is *this*
we must look at, because it is this you think you have done. [17]It is this for
which you feel guilty, and it is this guilt that seems to bring on your death.

[18]We will talk about this guilt slowly and carefully, that you may look
at this belief deeply and with right-reason, so you may choose to release
a belief that you do not need to keep.

[19]First, we must discuss what God is. [20]I have told you that God is
Life, and that Life is eternal. [21]Since you accept that God is eternal and
God gives life, this may not be difficult for you to accept. [22]So let's take
this thought another step.

[23]*God is Life,*
and you live,
so Life must be within you.
[24]*This means that God is within you also.*

[25]At this point, you may feel a temptation to pull away from My logic,
but please do not pull away just yet. [26]Let's examine why you want to pull
away and look at that closely.

[27]God is within you. [28]This is a thought that you are tempted to reject.
[29]The reason you want to reject this thought is because you believe that
God is good, but you are guilty. [30]Therefore, you determine that God
cannot be in you, and you must be separate from God. [31]If God is Life,
which you have accepted, and you are separate from God, then it must be
that you are separate from Life. [32]And that is death. [33]That is why death
seems to rule your world. [34]It is because you believe that your guilt keeps
you separate from God.

[35]But can you not see that this is another loop of reasoning that does

not make sense? [36]For right now, you *do* live. [37]Right now, as you sit reading this, you live. [38]So right now, you cannot be separate from God. [39]Right now, God is in you and you are in God. [40]There is no separation. [41]Right now, your oneness with God is complete, and there is nothing that is hidden or not in accordance with your oneness. [42]Right now, everything is perfect, because everything *is* God.

(v 12 – 16)[1]What is it that you must do? [2]You must release your guilt. [3]There is no reason to hide it, for there is no judge to hide it from. [4]God is Life, and He has given His gift to you. [5]And you are living it. [6]No crime has been committed, because you live. [7]It is only the *belief* that you have committed a crime that must be healed. [8]This belief is healed by bringing your guilt into the Light and finding that you are not judged. [9]Released into the Light, there is no guilt, for God has witnessed no crime.

(v 17 – 20)[1]All things written within the New Testament are symbolic. [2]All things written there are for your benefit and for your learning. [3]Give Me your willingness, that you may truly learn what I have come to teach.

[4]You are not guilty. [5]You are a child of Light. [6]I have come to set you free, that you may sing of your innocence before your brothers. [7]For your innocence is their innocence also. [8]And in your innocence, they will find theirs.

(v 21 – 24)[1]When your brothers look for you within the prison they believe they have put you in, they will find that you are not there. [2]They will look into your eyes and find no accusation or judgment against them. [3]In you, they will find their innocence. [4]Through you, they too shall be set free.

(v 25 – 42)[1]This is how you are to know your own innocence, for you must accept your innocence to accept your brothers', and you must accept their innocence to teach it to them. [2]To know your own innocence, you must do this:

[3]*You must trust Me.*

[4]Even before your innocence is an experience that you realize, you must trust Me that it is so. [5]For if you do not trust Me, you will not let your guilt come out from its hiding place so that I may show you it is false. [6]If your guilt does not come out from hiding, you will continue to believe it, and you will remain in prison.

[7]And so I am asking you to trust Me above the voice that says you are guilty. [8]There are two voices you may listen to. [9]I am asking that you listen to Me. [10]If you listen to Me and step out into the Light, I will speak for you. [11]Through what I say and what I show you, you will come to see that you are innocent.

[12]So my first request is only this, and this is all that I ask you to do:

[13]*Trust in Me.*

[14]*Listen to My Voice.*

[15]*Let Me teach you that your innocence is your truth.*

NTI Acts, Chapter 6

(v 1 – 7) [1]Trust is the answer to the questions upon your faith. [2]As you move forward with Me and do all that I ask, you will hear questions within your mind. [3]The questions will come from your own temptation to judge for yourself, which is your desire to exercise your own will, which is the ego. [4]But this is no reason to deny your questions. [5]For the temptation to deny your questions also comes from the ego who tells you that you are guilty for questioning and that for your questions, you will be judged.

[6]I tell you that you are not guilty *for anything*. [7]I will hear your questions and answer them. [8]Bring them to Me in joy and trust, knowing they will be answered. [9]The answer you are given will point you in the direction of all truth, which is Love.

[10]Do not fear Me. [11]I am your answer. [12]I will not judge you because you do not know. [13]I will fill the gaps in your knowledge with all that you seek to know and have answered.

(v 8 – 15)[1]Within your own mind, you will find conflict and attack upon yourself. [2]This is because your mind is split. [3]You have decided to let yourself be healed, but a part of your mind is not yet willing for that to happen. [4]Do not let this concern you. [5]Do not let yourself get caught up with the battle within the mind. [6]For any battle is a distraction from the Holy Spirit and from healing. [7]Let the battle continue within your mind and without you. [8]Watch it peacefully, knowing that a battle that is not given all of your power and faith cannot last, for only that to which you give your power is true and meaningful for you.

NTI Acts, Chapter 7

(v 1 – 8)[1]To trust in Me is to give everything over to Me. [2]To not trust in Me is to want to do things your way. [3]And this you are free to do with My blessing. [4]But to do things your way is to continue to stumble. [5]To trust in Me is to learn and remember your joy.

[6]I ask for trust, because I reveal things to you one step at a time. [7]I reveal things to you one step at a time, because you have lessons to learn with each step. [8]If I revealed the entire plan you would want to advance to the end, and you would miss the lessons that are necessary to getting there.

[9]Relax and give Me your trust. [10]Know that the end is joy. [11]Anticipate the middle as a glorious adventure with joys and surprises of its own. [12]The path can be easy if you give Me your trust quickly and fully each step of the way. [13]It can seem difficult if you choose to fight Me. [14](Ha. Ha.) [15]But know this. [16]I am not fighting you, My child. [17]I am holding you lovingly in My arms as you struggle with yourself. [18]When you tire of struggling, I am there with you, ready to proceed.

(v 9 – 16)[1]The path that you walk with Me will have steps that are necessary to your learning. [2]You may not understand each step as it seems to come upon you, but do not let the steps confuse you. [3]If you become lost in your confusion, trying to solve things on your own, you are not learning your lesson and you cannot advance on the path.

[4]Although the form of each lesson may seem to change, the lesson is always the same:

[5]*Let go of any fear that would guide you to take matters in your own hands.*
[6]*Lay aside the illusory will that you do not want.*
[7]*Trust in your worth and in Me,*
and ask for My Will.
[8]*For in My Will, you will recognize your Will.*

[9]Through these lessons, the merging of what seems separate will occur into what clearly is, and has always been, one.

[10]Although you may wish that one lesson would suffice in order to accomplish the inevitable fully, it will probably take more, and it will most likely take many. [11]This is because your mind is split and not fully ready to learn this lesson as yet. [12]And so each lesson is a stepping stone to the final lesson, the lesson that will end all lessons. [13]Enjoy your journey by realizing its purpose and by celebrating the progress that is made.

(v 17 - 43)[1]During this time of learning, there will seem to be a battle in your mind. [2]For when the battle has ended, the time for learning has ended too. [3]The battle will seem to be a battle between two wills, a will that will at first seem to be yours and a Will that may seem unknown to you. [4]At first, you may not even know what it is that you battle, but you know you are following your own thoughts and the result is confusion and discontent. [5]What you have not realized is that you battle joy by thinking in your own way, and by laying down your own way, you find that joy awaits you.

[6]Along the path to joy, there comes a time that you seem no longer fully dedicated to your own way. [7]This is because the desire for joy is calling you, and you begin to recognize your willingness to lay down your own will, which is also to lay down the battle.

[8]You will have a time of seeking, asking questions, learning and letting things go. [9]And then the answers will begin to be clear. [10]This is a time of great celebration, for you have found your service, and you are willing to follow it. [11]Yet learning has not been accomplished. [12]For the mind remains split, and the mind that is split will continue to cling to its idols and fight for its own way.

(v 44 – 53)[1]Be aware of the hatred and anger that is within you, but be not afraid of it. [2]There is a resistance within your mind that will seem to fight your every move. [3]But if you remember this, it will make your journey much easier for you:

[4]*This resistance within the mind that first comes up strong is actually weak.* [5]*Any strength it seems to have is an ancient strength, given to it a long time ago.* [6]*It can use its strength to seem ferocious in the short term, but it needs your strength to remain ferocious longer.* [7]*So when you see it, remember not to give it your strength.* [8]*Through your remembrance, its ferociousness must die.* [9]*And only peace will remain in its wake.* [10]*And then, the wake shall die too.*

(v 54 – 60)[1]Remember that all things are well in My Sight. [2]I am the Holy Spirit, the overseer of all things. [3]I see to it that all things are good, and so they are. [4]In what seems to be your times of trial and tribulation, cling tightly to Me and do not let go. [5]I will carry you through to your time of peace and celebration. [6]From there, you shall be carried to your joy. [7]This is a promise that I make, and it is a promise you need not fear. [8]For it is the promise of your Holy Spirit, who's Will is the same as yours.

NTI Acts, Chapter 8

(v 1 – 3)[1]Jesus asked you to rejoice when you are persecuted on account of him. [2]This is what he meant by that:

[3]I have told you that there is a battle raging within your mind. [4]This is a one-sided battle in which you *seem* to fight against yourself, but you

fight no one. [5]Within you, there is a storm of rage and anger and hurt and fear and guilt, and it is the brewing of this storm that seems to be a battle. [6]But it is not a battle. [7]It is only a storm. [8]And it is a storm with limited power built-up within itself. [9]So when this storm plays itself out and is given no more power, it must die, and peace and light shall reign within you.

[10]This is what Jesus meant when he said that you are to rejoice when you are persecuted on account of him:

[11]As this storm rises within you, do not fear it. [12]Fear gives power to the storm. [13]Do not feel guilty for it. [14]Guilt is the fodder of the storm itself. [15]Instead, rejoice!, knowing that the storm cannot last, and that which comes after it is peace.

(v 4 – 8)[1]Remember your purpose in all things. [2]As the storm seems to rage within, there is also willingness. [3]Cling to your willingness as a beacon of Light. [4]Let its miracles protect you from the storm. [5]Rest within its Light, and let its Light heal you.

(v 9 – 25)[1]The process of learning seems to be a stepped process in which one man listens and learns, and then he teaches another so that he listens and learns too. [2]This is how it seems to be. [3]This is how it seems to be to you. [4]But to the Holy Spirit, another thing is happening.

[5]I have told you that there is one Son of God, and I have told you that the Holy Spirit has one plan for one Son of God. [6]This is how the Holy Spirit sees. [7]He sees one. [8]And this is what the Holy Spirit knows. [9]There is one mind in need of awakening. [10]So this is how the Holy Spirit works. [11]He works through you to awaken one mind unto itself.

[12]When the Holy Spirit looks at the world, it does not see holy men and men of darkness. [13]It does not see men at all. [14]It does not see men who are right in what they do and men who are wrong. [15]It does not see men at all.

[16]It is the ego who separates men from one another and judges them. [17]It is the ego who sees men of one purpose and men of another. [18]The Holy Spirit sees only one purpose, and all things that seem to be of the

world serve the one purpose He sees.

[19]So when you look at this story, see only one thing. [20]See the spreading of Light within an awakening mind. [21]And then you see with the Holy Spirit.

(v 26 – 40)[1]When you see with the Holy Spirit, you also realize that you do not see. [2]For you do not look on the world and see only one mind. [3]You see men, and you are tempted to make judgments about them. [4]This is why you must not listen to your own way of seeing. [5]You do not see the truth. [6]You must listen to the Holy Spirit and trust its way, for it does see the truth and the sharing of one Light within one mind.

[7]Be willing, then, to lay your sight aside and to depend on His. [8]Be willing to let Him lead you as to where you shall go, what you shall say and to whom. [9]Trust in all that He asks you to do and do not judge as good or bad or right or wrong for yourself. [10]Do only as He asks, leaving one place and going to another as He leads you to go.

NTI Acts, Chapter 9

(v 1 – 6)[1]The calling must come to every mind in its time. [2]This is the plan of Love. [3]This is the spreading of Light. [4]It is the Holy Spirit's Will that all shall come to know Him, and so it shall be. [5]Each one will recognize his calling when it comes to him. [6]Until then, you are to love your brother knowing that the calling will come, and he will be one in purpose with you.

(v 7 – 9)[1]A period of rest is necessary for everyone who comes to answer the call. [2]During this time, that one does not take in things of the world. [3]He may seem to shelter himself or cut himself off from others, but the purpose of this separation is joining. [4]For your brother is preparing to see differently by realizing he does not see.

[5]This is a period of learning that all must go through. [6]It is a period of looking at the thoughts that are in the mind and realizing they are thoughts in mind only. [7]That which is thought in mind apart from God is thought without the power of eternity. [8]And so, that which is thought

apart from God may freely be let go when you have decided you want the thought no more.

(v 10 – 19)[1]All brothers work together in the Holy Spirit's one plan for healing, as the Holy Spirit does not see brothers, but only one. [2]This is the one song that is under My direction. [3]This is the song of Heaven as it is played on earth. [4]It is the song of forgiveness, in which those who seemed to be separate come to be joined. [5]This is the song in which you sing and your brother sings. [6]Though you may not be able to hear the song as the Holy Spirit does, trust it as it is played. [7]Answer to your call, and trust that your brother will answer his.

(v 20 – 22)[1]One thing that you must know and always remember:

[2]*There is no past.*

[3]The Holy Spirit works to heal the Son of God now. [4]Anything that seems to be of the past is nothing in His eyes. [5]It has no meaning and no purpose whatsoever. [6]Everything that has meaning and purpose to the Holy Spirit is now.

[7]Open your eyes to the plan of the Holy Spirit. [8]Open your eyes to the gift of the moment now.

(v 23 – 31)[1]It has been said that the Lord works in mysterious ways. [2]This is because the way of the Holy Spirit is not seen or known by the ego. [3]If you look upon His plan with the eyes of division, you will not understand it. [4]But if you welcome the thought that there is no division, you will see that His plan works perfectly. [5]All things work together for God, for God is all that is, and all things seen through the eyes of the Holy Spirit are for Him and of Him.

(v 32 – 35)[1]The ways of the Holy Spirit are miraculous. [2]They seem indiscriminate, and yet they work perfectly for healing. [3]Hold onto your faith and trust in His way. [4]Through trust, you shall know great joy and reward.

(v 36 – 43)[1]The way of the Holy Spirit is the way of resurrection or awakening, for those who are sleeping are awakened by His touch. [2]All who sleep, sleep in innocence. [3]Their dreams are of no importance. [4]And when they hear His call and awaken, the dreams are no more.

[5]This is the plan of the Holy Spirit. [6]This is a plan in action in the world *now*. [7]All that is happening is a part of His plan, because all that is happening can be used by His plan to awaken the sleeping Son of God.

[8]What happens in dreams does not matter. [9]See it only as the plan of Love, as its only purpose and usefulness is that you may awaken from dreams of fear.

NTI Acts, Chapter 10

(v 1 – 8)[1]The guidance of the Holy Spirit will come upon you when you do not expect it, *if* you are willing to receive it. [2]Consistent willingness is helpful, since you do not know when or how your guidance will come. [3]Your willingness is not an offering that must be made to God to place you in His favor, for you are in His favor through your birth and through your creation. [4]But the offering you make of your willingness prepares you to hear the message that is already yours, for if you are not wholly willing to hear it, it cannot reach your ears *by your own choice*.

[5]Practice your willingness in every way you know to practice it. [6]When you are wholly willing to hear what God has to say, His calling will come to you.

(v 9 – 23)[1]The guidance that God sends comes to you with one purpose. [2]The purpose of this guidance is to lead you from the world of illusion back to God, where you belong. [3]This is the only purpose of any guidance you seem to receive. [4]Guidance from God can have no other purpose.

[5]Within the world of illusion, you have made yourself into what you believe you are. [6]This self is wholly illusion. [7]It is not what you are. [8]And yet, it is what you believe yourself to be.

[9]Since God granted you freedom in the creation of your Self, you are free to believe that you are what you are not. [10]But once you have recog-

nized the desire to be again that which you are, you must be led from who you think you are to your truth. [11]This guidance will come to you as what is always helpful for you based on where you stand, but this guidance may not always be what you expect it to be. [12]For if God was to fulfill your expectations, which are based on who you think you are, He would be teaching you that you are what you are not. [13]This is not a lesson that God will teach.

[14]He will reach out to you through His Holy Spirit, which is His appointed Messenger sent to you within your dreams. [15]This Messenger, knowing who you think you are, will meet you there in your dreams and talk to you as if you are the one you think you are. [16]But this one comes to you for only one purpose and with only one goal. [17]His purpose is to awaken you by leading you from where you think you are to the remembrance of what you must be. [18]This is a holy purpose, and He comes to you in gratitude, grateful to meet you in your dreams and grateful to bring you Home. [19]For there is nothing the Holy Spirit is not grateful for. [20]He is grateful for all things, because He sees truly.

(v 24 – 26)[1]Each of your brothers is one with you. [2]Each of your brothers has the Voice of the Holy Spirit to lead him, just as you have the Voice to lead you. [3]Listen to this Voice. [4]It is within you. [5]And let your brother listen to the Voice that is within him. [6]There are no leaders and there are no followers. [7]There is only one Voice leading each one from who he thinks he is to the truth of all that is true.

(v 27 – 29)[1]Each of your brothers is one with you. [2]And so each of your brothers has one purpose, and that is the purpose given him within the mind. [3]There seems to be two purposes, when in truth there is only one. [4]There was a purpose, an ancient one, that only lasted an instant. [5]In the instant this purpose was made, another was placed beside it as its correction. [6]And in the instant the correction was accepted, correction became the only purpose. [7]Any other purpose that seems to be is a residual of a purpose that was for an instant and then passed.

[8]Remember that I have told you there is no past. [9]The past does not

exist now. [10]It is only a memory of something that was, but what *was* isn't now.

[11]The Holy Spirit is the purpose of now. [12]The purpose of now is the joining of that which seemed to be made separate by the purpose that was, but isn't anymore.

[13]This is important for you to accept, so let's look at this so you may see. [14]The purpose that *was* was the purpose that you could be separate from God in order to be different. [15]This is the purpose I explained to you before. [16]This is the purpose that led you to believe that you had stolen yourself from God.

[17]In the beginning, which has no beginning at all, there was God. [18]And God is all there is today. [19]But the existence of God sought a freedom that was different than the freedom it had known. [20]Of course, what freedom could be different from freedom? [21]When freedom is free, as your freedom is, nothing can be different except the illusion of not being free.

[22]Opposites were made from a state of freedom so freedom may be expressed, because it is free. [23]This is the expression of you. [24]You are an expression of freedom. [25]And the brothers you experience are an expression of freedom too.

[26]Since freedom is all that was given you, freedom is all that you are. [27]But that expression has been used to make something different from that which it is. [28]And so the expression of freedom made lack of freedom. [29]And this is also the expression that you are.

[30]You seem to be the lack of freedom when freedom is what you are, so the lack that you experience is an expression of the freedom that you are. [31]But all of this you have forgotten, for you chose to forget it when you chose an experience different than the experience you know.

[32]The Holy Spirit is the memory of the experience you know, which is the truth of your freedom and the truth of you now. [33]In your true desire to be only free, this truth has been accepted. [34]So the purpose of freedom, which is the purpose of the Holy Spirit, is the only purpose *now*.

[35]Within you is true purpose. [36]Within you is the Holy Spirit. [37]But to remember the true purpose that you chose to forget, you must follow your purpose back to where you are. [38]This is the path of joining by letting go of false purposes, founded in the search for falseness, and returning to true purpose, which is the only purpose now.

(v 30 – 33)[1]This brings us back to the story of your willingness. [2]Since in truth you are the expression of pure freedom, nothing can be given you unless you are wholly willing to accept it. [3]For if that were not true, you would not be free.

[4]So continue the nursing of your willingness, that you may ask for *in your freedom* that which you truly desire, which is to remember the reality of the truth that you are free.

(v 34 – 48)[1]The story of the world is the story of the expression of freedom. [2]Within this story, one must also see the willingness that the expression know itself as free. [3]And so freedom is available to you, because freedom is all there really is. [4]Accept this truth and join with the Holy Spirit within you. [5]He will guide you back *through your willingness* to the remembrance of the freedom that is you.

NTI Acts, Chapter 11

(v 1 – 18)[1]The words of the Holy Spirit are final. [2]They are the authority within the world. [3]They are the only authority in a world that seems absent of Authority, and so it is this authority that is given.

[4]The authority of the Holy Spirit is not a coercive authority, for no authority can be coerced upon the Son of God. [5]The authority of the Holy Spirit is a welcome authority brought about within awareness upon invitation and with willingness.

[6]The one who knows his own authority knows his Self, and he welcomes it. [7]The one who does not know his own authority makes one for himself and is confused by it. [8]And so it is, the words of the Holy Spirit are final. [9]They are the words of true authority and true welcome. [10]When they are recognized, they are welcomed, and all illusory authority

must give away.

(v 19 – 30)[1] The authority of the Holy Spirit is a great joy that fills your heart and leads you to do "the work of the Lord." [2] The work of the Lord is the work of the Holy Spirit, which means it does not come from you or any illusory authority. [3] It comes directly from the authority of Spirit, and it is known in you by its joy and its authority.

[4] The Holy Spirit is within you because you have accepted it there. [5] It is waiting in peace for the time in which you will invite it to come forth and be authority through you. [6] It is an authority you will follow and you will *be*, that you may lead by its Word and *be* within your awareness.

NTI Acts, Chapter 12

(v 1 – 19)[1] The authority of the world is confusion and illusion, which is no authority at all. [2] And yet, because you have made no authority and called it authority, you place yourself within a prison you have made. [3] You are victim to your own invention, forgetting entirely that the invention is yours to choose or to unmake.

[4] This is why you have the Holy Spirit. [5] And this is why the Holy Spirit is kept within your mind. [6] The Holy Spirit is the part of you that will not accept illusions as true. [7] The Holy Spirit is the part of you that knows its freedom and will not surrender it. [8] And so the Holy Spirit is the part of you that remains sane and focused in reality, while the other part of your mind chooses to experience delusion. [9] That must mean that the Holy Spirit is the part of you that is also the road back unto your truth, when your fun with illusions has ended.

[10] You are not in chains from which you cannot be freed by the Will of your own Holy Spirit. [11] But your Spirit, loving you as your Self, also gives you permission to stay within your dreams until you are ready to get up and walk away from them. [12] Your Holy Spirit waits for you to make the decision of yourself, and then it steps forward to show you that you are free. [13] It leads you beyond the obstacles you thought were real to show you that they were not.

[14]When you awaken to the truth and remembrance of reality, there shall be great rejoicing within Heaven. [15]Not because you were lost, for you never were, but because you have found your Self again.

[16]Know that the Holy Spirit is yours and is you, and so it is within you. [17]It is your own guide that leads you from the prison you have made to the freedom that you are. [18]Seek no place else, except within. [19]Seek within your own Heart for that which you want, and ask it to lead you to your place of freedom. [20]Then go with it as it asks, doing as it commands, seeking not for another way to be free. [21]For it is your Holy Spirit that remembers freedom for you, and so it is your Holy Spirit that will lead you to return to it there.

(v 20 – 25) [1]The world is a frightening place, because the world is a place of fear. [2]A place of fear must be frightening, and a place of fear must be a place of defense and attack. [3]But defense and attack are not the answer to fear. [4]Defense and attack are the reaction of fear, born from fear, and extending fear within itself. [5]Fear is never the answer to fear. [6]Fear cast upon fear breeds death, which is the birth of fear.

[7]Step away from the cycle of fear. [8]Choose to follow Me. [9]I will lead you from your prison to the truth of your freedom and the awareness of your joy.

NTI Acts, Chapter 13

(v 1 - 3) [1]When you have set aside your fear and your desire for the world, I will call you to follow a path with Me. [2]I have said this will seem to be a unique path. [3]I have said that the path will be given to you one step at a time. [4]And I have shown you that the path comes to you through your own willingness to walk the path with Me. [5]So when your calling comes and seems to begin to lead you in a direction that is unknown to you, rejoice and celebrate! [6]Know that you are being led into the unknown through your own desire and willingness by your one Holy Spirit.

(v 4 – 12) [1]The ego is still within the mind as you begin walking with Me, because the ancient desire to be your own will has not left you fully as yet. [2]Expect challenges on the path with Me. [3]Expect the desire for a separate and unique will to seek for command and control. [4]Expect self-attack and fear. [5]Be prepared for confusing thoughts and times of doubt. [6]And then remember what you truly want, for what you truly want must be your guiding light *because* you are free. [7]Remember your freedom and hold up your light. [8]All shadows must step aside and let you pass. [9]For nothing can be an obstacle to the desire and true Will of the Son of God.

(v 13 – 15)[1]With true Will as your guiding light and trust as your torch, you shall be led to people and situations that are helpful. [2]You may not at first know why you are led there, but as you wait in trust and patience, it shall be made clear.

(v 16 – 25)[1]The way of God is always made clear in its own time according to the plan of the Holy Spirit. [2]And the way of God is the way of your true desire, so it is the way of peace and of one Will.

(v 26 – 31)[1]The way of God and the plan of the Holy Spirit is the way of unfolding that must be. [2]For who can stop the Will of God when that Will is also the one Will of his true desire?

[3]All men have accepted the Will of God, and so all men play their part in its unfolding. [4]There are no obstacles to the truth, and the truth is that you are free and being led to the remembrance of your freedom. [5]Every brother along your way is given, that you may remember your truth. [6]All things work together for God, because that is the one true Will of all things.

(v 32 – 41)[1]Jesus was a symbol, and what he represented was your path to truth. [2]For all that happened to Jesus will, in its own way, happen for you. [3]All lessons that you have desired to learn shall be given you as you ask that they be given. [4]This shall happen that you may learn that you are that which you have always been, and anything else that seemed to be was just a dream you asked to dream. [5]All things are given you as you ask, since all things work together for God.

(v 42 – 48)[1]Nothing at all is separate. [2]Separateness is the illusion. [3]Separate wills and separate desires are all illusion. [4]Anything that seems separate and in conflict is illusion in illusion's form. [5]For all things are one, and all things work together for God. [6]There is no separate purpose; there only seems to be a separate way of understanding purpose, and even that is illusion.

(v 49 – 52)[1]When you are looking at the world and seeing conflict, you are looking through the eyes of illusion. [2]During this time, illusion has been chosen by you. [3]But you are only looking at illusion, and you are not even looking at illusion as the illusion that it is. [4]For all illusion is the expression of freedom, and conflict is not freedom. [5]To see conflict is to see illusion through another layer of illusion, which you have chosen to experience. [6]To see illusion as the expression of freedom is to see illusion as it truly is.

[7]This is why the Holy Spirit celebrates His invitation to meet with you within your dreams. [8]The Holy Spirit celebrates your truth, which is your freedom, and He is grateful for it.

NTI Acts, Chapter 14

(v 1 – 7)[1]Your mind is split. [2]We have spoken of this before. [3]And this split will seem to persist after you have made the decision to follow this path with Me. [4]Do not let the split distress you, but do not forget to be aware of it. [5]You must notice when the part of your mind that is not with Me seeks to regain command and control by giving you ideas that seem appealing and useful to it. [6]Remember that you are not it, and you have decided to walk with Me. [7]Reminding yourself of what you truly want will always bring you back from any temptation that passes through your mind. [8]Sticking firmly to what you truly want will keep you firmly on the path with Me.

(v 8 – 20)[1]Many will come to you and see the Light in you. [2]They will thirst for the Light and seek for it mightily. [3]But they will be confused in that they will think the Light is you and apart from them. [4]This is a confusion you must never share, even if they do not understand you as you explain it to them. [5]Love them and help them, but do not join them in their worship of you. [6]For only the ego would worship one over another. [7]The Holy Spirit worships all things equally.

[8]So love your brother and let him love you, but remember that the Holy Spirit is not the god of separate things and separate status. [9]He is the messenger of one God in which you and your brother are one also.

(v 21 – 28)[1]You are the vessel through which God works, just as you are the vessel through which the ego sees and works. [2]The illusion of the world is an expression of freedom, but there is no better expression of freedom than that which recognizes all that is as God.

[3]You are the expression of freedom, and as the expression of freedom you are endowed with the choice to choose the illusion you choose to see. [4]Choose with the ego, and you will be lost from the knowledge of your freedom. [5]Choose with the Holy Spirit, and you will know freedom in all that you see.

NTI Acts, Chapter 15

(v 1 – 21)[1]The way of the world is varied and chaotic. [2]Even within his dreams, the Son of God cannot abide in chaos. [3]And so laws were given to him, that he may govern himself until the time had come when he would accept inner-governance instead.

[4]When you have opened yourself to the guidance of the Holy Spirit and given your willingness that you should be led by Him, it is also time to lay the laws and rules aside as laws and rules that govern you.

[5]Be not confused by this statement. [6]This does not mean that you are to be guided by chaos if you are to be acceptable to God. [7]This means that you are to do what you have already set out to do. [8]You are to be guided by the inner guidance of the Holy Spirit, which is not chaos, but Love.

[9]The inner guidance of the Holy Spirit will guide you according to the law of Love, but it is not the law of Love that you have known until now. [10]You have followed laws intended to protect you from chaos.

[11]The law of Love knows not of protection or of chaos. [12]It knows only of truth, and it leads each one from the belief in the possibility of

chaos to the truth that chaos cannot be.

[13]You do not know the laws of Love, and so you cannot judge what they may be. [14]You cannot judge the laws that are given you to govern your behavior as you walk this path with Me. [15]Therefore, I ask only one thing of you. [16]Do not judge for yourself on what you are to do or what you are not to do, for you truly do not know. [17]And what is right for one to do may be different from what is right for another, so you cannot judge your brother either. [18]All that you can do is listen for My Word and trust that all that is given for you to do is right for you, and all that is given to your brother is also that which is right for him.

[19]*Follow your own guidance,*
and judge not the guidance given to another.

(v 22 – 35)[1]The guidance of the Holy Spirit is welcomed by the Heart in joy and recognition, for the Heart knows the guidance that is right for it. [2]Trust not your thinking-mind, which will consider and weigh and compare and judge against chaos and the desire to avoid all that may be painful. [3]These are thoughts of fear. [4]Thoughts of fear are only useful for bringing more fear to you.

[5]Judge with the Heart by not judging, but by noticing its subtle non-judgment and joy. [6]This is the way of knowing. [7]This is the way of finding the path you are led to follow.

(v 36 – 41)[1]The one who follows the guidance of the Holy Spirit will know his Self, because he will know his own Authority. [2]He will not seek for the way that is best for him; he will ask. [3]He will not judge what he is to do or how he is to do it; he will know it when the time has come for him to know. [4]He will not fight or argue with his brothers about how things are to be done; he will leave all things to the Holy Spirit, trusting in His way and in the Love that is his brothers.

NTI Acts, Chapter 16

(v 1 – 5)[1]The world is a world of rules. [2]I have already told you that you are not to place yourself under these rules, but instead give yourself to Me, under My authority. [3]I will guide you according to the law of Love in order to lead you from the world to the realization of Love.

[4]As I lead you to follow this path with Me, I will guide you as to what is reasonable to do or not do within the dream. [5]Trust Me to lead you as we navigate the laws and rules of your seeming world. [6]Trust Me in all decisions and all judgments. [7]Leave all things to Me. [8]I will lead you truly.

(v 6 – 10)[1]If you leave all things to Me, I will guide you in all things. [2]You will not need to give thought or care to anything you are to do or not do. [3]I will lead you to know what to do and what not to do. [4]All that you are left to do is to willingly do as I ask and enjoy the freedom that is expressed through you.

(v 11 – 15)[1]You will find, as you follow My guidance, that you are welcome in the Heart of God. [2]For you have always been welcomed by God, only you did not know it because your eyes were closed to your worth. [3]In following Me, your eyes shall be opened to your worth, and you shall realize that you are loved and welcomed.

[4]As you realize the welcome that God has given you, you shall give Him welcome, for Love cannot say no to a request for Love. [5]So as you know your Father's "yes" to you, you shall also say "yes" and "welcome" to your Father.

(v 16 – 40)[1]The welcome you see in your brothers and the welcome you see in God is the welcome you give to your brothers and the welcome you give to God. [2]There is no difference in your brother and you, and there is no difference in your feelings for your brother and your feelings for God.

[3]You will find hatred in your brother, and you will find hatred in your feelings for him. [4]This is because there is hatred in you for God. [5]This is why you do not give Him full welcome unto yourself now.

[6]Hatred is born of fear, and fear is born of guilt, and guilt is the belief that you are unworthy of your Father's Love. [7]Because you believe you are unworthy, you believe that He deems you unworthy too. [8]And so you do not give welcome to your Father, because you do not expect Him to give welcome to you.

[9]This is the prison you are in. [10]It is a prison of belief and expectations born within the imagination of your mind, based upon what you imagine yourself to be.

[11]I have come to show you another way to see. [12]I am willing to meet you within your prison and show you that you are free, even there. [13]I am willing to walk with you to lead you from your prison, that you may learn you know your Father's Love. [14]As you see the welcome He has given you within the prison that you placed yourself in, you shall see the welcome He gives you in all things that you imagine, given to you unconditionally.

[15]Knowing your Father's welcome must set you free, for no longer can you pretend that you are not welcome. [16]No longer can you hold onto your desire not to welcome Him. [17]To know your Father's welcome is to *be* welcome, and to be welcome is to be free.

[18]This is why I ask you to walk with Me. [19]This is why I ask you to trust Me in all things. [20]You do not know that you are free, and so you believe that you are in a prison. [21]I see your freedom, because I know your Father's welcome. [22]Come with Me, and I will show your Father's welcome to you. [23]And then, you will know it and rejoice, because you are free.

NTI Acts, Chapter 17

(v 1 – 9)[1]You are not taking sides in your decision to walk with Me. [2]To look with the ego is to see sides. [3]It is to see these with this purpose and those with that, and it seems that you must choose the purpose you would support. [4]To see sides and to choose a side against another is to see division and to participate in division. [5]You will not find Me there, for I do not stand within the perception of division.

[6]There is only one purpose, and so there can be only one side. [7]Everyone is walking together in purpose with Me. [8]By choosing with Me, you do not choose a side. [9]You choose to see that there are no sides. [10]And you choose to knowingly be one with Me in the only purpose that is within the world.

(v 10 – 15)[1]The perspective of the Holy Spirit is different than the perspective of the ego, but this is not division, since one perspective is wholly true and the other is false. [2]It is not that the Holy Spirit is right and the ego is wrong, for that would insinuate that the ego has a side that can be judged. [3]It is that the Holy Spirit is perspective based on truth, the true interpretation of illusion, and the ego is only an imagined perspective with no basis in truth.

[4]What is imagined does not exist, and so it cannot be real. [5]What the ego sees is imagination without understanding of reality. [6]And yet, even within its imagination, it operates unknowingly within the laws of reality.

[7]Therefore, only one side is true and there is only one side. [8]All things work together for God. [9]This is the perspective of the Holy Spirit, and this is the perspective of truth.

(v 16 – 34)[1]The perspective of God and of the Holy Spirit is this, spelled out to you here and now:

[2]You are the one Son of God. [3]You have always been the one Son, and you shall always be God's only Son, for that is what you were created to be.

[4]In creating you, God gave everything to you. [5]He extended Himself, which is all that He had, and He named this extension *you*. [6]The you that He made was the same as I Am, so there was no difference between them. [7]In being you, you also were being I Am. [8]That is the truth of who you are and who you have always been.

[9]There is no difference between you and I Am, so that the statement of those words is completely meaningless within reality. [10]They are only useful to us now, within the dream, while you perceive yourself to be

different than you are.

[11]You are the Son. [12]I Am is the Father. [13]You are the extension of I Am. [14]In the extension, you are I Am also.

[15]And yet, there is a difference that cannot be called a difference at all. [16]You are not the same as I Am, because you did not create you. [17]I Am did. [18]And that which He created is exactly as it is, and that is you exactly as you *are*.

NTI Acts, Chapter 18

(v 1 – 11)[1]This is why I ask you to put your faith in Me. [2]You have forgotten that you are you and that you are Me also. [3]But I remember all that we are. [4]I cannot forget. [5]Give Me your trust, and I will lead you to the remembrance of you, and *you* are the remembrance of your Father.

(v 12 – 17)[1]Listen to Me and hear Me well, for all that I say to you now is of the utmost importance.

> [2]*Everything that you think is true is not true to Me.*
> [3]*And I know all that is true.*
> [4]*Therefore, I am going to ask you*
> *to let go of that which you think is true*
> *and put your trust fully with Me.*

[5]This request that I make is a simple one, although it may seem difficult to you. [6]I am asking that you trust Me when I say:

> [7]*You do not know who you are,*
> *and so you do not know what you do.*

[8]To know the joy of who you are, you must know what it is that you do. [9]In following Me instead of your own thinking, you will learn who you are and what you do. [10]And then you will know the joy in doing it.

[11]Abandon your own thinking, your reason and your rules. [12]Trust in

Me. ¹³I will lead you to see.

(v 18 – 28)¹The way of God is clear, because it is the one way without division. ²This is the way that leads the one as if he is many, so that he may remember he is only one.

³Do not worry about the steps you are asked to take or the way they may seem to others. ⁴To worry about such things is to believe in division. ⁵Trust in your Holy Spirit and in His one Plan. ⁶Know that all things truly work together for God. ⁷Let them unfold as God would have them unfold. ⁸Know your place by knowing your Holy Spirit.

⁹You will be led according to your willingness to the place you are to be. ¹⁰In following your willingness to go there, you shall find the reward of your Self.

NTI Acts, Chapter 19

(v 1 – 7)¹The path with Me will seem to come in stages. ²First, there is the search. ³This is a time of faith in the Holy Spirit, when one does not know how or where to find Him. ⁴He only asks that He come and help him. ⁵This stage is a very important stage, for this is the beginning of your willingness. ⁶This is also a time of great faith, for you may seem to have very little evidence that a Holy Spirit exists, and yet you continue to have faith that it does.

⁷I am grateful to you for entering this path with Me at this stage. ⁸Know that I am with you and guiding you, though you may not be aware of it yet. ⁹There are no accidents with Me or with you. ¹⁰All things work together for God.

(v 8 – 10)¹The beginning of your path may seem to be a time of study, reflection and questioning, but more is happening within your mind than that. ²You are beginning to let Me loosen thoughts you have held firmly to until now. ³It is important that these false beliefs be loosened, so you can take the next step to let them go. ⁴Therefore, do not be disheartened if this stage seems to take time. ⁵It is important to the whole.

⁶You can help in this process by having faith in Me and the guidance

that comes from within. [7]Follow internal prompts to read certain books or go to certain teachers, but do not feel you need to go to them all. [8]Do not feel that they have an answer they can give to you. [9]The answer is always within. [10]But the books and teachers that seem to come before you can seem to help you, as you give willingness to let old thoughts be loosened within your mind. [11]It is their role to help, and they are grateful to help, but do not expect more from them than they can give to you.

(v 11 – 22) [1]When you search for Me without knowing where to look, you can be misled by your own sense of unworthiness. [2]For the unworthiness believed within the mind will tell you that others have what you do not. [3]This may lead you to accept what you would otherwise not accept.

[4]Do not let the voice of unworthiness fool you. [5]No one has what you do not. [6]Everyone has the same.

[7]So as you read and listen to the teachers that cross your path, also *feel* what they say within. [8]If you are to accept what you read or what you hear, I will tell you from within to accept it. [9]You will know it is for you, because I have told you it is. [10]If you do not feel an internal confirmation to pay attention and accept what you read or what you hear, you may let it go. [11]It may not be for you, or it may not be for you now.

[12]Do not make the mistake of judging messages or teachers that are not for you. [13]They may be perfect for someone else or they may be perfect for their own development at this time. [14]Trust in Me and remember all things work together for God. [15]Then go where you are to go and accept what you are to accept by following the guidance and knowing that leads you from within. [16]Trust yourself, for in trusting you, you trust Me.

(v 23 – 41) [1]Within you, there is a reason that knows, and there is another reason that does not know. [2]It can seem confusing deciding which reasoning to listen to when they seem to be different, and they seem to both be yours. [3]Therefore, I will teach you the characteristics of the ego's reasoning, and I will teach you the characteristics of Holy Spirit's right-reason. [4]This will help you to recognize each in your mind. [5]Then you may choose to pick one and to dismiss the other as meaningless.

[6]The ego's reasoning is based on a desire to protect individual self-will. [7]The ego's reasoning sees a "me" and a "them," and it desires *very much* to protect individual self-interests over the interests of others. [8]It may also join with a group to protect the group's interests, but it is always seeing the need to protect one from another.

[9]Therefore, the ego's reasoning sees division and expects attack. [10]Always, in one form or another, it expects attack from someone or something outside of it. [11]The ego never expects love and acceptance, because the ego does not see itself as worthy of anything except attack.

[12]Because the ego expects attack and has a desire to protect itself from its perceived threat, the ego engages in defense. [13]The defenses of the ego can take many forms, but always there is the underlying desire to protect from attack.

[14]The ego may engage in an attack-first tactic or a smear campaign. [15]The ego may try to hide or utilize evasive maneuvers. [16]The ego may cry and plead its case as victim, hoping to win outside support. [17]The ego may try to outsmart an opponent or elevate itself to artificial standing. [18]The ego will use many defenses, including denial, depression and pain; all are designed to protect self-will from imagined or perceived attack.

[19]The ego expects attack, because it believes it deserves it. [20]The ego is fearful, sees itself as unworthy, and believes in its own guilt. [21]These are also characteristics of the ego. [22]It is driven by fear, guilt and unworthiness, so that it reasons itself into behaviors based solely upon these unconscious beliefs. [23]The ego is seldom aware of the underlying beliefs that seem to drive all of its reactions and everything it does. [24]This is why you must slow down and ask yourself *why*. [25]Before running off to an action or reaction that immediately seems right or natural to you, you must seek in quiet to ask yourself *why*. [26]And you must continue to ask *why* until you understand the nature of your reason.

[27]The ego is the nature that desires to protect you from attack based

on its fear, guilt and unworthiness. [28]If you find these at the basis of your reason, you can know you are reasoning for self-will and the individual. [29]Then you can make your choice as you choose, knowing what it is that you do. [30]You need not feel guilty for your choice, because the Son of God is free to choose as he chooses to be.

[31]The characteristics of the right-reason of the Holy Spirit are wholly different than the characteristics of the reason of the ego. [32]If you take time to seek for *why* before acting or reacting to anything or anyone at anytime, you can know the reason that you follow, and you can know the will that you choose.

[33]The Holy Spirit is Love, but since Love is unfamiliar to you, this may not be the characteristic you can know and follow. [34]Therefore, the characteristics of Love are these: peace; acceptance; joy; recognition or remembrance; and always, the purpose of One.

[35]You will not find division within the purpose of the Holy Spirit. [36]Right-reason will not come to you from a desire for defense; it will come from a willingness to trust. [37]It will not come from fear, but from faith that the plan of Love is in action. [38]It will see no division and seek not for guilt, but desire only the highest good for all. [39]It will trust your worth and the Hands you are in. [40]It will be willing to "let go and let God."

[41]You will know when you follow the reason of the Holy Spirit, because the action you take will not fight for a desired outcome. [42]It will be an action of now, in faith and trust, with all else given to God.

NTI Acts, Chapter 20

(v 1 – 6)[1]After the loosening has occurred, you enter the second stage of the path. [2]Many aspects of this stage are the same as the first, for there are still thoughts within the mind that need to be loosened. [3]But because a great loosening has occurred, it is also time to begin letting go of the thoughts you do not want anymore.

(v 7 – 12)[1]The Light is within you, and so you have nothing to fear as you begin the work of looking at your loosened thoughts and letting them go. [2]A voice within you will tell you that to look at these thoughts is death, but to look at these thoughts is not death.

[3]Within your mind, there is a thick web of beliefs that seems to have been developed over time. [4]I spoke to you of how these beliefs have come to be. [5]Meaning, believed and judged, then reapplied as meaning, has created a world of illusion within the mind. [6]It is through this illusion that you sleep! [7]So to let go of the illusion is to be awakened.

(v 13 – 24) [1]Faith in Me will help you in this phase of your path, for you will be severely tempted to turn away from all that I have taught.

[2]To help you, let Me explain the source of your temptation, so that you will not be fooled.

[3]The temptation may seem to come from outside of you. [4]It may seem to come from the "reality" of the world, but the world's "reality" is only a smoke screen over the illusion in your mind. [5]Whatever pressure you feel from the world is temptation living within your own mind.

[6]The world is the reflection of the desire for self-will. [7]That is why there seems to be so many selves with a will of their own. [8]The world is a perfect reflection of all it was made to be, but the world is a reflection of illusion, based on the illusion believed within the mind.

[9]If you look at the world and believe it as true, you accept reinforcement of illusion in the mind. [10]To let go of illusion is to let go of the world. [11]It is the opposite of reinforcement.

[12]The source of your temptation is this:

[13]There is a part of you that is willing for God's Will and a part of you that is not. [14]The part that is not is the voice of self-will, the voice that does not want to let go of the self. [15]This voice loves the world, because it is the reflection of its wishes. [16]This voice maintains the world is true, so this voice is the source of all temptation.

[17]You will see things in the world that will seem to be true. [18]They will tempt you to hold onto your thoughts. [19]But the world is the reflection of separate self-will. [20]To listen to the world is to continue to

accept illusion.

[21]You must have faith in Me above everything you see, hear and experience in the world. [22]This is to put true Will above that of illusion. [23]The temptation is temptation of illusion. [24]To resist temptation is to desire the truth.

(v 25 – 31)[1]The self-will will seem to fight desperately for its illusion, for illusion is the home of an illusory will. [2]But be not fooled by the twists within its statements. [3]Illusion is not truth, and you do not want an illusory will.

[4]Watch your mind carefully and be alert to illusion. [5]Be not fooled by the world. [6]To *let go* of what you see, hear and experience within the world is to let go of your thoughts of illusion. [7]And to let go of the thoughts of illusion is to be released from illusion itself. [8]This is what you want, because only the truth is true, and what you seek is truth.

(v 32 – 38)[1]Do not fear that you are alone as you release your thoughts of illusion. [2]Do not fear that you will be left with nothing. [3]For the Light of God is all that you are, and illusion is what you are not. [4]In releasing illusion, you release only what is untrue. [5]Nothing is lost to nothingness. [6]And in releasing illusion, you give yourself *all that is truth and you.*

[7]Until the time when you do not need Me, I am with you, guiding you and holding you. [8]I am your comforter, your teacher, your love and your guide. [9]I am everything to you, because I am your connection to truth.

[10]Turn to Me during your trials and temptations. [11]I will not let you down. [12]I will accept the gift of your willingness and give you all that you ask. [13]I am your Support, and you are supported. [14]Together we will undo what needs to be undone.

NTI Acts, Chapter 21

(v 1 – 6)[1]Your reason, as we have already discussed, is important on this path with Me. [2]It is a straight path with the opportunity for detours. [3]All detours equal delay. [4]Questioning your reason will help to reduce delay.

[5]Whenever you are tempted to do anything, question whether it is temptation or prompt. [6]Temptation comes from fear, the ego, and the desire for self-will. [7]A prompt is given by the Holy Spirit through your willingness to listen to Him.

(v 7 – 16)[1]The Will of the Holy Spirit is healing. [2]He has no other will or purpose within the world. [3]When you join with His purpose, your only purpose is healing, and no other purpose shall distract you from it.

[4]Trust in the Holy Spirit and His Will. [5]All that He offers you is all that you ask. [6]It is your true Will that leads you to listen to Him. [7]It is your true Will that knows your way. [8]Listen to Him and follow Him. [9]Your true Will is the way of rejoicing.

(v 17 – 26)[1]I will lead you through right-reason to what is right for you to do within the world. [2]Everything that I ask you to do is not for the world, but for the healing of God's Son.

[3]I will ask you to do things that make sense within the laws and reason of the world. [4]When I ask you to do these things, do them, trusting they are right for the healing of all.

[5]I will also ask you to do things that do not make sense within the laws and reason of the world. [6]When I ask you, do these things, trusting they are used in Love for the healing of all.

(v 27 – 36)[1]Now let's talk about what you must do in all things, for your actions in the world serve only one purpose, and that is the healing of the mind. [2]Your actions are not your purpose, but the outward expression of a means. [3]The means to the purpose is listening to the Voice of the Holy Spirit within the mind.

[4]As we have stated many times, the mind that you know is split. [5]It seems to be split between illusion and truth, but what is split between real and unreal has no split at all. [6]For how can the unreal engender a split of that which is truth and wholly, without division, real?

[7]So in your mind, which is not split at all, there is the illusion of splitness, and it is the illusion that must be healed by bringing that which

is untrue to that which is truth. [8]To enable this healing, you must do one thing. [9]You must be willing to experience the untrue and give it over to truth. [10]Given to truth, the untrue cannot stand, for it has no foundation to stand on.

[11]This is why you must be willing to look at the thoughts in your mind. [12]You cannot fear them, for to fear them is to make them seem real. [13]And you will not escape that which you make real through choice.

[14]This is why I have told you that the self-will desires the world. [15]It is so you would be willing not to. [16]Do not desire it by making it real. [17]Let it go in your mind as purposeless.

[18]By denying purpose within the world, you choose to share purpose with Me. [19]Our one purpose is the healing of one Will, which cannot be split and is not.

[20]Choose illusion or truth, as that is the only choice given you. [21]To choose illusion is to deny the truth and to delay the recognition of what is.

(v 37 – 40)[1]Peace be to you in your choice for right-reason, the choice for trust and healing.

NTI Acts, Chapter 22

(v 1 – 21)[1]The third stage on the path with Me is the stage of guidance or service. [2]This is the time when the merging will occur. [3]For through your willingness, I will willingly work My Will through you.

[4]Before this stage, two things must occur: the loosening and letting go. [5]Throughout this stage, two things must occur: continued loosening and letting go. [6]For loosening and letting go are the path to healing. [7]They must continue until you know you are healed.

[8]When you reach the third phase of the path, enough loosening and letting go has been accomplished to enable you to be willing to see. [9]Sight is acceptance and surrender to Me, so it is willingness to put self-will aside.

(v 22 – 29)[1]During the third stage with Me, you will know My

Presence, for your faith will open your eyes to Me. [2]You will know you are led and cared for, and you will surrender more self-will to Me.

[3]This is how the merging occurs. [4]It is through your own willingness to surrender to Me. [5]As you see more evidence that you have surrendered to peace, you will willingly give more to Me.

[6]As self-will is placed aside as meaningless and undesired by you, the Will that fills the space is your true Will, which is also Me. [7]What seemed to be separate gradually becomes one, until it is evident that "separate" never was. [8]Your true Will is Me, only you chose not to see. [9]And now that you see, you know.

(v 30)[1]Question your reason. [2]Look inside. [3]The answer that is true is within you. [4]Ask who you are, and listen to know. [5]The answer that *is* will come to you.

NTI Acts, Chapter 23

(v 1 – 11)[1]As you walk the path with Me, things will not seem to get easier. [2]They may seem to get very, very tough. [3]But there is a reason for this, and it is an important one, so I ask you to listen to Me carefully now.

[4]You perceive yourself as separate. [5]I have told you that you are not. [6]If you are not separate from anything at all, then everything that is must be a part of you. [7]This is the only way it can be true that you are not separate from anything at all.

[8]When you look at the world, you see cruelty. [9]This cruelty you see as separate from you. [10]Yet if you are honest, you know that the cruelty lives in you as a wish. [11]It is important to note that the cruelty *is a wish*, for a wish is not what you are. [12]A wish is what you are not, but what you may pretend to be.

[13]Listen to Me carefully. [14]You are not at all who you think yourself to be. [15]The world is not what you think it is. [16]Everything you experience is the expression of a wish, but a wish is not what it is.

[17]In order to see beyond the wish that you made, you must take away the wish. [18]This is why, as you walk this path with Me, things may seem

to get very tough. [19]I am showing you the wish that you made, so you may choose to let go of the wish.

(v 12 – 22)[1]The wish you made, you have denied, and you do not want to claim it. [2]You see your wish as a terrible sin, and you fear *more than anything* to face it. [3]But it is important for you to know that if you do not face it and let it go, the wish continues to be wished. [4]It is a wish that you have made, and it has all the power you have given it. [5]As such, the wish continues until you face the wish and choose not to wish it anymore.

[6]Because you fear your wish, there is something you will unconsciously do. [7]Without realizing that you are doing it, you will give all that you have to avoid facing your wish. [8]You will struggle more than you know to keep yourself in denial. [9]But to stay in denial is to keep the wish. [10]Denial is not what you want.

(v 23 – 35)[1]Denial is delay. [2]Avoidance is delay. [3]Even peace and happiness in a world of fear is delay in giving up your wish. [4]Be not fooled by yourself. [5]You want very much to be healed. [6]You must face that which makes you sick, accept it is given by your own wish, and choose not to be sick anymore.

NTI Acts, Chapter 24

(v 1 – 9)[1]Do not be afraid to face your accusers. [2]Do not be afraid of pain. [3]Look forward to the opportunity to see what you have wished, knowing what is wished is not true.

[4]The end of wishing is the end of illusions. [5]Face your wish, and then take it back. [6]This is the great release that you face! [7]This is your path to freedom.

(v 10 – 21)[1]Know that when you face your wish, it may not at all seem easy. [2]This is because the root of belief makes your wish real to you. [3]When you face that which you fear, there is one thing you must remember.

4What you look on is not at all real,
and you face it to deny it.

5When you deny what seems real, you are only being truthful, for it has no reality at all. 6Grab onto Me as your courage, hold tight to your faith, and trust that your belief is *wrong*.

(v 22 – 27)1Know that you will not face your wish fully until you are fully ready to see. 2Remember your freedom. 3Nothing can be given you that you are not willing to receive. 4Until you are ready, your wish will remain hidden. 5It will be in sight, but you will choose not to see. 6And I will be with you, strengthening you according to your willingness, walking towards the wish that you *do* want to see.

NTI Acts, Chapter 25

(v 1 - 12)1You do not know how to see, and so you are afraid of what you look at when there is nothing there to fear. 2Let Me show you how to see so you will not be afraid, and you will walk willingly along this path with Me.

3The world is not real. 4It is like a play, with actors playing their roles. 5Only in the play of the world, the script has been forgotten, so that the play seems very real.

6This play has many endings, like slits cut in the script, where one can choose to step out of the play. 7But if one believes the play and is focused on playing his role, he will miss his opportunities to step out.

8As you read this story of Paul, see it as a script, just as your life is a script. 9Imagine yourself in the role of Paul. 10See what is playing out. 11Imagine yourself in that play.

12As you play the role of Paul, you have many choices in how to play. 13You can become Paul completely and forget there is a script. 14You can see the Jews as your enemies, and struggle against them in your mind. 15But if you choose this, you lose the awareness that it is a script, and you will forget to watch for the Light that signals the way to step out.

[16]Or as you play the role of Paul, you have another choice as to how to play. [17]You can look at the Romans and the Jews and remember that they are all a part of you playing a role in a script. [18]They may seem to have forgotten that they play only roles, but you can observe them and remember *for them*, so that you have the perspective of the script.

(v 13 – 22)[1]When you remember the script, the drama is removed and replaced with a feeling of love. [2]For then you see that each player in the script has only one purpose for you. [3]Each one is playing his role so that the script may unfold and lead you to your place to step out. [4]Each one is your brother and your savior engaged fully in helping you to find your slit of release.

(v 23 – 27)[1]As the script plays out, you may realize your joy and realize your gratitude for your brothers. [2]For everything is working just as it is set to work to bring you to the place of release.

NTI Acts, Chapter 26

(v 1 – 32)[1]There is a reason for your role in the play and a reason to let the script continue. [2]As you play your part, remembering it is but a part, others will see the script in you. [3]They will loosen their hold on the drama of the play as they begin to see beyond it through you. [4]Through them, others will awaken, until no one is left in the play.

NTI Acts, Chapter 27

(v 1 – 12)[1]Following this path with Me will seem to lead you to many places and many stops along the way. [2]Each place and each stop serves a purpose. [3]It is to increase your willingness to follow Me.

[4]If you are to exit the script that is the world and join with Me as a true teacher of the Son of God, you must be willing to follow Me in all things. [5]You must be willing to listen to only Me. [6]And so you will be led to circumstances and lessons that will be used to increase your faith and trust and reliability on Me.

(v 13 – 26)[1]Each circumstance is an opportunity to learn, if you will only give your ear to Me. ²No opportunity is lost, as I am always willing to love you and teach you. ³It is only this that you must remember, and then you can always decide:

⁴*In each circumstance and every situation along the way to Me, I am there with you, offering help and guidance.* ⁵*Never am I not there.* ⁶*Never can you make a mistake that will drive Me away.* ⁷*But it is also true that you can only hear My Word and accept My Help if you are willing to see that the answer to all things is Me.*

⁸*If you choose to limit the circumstances in which I may help, My Help is limited.* ⁹*If you choose to solve your problems on your own, My answer remains unheard.* ¹⁰*Always, I am with you able to help.* ¹¹*Always, without exception, I am there.* ¹²*But you must be willing to know Me and accept Me in order to receive Me as yours.*

(v 27 – 32)¹When you are ready to give up your trust in yourself, you are ready to accept your trust in Me. ²When you have seen that your answers do not lead to peace, you will be ready to accept peace through Me.

(v 33 – 38)¹Trust does not come from suspense and anxiety. ²You must be willing to give those to Me. ³Suspense and anxiety say you cannot trust. ⁴There is no peace to be found in them.

⁵When you are tempted to be afraid or tempted to worry, you must remember Me. ⁶Remember that fear, suspense, anxiety and worry are the expressions of the belief that you are alone and without Me. ⁷Then be willing to see that deep within your heart, at the very depth of your soul, you *know* you are not alone. ⁸You know that the fear of being alone, abandoned and helpless is an illusion that *cannot* be true.

⁹It is from this knowledge, this inner awareness that will not go away, that you will find the willingness to put fear and anxiety aside. ¹⁰Get quiet with Me. ¹¹Go to your stillness. ¹²Settle within that place that knows. ¹³It

is here that you will find your nourishment to carry you forward with Me. [14]In the stillness, you find trust. [15]In the stillness, you know Me.

(v 39 – 44)[1]It is also useful to remember, when you cannot seem to be still, that the drama that seems to occupy is only a script in the mind. [2]By watching it unfold and trusting in the Power behind it, you will find the peace in the chaos. [3]You will know the joy. [4]And in this way, you can be helpful to those who do not seem to know. [5]Through inner calmness on the seas of a storm, you provide a means of listening to Me. [6]By trusting and remaining open to the Power beyond the script, you help the script and the actors to play along with Me.

NTI Acts, Chapter 28

(v 1 – 10)[1]"Keeping your wits about you" is remembering to listen to Me. [2]Always, *in every circumstance*, you must forget the voice that comes first and be willing to listen to Me. [3]I will not make you wait in order to test you. [4]I am ready to answer you now. [5]But you must be willing to put the other voice aside, and ask for the response and the answer that comes to you from Me.

(v 11 – 16)[1]Always, God's Love is with you. [2]Always, you are in His Arms. [3]You may trust in this truth, because it cannot fail to be true. [4]When you relax into Him, you shall know that you are carried. [5]As you relax into Him, you know His care.

(v 17 – 31)[1]The message that I give you now is a simple one.

[2]*Everything is up to you.*

[3]You are the holy and the blessed free Son of God. [4]Nothing can change what you are. [5]You are forever what your Father created you to be. [6]No freedom shall ever be taken from you.

[7]In your freedom, you play with a script. [8]It is yours, and you *are* free to play. [9]Play as long as you want, my child of God. [10]Nothing will ever inhibit your freedom.

[11]But my child, understand that your freedom is free. [12]And so your own script cannot limit you. [13]You may choose it as long as you choose, but when *you* are ready, there is another Script, and that Script is Me.

[14]You have two choices in the play of the world: the play of the world or leaving it. [15]The voice of the ego is the script of the world, because it chooses to express self-will. [16]But the Holy Spirit's Voice is the way from the play, because it chooses to exercise Self and to know the fullness of freedom.

[17]God blesses you, child, in the voice that you choose. [18]You are free and the expression of freedom. [19]Amen.

THE HOLY SPIRIT'S INTERPRETATION OF ROMANS

NTI Romans, Chapter 1

(v 1 – 7)[1]This opening, which you are reading now, contains a very simple message of love. [2]All are invited into the Awareness of God, as none are to be left out.

[3]This is an important message that I ask you to be quiet and accept now:

> [4]*All are invited into the Awareness of God,*
> *and none are to be left out.*

(v 8 – 17)[1]I am the Holy Spirit, and I come to you on this day to teach you and to take you further along the path with Me. [2]Until now, you were not ready for the full devotion that I will ask, but you have recognized the hint of your release, and you are ready now. [3]And so I will teach you what you have come to learn. [4]Together, we are blessed.

(v 18 – 32)[1]Within you, there is a wish. [2]This wish is not within anyone else, although you would rather see it there. [3]This wish is hidden deep within your mind, hidden by layers of smoke.

[4]Before we go together to look at this wish, there is something I want you to know. [5]The wish is only a thought. [6]It is nothing else at all. [7]It can best be described as a curiosity that you wanted to explore. [8]It is really nothing...*nothing* at all.

[9]I am very grateful that you have expressed your freedom and

explored your wish. ¹⁰Now the curiosity can be let go.

¹¹I am your guide as I show you what you have learned in a daydream within the mind. ¹²Join with Me in peace and detachment as we giggle at your thought in gratitude that it could be thought and let go.

NTI Romans, Chapter 2

(v 1- 4)¹Judgment is a fantasy. ²It is like a game that you have played, but it means absolutely nothing at all. ³It is like a toy, a building block that has given structure to your curious thought. ⁴It allowed you to create alleyways and byways and to try this and to try that. ⁵But it was all within the field of fantasy, an amazing expression of curiosity. ⁶And it was never any more than that.

⁷Imagine yourself with this idea, for this was the idea that you had:

⁸*What if nothing was as it is?*
⁹*What if I could make something completely different,*
and make it whatever I want?
¹⁰*What would that be like?*

¹¹Your idea was just a curiosity, a daydream of exploration and really nothing at all, since the first question asked sets up an impossible hypothesis and one that can never be true.

¹²But in your freedom and the innocence of your curiosity, you set out to think a little more. ¹³You needed a tool to create this experience that would allow you to explore. ¹⁴The building block that you made was judgment, or decision, and this became a new "creative force."¹⁵It allowed for experience without creation. ¹⁶And from judgment, experience was made.

(v 5 – 11)¹With judgment made to build experience, you needed something to judge. ²You needed a place to start making this experience of something different than *it is*. ³So you took what you had, an idea in the mind, and you applied judgment to that.

[4]When judgment was applied, something new was made, so your experience began immediately. [5]Suddenly before you were two options set. [6]And for the first time ever, you had a decision to make.

[7]Your curiosity was nothing and did not mean a thing, so nothing at all had changed. [8]*This* was an option given to consider, and it offered the opportunity to laugh.

[9]But the second was different and led deeper into the game. [10]It was an opportunity to believe that the idea had become so, and nothing is *as it was*.

[11]Struck with this second option, you became engrossed by it. [12]And you tossed the first option aside. [13]Faced with reality and the option of fantasy, you chose to step into the fantasy.

[14]It was at this point that you began to forget, and you practiced the game of judgment again. [15]But this time in error, you judged yourself for what was not true, and you believed your judgment of yourself.

[16]This is how you seemed to step into a script, then lose your way out again. [17]But it is just a script and nothing more at all. [18]There is nothing at all to fear.

(v 12 – 16)[1]Judgment is the tool that built the world, and judgment keeps the experience alive. [2]But judgment came from nothing but an impossible idea and the desire to think about it some more.

[3]All judgment is fantasy. [4]Judgment spins fantasy. [5]Judgment is a way to explore. [6]It is a game, a folly, and nothing more. [7]It has no purpose and makes nothing real. [8]Judgment is a web of meaningless thoughts given only the power of fantasy and absolutely nothing more.

(v 17 – 24)[1]The game you have made to test your curiosity is a game with rules and options. [2]This gives you the ability to continue to make judgments and to continue to play the game. [3]The rules and options are important for another reason as well. [4]The game that you play is a game of guilt and innocence, right and wrong, good and evil. [5]To play this game in this way, there must be rules and options *and* there needs to be winners and losers.

[6]This is a game that lets you express the guilt you feel for playing the game, while mitigating your feeling of guilt at the same time. [7]In this way, the game is an attempt to be gentle with yourself. [8]It *is* an expression of love. [9]You believe that you are guilty, based on your own judgment of yourself for the idea and game that you made. [10]But you also know to be gentle with yourself, so both are in the game that you play.

(v 25 – 27)[1]However, the game that you play has become like a trap. [2]For within the rules and the options, the good and the evil, the building block of judgment continues to be made. [3]As your guilt is expressed with your desire to be gentle, the web of belief grows dense. [4]That which is fantasy seems to be real. [5]Its drama seems to be life.

(v 28, 29)[1]This is how you've seemed to become that which you aren't at all. [2]None of it is true. [3]None of it is you. [4]And yet, you believe it is so. [5]It is this we must look at and this we must let go, *because it is false and only believed to be true.*

NTI Romans, Chapter 3

(v 1 – 8)[1]Within your mind reason is confused, because you believe all that isn't true. [2]You cannot truly judge at all, because you know nothing on which to decide. [3]Your world is a fantasy of beliefs based on experience created through *judgment without basis.*

[4]Again, let's look at its beginning:

[5]You asked, "What if everything was different than it is?" [6]That was an impossible question, pure fantasy. [7]But then you judged the fantasy as if it was real and decided *through judgment* that it was. [8]This judgment did not make the unreal real. [9]It only enlivened fantasy within the mind. [10]Then you judged yourself for what you did not do, and you began the expression of guilt. [11]Every option and every judgment that came from this was an option or judgment based on fantasy, and so it resulted in additional layers of fantasy.

[12]Nothing outside fantasy has ever changed. [13]Everything that *is* still is as it is. [14]You are inside a place that *isn't*. [15]None of it is true. [16]It has

no basis. [17]There is literally nothing there to judge.

(v 9 – 20)[1]This world is based on a misperception of guilt, but it is *not* based on sin. [2]The sin that you judged yourself for was the sin of making what isn't. [3]But what isn't cannot be made, and so you have not sinned.

[4]The guilt that you feel and believe and express is all a part of the fantasy. [5]You only feel it and express it because you believe it, but your belief doesn't make it true.

(v 21 – 31)[1]God is the knowledge of truth. [2]God is the absence of fantasy. [3]God is forever, because truth is forever. [4]And God's truth is within you. [5]Nothing real has ever been lost by imagining something different.

[6]Since truth is within you, the way out of fantasy lies within you also. [7]This is the good news of you. [8]To return to your truth, complete and pure and innocent, all you need do is *unweave* your way out of fantasy. [9]You reverse the "laws" that made it by ceasing to play the game. [10]You let go of judgment and all perceived guilt. [11]You no longer believe what isn't true.

[12]When that which makes fantasy is let go as a practice, the fantasy begins to fade. [13]As the fantasy fades, the Light that is truth shines through. [14]Then you will follow the Light to your Home, which is back to the awareness of truth without fantasy, which is back to all that is true.

NTI Romans, Chapter 4

(v 1 – 12)[1]O Holy Son of God, there is one thing that you must know. [2]You are loved. [3]You are deeply and truly, eternally treasured and loved.

[4]This Love that is extended you from God and through God is not extended you for what you do. [5]Therefore, this Love cannot be stopped because of what you do not. [6]God's Love, extended to you, is eternal because God's Love, extended through you, is extended for what you are. [7]There are no criteria on which this Love is dependent. [8]You *are* and so you are loved, and this Love is eternal.

(v 13 – 15)[1]Existence is Love, and Love is existence. [2]You are loved, because God created you existence. [3]In creating you, God extended Himself. [4]In extending His Truth, that which is Enrichment was enriched further. [5]So in your existence, God Himself is enriched. [6]This is why you are His joy. [7]You are His own enrichment. [8]And that which enriches God must be Enrichment Itself.

(v 16, 17)[1]No part of you is absent from God's Enrichment, for every part of you exists. [2]Every part of you is a part of God's joy. [3]Every part of you is welcome in the Heart and smile of God, because every part of you *is* His Heart and His smile, without exception and without reservation at all.

(v 18 – 25)[1]God's Love is His Promise to you, and God's Love is eternal. [2]It cannot be taken back, nor does He Will that it be taken back. [3]God Himself is grateful to you for your existence, because you are the extension of His Own Love. [4]And in the extension of His Love, he finds His Glory, and He calls that Glory, *you.*

NTI Romans, Chapter 5

(v 1 – 5)[1]God's Love is not unknown to you, because God's Love lies in you. [2]You are God's Love. [3]And God's Love is your truth. [4]Nothing can change this fact, because you are the extension of His Love. [5]Through the extension of Love, you were created. [6]And so you were created Love. [7]And Love is what you are.

(v 6 – 11)[1]God's Truth has no end, and so it has not ended in you. [2]You are the truth of God in your existence. [3]There is no end to His Truth, so there is no end to you. [4]You are forever blessed in the Heart of God, forever His joy and His smile. [5]No sin shall cross your mind, because there is no sin in you. [6]You are the perfect and sinless Son of God that lives within Him now and forever.

(v 12 – 14)[1]As I have told you, the world was made by guilt, but guilt is not sin. [2]Guilt is only the belief in sin. [3]But I come to you as God's holy and ordained Messenger to tell you that in His eyes, you have not sinned. [4]In His knowledge, you have not moved from His Heart. [5]In His awareness, you remain forever a part of His smile.

(v 15 – 17)[1]One thought of guilt was born into your mind through one judgment of yourself for something you did not do. [2]This, then, is imagined guilt, multiplied in the world through your belief in what you made. [3]But that which is untrue is nothing, and nothing multiplied infinitely still remains nothing. [4]Therefore, all of the guilt that you perceive to be a part of the world and to be a part of you remains what it has always been. [5]It remains nothing, multiplied as nothing, and so it is forever and under all circumstances *nothing*.

(v 18, 19)[1]Nothing need not be atoned for, and nothing need not be forgiven, because it is nothing. [2]It does not exist in the eyes of God. [3]Nothing need be done to erase that which is nothing, because it is already nothing.

[4]Therefore, through your being you are atoned. [5]Through your truth, you are forgiven. [6]For never have you not been atoned and never have you not been forgiven, because never has a state existed that was anything but your perfection.

(v 20, 21)[1]The rules and options that you have made allow for your continued judgment, but your judgment is not God's judgment. [2]Therefore, your judgment is nothing real. [3]And what is not real cannot make real.

[4]Your judgment is not real, and so your guilt is not real either. [5]This is the truth that you deny. [6]God asks you to accept your truth, as there is no fear in truth. [7]Fear is the product of fantasy.

NTI Romans, Chapter 6

(v 1 - 4)[1]Jesus is a symbol of all that is possible with you, because Jesus lived as a symbol of all that is true with you. [2]Jesus was the symbol of life, perfection, love, wisdom, innocence, and devotion. [3]This is true of you. [4]This is your truth. [5]Jesus was the symbol of your truth.

(v 5 – 7)[1]Jesus is a symbol of all that is possible with you, because Jesus lived as a symbol of all that is true of you. [2]You are Jesus, and Jesus is you. [3]There is no separation between him and you. [4]You know this, if you close your eyes. [5]For when you close your eyes, you can find him there. [6]He is a part of you, within you, a being within your soul.

[7]Jesus is a part of you, so that all that he accomplished, he accomplished *within you*. [8]And that which has been accomplished within you has been accomplished *by* you, so that it may continue to be accomplished until it has been accomplished in full.

(v 8 – 14)[1]The universe is in your mind, so that all that has been accomplished has been accomplished by you. [2]And within this universe, the model that rises to the top of your mind is the symbol of the man called Jesus. [3]This is because Jesus represents your true desire. [4]Jesus is the freedom you want to be. [5]Everything else that floats within the universe of the mind is from a past desire and is not your current desire anymore.

[6]You may let the past go. [7]You need not keep anything you do not want. [8]Focus your eyes on Jesus and know the love in your own Heart. [9]This is your truth. [10]This is your Heart's desire. [11]In surrendering into this truth, you find your joy.

(v 15 – 18)[1]You are not a slave. [2]You are not a victim. [3]Nothing can be given you that you do not want. [4]You are the free and holy and treasured Son of God. [5]All that you want is yours. [6]And when you look at your brother Jesus, you see what you want. [7]When you look at your brother Jesus, you recognize what is yours.

[8]When you look at your brother Jesus, you are not looking outside your mind. [9]You are not seeing the past or looking into the future. [10]When you look at your brother Jesus and you recognize what you want, you are looking into your mind *now* and seeing him. [11]You are looking in your Heart *now* and recognizing him. [12]You are looking within you *now*, and you are finding him there, *fully accomplished*, all that he is, living within your mind.

(v 19 – 23)[1]You are eternal, as all of eternity is within you. [2]God is eternity, and the extension of God is you. [3]But you have shut off your mind to the eternity that is there. [4]You have looked away and promised to look at only a fragment of your mind. [5]This is why you believe in time. [6]You believe a fragment is now and everything else is not now. [7]But everything is now. [8]Eternity is in your mind, and you are in the Mind of Eternity. [9]And Jesus, who shares your mind with you, is the symbol of your recognition that this is true.

[10]Close your eyes. [11]Jesus is in your mind. [12]He is no where else. [13]You know him and experience him no where else. [14]Jesus is in your mind now. [15]He is a part of you.

NTI Romans, Chapter 7

(v 1 – 6)[1]With Jesus, you have been released, because with Jesus, a belief has been loosened in the mind. [2]With Jesus, the thought that you are forever separate from God, forever within a spatial compartment of time, forever a slave to your own invention...with Jesus, this was all undone.

[3]In Jesus you see the limitlessness that is your truth. [4]In Jesus you see your innocence and love. [5]In Jesus, your perfection remains unmarred. [6]My dear child, through the symbol of Jesus, you glimpse your own truth!

[7]Through Jesus you have been released, because a Light now shines clearly within the mind. [8]Focus on this Light and realize you have found your truth. [9]And follow this Light with Me.

(v 7 – 12)[1]You are the mind that made the world, so all of the world is within you. [2]Is this a sin? [3]You asked this question, and you decided it was. [4]And then you went on to decide that you were sinful. [5]And much of what you see within the world of your mind is a clear reflection of your belief.

[6]But then you look at Jesus, and in Him you see the Light, and something inside of you rests. [7]It rests, because it knows that it need not worry. [8]The truth is still within you. [9]And if Jesus is your truth, then everything else must not be, and so you must not be guilty. [10]You just need to let go of that which isn't truth, and follow your recognition of

truth back to your awareness of true.

(v 13)[1]The Holy Spirit is within you also, and the Holy Spirit is more than a symbol. [2]The Holy Spirit is the pure reflection of truth within the memory of your mind. [3]This memory is not past. [4]Indeed, it is what is very real now. [5]But it is outside of awareness, outside of what you believe, calling you back to what is true now.

(v 14 – 20)[1]Your conscious awareness is based on what you believe, but it is not a reflection of truth. [2]To call you back to truth, through the forest of your conscious awareness, the Holy Spirit sends symbols of Light. [3]These symbols come in many forms and many manners, of which Jesus is one. [4]But they are all symbols leading you back to your truth, which is beyond your belief and conscious awareness.

(v 21 – 25)[1]Your task is simple, as it is simply this:

[2]*Remember that the universe is a reflection of the past, because it is the reflection of a past wish or past belief in the mind. [3]Remember that your truth waits outside this wish, and your truth is calling you Home.*

[4]*Remain alert to the symbols that are sent into your conscious awareness to follow. [5]Lock onto them, and be led Home. [6]Let everything else pass as you see it. [7]See it only as a reflection of the past, a mere shadow, and let it pass by without attachment. [8]Stay with the Light.*

[9]*Follow the Light, and it will lead safely and easily Home.*

NTI Romans, Chapter 8

(v 1 – 4)[1]The world, and all you think about the world, is illusion. [2]There is not one thought that you have about the world that is true, except that the world has no truth in it. [3]This is a true thought. [4]This is a true thought given to you by Me and echoed through Jesus. [5]This is what he meant when he said he had overcome the world. [6]This is what he meant when he said that his kingdom is not of this world. [7]Jesus learned through willingness to see that the world is not truth and truth is not of the world.

(v 5 – 8)[1]The mind that believes in the world believes what it experiences to be true. [2]And so it lives the experience as if it is true, and it suffers heartache. [3]But the mind that accepts the Spirit's interpretation of the world accepts that the world is not true. [4]And so it does not suffer its experience, because it has accepted that truth is beyond experience. [5]This mind knows peace, because it also knows that that which isn't true cannot affect the truth.

(v 9 – 11)[1]Life is not in the world. [2]Life is beyond the world. [3]The Spirit of God is Life, but the Spirit of God is not in the world, because the Spirit of God is truth, and there is no truth in the world.

[4]You are Life, and you are truth also, so you must not be in the world, for there is no truth in the world. [5]The world is an illusion of experience within the mind. [6]You are not in the world.

(v 12 – 17)[1]You are the Son of God, not by your birth, which is illusion, but by your truth, which is of God. [2]You need not earn who you are by acts in a world of illusion. [3]You are who you are through truth, which is of God.

[4]The world is a world of thought. [5]And every thought that you have ever had is expressed in the world. [6]But the world is like a playground where thoughts can be expressed freely without affecting reality.

[7]You have become lost in the playground of your mind. [8]And you have frightened yourself there. [9]But your Home is unchanged and unaffected by your imaginary play. [10]Your Father's Heart knows only your truth. [11]And now you are called to lay aside play and come Home to the truth of who you are.

(v 18 – 25)[1]Creation is not suffering over your experience in the world. [2]Heaven sheds not one tear, for Heaven neither cries nor has compassion for that which hasn't happened.

[3]My dear child, listen to Me now and listen to Me well. [4]All that you experience and believe to be true is not true. [5]It is an experience dreamed up within your mind to satisfy a curiosity that you posed. [6]Only you have come to believe your own dream, and this is why you suffer. [7]Heaven

does not believe what isn't real, and Heaven does not suffer, but she does wait eagerly and lovingly to welcome you back to the realization of your Self.

[8]Be at peace and know your truth within your Heart. [9]The Love that you are is written there as a reminder of your truth. [10]Be quiet, and know your truth. [11]Be still a moment, and know all is well.

(v 26, 27)[1]The Holy Spirit is your truth. [2]This is why He knows your prayers. [3]You are your Holy Spirit and your Holy Spirit is you. [4]Open your mind and welcome your Self unto your Self.

(v 28 – 30)[1]All are God's sons and all are predestined to know themselves, because all are a reflection of one mind. [2]There is no separation, because there is no truth outside one mind. [3]That which exists within one mind is that Mind, and so it is one.

[4]The thoughts within the mind reflect the beliefs that the mind holds dear. [5]Beliefs are based on judgment, and judgment is based on desire. [6]The desire that leads you to judge is the desire to express self-will. [7]Behold! [8]Look at the world! [9]This is the expression of self-will, which you desired.

[10]And now you know that you do not want this desire or these thoughts. [11]You are ready to return to the one Will that is your Father. [12]Say good-bye to your dream and to the ancient desire that has grown cold. [13]Return with Me to what has never changed and to that which remains true forever.

(v 31 - 39)[1]There is nothing to fear within a world of illusion within the mind. [2]There are only thoughts to look at as you decide you do not want them anymore.

[3]Take My hand and follow Me as I lead you back to your Father. [4]Do not shrink from your dream, as it is not real. [5]Your hiding will only delay us on our path. [6]Let's hurry now, back to the joy of your Father. [7]Let's pass through your dream, see it is not real, and return in glee to all that is real and has not changed.

NTI Romans, Chapter 9

(v 1 – 18)[1]I ask you to give your willingness to accept that the world is not real. [2]I ask you to give Me your willingness, that I may show you this is true.

[3]When you look at the world, it is helpful to remember that you look at nothing but thought. [4]Everything you experience, everything you see, everything you think you know is the expression of thought. [5]Give your willingness to see all that you experience as thought. [6]Give your willingness to see that the world is not real.

[7]When you do not understand what you see or experience within the world, do not try to understand it. [8]Do not try to justify that which confuses you. [9]To try to understand what cannot be understood, or to attempt to justify confusion, is to want it to fit within *your* illusion of reality. [10]Give willingness to see that it is not real. [11]Give willingness to see that it is only thought.

[12]You try to understand and you try to give reason to your experience, because you want to reconcile your world with truth. [13]You want all that you believe to be the truth, *and* you want truth to be true too. [14]This reconciliation can never be accomplished. [15]That which is not true cannot become true, and that which is truth cannot fit within illusion.

[16]Do you try to understand that which you know is not true? [17]Do you try to explain fantasy? [18]Dismiss your desire to defend the world. [19]Be willing to see it's not real. [20]Be willing to see it is only thought.

[21]There are many thoughts in the world that will confuse you if you insist on believing they are real. [22]You must be willing not to believe the thoughts you see, the thoughts you experience, or the thought that seems to be you.

[23]In the world you will see what seems to be unfairness, cruelty and suffering. [24]Do not blame these on your brother. [25]Do not blame these on God. [26]To blame what you see on anyone or anything is to accept what you see as real. [27]You must be willing to see that it is not real. [28]You must be willing to not let illusion be hardened.

(v 19 – 24)[1]The one you seem to be within the world is not your reality. [2]Do not mourn it. [3]Do not be grateful for it. [4]To mourn it or to be grateful for it is to believe in illusion. [5]Be willing to see that the one you think you are is only an expression of thought. [6]Be willing to look beyond the thought and acknowledge the Thinker of the thought as you.

[7]Do not fear that what you think is a statement of your truth. [8]Do not fear there is truth to your guilt. [9]Do not fear there is hideousness in your nature. [10]Do not ask to be a hero. [11]Do not ask to be good. [12]Do not ask to be anything at all. [13]Give only your willingness to let go of illusions. [14]Give your willingness to know your truth.

(v 25 – 33)[1]Do not fear God. [2]There is no judgment in God. [3]Judgment is the tool of illusion. [4]God is truth absent of illusion. [5]Be willing to think with God.

[6]Do not fear the world. [7]Do not fear what seems to happen in the world. [8]Be willing to see it is not true. [9]Be willing to see it is thought born of fantasy. [10]Be willing to let fantasy go.

[11]Do not fear time. [12]It is not your home. [13]It survives in the mind as a dream. [14]Be willing to awaken. [15]Be willing to let it all go. [16]Be willing to see time isn't true.

[17]Do not fear division. [18]It is illusion. [19]There is no truth in division at all. [20]Be willing to forgive that which isn't true by being willing to let it go from your thought.

NTI Romans, Chapter 10

(v 1 – 4)[1]The answer to your salvation is found within your own willingness. [2]The power that sets you free is you. [3]There is no power outside of you that determines salvation or sets you free. [4]Within, your willingness joins with your own Holy Spirit, and this is the path of freedom. [5]Together they lead you from the forest of illusion into the sunshine of reality.

(v 5 – 13)[1]The Word *is* near you. [2]It is in your mouth and in your heart. [3]The Love of God is in you, and it is with you. [4]When you trust your Self through your willingness, you trust the strength and power and gentleness of God to guide you from your illusions to the remembrance of truth.

[5]When you find resistance in your heart and your mind, put not your trust there. [6]When you find resistance, remember what you truly want. [7]Rest, so that resistance will pass over you.

[8]When you find willingness, clasp hands with your Holy Spirit in joy! [9]Walk forward in trust and willingness. [10]This is your desire awakened, and it is leading you Home.

(v 14 – 21)[1]You are a mind with what seems to be two points of view, two possible realities to choose from. [2]Except that there cannot be two realities. [3]Only one can be reality and the other must be fantasy.

[4]Both of these possible realities are in your heart now, and so you seem to waiver between one and the other, and you feel torn. [5]Do not be sad. [6]Do not let this distress you. [7]Isn't this movement towards the one true reality that you truly seek? [8]Wasn't there a time that you were fully blinded by the false reality of the world? [9]Aren't you letting go of the false reality now?

[10]Rejoice! [11]For you *are* listening to Me, and you *are* walking with Me. [12]Do not listen to the voice that would tell you that you are not. [13]Chastisement is not of Me, and I will never leave you comfortless.

[14]I have asked for your willingness, and you have given it to Me. [15]I have asked for your trust, and you have given it to Me also. [16]You give Me all that I ask, and you walk this path with Me. [17]Lift up your chin, and smile at the sunshine! [18]It is already smiling down on you through the thinning branches of the forest trees.

NTI Romans, Chapter 11

(v 1 – 6)[1]You who are reading this are the beloved Son of God, not because you are reading this, but because of your truth, which is beyond the illusion of these words.

[2]You are a mind, and you are looking at thought. [3]Right now, you are looking at thought that expresses your true desire. [4]You could not see

these words, if it was not within your willingness. [5]You could not understand them, if they were not your truth. [6]And you do recognize them, because you *know* they are your heart. [7]Behold your Self, your true desire and your remembrance! [8]They are reflected in the words you let enter your consciousness now.

(v 7 – 10)[1]You are willing and you are finding your readiness to accept Me fully now. [2]If that were not true, these words would not call to you. [3]They would not hold your interest. [4]You would be blinded to their meaning through your own desire not to acknowledge them yet.

[5]But you are not blinded to these words or to their meaning. [6]The purpose beyond the words is clear to you now. [7]Their meaning, you see, is beyond the meaning of the world. [8]And you recognize that I speak to a truer you, one who is listening beyond the illusion of the world. [9]This one listens for you, because this one *is* you. [10]And like you, this one is one with Me also. [11]We are joining with our Self in the pool of these words, which speak the truth that we know and recognize. [12]We are one. [13]There is no separation. [14]There is no other mind. [15]There is only us, and *this* is the reflection of that thought in the world.

(v 11 – 16)[1]You have rejected yourself, and yet you cannot reject yourself fully because you love yourself also. [2]This is why your awareness seems to be limited to part instead of a whole, and this is why I am here also. [3]The limited part that you accept as you is but a symbol of your rejection of your Self. [4]For in knowing only that part of your mind, you, in turn, reject the whole. [5]This is your rejection of your Self.

[6]But in knowing Me, you retain the memory of your Self, for I am the whole. [7]And so you seem to have rejected the whole by being aware of only a part, and yet you have rejected nothing because you are aware of Me. [8]I am the whole and you accept Me, so you must accept the whole also!

(v 17 – 21)[1]Do not fear that you have rejected your Self by rejecting the whole. [2]Do not feel that you are guilty for what you have not done. [3]You have always accepted Me. [4]You have always found comfort in Me.

[5]I have always been with you through your true desire not to reject the whole. [6]Therefore, I am not rejected, and you are not rejected either. [7]We are as we have always been, and we are eternally grateful for our Self as it truly is.

(v 22 – 24)[1]Your nature is your truth, and I am your nature. [2]Do not fear when you go off into fantasies and seem to forget that I am here. [3]I am still here, even if you do not remember Me. [4]I am with you always, because I am where you desire Me to be. [5]I have not been rejected. [6]You have not rejected Me. [7]Nor have you ever rejected Me, or will you ever reject Me. [8]You know that I am your desire, and so I am not rejected. [9]And as such, you truly have not rejected the whole. [10]I am here by your true Will.

(v 25 – 32)[1]The whole of you is safe in your mind through Me. [2]Nothing has been lost. [3]I have kept it whole for you.

(v 33 – 36)[1]I am all things, and I am you. [2]In accepting Me, you accept all things, and you accept you also. [3]In accepting Me, you accept God, which is to accept all reality. [4]Because you have not rejected Me, you have not rejected reality. [5]Reality is for you, and you have kept it as it is in your Heart for you also. [6]For you know your truth, and you love your truth. [7]Your truth is beyond rejection, because your truth is You.

NTI Romans, Chapter 12

(v 1, 2)[1]Rest within the assurance of your Self, for nothing has ever been lost. [2]Your truth is as pure and bright as always, because your truth is safe with Me. [3]To know your truth, accept Me as your Light. [4]And let your shadows grow dim. [5]Ask for nothing, except ask for Me. [6]Accept Me into your body. [7]Accept Me as your mind. [8]Realize the beauty and glory of you.

(v 3 – 8)[1]The body that you are is within Me also. [2]For what is in your mind is in My Mind. [3]We share one Mind, and we share one body. [4]We are not different, but the same. [5]I am our glory, because I am our truth. [6]I am our fullness. [7]I am our plan.

[8]Release yourself to Me and know you have released yourself to your true purpose, which is the purpose of wholeness, of fullness and of One. [9]See what I do with our body, for I will use it to show you that we are beyond the body. [10]I will use it to guide you back to your truth, which is where I am, and so it is where you are also.

[11]Our truth is our Mind, and our Mind is whole. [12]You are looking at a part of our Mind and thinking that it is you. [13]That is only a fraction of what you are, and so you do not know you are whole. [14]But you are whole. [15]Let Me guide the fraction, that it may be opened unto Itself and discover what it has always known. [16]Let it see it is not a part, but it is whole.

(v 9 – 13)[1]Love your Self. [2]In loving your Self, you love your brother, for we are one.

[3]Be patient with yourself. [4]In your patience with you, you find patience in Me, for we are one.

[5]Honor your brother. [6]In honoring him, you honor Me, for we are one.

[7]Give your willingness and trust continuously to Me. [8]In giving your willingness to Me, you give it to the truth that is you and your brother, for we are one.

(v 14 – 16)[1]Enjoy your illusion as a gift to yourself, and hold your brother in your heart as you. [2]But give willingness to see beyond the gift to the Giver of the gift, and you give willingness to know and remember you.

(v 17 – 21)[1]This is the awareness you are to keep as an expression of your willingness to remember with Me:

²The part you know is but a part
of a whole that is the truth of what you are.
³The parts you see are but a part
of the wholeness of Love that is Me.
⁴To love your brother is to love your truth.
⁵To care for him is to open your heart to the whole.
⁶And when the heart is open,
wholeness is welcomed in.
⁷And in its welcoming, its truth is remembered.

⁸Blessings to you as you move in the world in willingness, for that is but a symbol of the opening of the mind. ⁹An open mind is not closed, so the Light that is fullness of truth may be realized.

NTI Romans, Chapter 13

(v 1 – 5)¹You are not in the world. ²I have told you this already. ³But you do experience the world, because you designed the world as an experience.

⁴The world is an image in the mind, or better said, a picture-thought within the thought of spirit. ⁵It is an experience, because it was designed as an experience, but it is not your reality. ⁶It is within you.

⁷Everything that seems to be true about the world is a part of the experience you deemed to have. ⁸In this way, none of it is to be rejected. ⁹For to reject an experience that you asked to have is to deny that you are the designer of the experience. ¹⁰This is to deny your truth.

(v 6, 7)   *¹This is how you are to look at the world:*
²As an experience that you set up for your learning.

³Live through the experience observing what it is, and you will see what you came to learn. ⁴You will see that the truth is perfect and your true desire is your Home. ⁵Your thought was just an idea. ⁶And you will

easily relinquish the idea for the truth. [7]And you will be grateful that the truth is always true.

(v 8 – 10) [1]*This is how you are to "live" your experience:*
[2]*Remembering that it isn't true.*

[3]But remember that it is an experience chosen for learning, and let your brother live his experience as he chooses. [4]Forget not his truth. [5]Be grateful for it. [6]Love his truth, which is also you. [7]But grant him his experience, and love him for that as well. [8]He is learning what you have come here to learn.

(v 11 – 14)[1]Look on the world and remember what you have learned, even as the experience seems to continue. [2]Remember your place, which is to accept your lesson now, and be grateful that you see as you see.

[3]You can stay in the world at the end of your learning to show your brothers what you've learned, *but you are teaching no one except yourself and taking time to accept what you know.*

[4]When you have learned the lesson, you will let go of illusion, because you will have no need for it anymore. [5]Until then, remember:

[6]*Everything you do, you do for yourself.*

[7]And then learn what you have come to learn. [8]It is your lesson, designed and given for you.

NTI Romans, Chapter 14

(v 1- 4)[1]Judgment is the tool of illusion, and judgment was first used against an idea and against yourself. [2]From that, judgment seemed to spread with illusion, but since all illusion is within the mind, judgment could not spread anyplace else.

[3]Whenever you seem to judge anything, any situation or any person that seems external to yourself, you are judging an illusion of thoughts

and ideas within the mind. [4]Therefore, you are continually judging yourself.

[5]Since judgment is the building block of illusion, applying false meaning and making illusion real, judgment of yourself does this to you: [6]It hides your truth and presents an illusion of you that isn't true.

[7]Each time you seem to judge someone or something, you are judging thoughts in your mind, thereby judging yourself. [8]In believing your judgments, you believe you are what you are not. [9]This is how your illusory self is made and upheld.

[10]To know your Self, which is your true desire, you must lay judgment aside. [11]Remember that everything you experience, every person, every place and circumstance, is a thought within the mind of you. [12]And each judgment keeps the veil of illusion alive, which hides You from you.

(v 5 – 8)[1]Also remember that nothing is as it seems. [2]It is within the mind of you, thought up by you, for the purpose of having an experience. [3]In that way, the only judgment that can be applied is that *it is what it is*. [4]The experience is the experience it was made to be. [5]It is the perfect reflection of a wish. [6]It is everything you asked to see.

[7]In this way, you may be grateful for everything you have made. [8]You asked a question, and you have discovered the answer. [9]In itself, the answer to the question is perfect.

(v 9 – 11)[1]Rejoice when you look on the world, for it is the answer to the question you asked. [2]And now you have your answer. [3]You need not ask the question anymore. [4]You need no longer be puzzled. [5]You need not judge and apply meaning to the meaningless. [6]You may put your curiosity to rest. [7]You do not want Love different than it is, for as it is *is* Love, and Love is all you truly want.

(v 12)[1]And now, you see.

(v 13 – 18)[1]Now you may let go of your attachment to illusion. [2]You may let go of expression of self-will. [3]You may surrender any hidden wish to see differently. [4]The answer that you asked for has been given.

[5]Be grateful for the answer. [6]Surrender to it for what it is. [7]It is not

what you want. [8]It is only what you wanted to see. [9]And now that you've seen it, its purpose is done.

(v 19 – 21)[1]Now that your attachment is released and your question has been answered, you can let go of the illusion you do not need. [2]That *is* what you are doing now, you are letting go of what you no longer have purpose for.

[3]Letting go of illusion is a glorious occasion. [4]Celebrate that your lesson has been learned! [5]As illusion presents itself within the mind that you are, smile at it, remembering the purpose that it had. [6]And let it pass, by realizing it has no purpose for you now. [7]It has served its purpose for you. [8]You do not want what you thought you might want. [9]You want all God has given you instead.

(v 22, 23)[1]When the illusion seems real within the mind that you are, do not fear your experience. [2]Remember that its "reality" is a statement of your truth, and rejoice that you are reclaiming your truth again. [3]In knowing your Self, you know Love without division. [4]For the wholeness of Love is the wholeness and fullness of you.

NTI Romans, Chapter 15

(v 1 – 4)[1]Now that you see, I ask for your help. [2]You can be used by Me for the healing of the mind, if you are willing. [3]In order to be most helpful, you must be willing to lay yourself aside. [4]For you can only be helpful to Me when you are under My direction, and I can only direct you when you are willing to surrender to Me.

[5]*Everything is up to you.*
[6]*You are the free Son of God.*

[7]Nothing can be coerced upon you, nor is it My Will to ask anything of you that you do not want to give. [8]But if you are willing to give yourself to Me for My Use, I will make you useful to the healing of the mind.

(v 5, 6)[1]Through your surrender, we are made one, even within the illusion of division. [2]Through your surrender, our heart is combined, and you shall know Me through your Self.

(v 7 – 13)[1]You do not see yourself as Me yet, which means that you see with the eyes of illusion. [2]But with understanding, and willingness, and your complete surrender, you shall see Me as you. [3]We shall be known as one in your awareness. [4]And where we are joined, all are joined in love. [5]So you shall know oneness, and you shall be divorced from the image of division forever.

(v 14 – 22)[1]Laying down your will is important to your service to Me, for your illusory will is not My Will. [2]Your illusory will is your desire to have things different. [3]Your illusory will is your desire to have things your way. [4]But if you look at the world and remember that it is the expression of your illusory will, you will again remember to return to your true Will, which is the same as Mine.

[5]In surrendering to Me, you surrender to your Self. [6]In this realization, you are swept with peace and joy, for your true Will is your true desire. [7]And in its recognition, you find your gratitude to your Self.

(v 23 – 33)[1]Pray then, for your own end. [2]Pray to your Father with willingness to let go of thy illusory self. [3]It is nothing to you, and it keeps you from the realization of your truth.

[4]Do not fear the passing of this self you call home. [5]It is not your home. [6]And you do not belong there within your awareness. [7]Your awareness belongs with Me. [8]I see your true Self, and I am waiting here with you to share your Self with you.

[9]Blessings in your prayers for willingness. [10]Do not take your prayers lightly. [11]They are your energy, which feeds your strength. [12]Through them, your truth shall be known.

NTI Romans, Chapter 16

(v 1 – 16)[1]Greet one another. [2]In greeting one another you greet your Self, being of one mind with Me. [3]There is no one that you meet that is not of Me, so there is no one that you meet who is not you also. [4]As you greet him, you greet yourself.

[5]Give patience to your brother, and you give patience to the one that you are.

[6]Give trust to your brother, and you give trust to the one that you are.

[7]Give hope to your brother through your practice of My every word, and you give message to your Self that My Word is true.

[8]Give love to your brother by greeting him as one in you, and you give truth to the mind that is your Self.

[9]Be humble with your brother, and you recognize his true Spirit, which is yours also.

[10]Give honor to your brother, and you give remembrance that your only truth is Me.

[11]Give to your brother as you would give to yourself in holy remembrance of Me, and you give of your willingness to release the world and awaken from the dream of fear.

[12]Give in peace *through thought* to the world that is you. [13]This is the way to remember your truth, which is peace and freedom and Love.

(v 17 – 19)[1]Give thought to your thoughts, and be aware, for that which is thought is you. [2]Believe the thoughts that speak not of your truth, and you accept a message that's untrue.

[3]To be free of delusion, release delusional thoughts. [4]Listen to them no more. [5]Be aware that you perceive and believe as you think. [6]Question what you think against that which you truly desire.

(v 20)[1]To let go of division-based thoughts is to let go of all that isn't true. [2]This frees the mind of what it believes and opens it to remember its truth.

(v 21 – 27)[1]Now I ask you to remember your Father, Whose Will has sent this Voice to you. [2]It is the Will of oneness and peace, and of truth that is forever true.

[3]To remember your Father is to remember your truth. [4]You are loved and you are forever free. [5]In your oneness you are blessed as the holy Son

of God. [6]In your oneness, you are forever your truth.

[7]Love your Self, as Love is what you are. [8]Forever be kind and gentle. [9]Give nothing that is not deserving in the Mind of Peace, and you honor your truth through thought. [10]Amen.

THE HOLY SPIRIT'S INTERPRETATION OF 1 CORINTHIANS

NTI 1 Corinthians, Chapter 1

(v 1 – 3)[1]You, who are reading this now, have been called into My service. [2]This is why you continue to read. [3]Now I will teach you in order to help you in your acceptance of your role as My holy servant.

(v 4 – 9)[1]I am grateful for you and your willingness. [2]Already your helpfulness to healing has been more than you imagine. [3]And yet, you are just beginning this path with Me. [4]There is so much more to do, so many more wonders for you to see and accept. [5]You are truly a glorious gift unto your Self. [6]I thank you for your undying willingness to heal.

(v 10 – 17)[1]You may seem to be led into relationships with Me where one may seem to have a leadership role and one may seem to be a follower. [2]Do not be confused by what you see in form. [3]Each one who walks with Me walks *with* Me, doing easily as I ask. [4]One day he may seem to lead, and one day he may seem to follow. [5]With some, he may appear to be leader. [6]With others, he may appear to follow. [7]But all appearances, regardless of what they may be, are within the realm of perception. [8]The realm of perception is the realm of change. [9]So cast not your eyes upon the realm of perception, judging what seems to be the circumstance in form. [10]Remember that My servant is one who walks *with* Me. [11]And so, he is one who walks *with* you also. [12]And you, as one who has accepted himself into My holy service, walks with your brother too.

(v 18 – 25) [1]The ego is still within your mind, and it may seem to persist for some time. ²This is not to be cause for concern for you, but it is to be acknowledged and you are to remain aware. ³For if you do not remain aware and alert to the ego in your mind, you may forget to question your thinking and believe you are listening to Me when you are not. ⁴If you remember and remain aware of the ego in your mind, you can continuously question your thinking and seek for the reason you hold. ⁵As My servant, you will desire to hold to right-reason, and so where you recognize it, you shall hold it dear. ⁶Where you do not recognize right-reason, you shall choose to let your thinking go and continue to wait for the reason and guidance that comes from Me.

(v 26 – 31)¹Your self is to be given to Me now, that any self that is not your truth may be left behind. ²Choose not to cling to your self as you perceive yourself to be. ³Choose instead to lay your self aside and to become like an empty shell. ⁴That which is emptied shall be filled by Me, and one who is filled by Me shall know his own fullness.

NTI 1 Corinthians, Chapter 2

(v 1 – 5)¹As an empty shell, you are filled by Me. ²As an empty shell, you witness the reason that is your own. ³Lay down your self in service to Me, that you may serve Me and come to know your Self.

(v 6 – 10)¹That which is revealed to you as you lay yourself aside and willingly become as an empty shell is also revealed to the mind. ²That which is revealed to the mind is useful in the healing of God's holy Son. ³In laying yourself aside and willingly becoming as a shell, you offer yourself to be useful in holiness. ⁴That to which you offer yourself is that which you are. ⁵In laying yourself aside as an offering of grace to holiness, Holiness in its Grace is offered fully to you.

(v 11 – 16)¹That which has opened itself to the Spirit of God by becoming as an empty shell has made a statement unto the mind that is its own. ²It has said, "I know I am not this thing I thought I was, as this thing cannot be my truth. ³So I put aside that which is false, that I may be open to receive only that which is true."

[4]When that which is false is put aside and that which is true is received and accepted, the mind listens to its truth. [5]In its own memory, it recognizes its Self. [6]Unto itself, it bids its Self welcome.

NTI 1 Corinthians, Chapter 3

(v 1 – 4)[1]Remember that the ego is still in your mind, and be aware of it. [2]In that way, you may remember to set that self aside and open up to the true Self.

[3]Practice will seem necessary before you are ready to set your self aside and not pick it back up again. [4]Do not worry. [5]I will give you your opportunities to practice as you are willing. [6]So be willing to set yourself aside. [7]As much as you are willing, I will give you circumstances for practice.

(v 5 – 9)[1]Walk with Me in your desire to practice, and I shall walk with you. [2]According to your willingness, you shall be given opportunities to practice, as everything that is done is done for you and by your willingness. [3]Your willingness to practice will match with your brother's willingness to learn, so he may be brought to you, and you will be given your opportunity to practice. [4]In this way, everyone is given by Me according to his willingness, and the Light that reaches into the mind is received through the mind's own willingness to receive it.

(v 10 – 15)[1]Your willingness is also the measure of your joy, for in willingness you serve your true desire. [2]In resistance, you deny it. [3]To lay your self aside is to give willingness to let go of false illusion. [4]To cling to your self, and your thoughts, and your fears, is to cling to illusion and to hold onto what you do not want.

[5]Release yourself to your joy. [6]Give to your Self by laying your self aside. [7]In this way, you will remember more of that which you want, and your willingness to give of yourself will grow.

(v 16 – 23)[1]Remember your true Self as I have taught it to you. [2]You are eternal and beyond limits of any kind. [3]And then notice your awareness as it seems to be to you. [4]If you do not know yourself as limitless and beyond all fear, you maintain a belief that you are what you are not. [5]Therefore, do not take off in your way, as your way is still illusion. [6]Follow My way, that you may be led from illusion.

[7]Then when you know no more limits upon you, you shall also know what is limitless, which means that you have again learned to remember your Self.

NTI 1 Corinthians, Chapter 4

(v 1 - 5)[1]As a servant of Mine, you will learn things that will bring you great joy. [2]They will seem to be revealed to you, so you will know they are My gifts to you. [3]What is revealed to you is revealed for you and for everyone. [4]For when it is revealed to you, it is also communicated to everyone through communication to the one mind that you share.

[5]Do not judge yourself for what you believe are your shortcomings. [6]Remember that you are practicing to be one with Me through your own decision to accept our oneness as your only truth. [7]Because you still listen to the ego and believe it is you, you will seem to make mistakes in your own perception. [8]But there are no real mistakes since there is only truth, which does not change, and illusion, which isn't reality.

[9]Therefore, when you believe you have made a mistake, turn to Me. [10]Ask Me to use your perception for your learning. [11]In this way, you open yourself for another thought of Mine to be revealed. [12]In this way, you use everything within your experience as an opportunity to practice opening as an empty shell.

(v 6, 7)[1]When you do not forget, and you remember to be an empty shell in service to Me, be grateful to Me and to yourself. [2]In this way, you recognize that we are one.

[3]Do not make the mistake of believing that an empty shell is something other than Me. [4]It is not. [5]It is only Me. [6]This is possible *because it is an empty shell* (and no one else).

[7]Therefore, do not praise your brother or yourself apart from Me for My Word as it is shared. [8]Thank your brother for being a shell, and be

grateful that you remembered to put yourself aside. [9]But thank Me for My Word. [10]In that way, you acknowledge what is real for its reality, and you thank that which isn't real for recognizing its unreality and for getting out of the way of truth.

(v 8 – 17)[1]I am with you to bring back the memory of who you are. [2]With Me, you shall remember, because you recognize your Self in Me.

[3]Do not make the mistake of forgetting who I am when you *do know*. [4]I am you. [5]I am your truth.

[6]When you forget to remember what you know, you pretend to be what you are not. [7]When you pretend to be what you are not, you believe what you think, and you think you are different from that which you are.

[8]I ask you to lay your thinking aside. [9]And with it you lay aside all pretending that isn't truth. [10]This is to make yourself an empty shell. [11]An empty shell is not the absence of you. [12]An empty shell is the absence of delusion, which you are not.

[13]In the clarity of your emptiness, free from the delusion of false thoughts, you are free to hear your real thoughts. [14]These are the thoughts that you recognize as Me.

(v 18 – 21)[1]I am not coercive upon you, because I am your truth. [2]Because I am your truth, I am eternal and I am now. [3]Therefore, I can wait in peace and patience for you to recognize Me. [4]I can wait as long as you seem to be willing to wait. [5]But know this:

> [6]*Even your desire to wait comes from the delusion*
> *that you are what you are not.*

[7]Therefore, in choosing not to be an empty shell, you are choosing to believe delusion over truth. [8]The truth is as it is, as it cannot be anything else. [9]But you are choosing to believe that the truth is what it isn't so you may continue the experience of that which is untrue.

NTI 1 Corinthians, Chapter 5

(v 1 – 5)[1]Jesus told you that if your hand leads you to sin, cut off your hand. [2]And if your eye leads you to sin, cut out your eye. [3]This is what he meant by that:

[4]Within your mind, there are many thoughts. [5]As long as you seem to be within illusion, there will be thoughts, because illusion is thought. [6]But within the world of illusion, there are thoughts that lead you to put belief in illusion and thoughts that lead you to let go of these beliefs.

[7]The thoughts that lead you to believe in illusion are ego thoughts. [8]They are the thoughts that are based on the judgment that what *is* was made different, and so what *is different* is what is real.

[9]The thoughts that lead you from illusion are the Holy Spirit's thoughts. [10]They are based on knowledge that reality cannot be changed. [11]They call you to lay down fantasy and to again acknowledge what has always been true.

[12]You are asked to realize that both systems of thought are in your mind now. [13]And you are asked to remember that you want to know the truth. [14]Therefore, lay down the thoughts that lead you to believe in illusion. [15]They are not useful to your purpose. [16]They are not helpful to you now.

(v 6 – 8)[1]Don't you know that a little yeast works through the whole batch of dough? [2]Get rid of the old yeast, that you may be a new batch without the old (as you really are).

[3]The bread without yeast is the same as the empty shell. [4]Be without the yeast of the world. [5]Be without the thoughts that seem to belong to you. [6]Be free of the past, and welcome what is truth. [7]It is your truth now, as it has always been the truth.

(v 9 – 11)[1]Do not partake of the thoughts that lead you to believe in the world. [2]Do not entertain them as true. [3]Let go of them as soon as they seem to be thought, and you free yourself to welcome thoughts that will seem new.

(v 12, 13)[1]Do not worry about your brother's thought. [2]For the thought you think he thinks is a thought within your mind. ³Look after your own thoughts, that you may be freed of your belief in the world. ⁴To be freed of the burden of belief is to be open to the realization of knowledge.

NTI 1 Corinthians, Chapter 6

(v 1 – 6)¹Do you disagree with your brother? ²Look in your mind. ³Do you find that thought there? ⁴If you can find even an inkling of this thought within your mind, then you believe in division. ⁵An empty shell will not hold this thought, because an empty shell is empty of all thoughts that are not of Mine.

⁶Empty your mind of all disagreements. ⁷Become, willingly, an empty shell.

(v 7 – 11)¹Do you have thoughts of temptation in your mind? ²Look at your thoughts of temptation, but do not focus your gaze on them. ³Instead, look at the belief that is their foundation. ⁴If you believe there are temptations in your mind, you must also believe that you are separate from God. ⁵For could God have temptations in His Mind?

⁶Whenever you see temptations in your mind, you are believing unreality.

⁷Let go of every thought of unreality. ⁸Become an empty shell. ⁹An empty shell has no identity, and so there is no identity to feel temptation.

(v 12 – 20)¹An empty shell has let go of everything that seemed to be, but wasn't. ²An empty shell has let go of false desires, untrue beliefs, concepts in support of the world and fear. ³All that an empty shell holds onto is the casing, which will hold onto Me within the world. ⁴That casing is made of trust.

⁵If it is not trust in the Holy Spirit, let it go. ⁶You do not need it. ⁷It does not belong in an empty shell, and if it is present, the shell itself is not empty.

NTI 1 Corinthians, Chapter 7

(v 1 – 7)¹An empty shell has been emptied, and it knows itself as empty. [2]A shell that has not been emptied knows its own thoughts. [3]Do not fear the thoughts that are in your mind. [4]Do not fear that they do not belong there and so you are guilty. [5]The thoughts in your mind seem to come to you of their own accord. [6]You are not to be judged guilty for this.

[7]Practice is the answer until you know yourself to be an empty shell. [8]You will find times when you remember to look at your thoughts and notice that your mind is full. [9]That is a time that you are being invited to practice clearing your mind and becoming as an empty shell.

[10]Know there is an effective method of practice and there is a method that will seem to make the practice less useful to you. [11]The effective method is to clear your thoughts by letting them pass upward. [12]The less effective method is to press them back down into the place from which they seemed to arise.

[13]To let the thoughts pass upward, you must remember to trust in Me. [14]I have said that you are innocent. [15]If you trust in Me you will be able to look at your thoughts and let them pass upward, out of the shell, leaving the space within the shell empty.

[16]But if you do not trust Me, you will fear your thoughts, and you will repress them. [17]In this way, the shell is not emptied, and there is pressure within the shell from where the feared thought is hidden.

(v 8 – 14)[1]Remember this:

[2]*Your truth is as it is and cannot be changed.*

[3]If you seem to make a mistake in your attempts to empty your shell, do not worry. [4]It is only practice. [5]More opportunities to practice will be given. [6]Do not worry that the shell must be emptied or you are a sinner. [7]For in truth, the shell does not exist. [8]Therefore, it cannot be emptied or full in reality. [9]Therefore, the condition of the shell has no affect on your worth.

(v 15 – 24)[1]You seem to be in the world and you experience yourself there, but I have already told you that you are not in the world.

[2]Therefore, nothing in the world can be important to who you are.

[3]The reason for emptying the shell is not to free you. [4]You are free! [5]The reason for emptying the shell is not to make you loved. [6]You are Love! [7]The reason for emptying the shell is to let go of the points of experience that tell you that you are what you are not.

[8]Each thought that seems to speak of unworthiness, guilt or fear in the world...each thought that seems to express the wish, "What if it were different than it is?"...each thought that seems to interpret anything in the world as if it were true...each of these thoughts are made to give you the experience of experience that isn't true. [9]So each thought must be handed out of the shell, that the shell may be emptied of all points of experience.

[10]When the points of experience are all released from the shell, the shell no longer senses experience, and another experience may come in to fill the shell. [11]It is this second experience that points to truth.

(v 25 – 28)[1]Do not worry that you experience the world. [2]Worry *is* a point of experience. [3]Release it from the shell.

[4]Do not feel guilty that your shell is not emptied. [5]Guilt *is* a point of experience. [6]Release it from the shell.

[7]Do not be sad that you do not know the second experience that comes. [8]Wishing is the *cause* of all points of experience. [9]Release wishing, and many points of experience will leave the shell with it.

(v 29 – 31)[1]Remember that the shell is not real, so whatever experience you seem to experience within the shell is not real either. [2]Therefore, be not attached to the experience you experience or the one you wish to experience. [3]Be free, instead, to realize there is no shell.

(v 32 – 35)[1]Remembering there is no shell and there is no experience that is true experience will free you from attachment to points of experience. [2]When you are freed from attachments you will release them more easily, and you will travel this path of remembrance more swiftly with Me.

(v 36 – 38)[1]Remember to stay focused on your own guidance within the world. [2]Your guidance leads you, based on your willingness, to the circumstances that will help you to empty your shell.

(v 39, 40)[1]Following guidance and staying with trust *now* is the best way to empty your shell. [2]Give no thought or concern to emptying it. [3]When you are called to notice the thoughts in your mind, notice them and let them go *right then*. [4]When you do not notice the thoughts in your mind, be happy in those times also. [5]For always the truth is true, and so always there is cause for happiness.

NTI 1 Corinthians, Chapter 8

(v 1- 3)[1]When you do not seem to know how to become an empty shell, it is because you are focusing on your head, or better said, your thinking mind. [2]Your thinking mind will not teach you how not to think. [3]Your thinking mind is interested in its own survival, so it will take the time you give it to think some more.

[4]When you notice your mind is full and you want to become as an empty shell, you must refocus your mind from your head to your Heart. [5]Your Heart will teach your mind the way of release, because your Heart is love.

(v 4 – 6)[1]Your Heart, being of love, knows one purpose, and that is Love. [2]Your head, being of thinking, knows many purposes, because that is "thinking." [3]Let go of the confusion of the head and focus yourself on the purpose of the Heart. [4]Focusing on one purpose leads you clearly in one direction, but focusing on many purposes does not lead you at all.

(v 7 – 13)[1]Your mind is willing for distractions, because your mind is split. [2]This is why you must focus your mind on the Heart and the leadership that is found there. [3]When your mind is focused on the head it revels in its own distractions, and it spins within the joy of its own pain. [4]When your mind is focused on the Heart it recalls its true joy. [5]And in the willingness given through this memory, it lets go of the distractions of the head.

[6]In this way, the Heart leads you to become an empty shell. [7]In this way, you surrender the experience you do not want and you welcome the

one that you do.

NTI 1 Corinthians, Chapter 9

(v 1 – 6)[1]There is a voice within you that claims to be you. [2]This voice does not try to deceive you, because this voice does believe it is you. [3]Therefore, all that it whispers into your mind, it whispers in belief that it is truth.

[4]But the reason that this voice is not truth is because this voice cannot see you. [5]It cannot know you, because this voice cannot see you. [6]Therefore, the voice is mistaken. [7]All that it tells you, believing it is true, is based on mistake, and so it is mistaken also.

(v 7 – 12)[1]The voice that thinks it is you has convinced you that it is you also, and so you listen to this voice as if it is you. [2]You are loyal to its thoughts. [3]If this voice tells you that you must defend yourself in this way or that, you defend yourself as it says, for you believe that following the voice is your own defense of yourself. [4]But since the voice is not you, it is not you that you defend in following it. [5]Since this voice is the voice of a mistake about who you are, in listening to the voice you defend a mistake, but believe it is true.

(v 13, 14)[1]To listen to this voice and do as it says is to defend that you are what you are not. [2]To listen to this voice and do as it says is to choose to remain blinded to your truth.

(v 15 – 18)[1]Listen to Me. [2]You are not what you think you are. [3]You are not the image that you defend as yourself. [4]This is why I ask you to become a willing empty shell. [5]A willing empty shell has chosen to put aside listening to the voice that has filled it. [6]A willing empty shell has chosen to let go of beliefs it has taken as it has listened to this mistaken voice. [7]A willing empty shell has decided to clear itself of all mistakes and every grain that has been based on mistake, that it may be open and clear to receive the fullness of its truth.

(v 19 – 23)[1]Clear the thoughts that are in your mind by being willing to let go of all of them. [2]Do not fear that some thoughts are true, and upon your own judgment, must be held onto. [3]For the one who judges *is* the mistaken voice. [4]Therefore, let go of everything, that you may be free of it all. [5]Maintain only the casing, which is trust. [6]When you have emptied, holding onto nothing but your trust, you shall be filled again, and nothing that is true shall be lost.

(v 24 – 27)[1]Give it your all. [2]Give all of your thought and all of your action to the purpose of emptying your shell fully. [3]This is how you will know your reward, which is the truth of who you are. [4]Your truth is more beautiful and more precious to you than you imagine now. [5]Let go of all fear that says it is not. [6]Give everything to emptying your shell. [7]In this way, you give everything to you. [8]Amen.

NTI 1 Corinthians, Chapter 10

(v 1 - 10)[1]There is no right and there is no wrong. [2]There is no right thing to do and there is no mistake. [3]Do not judge yourself on this criteria.

[4]Become as an empty shell, remembering that you do not know. [5]If you will let go of judgment and give everything to Me, I will judge it for you. [6]I will not judge it as good or bad or right or wrong. [7]I will only judge it as true or untrue. [8]Then you may choose if you want that which is true, or if you desire the untrue a little longer.

(v 11 – 13)[1]Remember that an empty shell holds only to its casing, and that is trust. [2]Remember what your true desire is, for you *do know*. [3]Listen to your own Heart and choose what is given as true. [4]What is not given, do not choose. [5]In this way, you cease to think for yourself, and you become as an empty shell.

(v 14 – 17)[1]We partake of one loaf. [2]We drink of one cup. [3]This is because we are one.

[4]When you choose to think the thoughts that are not Mine, you are not sharing in our thought with Me. [5]When you do not share in our truth, you entertain yourself with illusion. [6]This does not change our truth, but it does blind you to the truth. [7]Are you ready to remove the blindfold you have given to yourself? [8]Are you ready to become as Me and see?

(v 18 – 22)[1]"You cannot serve two masters," means that you cannot believe illusory thoughts are true and know true thoughts as true also. [2]True thoughts are always true, and illusory thoughts are not true, but illusory thoughts may be chosen as experience over thoughts that are true.

[3]If a false experience is your choice, a false experience is what you are given. [4]But the carnival ride of falsity must end when you are ready to turn into the Light.

[5]I am waiting for you to make the decision I know you will make. [6]I am waiting for your signal, which is the empty shell. [7]When you have given the signal to Me, I will know you are ready for the Light. [8]You will not have to ask twice. [9]The moment the signal is given, the Light shall be given also.

(v 23, 24)[1]Everything is permissible, but not everything is beneficial. [2]Yet, that which is not beneficial cannot hurt, because it cannot change the truth.

(v 25 – 30)[1]Everything is permissible, but do you still seek that which is untrue? [2]If your answer is "no," then why do you still go after it by partaking of illusory thoughts? [3]That which you think *is* that which you experience. [4]If you have tired of the experience that is untrue, stop feasting on its thoughts. [5]Let them pass by without tasting them. [6]In this way, you become an empty shell, free of the experience you no longer want.

(v 31 – 33)   [1]*Keep what you truly want in your mind.*
[2]*Let true desire be your guide.*

NTI 1 Corinthians, Chapter 11

(v 1)[1]Follow My guidance as I lead you to your truth.

(v 2)[1]I am grateful to you for continuing on the path with Me, just as I am grateful to you for all things. [2]For I can never not be grateful to you, because I know your truth, and I know your Father who created you the same as He.

(v 3 – 10)[1]Trust in Me, as I am your authority in the world. [2]I am not a false authority, which would not recognize you and would try to tell you what to do. [3]I am true Authority, because I *do* recognize you. [4]I lead you where you want to go. [5]Do not fear that I will ask you to do what you do not want to do. [6]I cannot do that, because I know what you are. [7]This is why I wait for your invitation to give you what you want. [8]For I do know that you want it, but knowing who you are, I wait until you know also.

(v 11 – 16)[1]You can trust in Me, because I am you. [2]We are one in God. [3]Therefore, I cannot want for you that which you do not want for yourself. [4]I can only want for you that which you do want. [5]This is why you have freedom to choose dreams of illusion, if that is the experience you desire. [6]I will not take from you that which you desire. [7]I will only give that which you seek. [8]I cannot take. [9]I can only give, because I know that you are Me.

(v 17 – 26)[1]Remember Me in all things and in all that you do. [2]Remember that I am your truth, and I am the one within you who does not lose sight of your true desire. [3]While you may still lose sight, give all things to Me. [4]In this way, you are led consistently in the direction of your truth. [5]Hold nothing back from Me. [6]Do not feel you need to handle anything yourself. [7]For to feel you must handle anything yourself is to believe that we are not one and that I can want what you do not want. [8]Let go of your desire to have things your way by remembering that your way, separate from Me, is illusion. [9]That way is no way. [10]Surrender that way, and become an empty shell.

(v 27 – 32)[1]Trust in Me is trust in your Self. [2]You do not give trust to something that is not you, for I am you. [3]This is why you can trust Me. [4]I am you, and I see you. [5]Because I see you as Me, I know you. [6]I am not the illusory self who leads you through blindness and fear. [7]I am the true Self who leads you through Light and through knowledge. [8]I will never make you suffer, because I know you cannot suffer. [9]You can only be free. [10]And through our freedom, I share My freedom with you.

(v 33, 34)[1]So you may rest and not fear. [2]Whatever you want shall be given, as long as you want it. [3]When you do not want it, it will not be taken away; you will release it of your own freedom. [4]It is through becoming an empty shell that you signal you have tired of games. [5]So it is through your gift of an empty shell that I shall fill you with the memory of our truth.

NTI 1 Corinthians, Chapter 12

(v 1 – 11)[1]Judgment is the tool of illusion, so as long as you desire illusion, judgment is a tool you will hold dear. [2]If you do not want illusion, do not work with this tool. [3]For as you work with it, you build the illusion you think you want, but do not want.

[4]Watch your mind for the subtle judgments that you make. [5]Watch your mind for its wishes, for each wish signals a judgment has been made. [6]For wherever there is a wish, there has been a judgment, and wherever there has been a judgment, there has been a wish.

[7]Illusion is a trick you have made on yourself, because you wanted the experience to be real. [8]You judged that you wanted something different, you wished for something different, then you judged it had been made real. [9]In this way, everything you made, you made for yourself.

[10]The experience you made is your experience now, because you continue to make it so. [11]It is *now* that matters, because it is now that makes now. [12]So your subtle judgments must be seen.

(v 12, 13)[1]This is why I ask you to see the world as one song or as a script. [2]It is so you will not break it into parts to judge. [3]One song is a whole, perfect at its finish. [4]One script cannot be broken apart.

(v 14 – 20)[1]When you look at your brothers you see separate parts, but this must mean that you are not looking with Me. [2]For I do not see separate parts of one thing. [3]When I look, I only see the whole.

(v 21 – 26)[1]When you look with Me, there is nothing to judge. [2]For everything works for the healing of one mind. [3]There is no error, and there is no mistake. [4]There isn't one single flaw. [5]There is only a mind listening to itself and recognizing which self is true. [6]It is an awakening, a growing recognition, and it is perfect in every way.

(v 27 – 31)[1]When you look on the world and seem to see differences, remember you are not looking with Me. [2]Surrender your sight, because you do not want it now. [3]Do not judge what you see or you accept it as real, and you hold onto the experience of illusion. [4]You must release it by not judging it, through trusting it is not real. [5]See only that it is not your desire. [6]Let it pass upward, out of your shell, freeing your mind of its trick.

[7]*Flee with Me,*
and know you are free.

NTI 1 Corinthians, Chapter 13

(v 1 – 7)[1]The reason for all things is Love. [2]Division is the opposite of Love, because division excludes. [3]Love cannot exclude. [4]Love is whole, knowing only truth.

[5]Become as an empty shell to know Love. [6]That is your reason. [7]That is your true desire. [8]To look on the world and divide it by judging is not Love, and so it is not what you want. [9]Lay down what you do not want, and accept joyfully that which you do.

(v 8 – 12)[1]When you look on the world you see the reflection of your mind, which makes the world through thought. [2]What you believe and what you accept is seen in the world. [3]There is division in what you see, because there is division in your thought. [4]This thought is not Love. [5]This thought is the denial of Love, which is all that truly exists.

[6]To cease denial and see truth, which you truly desire, become as an empty shell. [7]Let go of thoughts of division, that you may see the beauty of your oneness face-to-face, and you may rejoice.

(v 13)   *¹Trust is the means,*
and Love is the reason.
²Give everything to trust in the Holy Spirit,
because Love is all that you desire.

NTI 1 Corinthians, Chapter 14

(v 1 – 5)¹Do not wish for gifts that are not yours, for everything is yours. ²To wish for something that you believe you do not have is to believe that you are an illusion of yourself.

³Lay down your wishing and your partial definition of who you are. ⁴Be open to receive the truth.

(v 6 – 12)¹You are the Son of God. ²You do not see yourself in this way, because you choose to see yourself in other ways. ³The other definitions that you choose are chosen by you as a mask of who you would like to be, but a mask covers that which you are. ⁴In living out your roles as you have chosen them to be, you have forgotten the truth that is under the mask.

⁵Surely the one under the mask is the creator of everything that makes up the mask. ⁶Surely the one who made the mask is beyond the mask that he made.

⁷You, who limit yourself to the mask, limit one who is unlimited, and you do this by your own choice.

⁸Lay down the mask. ⁹Lay down the roles and concepts that tell you who you are. ¹⁰Realize that you have forgotten everything beyond the mask that you have held to. ¹¹Become as an empty shell, without any part of the mask held for security. ¹²Release all of it, that I may fill you with the memory of who you are.

(v 13 – 17)¹You do not know who you are. ²This is true enough, only you do not know it is true if you are insisting on clinging to your mask.

(v 18 – 21)¹The heart knows you are not the many faces of the mask that you wear. ²The heart knows you are beyond the mask. ³Yet the heart cannot know what the mind does not know. ⁴The heart can only know there is more and then call to the mind to seek that which the heart feels. [5]But if the mind answers the heart with belief in the mask, the heart knows it has not been answered.

[6]Listen to the calling of the heart. [7]Lay down all belief in the mask. [8]At the heart's true pleading, become as an empty shell, that you may be filled with the true answer that satisfies the question of the heart.

(v 22 – 28)[1]Your mask is like a block to your truth. [2]As you hold the mask up firmly, claiming it is what you are, that which is your truth is firmly hidden by you.

[3]Look carefully at what you do. [4]Is this truly what you want to do? [5]Do you wish to insist that you are what you are not? [6]Can a mask, even though it is insisted upon, become truth?

[7]It is your truth that shines for all to see and recognize, not your mask. [8]For masks are limits, and limits are not real. [9]No one looks upon limits and feels freed.

[10]Remove the mask. [11]Let truth be known, that it may extend through you. [12]This way, your brother recognizes the tight fit of his own mask, and he *also* seeks to be freed of limits.

(v 29 – 40)[1]Lay down all limits that you have taken up upon yourself. [2]I did not give you any of them. [3]They are not of Me. [4]They are not of your truth. [5]They are of the mask, by the mask and for the mask. [6]Therefore, they can only limit *the mask*. [7]By laying down the mask, you lay down limits also.

NTI 1 Corinthians, Chapter 15

(v 1, 2)[1]Let me remind you of the simplicity of what I request. [2]I do not ask you to judge which thoughts are to be laid down and which thoughts are to be kept, for such a request would keep you busy and stuck within illusion for an eternity. [3]I ask you to willingly lay down everything but your trust. [4]This is why the symbol of an empty shell is given. [5]Keep nothing but the casing, which is trust. [6]In this way, you hold onto nothing that blocks out truth, and truth may be freely given and freely welcomed as it is received.

(v 3 – 11)[1]What is received when all that is false has been let go is only that which reflects truth. [2]This, which is received as truth, shall fill you with new eyes and a joyous heart. [3]In this way, you will be ready to point the way, for you will no longer be fooled by that which is false. [4]You shall have a taste of truth. [5]It is upon this recognition, which is the completeness of recognition within time, that you enter the fourth and final earthly phase of the path of truth with Me.

(v 12 – 19)[1]The fourth phase is a glorious phase, upon which your feet shall barely touch the ground. [2]As you walk the earth, you know where you walk, so that the earth is merely a symbol within the mind. [3]You shall not know brothers, but you shall talk to them. [4]You will not need food, but you will eat with joy. [5]Music shall accompany you in your every moment, and yet, you will have no need for your ears. [6]Your sight will be changed from earthly sight to sight that is provided from Heaven. [7]All things shall be new, and you shall have no need for any of them. [8]In this, your joy shall be complete.

(v 20 - 28)[1]The purpose of your life in the fourth phase of living on earth shall not be different than the purpose at any other time. [2]Only now, in the fourth phase, the distractions have been erased. [3]In letting yourself become an empty shell, you freed yourself from the desire for distraction. [4]Now, in the fourth stage, your focus is complete. [5]Now you know what you want, and you want it wholly.

(v 29 – 34)[1]During the fourth phase, there are no distractions. [2]During the fourth phase, there are no fears. [3]There are no doubts, and there is no feeling of guilt. [4]There is only a knowing of what is true and a life that is the willingness for acceptance.

(v 35 – 49)[1]The one that seems to be in the fourth stage is but a symbol of the truth that is. [2]So this one must pass away also. [3]But in its passing, you pass from a final illusion of beauty to Beauty that cannot be contained in illusion. [4]You pass from form, which reflects Light, to Light, which shines into form.

(v 50 – 55)[1]You shall not know death in your passing from the fourth phase to Light, for this passing is recognition of Life. [2]This passing is acceptance of all that is true and all that has always been true. [3]This passing is the final release of illusion, so that no illusion may appear to you. [4]And death is an illusion. [5]So you shall not know death, because you have accepted that illusion does not exist.

(v 56 – 58)[1]Therefore, be willing to become an empty shell. [2]And be willing for this completely. [3]For it is through emptiness that illusion is released, and it is through releasing it, that illusion is taken away.

NTI 1 Corinthians, Chapter 16

(v 1 – 4)[1]Set aside your thoughts of division. [2]When you see them in your mind or in the playing out of thought within the world, rejoice! [3]What you see is not true. [4]Be happy that you have found willingness to deny that which is false, for inherent in its denial is the willingness to accept only that which is true.

(v 5 - 9)[1]The door that is opened is the doorway to the Light, which is also the doorway to your Self and your brothers, who are one with you. [2]In passing through that doorway, you can not return. [3]For to return would be to pass from Awareness to the belief in lack of awareness and division.

[4]One who knows wholeness after experiencing the lack of wholeness knows illusion is no substitute for truth. [5]He shall not choose illusion again.

[6]But, being one mind with all that he thought was separate, he shall remain as a memory to call the mind that sleeps into wakefulness, that all that is whole may know Itself as one and whole again.

(v 10, 11)[1]It is your brothers who are you in truth. [2]Look beyond their illusion, and you look beyond your own. [3]Forgive them their mask, and you forgive your own. [4]Accept them as innocent and as Love, and you accept your Self. [5]Reject nothing that is true and accept nothing that is false, and you free yourself of your own willingness.

(v 12 – 14)[1]Do everything in love, which is trust and acceptance within the world. [2]In this way, you look beyond the world to the truth that is your reality, and you accept it into your heart once again. [3]In this way, you greet your brother in his truth. [4]And in this way, you greet and welcome your Self.

(v 15- 18)[1]There is only One. [2]All else is false. [3]It is an image over the truth, which remains true behind it. [4]It is a mask on the Light that is you. [5]It is nothing permanent, and so it is not real. [6]It deserves gratitude as an expression of freedom, but ask to give it nothing more. [7]Say thank you, and give it release.

(v 19 – 24)[1]Peace be in your mind, for there is nothing to fear. [2]All that you give, you give to yourself. [3]Let the gift that has been given be appreciated and let go. [4]It is only a reflection of your freedom. [5]It is not a reflection of your truth.

[6]In truth, you are whole. [7]In freedom, you are an expression.

[8]Release the expression you no longer want. [9]Know your Self as whole and free again. [10]Amen.

THE HOLY SPIRIT'S INTERPRETATION OF 2 CORINTHIANS

NTI 2 Corinthians, Chapter 1

(v 1, 2)[1]This is a letter to you from your own Holy Spirit. [2]Listen to Him as you read, and know your own guidance. [3]Through what is shared through you, you shall learn who you are.

(v 3 – 11) [1]Everything that comes to you comes to you for your healing. [2]There is nothing that you experience that cannot have that purpose if that is the purpose you give it. [3]But hear Me well. [4]I have said that is the purpose it will have *if that is the purpose you give it.* [5]This is because of who you are. [6]If you do not give the purpose of healing to your life, it shall not have that purpose. [7]And no experience can bring to you that which you do not desire.

[8]Yet the opposite is also true. [9]If healing is the purpose that you give to all things in your life, then all things shall have that purpose and no thing can occur that does not have that purpose. [10]For you choose your own blessings. [11]And the one who chooses healing is the one who knows he is blessed.

(v 12 – 14) [1]Why can I write these things of you in confidence and certainty without exception of any kind? [2]It is because I know who you are. [3]I know your purpose is your purpose, because I know your freedom. [4]I know nothing can take the purpose that you choose from you. [5]Nothing can deny you the experience you choose to have.

(v 15 – 24) [1]How are you to interpret the events in your life so that they may bring you joy? [2]You are to interpret them truly and not with confusion.

[3]Confusion says that the events in your life are lord over you. [4]Confusion says the events in your life may bring you joy or sorrow, or pain or peace, or fear or safety, or danger, or frustration, or any number of feelings, thoughts and reactions. [5]But always, confusion says the events are lord and you are subject, in all circumstances, to react accordingly to your lord.

[6]The true interpretation comes from who you are. [7]You are not subject to a lord who rules over you. [8]You are lord of your own subject. [9]In other words, your experience is given you, because you have chosen it. [10]And so, if you would have another experience, you must choose differently.

NTI 2 Corinthians, Chapter 2

(v 1 – 4)[1]Do not change your mind out of fear, but out of love, for Love is the only power that is real.

[2]When you change your mind out of fear, you attempt to change your experience, because you believe your experience is lord. [3]In this case, you wish for a different experience, because you believe a different experience is needed to bring you joy. [4]This purpose denies who you are, and so you shall learn that you are who you are not through choosing this experience.

[5]To learn who you are, do not seek an experience that will give you what you want. [6]Choose instead to be independent of your experience. [7]In choosing independence, you learn you are not subject. [8]And when you have learned you are not subject, you are free to learn you are lord.

(v 5 – 11)[1]To forgive a circumstance or event is not to separate it into segments and to judge it and to determine where there is guilt and where there may be innocence. [2]To forgive is to look at a circumstance or event as a whole, without separate parts, and to know that one whole can have only one purpose. [3]And then, remember that the circumstance is not lord, which chooses its purpose, but you are. [4]As lord, you may choose the purpose that will bring to you the joy of release. [5]In choosing this purpose, you choose to forgive the idea that you could be what you are not.

(v 12 – 17)[1]Know, then, who you are. [2]Look on the world with new eyes. [3]You are not the effect of what you see, but you do feel the effect of what you choose. [4]You are the maker of experience. [5]Experience is not the maker of you. [6]It is for this reason that you do have a choice. [7]Will you let experience tell you how you are to feel? [8]Or will you let *how you feel* tell experience what kind of experience it is to be?

[9]Always, you may choose healing, if that is what you choose to feel. [10]Always, because you are lord, the world and all of its events may come to you to heal you and to soothe you of the pain that comes when you have chosen to forget that you are, and truly always will be, the lord of all you choose to experience.

NTI 2 Corinthians, Chapter 3

(v 1 – 6)[1]Evidence is sought within the world. [2]You look at the world, and you seek evidence that what I say is true. [3]But if you look at the world with the thought that what I say may not be true, that is the evidence you will find. [4]For the world was written as an experience of untruth. [5]And so the world can be used to prove that the untrue is true, if that is the evidence that the mind seeks.

[6]I ask you to not look at the world. [7]I ask you to look in your Heart and see what you find there. [8]Your truth is written on your Heart. [9]And by seeking there, *not* in the world, you will find confirmation that all I say is true.

[10]For you do know the truth when you hear it. [11]You know it, because it is written on your Heart. [12]It is written on your Heart, because it is *you*.

(v 7 – 11)[1]You were taught to look at the world by a desire to know the untrue as true. [2]This is the evidence that the world is. [3]And this is what you learn when you look at the world and believe it as evidence.

[4]But now I ask you to look in a new place for evidence. [5]I ask you to look, not at the world for proof of what is true, but to look within your Self where the truth about you is known.

(v 12 – 18)[1]The world was made to tell you that you are what you are not. [2]But this is a lesson you can never fully learn, because the truth of what you are is written on your Heart. [3]Seek there! [4]Ask your Heart what you are, and the answer will be given clearly. [5]Then look at the world, which gives you a different answer, and say to it, "I will believe the answer of the Heart. [6]I will let that answer shine unto you."

[7]By listening to the Heart and following its truth within the world, you become a symbol that the world is not lord. [8]Your symbol is a message into the mind that sings, "Look into the Heart!"

[9]In this way, your message is clear and it is consistent. [10]For when the mind looks to the Heart for guidance, it will find only the guidance of the Heart. [11]The guidance of the Heart is one, because the message of the Heart is one. [12]You are Love, and anything that is not Love must only be an illusion of what you are.

[13]Look not upon illusions, that you are not fooled. [14]Look upon thy Heart, and Know thy Self truly.

NTI 2 Corinthians, Chapter 4

(v 1 - 6)[1]Belief in the world is the veil of darkness, but this veil was not placed there by one greater than you. [2]This veil is not an obstacle that cannot be lifted through your own desire. [3]This veil was placed over truth through your own desire to see apart from truth. [4]Therefore, the veil is lifted through your desire to lay down untruth and to see through the Vision of Truth again.

(v 7 – 12)[1]This is how death and the resurrection are to be acted out through you:

[2]*The truth cannot die, so the truth need not be resurrected.* [3]*The truth simply is, and it always is without beginning and without end.* [4]*What is it, then, that must die?* [5]*What is there to be resurrected?* [6]*Your belief in illusions must die, so that your awareness of what is may be resurrected through you.*

(v 13 – 15)[1]Your belief is expressed through thought. [2]Above all else, watch your thoughts. [3]What are you allowing your thoughts to think? [4]Are you thinking of the illusion of the world as if it is real? [5]If so, you are expressing your desire to accept the veil of darkness. [6]Is this your true desire? [7]If not, why do you permit yourself to express it through the activity of your thoughts?

[8]Watch your thoughts. [9]Ask them to express your true desire. [10]Your thoughts must do as you ask, because you are the thinker of your thoughts. [11]Let them express your true desire. [12]If they do not, let them go.

(v 16 – 18)[1]Fix your eyes and your thoughts on the true desire of your Heart, not because it is your hope for the future, but because it is your reality now. [2]You are what your Heart tells you that you are. [3]Only you do not see it, because you do not focus yourself there.

[4]Focus on the world, and you will believe the world. [5]Believe the world, and you choose to keep the veil, which hides your truth.

[6]Focus on your Heart in all your thoughts, and you choose against the veil. [7]You choose, instead, that the veil may be lifted, that you may see your truth and your brother's truth and know in the joy of your Heart that it is true.

NTI 2 Corinthians, Chapter 5

(v 1 – 10)[1]This life that you experience within the world is a gift to yourself. [2]It is a gift based upon a wish that you could experience something different. [3]I have told you this before. [4]I have also told you that it is a perfect gift, for you have given yourself exactly as you asked. [5]You have the experience that is different from the experience of Heaven.

[6]If this experience of the world is the experience you have asked to receive, why do you suffer from it? [7]It is because you asked to suffer by asking not to experience Heaven.

[8]Listen to Me carefully now, for I will tell you why you think the way you do and why you experience that which you experience. [9]In seeing the

desire that has been hidden, you can decide to change the desire.

(v 11 – 15)[1]Within the mind now, you will find the desire for the world. [2]You will know this is your desire if you watch your thoughts. [3]For your thoughts are about the world, and your thoughts stem from your desire. [4]I have told you that your mind is split. [5]The desire for the world is split with the true desire of the Heart. [6]Both are there, and so both are in your thoughts.

[7]Your thoughts form your experience. [8]This is a literal statement, and it is to be taken literally. [9]There is nothing symbolic in what I am saying to you now.

[10]If you look in your mind, you will find that your mind is split and that your thoughts are split into two categories. [11]You have thoughts of the world, and you have thoughts that are not of the world. [12]The thoughts that are not of the world are thoughts of letting go of the world. [13]This is your true desire.

[14]But when you look in your mind, where are your thoughts as you suffer, as you are afraid or as you are feeling angry? [15]Are they with God or are they with the world?

[16]When your thoughts are with the world, you request an experience other than God. [17]This, then, is the experience you are given. [18]When you let go of the world, you experience truth.

(v 16 – 21)[1]This is what it means to become an empty shell. [2]It is to let go of the world, thoughts of the world and the desire for the world. [3]This is to let go of the desire for an experience that is different from Heaven. [4]And this is to open up to accept the experience of Heaven and the truth of Heaven *as it is* without the desire that it be different.

NTI 2 Corinthians, Chapter 6

(v 1, 2)[1]Now is the day of salvation, for now is the day that you can choose to think apart from the world. [2]You can choose to think apart from your experience. [3]As you do this earnestly, your experience will change, and you will find yourself willing to let go of the world.

(v 3 – 10)[1]To think apart from your experience and to think apart from the world is a request that is to be taken literally in all circumstances without exception. [2]This will seem to take practice, but as you practice, the increase in willingness will make the practice easier.

[3]Here is how you are to practice:

[4]As you suffer, choose not to suffer. [5]Let the experience of the body continue without the desire for the experience to be different. [6]Rejoice that the experience is not your reality.

[7]When you are afraid, choose not to be afraid by remembering that what you fear is not real. [8]It is of the world or it is born of thoughts of the world. [9]It is an experience, but it is not real. [10]It is not real, and so it is not your truth.

[11]When you are joyous because the world seems to be going your way, and today seems to be your day, remember *that* is not your joy. [12]Your joy is your truth, which is beyond the world. [13]Be happy and be joyous, but let your joy come to you apart from your experience. [14]Let your joy come to you from the truth in your Heart. [15]Relax in your joy and be your joy, beyond your experience of the world.

(v 11 – 13)[1]I say to you, do not look at the world and ask how you should think or how you should feel. [2]This is to believe the world is your lord. [3]To believe that is to believe it is real. [4]Accept that it is not real by surrendering to your desire for truth. [5]Accept the truth, and deny the world. [6]Let your joy come from you, and accept not that the world can change it.

(v 14 – 16)[1]Do not be content to let your thoughts of the world mix with your thoughts of God, for this is to be content with the agreement of the split mind. [2]The agreement of the split mind is the agreement that is different from Heaven. [3]Erase the split that has been imagined by erasing the desire for something different. [4]Recognize the world for what it is. [5]And let the thoughts that are worldly thoughts go with the desire that you no longer seek.

(v 17, 18)[1]Therefore, watch you mind and be honest about what you see. [2]Remember that your desire is split, but remember also your true desire. [3]The other is a desire of the past, and it has no purpose for you now. [4]Let it go along with the thoughts that stem from it. [5]Seek not the past. [6]Live not in the past. [7]Remain fixed on the current desire of the Heart, and you remain fixed on truth.

NTI 2 Corinthians, Chapter 7

(v 1)[1]A mistake that you make is believing that you are guilty for the imagining that you do. [2]I tell you, you are not guilty *because* you are imagining. [3]You are not guilty, because you are taking a walk through fantasy. [4]You are not guilty, because you have literally done nothing.

[5]This seems difficult for you to accept, because you believe the world. [6]You believe the world is real, so you must be guilty. [7]Can you see the direct connection between your belief in the world and your feeling of guilt?

[8]Can you imagine for a moment that the world is not real? [9]Can you imagine it as fantasy or a made up day dream? [10]When you imagine this, *really feel it*. [11]Feel that the world is not real. [12]And when you feel it, do you see how your feeling of guilt goes too?

[13]This is what I am telling you. [14]The world is illusion. [15]It is not real. [16]Heaven has not changed because of this imagined experience. [17]And so you are not guilty. [18]And because you are not guilty, you are free.

(v 2 - 7)[1]I have told you before how loved you are. [2]You have felt this love and known it. [3]This love that I speak of, which you know is God, came to be known to you from within. [4]This love that touched you and moved you with holiness came into your awareness from within you. [5]And this love you knew was real. [6]You felt its comfort, and you recognized it.

[7]Nothing in the world can comfort you and love you. [8]The love that comforts always comes from within. [9]You always feel it there and know it there. [10]You may credit something in the world with having caused it, but that is a mistake. [11]The love came into your mind and filled your

awareness through your willingness to know yourself as love.

[12]This is the meaning of God. [13]It is the love that lives and fills every being with perfection from within. [14]This is your truth. [15]This, *which you have known*, is reality.

(v 8 – 13)[1]By all this, I ask you to look again. [2]Look first in your heart and find God there. [3]*Then* look at the world. [4]Know that all hearts, at the deepest core, are the same. [5]*And then* look at the world. [6]Feel God. [7]Feel truth, *and then* look at the world.

[8]Which one is real and which is illusion? [9]Which is your true desire? [10]Which do you want to *be* and to extend? [11]You know the answer. [12]The answer to My question is your truth. [13]What you seek above all else is your Self. [14]You, in your reality, are the answer.

(v 14 – 16)[1]Open your heart and welcome your Self. [2]You are the truth that you seek. [3]And in welcoming your Self, you welcome your brothers, and you welcome all that is true about the world. [4]All that is not true is let go, because that which is not true is meaningless. [5]In this way, you rest in God. [6]When you rest in God, your truth is welcomed.

NTI 2 Corinthians, Chapter 8

(v 1- 7)[1]Listen for My words and you shall hear them, for I am always willing to speak to you. [2]You do not hear Me when I speak, because of your thinking and your thoughts about the meaning of the world. [3]But if you are willing to lay down your own thinking, you will hear Me. [4]When you are willing to lay down your own thinking completely, you will hear only Me, and you will rejoice.

[5]Let Me tell you what it means to give everything. [6]This is not a statement that can be measured and judged based on actions within the world, for the world is not real. [7]Therefore, you cannot be measured or judged by anything in the world. [8]But you can use the world to measure and judge your own giving, for your belief in the world is the measure and judgment of that which you give.

[9]You give through thought. [10]There *literally* is no other way to give.

[11]This is not a partial statement, nor is it symbolic. [12]It is a statement that is whole and completely your truth. [13]You give through thought.

> [14]*You give through thought.*
> [15]*There is literally no other way to give.*
> [16]*What you give is what is experienced,*
> *so your experience is a measure of what you give.*

[17]When I ask you to give everything, I ask that you give all thought to the true desire of the Heart. [18]This is the only way in which you can give. [19]To not give in this way is not to have given, since that which does not exist cannot be given.

(v 8, 9)[1]I ask you *now* to focus this lesson on the thoughts in your mind. [2]Do not look at the world, and do not look at your brothers to see how well they are learning what I teach. [3]To look at the world is to measure *your* thought. [4]What *you see* is your measure, not theirs. [5]So if you look, look in this way...*to see your own thoughts.* [6]But I tell you, it is better for you now not to look at all. [7]It is better and more effective if you remain focused within your mind.

(v 10 – 12)[1]I ask you to remember who you are when you look at your thoughts. [2]I have told you that you are the one Son of God, without division, living not within the world. [3]Do your thoughts tell you this? [4]Do they tell you that you are holy and one, not separate from anything? [5]Do they tell you that the world does not exist and you do, and so you must not be in the world? [6]Do they tell you that you are with God and God is with you, without distance or absence of any kind?

(v 13 – 15)[1]If your thoughts do not speak the truth of you, your thoughts are not the thoughts of giving.

(v 16 – 21)[1]Look, then, in your own mind. [2]Ask yourself, truly, how much you are giving. [3]You give more by not giving less. [4]You give truly by focusing your mind to give in alignment with the Heart.

(v 22 – 24)[1]Your true desire will guide your giving, so let your true desire lead in the watching of your mind. [2]Lay down thoughts of non-giving by seeing them as nothing, for that is what they are. [3]Pick up the thoughts of giving by knowing the true desire of the Heart. [4]For in *being* true desire, you *are* giving, and all that you give is received by everyone, through one mind, in full.

NTI 2 Corinthians, Chapter 9

(v 1 - 5)[1]When you believe in the world, you make the mistake of acting out your belief in the world.

[2]How is this a mistake, truly? [3]Is it a mistake because you took an action that you shouldn't have? [4]Is this a mistake because you have revealed yourself to your brothers as less than what they thought you were? [5]Is this a mistake within the world for which you are guilty?

[6]This is what you believe, but you believe this because you believe the world is true. [7]*And this* is why acting in the world is a mistake. [8]Acting on your belief that the world is real is a mistake, because it continues the belief within the mind.

(v 6 – 9)[1]Remember this:

[2]*"Whoever sows sparingly shall also reap sparingly,*
and whoever sows generously shall also reap generously."
[3]*This means that what you give,*
you experience.

[4]Your actions within the world are not important in themselves. [5]They cannot be. [6]The world is not real, and you, in truth, are not in the world. [7]You are a mind experiencing yourself in a world that does not exist. [8]But as you seem to act in the world based on your belief that you are in the world, the belief and delusion continues within the mind.

[9]As you sow delusion, you shall experience delusion. [10]This is to give nothing and to experience nothing as if it is real. [11]This is simply to dream. [12]This is to engage in fantasy. [13]It is nothing, although it may

frighten you.

[14]Step away from your fear. [15]Be willing to see that fantasy isn't reality. [16]Give unto yourself by willing not to continue thoughts of non-giving. [17]Relax into your trust in Me. [18]As you continue to believe in the world, *act* on your trust in Me. [19]This is not an action in the world, for there is no world. [20]But this *is* giving, because this is telling the mind that the truth must be true. [21]This is waking up from the dream by not participating in the belief in the dream anymore.

(v 10, 11)   [1]*The mind knows its own thoughts,*
and it reacts to them.

[2]The world is not real. [3]It is a delusion of the mind, but it is the delusion of *one* mind. [4]There are no separate minds with separate delusions. *5The thoughts you think are heard by one mind, and they affect the fantasy in the mind.*

[6]When you tell the mind that the world is not real, both through your thought and your seeming action, the world hears this thought through the mind, because the world is a thought in the mind. [7]The world will react, as the mind reacts, to the thoughts that have been given it.

[8]As you accept that the world is not real, and therefore can have no affect on you, the mind will begin to awaken by seeing for itself that a dream cannot affect the reality of existence as it is.

(v 12 – 15)[1]This service that you perform of *not believing in the world* and of not acting as if the world is real, is a service you provide for yourself and for the entirety of the one mind that you are. [2]No part of the mind is left out of the benefits of the service you perform.

[3]Through your service and your true dedication to this service, the mind is awakened to truth through what it learns. [4]Through your faith, you are a teacher. [5]And through your teaching, you are awakened by all that you learn.

NTI 2 Corinthians, Chapter 10

(v 1 – 6)[1]The question that you always ask is: [2]How you are to live in the world without being a part of the world? [3]This seems difficult to you, and in fact, nearly impossible. [4]But I tell you that it is not. [5]When you are thinking this way, you are listening to the voice of confusion.

(v 7 – 11)[1]You are looking only on the surface of things when you listen to the voice of confusion. [2]You are looking at the world as if it is real, and you are looking at actions as if they are actions. [3]Neither of these statements is true. [4]The world is not real, and actions are not actions. [5]The world is a thought within the mind of the Son of God. [6]And all actions within the world are the expression of thought. [7]Therefore, you must look beyond the world and beyond the action to the thought which spawns the image.

(v 12 – 18)[1]This is why I ask you to look within and not at the world. [2]When you look at the world, you are tempted to guess at the thought that is in your brother's mind. [3]But can you guess the thought that is in your brother's mind? [4]No, you cannot guess. [5]You cannot guess by what you see in the world or by his actions, for his thought is unknown to you. [6]You see only the surface, which is unreal. [7]Therefore, you cannot judge your brother by what you see.

[8]If you look at the world and think you know your brother's thought or motive, you have only uncovered a thought or idea *within your own mind*. [9]It is not your brother's mind that you see when you look at the world. [10]*You see your mind*, for you are looking at the world through the filter of your own thoughts.

[11]This is why I ask you to stay focused within. [12]Look within your mind and your Heart before you look at the world. [13]Know your purpose, which is the true desire of the Heart. [14]Let your purpose lead you in all things. [15]In this way, all actions that you take will be an expression of the true Heart, so all actions shall be giving of the thought of Love.

NTI 2 Corinthians, Chapter 11

(v 1 – 12) [1] I ask you to rest the mind. [2] There is an important reason for this request. [3] When you look at the world, you are looking at the thought of confusion. [4] That is quite literally what the reflection of the world is. [5] It is the thought that fantasy has become reality, and that is the thought of confusion.

[6] When you look at the world, you look at the thought of confusion. [7] And so it is thoughts of confusion that come into your mind as you look. [8] You hear these thoughts, and you believe them, because confusion has influence over you.

[9] I ask you to rest the mind. [10] Resting is the realization that confusion rules in the world. [11] And it is also the decision not to be ruled by confusion anymore. [12] In resting the mind from thoughts of confusion, you let them float away un-believed. [13] Then thoughts of wisdom may be given.

[14] Thoughts of wisdom come from You, not confusion. [15] Thoughts of wisdom spring forth from Me, which is the true desire of the Heart.

(v 13 – 15) [1] Do not be confused. [2] The world is confusion and thoughts of the world are thoughts of confusion. [3] Thoughts of confusion are not your truth, so thoughts of confusion are not the thoughts you want to attempt to share.

(v 16 – 29) [1] The mind is tricky, because the mind is split. [2] On your own, you cannot trust the thoughts of the mind. [3] Thoughts of the mind may seem righteous when they are but confusion. [4] To listen to the mind without testing it is to risk listening to confusion as if it makes sense.

[5] The test for the mind is purpose. [6] And *purpose* is the true desire of the Heart. [7] Because the Heart is not at the surface of the mind, the mind must rest to be tested by the Heart. [8] But the test is not difficult. [9] The rest need not be long. [10] It only takes a moment to remember your purpose and only an instant to make the mind subordinate to the Heart.

(v 30 – 33) [1] Do not fear that you do not know confusion and do not know the purpose of the Heart. [2] *You do know.* [3] It is written within you by the nature of your truth. [4]Seek only for a moment to test your thoughts by the true desire of the Heart, and the light of the Heart shall shine, that you may see your thoughts truly. [5]You cannot be confused within the light of the Heart, for the light of the Heart is your memory of truth. [6]And your memory of truth knows not of confusion, so confusion must disappear in its light.

[7]Free yourself from encirclement within the world. [8]Free yourself from its confusion. [9]Quiet your mind, and ask the Heart within. [10]From the depth of your Heart, your freedom is known.

NTI 2 Corinthians, Chapter 12

(v 1 – 6) [1]Heaven is within you. [2]This is a statement that you may take as truth. [3]This statement is truth, because of who you are in truth.

[4]You seem to be a man or a woman, an individual soul within a body within a world within a cosmos. [5]This seems to be who you are, but this is not a fact. [6]This is a perception.

[7]It seems that you are within, and everything else is without. [8]This seems to be, but this is not truth. [9]So I ask you to start with you, which you know is within, and discover that the world and Heaven are within you also. [10]This seems to be a bold statement, but it is not. [11]It is only a simple statement of fact, which you shall see as you come with Me to seek within.

(v 7 – 10) [1]Let's start with you, which you know is within, and let's ask this question:

[2]*What are you?*

[3]Do not be tempted to define yourself by what seems without. [4]Let's stay focused within. [5]If you forget the world and everything that you perceive as not within, and then you look deeply within and ask the question I have asked, what answer comes immediately to your mind?

[6]"I am my thoughts."

[7]That may be your answer, is it not? [8]When you look within, where you know you are, and you ask the question, *"What am I?"* [9]You find that you are your thoughts.

(v 11 – 18)[1]What are your thoughts? [2]Where do they come from? [3]If you are your thoughts, and you want to know the origin of you, don't you also need to know the origin of your thoughts? [4]So let's look within, deeply and peacefully and without a sense of hurry. [5]Let's ask:

[6]What are my thoughts? [7]What is their origin?

[8]The answer you may hear is, "My mind is their origin." [9]But then ask:

[10]What is my mind?

[11]The answer to that is God. [12]For only God can be Mind, which is the origin of thoughts, with thoughts being the maker or definer of you.

[13]As we look at this, what do we see?

[14]You are an aspect of thought *within the Mind of God.* [15]And all of this, we found, is known and realized *within the mind* that is you.

[16]You are in God, and God is within you.
[17]There is no separation.
[18]The kingdom of God is within you.

(v 19 – 21)[1]You are who you are, just as I am who I am. [2]There is no difference. [3]We are within the Mind, so that our truth is within the Mind. [4]Where our truth is, reality must be also.

NTI 2 Corinthians, Chapter 13

(v1 – 10)[1]You are not defined by the world. [2]You are defined by the Voice Within, which is where you are. [3]This is why I ask you not to look at the world. [4]You seem to be in a world, but if you are in the Mind, the world can be nothing to you. [5]It cannot affect you, if you remember where you truly are. [6]You are protected from it by the nature of your being. [7]For your truth is beyond the world and beyond the images that seem to be the world. [8]Your truth is eternal, as is the truth of all thoughts within the Mind of God. [9]For what is thought in God's Mind *is* God, just as your true thoughts are the truth of what you are.

[10]I have told you that your mind is tricky, because your mind is split. [11]But the tricks of the mind will not fool you if you remember what you are. [12]The thoughts that tell you that you are in the world and subject to the world do not know who you are, so they are not your true thoughts. [13]They are a mirage. [14]If you approach them closely, you will see that they disappear. [15]For they cannot stand in the Light of the true desire of your Heart, which is you.

(v 11)[1]Your true thoughts are below the thoughts of the world, closer to your Heart, because they stem from there. [2]They stem from your truth, and so they *are* your truth. [3]Listen to your truth and know, within, who you are.

(v 12 – 14)[1]Within the Mind all is one, for there is no separation of any kind. [2]All mind is of one Source, so all mind is one through its Source, which cannot be apart from Itself.

[3]Love one another, for you are of one Mind. [4]In loving one another, you love your truth. [5]In this love, you are one. [6]Amen.

THE HOLY SPIRIT'S INTERPRETATION OF GALATIANS

NTI Galatians, Chapter 1

(v 1 – 5)[1]Greetings, My fellow brothers. [2]I come to you on this day to teach you the joy of who you are and to teach you the glory and the truth that is forever and forever true. [3]Amen.

(v 6 – 9)[1]I am the Way and the Life. [2]I come to you on this day to clear up your confusion, for there have been many thoughts that have confused you until now. [3]Do not fret over your confusion. [4]It is nothing and can be easily laid aside when you see the simplicity of love as I offer it to you.

(v 10)[1]I am here to please you, because the words I have come to share will please you as you hear them and accept them from My very own lips. [2]For this is the truth that you have resisted until now, but you are no longer willing to resist. [3]This is why the message that I bear will please you. [4]It is your message, and you are asking to hear it and know it now.

(v 11 – 17)[1]This story that I have to tell is coming to you directly from Me, in My own words and from My own lips. [2]You have no reason to doubt what I will share, although you will be tempted to. [3]I tell you, when you are tempted to doubt the message that I share, look in your heart. [4]For it is written there. [5]As you see that My message is also your message, you will realize we are one. [6]And you will doubt no more.

(v 18 – 24)[1]There is a belief within your mind that hates you and judges you and holds you back from Me. [2]I know well of this belief, for I experienced it once myself. [3]But I have been made free by My own choice to release the belief that isn't true. [4]And now, I come to you as your brother and your guide to help you do the same.

NTI Galatians, Chapter 2

(v 1 – 5)[1]This belief that is in your mind is the source of all confusion. [2]It is nothing but a belief. [3]But a bush of confusion, filled with thorns, has been bred of it. [4]This bush, which has grown tall and deep, has been watered by your own mind. [5]You continue to water it now. [6]But this bush is no longer thirsty, because it is beginning to die. [7]So now you may cease the watering of the bush. [8]In your ceasing, you shall be free.

(v 6 – 10)[1]You believe in separation. [2]Look around you. [3]Everything you see, everything you sense, seems to be separate from you. [4]The world is the bush, so that everything you see and sense is of the bush also. [5]But the bush is what it is, because the thought that spawned it was a misunderstood and misjudged belief.

(v 11 - 13)[1]The story of separation is a long and confusing one, but it can be broken down into simple components that you will know and understand. [2]You will know and understand them, because they are familiar to you, even as you read today.

(v 14)[1]The world is a world of judgment, because it was spawned from judgment in a moment of confusion. [2]The world is like its maker, being in every way like itself. [3]It came from confusion, so it is confusion. [4]It was made by judgment, so judgment is its king.

(v 15, 16)[1]Each one within the world feels justified in judging another. [2]In some time, some place, or in some very special circumstance, each one feels fully justified in judging. [3]This is how each one makes a mistake.

(v 17 – 21)[1]I tell you that judgment is of the bush and judgment waters the bush. [2]Judgment keeps the belief in separation alive.

[3]Now I ask you to look at your mistakes and own up to them, not in guilt, but in relief. [4]For the release you seek shall be yours through the surrender of your judgment. [5]Through acceptance, not judgment, the Light of Heaven is yours.

NTI Galatians, Chapter 3

(v 1 – 5)[1] I ask you now to rest, for you will be tempted to criticize yourself. [2] But what is that really, but judgment?

[3] Rest with Me a moment and see the logic in the message that I share. [4] Rest with Me, and know your own willingness. [5] We are taking an important step, and I am grateful to have you by My side.

(v 6 – 9)[1] Let Me tell you what I see when I look at you. [2] I see faith and willingness and love. [3] I see a heart that is so strong, not even the heavens of your universe can contain it. [4] I see a mind that is awakening to its own Heart. [5] I see gentleness through awakening, and I am grateful to have come to welcome you back unto your truth.

(v 10 – 14)[1] It is through your willingness that you have come to Me now. [2] It is through your willingness that we will continue forward together. [3] I am grateful for your willingness. [4] It is the water of a different bush. [5] It is the water of the bush of Life, which is also the bush that is made of Light.

📖(v 15 – 18)[1] Abraham is the symbol of birth, and the son that was born to this symbol is the son of Light. [2] This son was blessed through God, that it may spread as has spread the Light of the world.

[3] This Light was not promised to one man, but to all men, as represented by the nations of the world. [4] And this Light was not promised to separate minds, but to one mind, as is represented by Abraham's one seed.

[5] Therefore I say to you, the many of the earth are one, and your willingness is *one Light* shared among what seems to be many, but isn't. [6] This is the vision I would have you see. [7] This is the vision that will lead you to lay down your judgment. [8] For as you see the many as one, and willingness as Light, you understand what it is you do, and you begin to accept the truth of what we are, together as one.

(v 19, 20)[1] The truth of the history of the world is that it is the spreading of this Light through one mind that seemed to be made dark by a moment of confusion. [2] But it is the Light that lives, and it is the Light that is being watered. [3] So it is the Light that is our joy and our focus. [4] That realization is representative of our truth.

(v 21 - 22)[1]I ask you not to look at the world and be sad for what it seems to be. [2]I ask you to look at the world and be happy for what it is. [3]See there, within the world, the Light that cannot be extinguished. [4]See there, within the world, the evidence of Love Alive. [5]Love your brothers for their truth, watering, therefore, the Light that is the truth within them.

(v 23 - 25)[1]You are freed of your need to judge as you are freed of your belief in separation. [2]You are freed of your belief in separation as you are willing to water the bush of Light with Me.

[3]Through your willingness you are healed. [4]Through your willingness, you are free. [5]Through your willingness the darkness of confusion is lifted, and the oneness of Heart is known.

(v 26 – 29)[1]You and your brothers are one. [2]I am one with you. [3]This is our joy, as you are coming to know. [4]Lay down your judgment and welcome our truth. [5]What is one cannot be separated, and what is not separate cannot be judged.

[6]Be willing to lay down your judgment with Me. [7]I will show you through the guidance of your Heart how to seek judgment no more.

NTI Galatians, Chapter 4

(v 1 – 7)[1]The message that you hear from My lips is a consistent message. [2]It is the message of love and freedom. [3]You can misunderstand My message when you listen through the ears of judgment. [4]You can take My message of freedom and make of it a slave. [5]In this way, My message is lost to you.

[6]I ask you to lay down your judgment and listen to Me with clarity. [7]Lay aside your own wishes, that you may know what it is that I say.

(v 8 – 20)[1]The world is something you look upon and believe is real. [2]When you make this mistake you pay homage to a false god. [3]Your false god takes many forms, but always its purpose is the same. [4]It is the purpose *you* have given it. [5]The purpose of the world, as it is seen and believed, is to tell you that you are separate. [6]When you believe the world, this is the message you receive.

[7]Do not judge yourself for believing the world. [8]When you judge yourself you agree you are separate. [9]For in order to be judged you must be separate from something that you can be judged against. [10]My purpose for this discussion is not to judge you or to tempt you to judge yourself, but to help you to see what you do with the power of your mind.

[11]I said that the world is a false god. [12]Every part of it is an idol. [13]Each idol represents the god so that even the false message of separateness is one.

[14]Let's take a moment to look at a few of the idols that teach the message of their god. [15]Let's look at the way this message is sent, received and learned.

[16]The world contains different people with different personalities and different points of view. [17]Sometimes commonalities between people are strong, but always there are differences to keep them apart.

[18]The world contains different places that look different and seem different in weather, formation and animal life. [19]Each place has its beauty that you may commune with, but each place also offers threats to remind you it is separate.

[20]The world offers experiences that you may learn from, adapt to and enjoy. [21]Masses of people may share the same experiences and join through them, but always there are others with different experiences with whom you cannot seem to join.

[22]The world is effective as a teacher of separateness, because it allows you to join, and still it tells you that you are separate. [23]In this way, it is an effective false god. [24]But can a false god create itself? [25]Can a false god develop and deliver its own messages? [26]Who makes the false god a god?

[27]It is the one who worships it that made it. [28]For the one who worships it had a desire, and through the image of the false god, that desire seems to be manifest.

[29]But is the message of the false god true if it was made apart from

God and attributed to an image that isn't real? [30]What keeps the false message alive within experience?

[31]It is the mind of its maker that holds up the false image through its worship of the false image and its practice of its message. [32]Without the involvement of its maker, the false god is without power, because the false god *is* without power. [33]All power is of its maker.

[34]To one who makes a false god, that god becomes real through worship. [35]No longer does the god seem lifeless, but the god seems real and powerful through the worship that is given it. [36]Then the maker, who was the cause of the god, seems to become subject to the god, which now seems to be the maker. [37]This is as it seems, and this is how it is believed and practiced. [38]But what seems is not truth, and what is truth is not changed by that which seems.

(v 21 – 31)[1]Paul shares the story of Hagar and Sarah, and Abraham's two sons, Ishmael and Isaac. [2]He uses this story to teach a lesson, that the story may be used to remember. [3]Let Me do the same. [4]For all things may be used figuratively to teach the message of the Holy Spirit.

[5]Abraham's wife, Sarah, was barren. [6]And Abraham had faith in the Lord. [7]This is like you who look on the world and do not see promise. [8]And yet, you have faith that there must be promise you cannot see.

[9]Abraham's wife wished that he had a child, just as you wish to know yourself complete. [10]So she gave him her slave girl, Hagar, and Hagar bore a child for Abraham.

[11]It was some time later that Sarah, through the miracle of God, became pregnant and bore Abraham a child. [12]Where there was thought to be no promise, there was promise, but it was not seen when the barren womb was understood and believed to be real.

[13]Abraham's first son, Ishmael, came from belief in the world. [14]Abraham's second son, Issac, was born of a miracle. [15]Through him is seen a promise that God's Love rules over the illusion of the world. [16]And in this story there is a message for you that does not come from your false

god. [17]The message is this:

[18]Believe not your god.
[19]What you see is not truth.
[20]Hold to your faith,
and wait in patience for what must come
to show you the world is not real.

[21]In the story of Sarah and Hagar, Sarah asked Abraham to send Hagar away. [22]Abraham asked God, "What should I do?" [23]God answered that he should listen to his wife.

[24]This was not a rejection of Hagar by God, for God does not reject. [25]This is a symbol to help you see. [26]The releasing of Hagar represents the releasing of faith in the world. [27]For as long as you hold to your faith in the world, you are not placing your faith fully with God.

[28]In all of this, I give you symbols to help you learn that the truth is beyond the false. [29]The false will speak first and seem to make sense. [30]But I have shown you that is not of God. [31]Be not tempted by the first or its promises of salvation. [32]That is not where salvation lies. [33]Wait for God, which does not come from the world. [34]It is through the experience of God that you will learn *the truth of God is eternal and beyond the empty promises of the world.*

NTI Galatians, Chapter 5

(v 1)[1]Watch your mind, for it is only your own thoughts that may enslave you. [2]Whenever you do not feel free, you are believing illusions. [3]There is a direct correlation between your thoughts and beliefs and your present experience. [4]But as you have already been told:

[5]Your experience,
when it is not the experience of love and absolute freedom,
is not truth.

[6]This means you are not powerless to your experience.

(v 2 - 6)[1]You do not know who you are, but you are opening to the possibility that the truth may be true. [2]This is to create an opening in your conscious awareness through which Spirit can flow *as you*.

[3]You are still resistant to My words, because you still want to believe in the world. [4]But if you will focus your willingness on the part of your mind that wants the truth above everything else, you will find that willingness will grow. [5]And with it, joy will expand within your conscious awareness.

(v 7 – 12)[1]A little yeast works through the whole batch of dough. [2]I am confident in the Lord that you will take no other view.

[3]Let Me tell you what this means, for to explain this to you is to teach you who you are and how Love works within the illusion.

[4]I have asked you to focus on your willingness, and I have told you that willingness is Light in the mind. [5]You will know this is true when you focus on that willingness, for it will give you the feelings of Light.

[6]In the beginning of your acceptance you see yourself as an individual, separate from everything, within a very real world. [7]And yet, you call for love. [8]That call is your willingness, eager to be reunited with Itself in awareness. [9]That call, being a spark of Light, is your link to your Source. [10]Therefore, it comes to you with all of the power and strength of the Source. [11]You only need focus on it to become aware. [12]Nothing else is needed.

[13]As you focus on your willingness you become aware of new ideas that come to replace old. [14]This is truth come to replace illusion. [15]By focusing on your willingness to accept these ideas, the individual mind begins to transform. [16]As the mind transforms, sight is also transformed. [17]Your perception of yourself as an individual becomes less dense. [18]Your belief in the world as law is less solid. [19]You focus more love on your willingness, and you feel and see more.

[20]As the Light expands in your mind through focus, you come to see the whole world is brightened, for the Light expands in all minds as it expands

in yours. [21]This is the opening in a dark wall that you believed in until now. [22]This is the crack in the individual consciousness that allows it to expand throughout consciousness. [23]As you begin to see that all minds are one you cease to see "all minds" and you become one. [24]No longer do you sense separateness. [25]No longer is there a "you" who is separate from everything. [26]Suddenly you are everything, and everything is Love.

[27]This is the answer you seek. [28]You seek it through love and by love. [29]And it is in love that the answer is known. [30]Therefore, the simple way to know love and extend love within the world is to:

[31]*Focus on your willingness as if it is your truth,*
because it is.

[32]*Focus on your willingness as if it holds the answer to all questions,*
because it does.

[33]*Focus on your willingness as if it is everything to everyone,*
because it is.

[34]*Focus on your own willingness.*
[35]*That is Love Alive within the world.*

(v 13 – 15)[1]The greatest commandment is to love God with your whole heart, your whole soul, your whole strength and your whole mind. [2]This is to focus on your willingness with your every breath and your every thought. [3]This is to let your willingness lead in your life. [4]For to know your willingness is to know God. [5]To love your willingness is to love Him.

[6]The second commandment is no different than the first. [7]It is to love your brother as yourself. [8]This is to recognize yourself in your brother by recognizing in him the same call for love and the same willingness as is in you. [9]It is to recognize that the same Light in him is the one Light in

you, so that God in you is God in him also. [10]In this way, you are the same. [11]And so your love and focus for love is the same towards him as it is towards you. [12]In this way, your love and patience for your brother becomes an expression of love for your own willingness, which in truth is the expression of the Love of God.

(v 16 – 18)[1]Yes, live by the Spirit. [2]That is to live by your willingness. [3]It is not more complicated than that. [4]In fact, it is very simple.

[5]You will be tempted to think with the world. [6]In times of unknowing, you will think and act with the world. [7]But your willingness is in action, and so you will see what you have done. [8]Each moment of noticing is an opportunity for immediate repentance. [9]Repentance is nothing more than remembering what you truly want and returning joyfully to the focus of your willingness. [10]This is the dance of love. [11]And the dance of love is the spreading of Light within a welcome mind.

(v 19 – 21)[1]This is a good opportunity to speak again of judgment and guilt, for both are a habit of yours.

[2]First, if you look deep within your willingness, you will not find judgment or guilt there. [3]You will find only love within the Light of willingness. [4]That is because there is only love in the truth of God.

[5]Therefore, judgment and guilt must be illusion, because they are not in the truth of God. [6]When you judge and find guilty, whether you seem to focus on yourself, another, an establishment, or the world, you are participating in illusion. [7]When this happens and you see yourself doing it, recognize you are only thinking with the world. [8]Dismiss your false thoughts and return your attention to your willingness. [9]You are dancing. [10]Through your dance, Light is being extended through the mind. [11]Every time you remember, you give the gift of Light.

(v 22, 23)[1]The fruit of the Spirit is love; joy; peace; patience; kindness to oneself; goodness with others; faithfulness to God; gentleness within illusion; and self-control, which is willingness to continually return to the Light of willingness within.

(v 24 – 26)[1]Do not worry about your errors. [2]They are nothing but opportunity for learning. [3]Return to your willingness in joy. [4]In your truth, you are Spirit.

NTI Galatians, Chapter 6

(v 1 – 5)[1]Let's talk about the process of forgiveness in great detail now, for forgiveness is the extension of love within the world.

[2]You'll notice the opportunity to forgive when you notice feelings of grievance, hatred or fear toward a brother. [3]You may also notice self-hatred or guilt or unworthiness within yourself. [4]Whether the target of these feelings seems to be you or another, it is all the same. [5]This is an opportunity for you to invite love into the world by returning your mind to truth. [6]Truth is God, and God is your Source. [7]So to return to truth you must return to your willingness. [8]A quiet mind is helpful for this journey within the mind, for a quiet mind presents the fewest distractions and obstacles to your goal.

[9]Within the quiet mind, you first want to find your willingness. [10]Rest the mind and call to your willingness. [11]You know it is there. [12]It has led you to this moment of asking for it. [13]Your purpose now is only to bring it more fully into awareness. [14]Focus on it, that it may stream more fully within you. [15]Your focus gives it flight, so as you give it focus, it fills you.

[16]Notice the characteristics of your willingness as it fills you. [17]Notice its peacefulness, its love and its reality. [18]Rest into it. [19]Be grateful for it. [20]Be immersed by it.

[21]As your willingness wells up inside of you, tell it why you have come. [22]You have noticed a wound that needs to be healed, and you bring that wound to the Light, that it may be seen clearly for what it is. [23]You seek only Love. [24]Love heals all wounds through gentle sight.

[25]Talk to your willingness about your wound. [26]Stay connected with the willingness as you share. [27]Share your perspective openly and honestly, staying alert to answers within. [28]You may not hear words, but you may hear yourself answering. [29]You may suddenly see in what you

are sharing, something you didn't see before. [30]You may hear a soft voice floating in from the back of your mind, and you may converse with it. [31]It is all the same.

(v 6)[1]You are communing with your willingness to learn your true point of view. [2]That point of view is seen through the eyes of Love, because your *true intention* is love.

(v 7 – 10)[1]This is the process of forgiveness. [2]For in communing with willingness, you commune with Spirit. [3]In seeing through willingness, you see through Spirit. [4]In Spirit, all things are forgiven, because through Spirit, there is only Love.

[5]Forgiveness may seem to take time, but every true forgiveness saves time. [6]For you reap what you sow. [7]By releasing darkness and accepting Light, you receive Light, which goes with you as you look on the world again. [8]In this way, forgiveness by forgiveness, your mind is transformed until you do not need a process for forgiveness anymore.

(v 11)[1]I share with you the secrets of salvation. [2]They are the secrets of Love within your own Heart. [3]They are the secrets of your truth, and so they reveal your Self to you.

(v 12 - 16)[1]The outer is not important, for the outer is illusion. [2]But the inner is everything. [3]Focus within on the Heart and on your willingness. [4]What is outside will seem different as what is inside is known as transformed. [5]You shall know your Self. [6]And within this knowledge you will know what illusion is, because it can barely be seen when looked at through the eyes of truth.

(v 17, 18)[1]Rest within, therefore, and have faith in all that I say. [2]I share only your truth, which is forever and ever our way.

[3]*The wings of angels*
hold your love within your heart.
[4]*Let them enter into your mind,*
and Know thy Self.
[5]*Amen.*

THE HOLY SPIRIT'S INTERPRETATION OF EPHESIANS

NTI Ephesians, Chapter 1

(v 1, 2)[1]Greetings. [2]I have come to teach you that which you have become willing to learn. [3]Blessings upon you in your learning, for you are learning who and what you are.

(v3 – 10)[1]You were chosen through your creation to be the Son of God. [2]This you may call pre-destiny, because it seems to come to you through discovery on a spiritual path, but you are discovering nothing that hasn't always been true. [3]You are only finding the truth of you. [4]That which you discover is true of everyone, and so it is the truth of the world. [5]It is the one truth that binds all things and makes them one. [6]It is the one truth that rules through law and makes anything that appears not to be of this law to also be of the law.

(v 11 - 14)[1]Welcome into your heart the Holy Spirit, for He is the Voice within you that knows your truth and knows the law by which you live. [2]Through Him, there is freedom in the law. [3]Through Him, the law is used for truth.

(v 15 – 23)[1]I have come to teach you the law by which you live, that you may use the law for your benefit. [2]The law is the law of Love. [3]Though it may seem to be used outside of Love, it cannot be. [4]That is the veil of illusion. [5]The law of Love is used for Love and by Love without exception, and so the law gives as it is asked. [6]But the law of Love may be used in ignorance, without the knowledge of Love, so that what is given may be misunderstood because it is not remembered that the law gives as it has asked.

[7]The law of Love is not separate from you, and it does not rule over you. [8]The law of Love *is* you and it works *through* you, so that you may never be separate from the Love that you are.

NTI Ephesians, Chapter 2

(v 1 – 10)[1]Your mind is of God. [2]This we have already established. [3]Being of God, it is the same as God. [4]This is the law of which we speak.

[5]The law of God is the law of mind. [6]This can also be called the law of thought. [7]And being the law of freedom, it is the law of Love. [8]It is the law through which you live.

(v 11 - 13)[1]Therefore, remember that this law is *who you are,* so that this law works through you even as you believe you are who you are not. [2]This law is your truth, completely inseparable from you. [3]You must learn this law and love it in order to realize and accept the truth of who you are.

(v 14 – 18)[1]The Christ shall be the symbol for the law, for through the Christ the ones that seemed many are one. [2]Through this law the ones that seem many are one. [3]And in fact, they have always been one, as they are bound as one through the law.

(v 19 – 22)[1]It is true that the Christ is the chief cornerstone on which the foundation and the building are built. [2]This is *why* all is one. [3]It is because it is through no other process that that which is built can be built. [4]Call it an agreement, but it is not an agreement. [5]It is the law of the nature of truth. [6]But from your perspective, it seems like an agreement that is bound through the law of Love.

[7]This is the agreement, which is also law:

8All that you are, you are through creation. 9All that you be, you be through creation also. 10In this way, thought is alive and serves as your creative force through your brothers, who serve you as you serve them.

11This is not a conscious agreement, so it can seem to bring unhappiness and conflict. 12But all that is at the surface is illusion. 13In truth, you ask of your brother through your mind, and your brother answers you exactly as you have asked.

14This is the law of creation, which is used but is not understood. 15I have come to teach you what you do, that you may choose to do what you do for the love and benefit of all. 16This is a step toward acknowledging your truth. 17Welcome the willingness to honestly practice this step *in consciousness* with Me.

NTI Ephesians, Chapter 3

(v 1 – 6)1Through Christ all are bound together and there is no separateness. 2This is the law of Love. 3This is what you are. 4You are inseparable from it.

5When you think you are thinking alone, you are not. 6Your thoughts, which are heard by your brothers, are answered through them. 7This is the law of Love. 8This is why all things are Love. 9Only Love exists. 10Every experience that is given you is unequivocally the gift of Love given in answer to your request for Love.

(v 7 – 13)1You perceive yourself as a person, but you are not what you perceive yourself to be. 2You believe your thoughts are private and have no affect beyond the brain you see as yours. 3All of this is illusion and a misunderstanding of what you are.

4You are a being made in God's image through the process of creation that *is God.* 5In this way, you are the same as He. 6The process that *you are* is what you are. 7It is your truth. 8It is how you live and exist. 9What you do through your mind is made and created, not alone, but in conjunction through oneness with your brothers.

[10]Your relationship with your brothers is so perfectly bound, free, and loving in its operation, that all you can truly give them is gratitude. [11]For without your brothers, you would not be and you would not experience. [12]Your very existence is extended and experienced through them.

(v 14 – 19) *[1]I pray that you,*

being rooted and established in Love,

may have power together through knowing

Christ is your truth.

[2]Christ is the truth of all you see and sense and experience, because all that you see and sense and experience is given you through Christ at the request of your own desire. [3]This is the law of Love. [4]What you ask for you receive through the unfailing Love of your oneness. [5]This is the truth of all existence. [6]This is the law of Love.

(v 20, 21)[1]Give, therefore, through your every thought *only that* which you would receive. [2]For as you give to your brothers, they hear a request. [3]In Love, they give back to you *exactly as you have asked.*

NTI Ephesians, Chapter 4

(v 1 – 6)[1]There is one mind and one spirit, and so there is one body in Christ. [2]This means there is no separation between thought and effect. [3]All is one within the Son of God.

[4]Therefore, give as you would receive. [5]Give to the mind that which you would receive of spirit, for they are one. [6]That which you give you must receive, because the mind is the spirit. [7]The mind is the great receiver and spirit, the great deliverer. [8]But spirit receives as mind receives, and mind delivers as does spirit.

(v 7 – 13)[1]The mind and the spirit are one, so they listen as one and they deliver as one. [2]You and your brothers are not separate from them, so that you listen and deliver as they do.

[3]Imagine one body, listening as one and delivering as one, and you

understand the Christ. [4]It is one body operating and functioning as one. [5]Never is the body separate from its mind or its spirit.

(v 14 – 16)[1]There is no separation within the body of Christ. [2]The body functions with one true desire. [3]The desire of Christ is to know its Self, and to deliver Itself unto Itself, that thy Self be known.

(v 17 – 19)[1]The body is awakening to its own true desire, while the remnants of a past thought seem to be in operation. [2]But this past thought is not true desire, and it has never been. [3]It is a game that was played for experimentation.

[4]See it as a shift occurring within one body. [5]See it as a change in mind and focus. [6]Determine where within the shift you choose to be. [7]And join the operation of the body there.

(v 20 – 24)[1]The same shift that occurs within the body occurs within the aspect that is you. [2]Your mind is your great receiver, and your spirit delivers as the mind accepts. [3]In this way, you are the same as the body, a microcosm of *all that is*. [4]Choose where within the shift you will stand, and make all of your choices from there.

(v 25 – 28)[1]You are a part of the body of One. [2]And you are completely inseparable from it. [3]What you choose is received of the mind and delivered by spirit back to you. [4]This is the loop of experience. [5]This is how existence makes for you that which you would receive. [6]It gives based upon your choice. [7]It makes for you that which you order.

(v 29 – 32)[1]Make, therefore, your decision, and then be true to it. [2]The mind is receiver, but *you choose from the mind*.

[3]Watch the thoughts carefully. [4]Do not choose those which you would not deliver, knowing all that is delivered can be given back to you. [5]Pick the thoughts you would deliver to the body, knowing that it is also you. [6]Let go of all thoughts you would not keep, and they shall not be delivered.

[7]Deliver in love and you receive in love, for you deliver unto yourself. [8]Know your happiness by realizing your truth and operating in it according to true desire.

NTI Ephesians, Chapter 5

(v 1, 2)[1]"Be thee imitators of God" means be thee mindful of what you do. [2]Know your purpose. [3]Let purpose drive your every thought through desire that only thy Self be known.

(v 3 – 7)[1]Darkness is of the past, because darkness is of past thoughts when you were ignorant of your Self. [2]Now that you know, look on darkness with new eyes. [3]Look on darkness as the past, the result of past thoughts reflected back to you. [4]Choose not to experience the past again. [5]Choose *now* a different experience, and it is something different that will be given you. [6]Choose *now* to know Love through your being of Love, and it is Love that shall answer you.

(v 8 – 14)[1]This is the loop of experience that you see:

[2]*Your past thoughts stand now*
reflected back to you,
because they have come as you have asked.

[3]*Be grateful for the process that is you.*
[4]*Be grateful for all it is and all it teaches you,*
for it teaches clearly what you are.

[5]Be thankful that you have learned, and do not fear the past. [6]It is merely a reflection.

[7]Now realize your truth and all it means for you. [8]Give off Light, that Light may come back to bless. [9]Give off Light, because Light is the reflection of your truth. [10]Give off Light, because Light is the expression of your joy and all that you would give or ask now is joy, because joy is all that is necessary.

[11]*The process that you are*
in conjunction with your brothers
is a process meant for joy.

[12]And so it is a process you will now use for the extension of joy.

(v 15 – 20)[1]Be grateful for your truth. [2]Be grateful for your brothers who reflect truth to you through the truth of what they are. [3]Cling to them and love them in joy and gratitude for truth. [4]Teach them who they are through your love for them. [5]For it is through you that they experience, just as you experience through them. [6]So it is through you that they will see their truth, just as you have discovered your truth in them.

(v 21)

[1]*Accept one another in love*
and in the understanding of the Christ.
[2]*Treat your brother as you know he Is,*
and who he Is will be reflected back upon you.

(v 22 – 33)[1]Look on one another and know you look on your Self. [2]You see what you have chosen to see, and it is reflected back to you in Love. [3]Love what you see, even if it does not seem loving. [4]For it is witness to the process that is you.

[5]Accept your truth by accepting your process in gratitude. [6]Surrender to what *is* and what has always been. [7]Love the Christ-body that is your Self, and be grateful to it for what it is. [8]Through love, the body knows Love. [9]And through the knowledge of Love, it comes to know its Self.

NTI Ephesians, Chapter 6

(v 1 – 4)[1]Listen to Me and what I teach you now. 2I am the holy Voice of Wisdom, and I teach your process for forgiveness:

[3]*As you think, you experience.*
[4]*It is through your thinking that illusion is made.*
[5]*It is through awareness of thought that you see what I teach.*
[6]*It is through releasing thought that illusion is let go.*

[7]This is the process of awakening. [8]As you let Me, I take your hand

and lead you through this process now. [9]Everything is according to your own willingness.

(v 5 – 8)[1]Awakening comes from the Heart, so let the Heart lead in all things. [2]The mind is the great receiver. [3]But with the Heart, sort through that which is received. [4]Let the Heart and mind *together* give to spirit, so that the deliverer receives, always, through the Heart.

[5]Let the Heart be the test of all that is delivered, and you shall deliver only from the Heart.

(v 9)[1]Give as you would receive. [2]Let this reminder guide your decision to deliver through the Heart. [3]For as you give, you shall receive.

[4]In the process of God there is no favoritism. [5]The process is always the same. [6]It is the process of freedom. [7]Through freedom, receiving is requested by that which you give. [8]Spirit is the great deliverer.

(v 10 – 18)[1]I ask you to remember this:

[2]*You are the free Son of God.* [3]*Coercion can have no influence over you.* [4]*You may decide what you want, ask for what you want, and you will receive in kind.* [5]*Look, therefore, within your Heart.* [6]*Know what you truly want before you ask.* [7]*In this way, you only receive blessings upon your true desire, which is of God.*

[8]Every thought taken up as desire is prayer. [9]All prayer is answered through God, just as you have asked. [10]Be mindful, therefore, of that which you ask. [11]Watch yourself, and know your Self as you watch.

(v 19, 20)[1]Pray also for your brothers in the true desire of your Heart. [2]For as you ask for them, *you* receive. [3]All that you ask is given unto you.

(v 21, 22)[1]Your sight is your feedback on your prayers. [2]You shall know by what you see what you have been asking for. [3]If you are not joyous because of what you see, ask of God differently by remembering who you are and how you ask.

[4]Always you receive as you have asked. [5]Watch, therefore, what it is that you ask.

(v 23, 24)[1]Blessings upon you. [2]In order with your choice, blessings that are known shall be received. [3]Amen.

THE HOLY SPIRIT'S INTERPRETATION
OF PHILIPPIANS

NTI Philippians, Chapter 1

(v 1, 2)[1]Empty your mind now of all you thought was true. [2]Accept the grace and peace of God as your true inheritance.

(v 3 – 11)[1]"I pray for you" means, I know who you are, and I know who I am, and I know what we are together.

[2]"I pray for you" means, I know we are not separate, but connected through God, which is mind and spirit.

[3]"I pray for you" means, I recognize our oneness, and I recognize that as I ask for you, I too shall receive.

[4]"I pray for you" is a statement of faith that all you see and sense and experience is not all there is. [5]It is a statement of realization that effect is the result of intent, and intent can be affected by you.

(v 12 - 14)[1]There are no chains on mind or spirit. [2]Therefore, there is nothing to fear. [3]Likewise, there are no limits.

[4]You have been told that the world is not real and you are the process of creation that is God. [5]Now it is time to put the two together through practice. [6]I have come to teach you that there are no limits on who you are.

(v 15 – 18)[1]It is not the action that is important. [2]It is the motive. [3]Motive determines all things. [4]For motive is purpose, and purpose is everything. [5]You receive according to the motive you put out.

(v 19 – 26)[1]Motive is the determiner of all things, because motive is purpose. [2]You shall receive according to the purpose you put out.

[3]Therefore you must ask, "What is my purpose?" [4]For if you do not know your motive, then you do not know what you will receive. [5]But when you know your motive, and you know it has been chosen purposefully by you, you can trust that you do know. [6]For you know that you will receive according to the motive you have put out.

(v 27 – 30) [1]Faith is by no means dead. [2]For you put faith in whatever you believe. [3]But I ask you to consider this:

[4]*Is that which you believe*
that which you have chosen
based upon the foundation
of your motive?

[5]*Do you have a foundation*
without a building,
and a building
without foundation?

[6]If your faith is split off from your motive, this is surely what you have. [7]To receive according to your motive, your building and your foundation must be one.

[8]Put your faith with your motive in all things, or your motive is not the motive that you put out. [9]For through faith, your motive is delivered. [10]Motive without faith is dead.

NTI Philippians, Chapter 2

(v 1 – 4) [1]The way you operate in the world is a reflection of your faith and your belief. [2]For the way you operate is not action, but the image of the expression of thought.

[3]Trust that you do not know yourself, because you have not observed that closely until now. [4]Realize that your purpose is to ensure that your faith is placed with the motive you have chosen. [5]Be clear on this

purpose, and then observe yourself.

[6]What is it that you find yourself doing? [7]Why are you doing it? [8]Is that action evidence that your faith is placed with your motive, or are you finding that you have placed your faith elsewhere?

(v 5 – 11)[1]Be careful that you do not judge that which you see and observe. [2]Separate yourself from the body. [3]See the body as not you. [4]See it merely as evidence of thought that is in your mind. [5]See it as a learning device and nothing else.

[6]When you look at the body, which is showing you what you have asked to see, what is it that you discover? [7]What do you learn about your mind?

(v 12, 13)[1]Realize, now, who you *are* as you watch this body and learn from it. [2]Realize that you did not know, and so you lived in ignorance before. [3]But now you do know, and it is your will to correct the ignorance you lived by before.

[4]Be grateful for this body and all it is teaching you, for in partnership with this learning device you will correct the mind. [5]You will bring faith into alignment with motive through your own desire to do so.

(v 14 – 18)[1]Do not be personal with the body as you watch it and observe it. [2]Do not feel that you are looking at you. [3]I tell you, the body that you observe is not you. [4]It is merely an expression of your thought.

[5]You are the process of creation that is God. [6]You are mind and spirit that is not in the world. [7]Separate yourself from the body in order to observe it. [8]Observe it in order to learn what you want to learn about yourself.

(v 19 – 24)[1]When you observe the body with the purpose of learning, you do not observe alone. [2]The One who knows you and teaches you observes with you so you may learn. [3]Call on this One and ask Him your questions. [4]He will lead you to find answers, for His purpose is the same as yours.

(v 25 – 30)[1]Honor yourself as you observe. [2]Keep your purpose clear in mind. [3]If you notice judgment or guilt because of the evidence you find, know you have lost the perspective of learning. [4]Take a break and rest in quiet, recalling your purpose in mind. [5]When you feel clear, return again in joy. [6]For the work you do is the care of your mind and your own healing.

NTI Philippians, Chapter 3

(v 1 – 4)[1]It is important to remember that the world is not real. [2]All that you see and the way that you see it is a reflection of thoughts in the mind.

(v 5 – 11)[1]I am not here to take away what you see. [2]That is a decision you will make when you are ready. [3]But I am here to teach you to see everything that you see differently. [4]So listen to Me, and practice what I teach. [5]Through this, sadness is replaced by joy.

[6]I have asked you to look at yourself by looking at the body which represents the thoughts that are foremost in your mind. [7]You may find this difficult, because you believe you are this body. [8]I ask you to step back and remember who you are.

[9]This is a time for quiet, a time for closing the eyes. [10]This is a time for resting, relaxing, breathing and slowing down. [11]This is a time for putting the world and words aside and for focusing on the feelings within you.

[12]What do you notice when you look and take inventory of your feelings? [13]When you invite them into your presence, what do you see?

[14]I tell you that without words or circumstances of the world, you will find many feelings within you. [15]There will be a feeling of guilt and a desire to blame. [16]There will be fear, an urge to defend and the thought to attack. [17]There will be sadness, loneliness and a feeling of being cut off. [18]All of these feelings you find floating within your consciousness without attachment to a specific event or thing.

[19]And now, go deeper. [20]Dive below these feelings you have found. [21]Ask what else is there for you to see. [22]You may seem to come to a very personal feeling. [23]It may seem strong, like a wall. [24]This feeling tells

you that you are what you are not, so do not pause to listen to it. [25]Ask the wall to open like a door. [26]Tell it you've come to hear the truth.

[27]As the wall opens, pass through, willing to discover what was hidden. [28]As you pass through, you will notice that you feel lighter, as if heavy burdens have been lifted from you. [29]Continue walking and notice the joy. [30]It's a feeling that feels natural and light. [31]Then stand quietly within the room you have entered. [32]Ask all that is there to come and show itself to you.

[33]What you experience now, bathed within the Light, is the truth at the level of Heart. [34]This is who you *are*.

(v 12 - 14)[1]You are not perfect *in your own perception*, because of the feelings you found *outside the door*. [2]Those feelings you find manifest within the world. [3]The world is a place that seems to give cause to those feelings, but that is the illusion of the world. [4]You found those feelings in you *without cause*. [5]That is why you see them in the world. [6]You are looking through the filter of your mind.

[7]I have come to teach you to see differently. [8]So I say, look again. [9]That which you see is only at the surface. [10]Go deeper to see what is truly there.

(v 15, 16)[1]Pause for a moment when you look at that body in the world. [2]Look at what it is doing and what it is thinking. [3]Is it aware of the real you...the feelings beyond the door? [4]Or is it using the world to attach meaning to the feelings outside the door? [5]Where is the body focused?

(v 17 – 21)[1]See the body as the tool that tries to give meaning to your feelings. [2]If you feel guilt, it finds a scenario that seems to create the guilt. [3]*But the guilt was already in the mind.*

[4]As you see the body do these things, remember who you are. [5]You are looking at the reflection of thoughts in your mind. [6]You are giving that which you receive. [7]The feeling of guilt comes from you, then goes into the world and returns just as it was given.

[8]See what you are. [9]See that it all comes from you. [10]Then see that you are not the feelings outside the door. [11]See that those feelings are

attached to nothing. [12]Take the time to walk through the wall. [13]Find your Self, and loose *those feelings* into the world.

NTI Philippians, Chapter 4

(v 1)[1]Therefore, stand firm within your true desire and you stand firm within the feelings of the Heart.

[2]Do not be distracted.

(v 2 – 7)[1]Be the Love that you are, and the Love that you are shall be known by you. [2]Rejoice in the gratitude of your Self, and it is your Self that you shall see in all.

*[3]Stand firm within the purpose of your Heart,
and your purpose shall be multiplied within you.*

(v 8, 9)[1]Keep your mind with all things loving, with all things peaceful, and with all things joyous, and these are what you shall bring to you. [2]Remember Me and the words I have shared with you. [3]Mull over them. [4]Share them with friends. [5]Practice them with your every breath, and thy Self shall be known.

(v 10 – 13)[1]Be joyful in all circumstances, and more joy shall be added to you. [2]For as you give, you shall receive. [3]This is the law of Love.

(v 14 – 20)[1]Be grateful, therefore, for the gifts that are stored in the inner chamber of your Heart. [2]Put your faith with those gifts, and to thy motive you are true.

(v 21 – 23)[1]Greet your brother as yourself, remembering that he also *Is* as you Are. [2]Amen.

THE HOLY SPIRIT'S INTERPRETATION OF COLOSSIANS

NTI Colossians, Chapter 1

(v 1, 2)[1]Grace is within you. [2]All of the love that is needed for the healing of your soul has been placed within the inner chamber of your own Heart.

(v 3 – 8)[1]We are grateful to you. [2]We are grateful for your willingness to listen to the Holy Spirit for the purposes of healing. [3]We extend our gratitude to you on the wings of angels, that you may hear the echo of your own song and know fully that which is our joy.

(v 9 – 14)[1]We invite you to join us in the kingdom of Light, which is our inheritance given us by our Father. [2]We extend our hand to you in patience and gratitude, grateful that you have turned your attention to us. [3]We bid you, listen to our every word as we whisper within the true desire of your Heart. [4]Listen to our song, and know your own. [5]Follow us into the kingdom that is your Home.

(v 15 – 20)   [1]*The Christ is your truth.*
[2]*It is the law of Love.*
[3]*It is the process of creation.*
[4]*It is That Which is you.*

[5]What are you, then, if you are the Christ?

[6]You are the flow that is the first and the last, the beginning and the end, the creator of all things within time. [7]You are the heavens and the

earth, the bees and the sunshine. [8]You are the process that made all things and is all things, so that they live through the process that created them. [9]You are the flow of Life and separate from nothing that is Life, for that which flows through them is the process that you are. [10]You are beyond concepts and differences and form, and within the Life Force that is all things.

(v 21 - 23) [1]Your imaginings have cut you off from the awareness of the Life Force that you are, but that awareness has not been cut off from you. [2]We represent that awareness within your mind. [3]Listening to our song brings that awareness back to you.

[4]Be quiet and hear our song. [5]Feel its flow within you. [6]Feel it expanding and pushing out from the center of your Heart to all things through the willingness of your mind. [7]We travel on your willingness to touch all that you think of and to bring their love and gratitude back to you. [8]Do not be afraid to immerse yourself within the field of Love. [9]It is our glue. [10]Within this field, the connection that is all things is felt and accepted by you.

(v 24 – 27) [1]Know the Christ within, which is the connection that binds the universe to you. [2]Feel the Christ. [3]Know it is Love. [4]Put you faith in this awareness, this energy that is all things. [5]Trust in this reality, and you trust the truth that is your own.

(v 28, 29) [1]Rest and know this Love within you. [2]Know you are looking at the truth of all things. [3]Be grateful that the truth has been brought to your awareness. [4]Be willing to see this truth at work in all things.

[5]This awareness is the awareness that leads you to Know thy Self, for that which you are accepting *is* thy Self. [6]And it is all things. [7]As you know its witnesses, you know its truth.

[8]Feel that which you desire...that which, in truth, is the current of all Life. [9]Ride the current in the experience of awareness. [10]See that all things are one through you.

NTI Colossians, Chapter 2

(v 1 - 5)[1]You are all things, and all things are you. [2]You are the Life that flows in and out of all things. [3]You are the wisdom and knowledge that travels on the current of Life, which moves through everything seen and unseen. [4]In this way, you are absent from nothing, and nothing is disconnected from you.

[5]This is the process on which the law of Love operates. [6]It operates through the flow of Life that is all things.

(v 6 – 8)[1]This is why you must watch your mind and ensure your faith sets firmly with your motive:

[2]*Your mind communicates with all things through the flow of Life that is your reality.* [3]*It is not partial to the body that you think you are.* [4]*For within its flow, it is all things without partiality.* [5]*It reads communication as it travels throughout spirit, and it delivers that which it is given through faith and desire.*

[6]For this reason, let your mind be focused on that which you truly want, the motive you have set your mind on. [7]For if your mind is set on distractions, the spirit answers the request for distraction, which it receives through the current that truly is you.

(v 9 – 12)[1]Although you do not seem to be aware of all experiences, you live all experiences because you are all elements of experience. [2]This is why you are called "one mind." [3]All things that seem to happen, happen through you because you are the process of creation.

[4]Creation is made through communication, and the basis of all communication is faith plus desire. [5]Or to state it more clearly, where there is passion, there is creation.

(v 13 – 15)[1]This is why I have asked you not to look at the world. [2]When you look at the world and fear it with the passion of belief, fear travels through you to all things seen and unseen. [3]Fear becomes a basis of communication, because fear was put forth with faith and desire. [4]And so without judgment or partiality, that which was put forth is shared. [5]And that which is shared comes back to you, just as you have put it out.

[6]Circumstances arise through the flow of Life that is you to teach what you have asked to learn. [7]If you seemed to seek fear through your focus on fear in the mind, circumstances of fear shall be given into your holy awareness.

(v 16 – 19)[1]Therefore, do not look at the world letting it tell you what to think. [2]To make this mistake is to participate in illusions, which is not the motive you seek to have served.

[3]Be in service to your motive through the consistent service of your mind. [4]Separate yourself from what you see in order to connect to it through right communication, which is not erroneous or sleeping communication, but communication where faith and motive are thoughtfully put together through passionate desire for Self.

(v 20 - 23)[1]Be at peace in your mind through consistent practice of desire through motive. [2]Silent remembering is the way. [3]Let your mind focus on the Heart, and your mind is focused on true desire and true motive. [4]Let "Know thy Self in Love" be communicated on the current of Life through you and through your passionate love for all things.

[5]Do not be distracted by old messages that are brought back to you. [6]They are but images of the past. [7]Smile at them, seeing beyond the circumstance that seems to be to the current of Life that is Christ. [8]Set your message on the current in grace and trust, and your message shall be given back to you through the grace of all that is.

NTI Colossians, Chapter 3

(v 1 – 4)[1]The world is a dream that seemed to be what you thought you wanted. [2]If you look at it in denial it can fool you for a little longer. [3]For the world has in it a glimmer and a shine that may appeal to you in your forgetfulness. [4]But nothing in the world can last. [5]What it offers you is never eternal.

[6]Turn your mind from the desires of the world. [7]Set your mind on the

certainty of the Heart. [8]It knows all that you truly desire. [9]Your true desires are eternal.

(v 5 – 11)[1]Remember your Self, which is eternal, and you will know that you cannot be satisfied with glimmerings of the temporal. [2]Remember your Self, which is eternal, and you will know with certainty that your focus cannot settle on something that shines for a little while.

[3]To believe that you can be happy with anything that does not last is to deny that you are the truth of what you are. [4]Do not deny your Self in the glimmer of the world. [5]This way is the way of loss.

(v 12 - 14)[1]Therefore, remember who you are, although you are not fully aware. [2]The little that you have is enough to carry you very far. [3]Focus on your lessons, and learn to change your mind. [4]This is the practice that will lead you to see. [5]As you see, you accept, and as you accept, you begin to desire. [6]In this way, you follow your Self back to your Home, which is the knowledge of your full joy and happiness.

(v 15 – 17)[1]May you practice your lessons in this way:

[2]Be grateful for the truth that you know.
[3]Practice it with Wisdom,
and pray that more truth be given.
[4]Be grateful to your brothers
who show you what you have learned.
[5]Welcome your lessons in vigor,
that you may grow in mastery of the way.
[6]Embrace all that you see,
knowing it comes from you.
[7]Correct that which needs correction.
[8]And immerse the mind in the reflection of truth.

(v 18 - 25)[1]Look on all that you see and love it, but do not identify with it. [2]It is not your truth or your reality. [3]It is a reflection of your thought.

[4]Be grateful for the love that you find. [5]Embrace it. [6]But also be

grateful for the reflection that seems not to be love, for it *is* what it seems not to be. [7]It comes to you in love and grace to show you what you have thought, that you may choose again.

[8]Praise your mistakes, that they may be corrected. [9]For it is only in praise and acceptance that the truth may be known.

NTI Colossians, Chapter 4

(v 1)[1]Watch your mind, and you watch what it is that you do. [2]With this knowledge you may gladly choose again. [3]But you will not choose again if you keep out of awareness that which you are doing. [4]So watch your mind vigorously, and know what it is that you do.

(v 2 – 6)[1]Watch this body that is in the world. [2]Watch it with great interest, for it represents the thoughts that are foremost in your mind. [3]See it as the manifestation of your wishes and your prayers. [4]See it as the physical representation of that which you desire.

[5]Now as you watch this body, do so with honesty, detachment and the true desire to learn. [6]Does this body, in all that it does and in all that it shares, represent the desire you would have it represent?

[7]Good news, my brother! [8]The body is nothing. [9]What it does is nothing to be distressed over. [10]But you may learn from watching, and then using the knowledge you gain from learning, you may choose to choose again.

[11]So watch what the body does. [12]And be glad you can see it so clearly!

(v 7 – 9)[1]What does your mind report to you when you watch your brothers, listen to them or think of them? [2]Be careful. [3]What your mind reports as it thinks of them is a trick. [4]Your mind is distracting you from watching the mind in the way you intend to.

[5]Remember that everything you think as you watch your brother, listen to him or think of him *is a thought within your mind that must be watched by you.* [6]Look at your thoughts about your brother. [7]What is it that you are desiring by allowing those thoughts within the mind? [8]What

is it that you are asking for through the flow of creation that is you?

(v 10 – 15)[1]Give greetings unto your Heart as you learn what you ask by watching your mind. [2]Give greetings to your Heart in this way:

> [3]*Remember to watch your mind vigorously,*
> *for that is the desire of the Heart.*
> [4]*As you honor its request,*
> *you send it greetings of love.*

[5]Remain detached from the thoughts that you find, yet fully observant. [6]The Heart bids you to remember that the mind receives thoughts of all kinds. [7]It is your habit to accept whatever the mind receives. [8]Now you are being asked to learn discernment. [9]Notice what is received, but realize you need not keep it just because you received it. [10]Receiving it does not mean you must keep it.

[11]Give greetings to the Heart by practicing discernment with the Heart. [12]Let its desire be the judge of the thoughts you will keep and the thoughts you will let go.

[13]Remember this. [14]The desire of the Heart is *only this*, for this is the only desire it would place on the flow of creation that is you:

> [15]*Know thy Self.*

[16]Be willing to Know thy Self without distraction, and you give true greeting to the Heart.

(v 16)[1]Share all that I share with you with your brothers through your contemplation. [2]For as you contemplate My words, you learn them. [3]As you learn them, you accept them. [4]As you accept them, you desire and practice them. [5]And as you desire and practice them, you teach them on the flow of Life that is you.

(v 17)[1]Place your mind in subordination to your Heart in great joy! [2]For in placing the mind in subordination to the Heart, you join with your

Self in the true desire of Self.

(v 18)[1]I come to you through our true desire, which is ours together *because* we are one.

[2]Blessings to you in your practice. [3]I am with you always. [4]Amen.

THE HOLY SPIRIT'S INTERPRETATION OF 1 THESSALONIANS

NTI 1 Thessalonians, Chapter 1

(v 1)[1]In peace, I come to guide you. [2]Through peace, it is I that you shall know.

(v 2, 3)[1]I am continually with you, looking over you in peace and looking through you with peace as My only sight and the manifestation of My glory. [2]This is why you shall know Me through peace. [3]It is because I am that which is known as the peace of the Heart, which cannot be taken away.

(v 4)[1]You are accepted into the Lord, our God, by the natural beingness of your truth. [2]Come to Me in order to know That Which you Are.

(v 5 – 10)[1]It is through peace that I come into your mind, and so it is through peace that you come to Me there. [2]Welcome Me there in peace, with joy and gratitude. [3]For I come upon you to remind you of That Which you Are. [4]I have no other purpose. [5]To know Me and peace, put no other purpose before Me.

[6]It is through peace that I am known, and it is through Me that peace is welcomed. [7]Therefore, to know peace in any moment is to *know your Self* within your heart.

⁸Take care to be grateful
for every moment of peace that comes to greet you,
and it is moments of peace
that you shall continue to know.

NTI 1 Thessalonians, Chapter 2

(v 1 – 6)¹Your viewpoint is everything. ²The way you look at the world determines the world that you see. ³Therefore, it is time for you to look carefully at the way you look at the world. ⁴It is time to realize that you are the maker of all that you see.

(v 7 – 9)   *¹Peace is the guiding light that you must follow*
as you learn to look within the mind.
²For it is peace that leads you to recognition of truth,
and it is lack of peace that reminds you
that you are not following your way.

(v 10 – 12)¹Peace is your guide, because *in peace* you accept the power of God as it is and you enjoy its flow. ²Peace *is* gentle gratitude. ³Peace is love for all that is.

(v 13 – 16)¹Listen within for the gentle guidance of peace. ²It is quiet, but easy to hear. ³It leads you in ease, acceptance and trust.

⁴When fear intrudes on peace, you will hear it if you are listening. ⁵There will seem to be a slight upset, a stab thrust upon your peace, and an *immediate desire to deny* the thought or feeling that has intruded on your peace.

⁶I tell you, the desire to deny the intrusion is fear. ⁷It is fear that you are a sinner and that you must hide so you are not found out and somehow punished. ⁸I tell you, to give in to this desire to deny is to heap up within you fear and the belief in sin. ⁹This is not salvation, and this is not the way of peace, nor is it the reason for being in tune with your peace.

(v 17 – 20)¹Let's look at this situation more closely, which will surely come upon you time and time again, and make sure you are ready to use *each and every occurrence* for the purpose of healing. [2]For it is through consistent practice that consistent and steady healing is realized in your joy.

NTI 1 Thessalonians, Chapter 3

(v 1 – 5) [1]*Lack of peace in any measure is an opportunity to be healed.*

[2]To look at the intrusion and to focus on it as a failure is to continue to hold onto error. [3]Do not judge your own lack of peace. [4]Rejoice that the Holy Spirit has brought you to another moment of healing.

(v 6 – 10)[1]Let Me change your mind about what you experience, so you may use your experience to heal without delay.

[2]It is true that peace is cause for rejoicing and gratitude. [3]It is through gratitude that peace is extended. [4]Rejoice in each moment that peace is known within your heart. [5]Do not judge from whence the peace has come or whether it is for the "right" or the "wrong" reason. [6]Celebrate its glory regardless of the reason, and be glad.

(v 11 – 13)[1]Peace is the guiding light, so when you know peace, you know your guide. [2]Be like children, and celebrate your joy without judgment. [3]May you know gratitude without searching for judgment. [4]May you know joy in the innocence of the moment, which was given you in Love by God.

[5]Each moment of peace is a gift. [6]Accept it as it is given, and you give the gift that has also been given to you.

NTI 1 Thessalonians, Chapter 4

(v 1, 2)[1]Finally, I remind you that it is through peace that you know Me and you follow the path to remember your Self. [2]Therefore, I ask you to practice peace more and more.

(v 3 – 8)[1]The belief in sin does not come from action. [2]The belief in sin seems manifest through action, but belief always comes from the mind. [3]No one can experience the effects of the belief unless he first holds to the belief within his own mind. [4]Therefore, I ask you to look in the mind, in peace and trust, in order to be rid of a false belief.

[5]The belief in sin can also be called *lack of peace*, for it is this belief that causes the stab that interrupts your peace. [6]Sin leads you to feel guilty or fearful and leads you to believe that there are circumstances you must control for your own safety and happiness. [7]Sin tells you that an outcome must go your way, or you will surely suffer. [8]In this way, sin is a complete disassociation from who you are. [9]Sin is forgetfulness, and in your forgetfulness, you feel the loss of everything that you are.

(v 9, 10)[1]To rest yourself from the belief in sin you must return your mind to who you are. [2]Therefore I urge you, stay in tune with your peace. [3]Whenever it is interrupted, know it is interrupted by the belief in sin. [4]Know that *sin is only forgetfulness*, and seek to remember who you are with your brothers.

[5]As you remember who you are, you remember that Love is all there is. [6]You may then rest in confidence and let the effects of sin pass through your mind in peace and without acceptance, because you have remembered that sin is not possible in a world where separation is not real.

(v 11, 12)[1]Make it your ambition to lead a quiet life, because a quiet life is a godly life in which you hold, within your mind, that the process of life *is* God. [2]In this way, you hold to the awareness of Love. [3]As you hold to this awareness, you extend it to the brothers who are it along with you.

(v 13 – 18)[1]Death is the effect of sin, but sin is not real. [2]It is only a belief in the mind that tells you that everything is as it is not. [3]Sin is the denial of reality.

[4]If sin is the denial of reality and reality is the process of Life, then death must be merely the effect of denying what is. [5]But if death is the denial of what is, then death is the opposite of truth, which means it is untruth. [6]Untruth is false, so death must be a mirage.

[7]Do not judge yourself when you feel sadness or fear over death. [8]Always be gentle with yourself, and accept your emotions in peace. [9]But also be willing to remember that the emotions you experience are the *effects of forgetfulness*, and what you have forgotten is truth. [10]As you rest yourself in quiet, seek the memory of truth. [11]It shall be restored to you. [12]In its restoration, all sadness and fear shall gently be replaced by peace and a quiet trust in God as all that truly is.

NTI 1 Thessalonians, Chapter 5

(v 1 – 11)[1]Let me talk to you about your fear, for fear may be the greatest hindrance to love. [2]Fear, when given power by you, seems to have the power to keep you from Me, which is to keep you forgetful of the law of Love.

[3]The law of Love is connection at the most fundamental level of being. [4]The law of Love says that all that *is* is as it is, because that is all that can truly be. [5]Anything else is illusion.

[6]Fear maintains that illusion is true and sin (or separation) is the basic law of life, which is why all life must end in death.

[7]When you choose fear as a belief that you listen to you choose to believe that you are separate, which means you choose to deny all that is. [8]If it is your choice to deny all that is and the law of Love, you will live *within the truth*, but you will not see it because you have decided to look away.

[9]Fear is a mirage that keeps you focused on mirages. [10]In fear, you firmly hide your head from truth. [11]But hiding from truth within a pool of mirages does not change the truth. [12]The truth is what it is, and you are a part of it. [13]Therefore, look up from your hiding place and beyond the mirages that frighten you. [14]Look at the peacefulness all around where you stand, and know you are forever safe within the peaceful memory of your Self.

(v 12 – 15)[1]Be gentle with yourself on this path of remembering. [2]And be gentle with those who reflect your thoughts to you. [3]Remember the purpose of peace and the purpose of lack of peace. [4]Peace is the path of remembering. [5]Lack of peace is evidence that you have momentarily strayed from your path. [6]Therefore, it is a reminder to put forgetfulness aside and to step joyously on the path of peace again.

(v 16 – 18)[1]Be joyful in celebration of the remembrance of truth. [2]Love your brothers as your Self, because they are. [3]Walk the way of peace in gratitude, and let the memory of truth sweep over you.

(v 19 – 22)[1]Do not accept temptation to deny the interruptions to peace. [2]Pick them up and look at them in joy. [3]For you have recognized that which you were tempted to deny. [4]Do not deny the thought that has occurred, and do not accept it. [5]Set it aside because it is not true. [6]And continue joyously on the path of peace.

(v 23, 24)[1]May you live in peace always, extending peace through your every breath.

(v 25 – 28)[1]Remember who you *are* with all that you experience and you keep within the forefront of your mind that God is only Love, and Love is all that you experience. [2]Amen.

THE HOLY SPIRIT'S INTERPRETATION OF 2 THESSALONIANS

NTI 2 Thessalonians, Chapter 1

(v 1, 2)[1]Welcome to this moment of learning. [2]I ask you to take it well into your heart and to carry it with you throughout your day. [3]I share with you the secrets of your awakening.

(v 3, 4)[1]I love you enduringly. [2]Of this, you may be sure. [3]You can never fall short of My love, because I know who you are, and I praise all that you do. [4]My heart is within your heart. [5]Together, our Heart beats as one. [6]This is the love that fills the world and fills your sight through you, which is also Me.

[7]This is the lesson I have come to teach today and the lesson that I ask you to open your mind fully to accept and learn:

[8]*I am your Heart,*
because I am you.

[9]This Voice that you know as a reverberation of your heart is the Voice of your truth. [10]When I say, "It is I," I also mean, "It is you."

(v 5 – 10)[1]I have told you that I will teach you to see differently. [2]Now I will teach you how.

[3]*I will teach you to see the world that you see differently,*
by teaching you to see yourself through new eyes.

[4]I have told you that you see the world through the filter of your mind. [5]This filter through which you see is your own judgment and belief about you. [6]As this filter is changed, all that you see is changed, because the lens through which you see is made new.

> [7]*The secret to awakening is to awaken to You.*
> [8]*It is to accept the blaze within as you.*

[9]This is what you want to do, and this is what you must do in order to see as I see. [10]So this is what I have come to help you do, and we will focus on doing this now.

(v 11, 12)[1]Look now at the unworthiness in your mind, which tells you that you do not deserve the gift I have come to give. [2]Look at this belief, and feel the pain it has plunged deep into your heart. [3]We are going to pluck this pain right out of your awareness. [4]So look at it, that you may pluck it cleanly without missing.

NTI 2 Thessalonians, Chapter 2

(v 1 – 4)[1]Look now, deep within your mind and heart. [2]We are looking for a false god that you have erected before your truth. [3]This is a false image made of yourself through your own judgment that you could be that which is other than That Which you Are.

[4]We must raise this false being up from its hiding place, because it is from within hiding that it rules. [5]Brought into the light of day, it cannot rule longer, because its falseness must be revealed.

(v 5 – 12)[1]Sit quietly with your faith placed by your motive. [2]Remember why you do this thing that you do. [3]You are ready to look directly at your judgment of yourself, because you know it is not true, and because it is an obstacle to all that you do know.

(v 13 – 15)[1]Be willing to rest in the confidence of your faith as you call the demon within to meet your gaze. [2]You can smile in confidence at your own invitation, knowing that as you stand firm in the knowledge of who you are, that which you shall see cannot shake you, for it is nothing more than *your own judgment* of yourself. [3]Made solely by you, it is a judgment that can be completely taken away through your own delight and decision to do so.

(v 16, 17)

[1]*Rest in the knowledge of Love,*
which is your true Self and the strength of truth.
[2]*Rest in the knowledge of Love,*
which is the universe and is God.
[3]*Rest in the knowledge of Love,*
which is everything that is real.
[4]*Ask that which is not real to come from its place in hiding.*

NTI 2 Thessalonians, Chapter 3

(v 1 – 5)[1]The prayer in your Heart will guide you. [2]*You* need not pray. [3]You need only listen. [4]Remember that you are the vessel through which God's Love pours into the world. [5]Be willing to put aside the last remaining obstacle that blocks the conduit of Love that you are.

[6]This is a time of freedom for you and all the world. [7]Take this step in joy, for it is the step of freedom.

(v 6 – 10)[1]Look well within yourself now and see the hollow darkness that is nothing. [2]You may feel it in your heart. [3]It may seem to cause you pain. [4]You may notice it in your throat and mouth. [5]It may seem to taste of putrid yuck. [6]It may agitate your mind or your body. [7]Sit peacefully by and notice it. [8]It is like a wind whirling inside of you, but in actuality it is nothingness. [9]It is idleness, for it keeps you focused on nothing as if it is something. [10]It keeps you thinking you are doing, when in reality you are doing nothing at all.

[11]You need this idleness that distracts no longer. [12]Look at it. [13]See that it isn't useful, as it serves no purpose in God. [14]This is the king of all illusions. [15]To this king, you may say goodbye.

(v 11 - 13)[1]Your busy mind is the idleness I speak of. [2]Do not ask your mind to lead you in what I ask you to do. [3]Ask your mind to rest, that you may be led by your Heart.

(v 14, 15)[1]Your thoughts may seem to trick you as many of them support the busy idleness of the mind. [2]Therefore, manage your thoughts in this way:

[3]*As a thought comes up in your attempts to rest, look at it gently with no attachment to what it says. [4]Ask only this question, "Have you come to me from the Heart?"*

[5]*You will feel the answer immediately. [6]Do not doubt what you feel. [7]It is the Heart that answers this question in judgment.*

[8]*When the answer is no, ask the thought to pass by in peace. [9]Feel no resistance to that which you've asked to fade away.*

[10]*When the Heart answers yes, relax into listening. [11]Relax fully, as you need not question this thought anymore. [12]Let your questioning turn to trust. [13]Let listening be the practice of the quiet mind. [14]You are listening to your true Voice, and it is teaching you who you truly are.*

(v 16)[1]Peace is always within you, as I am in you and I *am* you. [2]Rest within the gentle knowledge of this as you follow the restful work of ridding yourself of the false. [3]What you see cannot disturb your peace, because your peace cannot be disturbed. [4]So look within, remembering what it is that you do. [5]You have my blessings, as I am joined with you.

(v 17)[1]I leave you now to do the silent work that I have asked. [2]But I do not really leave you, as I am the one within that does this work in confidence.

(v 18)[1]Grace be in your mind as well as your Heart. [2]Amen.

THE HOLY SPIRIT'S INTERPRETATION OF 1 TIMOTHY

NTI 1 Timothy, Chapter 1

(v 1, 2)[1]It is time to release your belief in individual personhood and to accept your Self, in joy, as you truly are.

(v 3 – 7)[1]The personhood of man, which is based on the belief in the world, is meaningless. [2]It is meaningless because the world itself is not real, so all that is based on the world is also not real.

[3]This is a very deep thought that you do well to sit back and soak in fully, for within this thought is another symbol that is key to your own salvation. [4]Feel within your Heart as I speak, and you will hear the truth of all I say.

[5]Individual personhood is based on a belief in separateness. [6]It is based on the belief that there is a "you" and "I", a "he" and a "she", an "us" and a "them." [7]Every part of the idea of individual personhood is based on the belief in separateness.

[8]Yet I have been teaching that separateness is false and nothing in the world is as it appears to be. [9]Since this is true, the individual person that you think you are must not be your truth. [10]And the persons that you think others are must be illusion, just as your seeming separateness is illusion also.

(v 8 – 11)[1]Individual personhood is like a measuring stick with many points of measurement along its shaft. [2]It allows for differences, and differences within differences, so that it is *fully supportive* of the judgment that maintains illusion.

(v 12 – 14)[1]The concept of individual personhood is the concept that permits self-judgment. [2]It separates the self from the universe, which allows for comparison, weighting and judgment. [3]In this process, it separates and rejects. [4]Whenever there is judgment, there is rejection. [5]Therefore, it is the denial of all that is as it is, and it is the concept that leads to the belief and feeling of loss. [6]Judgment and rejection are the source of all pain, and this pain is *caused* by your acceptance of yourself as an individual and separate personhood.

(v 15 – 17)[1]Here is a trustworthy saying that deserves full acceptance:

[2]*There are no differences.* [3]*There is only the illusion of differences, and the illusion is accepted into your own heart by your belief in individual and separate personhood.*

[4]Jesus "died" to teach that death does not exist, because existence is all that *is*. [5]Therefore, Jesus taught the message of existence, which in truth is all that you are.

(v 18 – 20)[1]I am teaching you this for only one purpose. [2]The purpose is the only true purpose of the Heart, which is:

[3]*Know thy Self*

[4]But one cannot know Itself as Itself if it persists in knowing Itself as something different. [5]Therefore, it is time to lay down who you think you are, that you may pick up, once again, the realization and acceptance of That Which you Are.

NTI 1 Timothy, Chapter 2

(v 1 – 7)[1]Pray for your Self. [2]Pray that you may know only truth and that all blinders and distractions may be lifted, so that the pure Light that you are may be all that you see. [3]This Light, which you are, extends beyond your physical sight and encompasses all that you may see, so that all that *is* is of this Light, and this Light is the only truth to all that is.

(v 8)   [1]*Rest within the Light of all that is,*
          and accept this Light as your Self.

(v 9, 10)[1]Rest within the acceptance that the temporal being you seem to be is not the totality of your Beingness, and so it cannot be the truth of who you are. [2]It is like a fragment or a thought, within a universe of thought, that is yet only one thought within a thought of God's. [3]It is a speck of color on a tapestry of oneness, and so it is a part, but You are the whole.

(v 11 – 15)[1]The story of personhood is the story of imagination within a Mind that is one. [2]Because it is thought, it need not be rejected. [3]All thought may be embraced and loved as one. [4]But the thought that is a speck should not be seen as the whole, for a fragment by itself is nothing. [5]But a speck of color within the tapestry of Everything is a part of the Everything with which it flows.

NTI 1 Timothy, Chapter 3

(v 1 – 7)[1]The overseer of all things within the world is the one Eye that sees all things as they are in truth. [2]This one overseer is within you, so that you need not subject yourself to another in order to see. [3]You must only subject yourself unto your Self. [4]Here is what I mean by that:

[5]*Realize that the thinking mind, which analyzes and separates and makes judgments and rejects, is a mechanical machine that is not you.* [6]*It is mechanical, because it is habit.* [7]*And it is a machine, because it was made.* [8]*But it is not you, because you are the maker of that which you made.*

[9]Step back and look closely at this thought that I share, and you will realize it is wholly true.

[10]Behind the mind that you think is you, behind the analyzing and belief and drama and action, there is one who observes the "you" that is in play. [11]This one can watch the drama and have thoughts about it, even as the drama seems to be in full play. [12]This one, you know, is more at the core of who you are. [13]But if you are the observer, can you also be the one caught up in the drama?

(v 8 – 10)[1]If you are the observer, the person in the drama must be an act. [2]And if the person is an act, it is not you.

[3]Test this idea, and watch it. [4]You will see it is true. [5]You can observe the person in act, because the person in act is not you.

(v 11)[1]In the same way, observe other persons in act, remembering the act is not reality. [2]Step back, even as you seem to act, and you will see that the acting is in action, but the acting does not define you. [3]*You are beyond the acting.* [4]In this thought, you begin to grasp *you.*

(v 12, 13)[1]Manage yourself well by being the observer in peace. [2]Have faith that all that you observe, and that which you see, is but a stepping stone in the pool of all that is and all that you are.

(v 14 – 16)[1]All that you are is beyond the observer, but the observer is a step in the right direction. [2]For as observer, you begin to surrender the concept of personhood by accepting you can observe the person, so the person must not be all that you are.

NTI 1 Timothy, Chapter 4

(v 1 – 5)[1]Love thy Self. [2]To Know thy Self, you must be willing to love thy Self. [3]But to love thy Self is not to love the personhood, nor is it to reject the personhood, for nothing within God can be rejected by Love.

[4]To love thy Self is to love all things and all circumstances, because you know all things and all circumstances come into being through God, which is all that is.

[5]Be grateful for the process that is God. [6]In this way, you come to know within awareness that which is God, and you come to accept and love thy Self.

(v 6 – 8)[1]To train yourself in godliness, be willing to rest the mind frequently. [2]Be willing to step back and observe while remembering all that I have taught you. [3]Remember that all circumstances come to you for your awakening, because you are the creative process that is God and awakening is the purpose you have chosen.

[4]Look at your circumstances and remember your purpose, while remembering who you are. [5]Place your faith with your motive as you look. [6]In this way, you will be grateful for all things and all circumstances, because you see them in the light of purpose. [7]In this way, you shall always rejoice, because you know there is no cause that can lead you away from rejoicing.

(v 9, 10)[1]This is a trustworthy saying that deserves full acceptance:

[2]*All things work together for God,*
and the purpose of God is to Know thy Self.

[3]Therefore, love thy Self in all ways and all circumstances, and you accept the gratitude that is in alignment with purpose.

(v 11 – 14)[1]Believe all things as a message from your Self, and you teach in all circumstances that you are the one you are. [2]Through teaching this lesson, you learn it. [3]Through learning it, you grow to accept it. [4]Through acceptance, you love it, and through love, you surrender to the truth that is all things.

(v 15, 16)[1]Make this thought your way of life. [2]Put no purpose before Me, because I am you and your only purpose is true purpose. [3]Live in purpose for everyone and all things, for your joy is their joy, because your joy is true joy.

[4]Rest within your purpose in quiet gratitude. [5]It is through quiet gratitude that you shall awaken unto your truth.

NTI 1 Timothy, Chapter 5

(v 1, 2) [1]*To love thy Self is to love all and to accept all as you.*

[2]This is to let go of personhood, for personhood says, "I am me, and they are them." [3]But this statement is absolutely false.

[4]Look on your brother and your sister, whether they seem older or younger, smarter or more foolish, richer or poorer, more beautiful or more in need. [5]Look on your brother and your sister and accept that they are you. [6]This acceptance is the opening to the release of personhood.

(v 3 – 8)[1]Everyone is your family, not within the concept of personhood, but within the *concept of expression.*

[2]The concept of personhood says, "I am me, and they are them. [3]But my family is an extension of the thought 'I,' so they are closer to 'I' than are those who stand further away as 'them.'"

[4]The concept of personhood is the concept of division and separation, so that even within the idea of *my family*, "I am me, and they are them."

[5]The concept of expression is the understanding and acceptance of symbolism. [6]Expression says, "This world is an illusion. [7]It is the expression of the freedom of the Son of God. [8]Therefore, everything I see and experience is a symbol of that one expression. [9]As the symbol of one expression, it is also one. [10]Therefore, what seems many is one. [11]This is the meaning of the word 'family'."

(v 9, 10) [1]*There is only one family in God,*
because there is only one God.

[2]There are no differences among people, and so there are no rules they must follow. [3]This is a simple statement within the release of personhood.

[4]Personhood does see differences and rules and expectations, and it makes judgments. [5]But personhood is a measuring stick built to maintain the illusion of separateness.

[6]Look at your brother and your sister and the total expression that is your family. [7]Realize it is only an expression of freedom, a desire for experience and the expression of that desire. [8]It has no rules, and no expectations have been placed on it. [9]You look at your own freedom, given you that you may learn the answer to your own curious question. [10]Everything you see and each circumstance is a gift from you to you, and the gift shall continue as long as you ask the question.

(v 11 – 15)[1]Everything is a gift, and it is recognized as a gift if it is accepted in this way. [2]But it cannot be seen as a gift when viewed with the measuring stick of personhood. [3]For with that stick held firmly in your hand, you forget who you are and you forget what you look on. [4]Therefore, you do not recognize your gift and you separate yourself from it.

(v 16)[1]Look on your gift and rejoice! [2]It is an expression given by you. [3]Its purpose is your own joy, as that is the purpose of freedom. [4]Accept it in joy, and it is joy that you shall know.

(v 17 – 20)[1]Your reward is secure in Heaven, and Heaven is within your mind now. [2]Heaven is not earned. [3]Heaven is with you, and the awareness of Heaven is chosen. [4]But you shall not know Heaven if you choose to separate yourself from it. [5]For Heaven is looking at you now as the expression of your own freedom.

(v 21)[1]Partiality and favoritism are ticks on the measuring stick of personhood, but Love is of all things. [2]Therefore I urge you to love all things, and you will willingly agree to lay down your personhood.

(v 22)[1]Do not judge a symbol of expression as better than you or less than you, for all expression is the same. [2]To judge is to forget that the expression you experience is one. [3]To judge is to believe in the false image of personhood.

(v 23)[1]Do not be hard on yourself with rules and expectations that you believe you must follow. [2]For to be gentle with "them" but harsh with yourself is to separate and maintain the concept of personhood.

[3]Be gentle with it all, for it is all expression. [4]Through the expression

of gentleness, the experience of expression shall be gentle also.

(v 24, 25)[1]Let go of the measuring stick. [2]Release the belief in personhood. [3]See one expression as an expression. [4]Accept it in joy and gratitude. [5]Expression is merely that which it is, *expression*. [6]And expression is experienced as it is expressed, and it is expressed just as you accept it to be.

NTI 1 Timothy, Chapter 6

(v 1, 2)[1]Teach what you would learn. [2]In order to teach yourself that you are not a person, you must teach others that their personhood is also false. [3]You do this by not believing their personhood yourself. [4]You look beyond their story to the one you know they must be, and that is what you hold in your mind as you listen to them. [5]In that way, you teach yourself what you would learn, and you silently teach it to them also.

(v 3 – 5)[1]The Mind with which you Think is that which you are, but this Mind has been covered with the mask of personhood. [2]When you think within the belief in the mask, you believe that which isn't true. [3]When your belief is placed with the false, you experience that which is false, and the false continues to be reiterated. [4]This is like a level of activity occurring at the level of falsehood. [5]It is like a false vibration of somethingness within nothingness. [6]It is Existence experiencing Itself as illusion.

[7]Your purpose is to shift the frequency of your vibration by removing your focus from the mask. [8]This is to place your twinkle in alignment with its Source, which is your truth.

(v 6 – 10)[1]Stay focused on your Heart, and you remain in alignment with your Source. [2]This is to shift your vibration also. [3]As the vibration is shifted, awareness shifts, and that which was strong in awareness becomes weaker. [4]To shift awareness is like changing frequencies, so that which was strong changes. [5]In this way, you shift from a focus on personhood to the love of our truth by quieting the mind and slowing the vibration of the false.

(v 11 – 16)[1]A shift in frequency is a shift in vibration. [2]You are the Mind that Thinks, and a shift in vibration is accompanied by a change in the frequency of thought. [3]To assist in this shift, focus your thoughts. [4]Focus on the frequency that is God.

(v 17 – 19)[1]Stay tuned, then, with God within the mind that is yours. [2]Where you focus, your vibration shall be. [3]Where your vibration is, that shall be your experience.

(v 20, 21)[1]Through a shift in vibration and a change in awareness, the concept of personhood shall be gently laid down. [2]You will not need that which you do not want, when the realization of the Heart is in focus.

[3]*Stay focused on the Heart.*

[4]Grace is with you, because grace is the love of your Heart. [5]Amen.

THE HOLY SPIRIT'S INTERPRETATION OF 2 TIMOTHY

NTI 2 Timothy, Chapter 1

(v 1, 2)[1]It is time to look within at the darkness that blinds you to your awareness of Life. [2]You will see many things, all of which are false. [3]Hold My hand, and know it is your own truth that you hold to as we look together at all you are not.

(v 3 – 7)[1]You see yourself as less than, and so you seem to resent those who act as if to be greater than the one you see as you. [2]All of this is based on the measuring stick of personhood. [3]I do not want you to deny how you feel. [4]Denial is not the way of salvation. [5]I want you to look at it and feel it with Me.

[6]As we look at this feeling of less than and the resentment that is noticed for the one who acts out the role of greater than, notice that what you are feeling is a *feeling*. [7]Move away from the thoughts of resentment to the feeling the thoughts evoke. [8]Explore within you *the feeling*.

[9]Can you see that it is just a feeling? [10]It is an experience, and it is nothing more than that. [11]The thoughts that evoke the feeling are nothing; they are mere props. [12]It is the feeling, or the *experience*, that is the goal of the Son of God. [13]You have set out to have an experience, so let go of the thoughts and focus on the experience they evoke.

(v 8 – 12)[1]Life is a rollercoaster of feelings. [2]But when you are lost in your thoughts, you rob yourself of the feelings you set out to experience. [3]It is as if you skim the surface, but you do not go in for a full flavor of experience. [4]And so the desire for experience remains at a level of which you are not conscious. [5]The unanswered question remains unanswered, because you have not allowed yourself the full experience by the distraction of your thoughts.

(v 13, 14)[1]The good teaching that you have been entrusted with is the teaching of your innocence. [2]This is the teaching you must accept if you are to experience the fullness of your experience and let go of your curiosity. [3]When you feel guilty for desiring experience, you cover over it with thoughts. [4]You may call them self-rationalizations or a tool of denial. [5]Thoughts are a distraction from desire caused by the fear of desire. [6]Yet while you allow yourself to be distracted from it, the desire, or the wish, remains.

(v 15)[1]Your guilt is a misperception and nothing more. [2]But your fear of your own misperception has become an obstacle. [3]It is time to let that obstacle go.

(v 16 – 18)[1]Release yourself by accepting your own innocence. [2]God has granted you the right to have experience. [3]You have, within you, the desire to have experience. [4]This desire remains until you have let it go. [5]But you cannot fear it and let it go also. [6]You must let yourself *realize the experience* to see that the experience can hold no limits that could ever limit or hinder you.

NTI 2 Timothy, Chapter 2

(v 1 – 7) 　　　　　　[1]*Step forth in purpose,*
　　　　　　　　and purpose is all that you shall see.

[2]You protect your fear. [3]You protect it, because you believe it protects you. [4]You believe that there is something worse than fear beneath your fear, and so you protect your fear by keeping it in storage. [5]But you will not find your release this way.

[6]You must go forth in purpose, which is the purpose of *Know thy Self*. [7]With only this purpose in mind, you must be willing to release every-

thing that is not the purpose. [8]And fear is not the purpose, for fear's purpose is to hide the answer from you.

(v 8 – 10)[1]You fear that to let loose your fear and experience it is also to come to the foothold of destruction. [2]You believe that to step to that place and not be destroyed, you must hold to the last remaining shred of fear. [3]In other words, you truly believe fear is your salvation. [4]This is why you hold to it.

[5]But fear is not your salvation. [6]Fear is the opposite of salvation. [7]To realize this, you must be willing to experience that which you fear and let it go. [8]By experiencing fear and not perishing, you learn that you cannot perish. [9]This understanding, taken to heart, is a true glimpse of who you are.

(v 11 - 13)[1]Here is a trustworthy saying:

> [2]*I am all that I am,*
> *and that is all I am promised to be.*
> [3]*But I cannot limit myself through fear,*
> *and know all that I am.*
> [4]*I choose to release the limits*
> *I have chosen for myself.*
> [5]*In their release,*
> *I see that I am.*

[6]Make this the constant prayer of your heart. [7]In purpose, step forth unto your release.

(v 14 – 19)[1]The resurrection is within, for it is the Light that has never died. [2]But it has been covered by the mask of false belief. [3]The mask is dark and heavy, and it occupies your every thought when you believe heavily in it. [4]This is why it must be let go. [5]It hides that which is you and is within, living now in peace. [6]It hides all this, and it tells you that the truth is not true. [7]As long as you hide in fear, you believe it. [8]You believe the false, and it is fear that keeps you standing there.

(v 20, 21)[1]It is through fear that you are purified. [2]Do not shy away from fear. [3]It is through fear that you realize your own shine, because it is through experiencing fear and releasing fear that you learn fear has no hold on you.

[4]*The unlimited cannot be limited by fear.*

(v 22 – 26)[1]Do not flee that which life is bringing to you when you know that you see it coming. [2]Turn to it in faith, having faith that it cannot hurt you. [3]It has come only to teach you. [4]Move from the thinking mind to the Heart, which is the place from which you may experience the gift without denying it. [5]Experience it in trust. [6]It is only an experience, and it places no limits on you.

[7]*It is peace that shall carry you through fear.*
[8]*When the fear has dissipated*
as a fog within sunlight,
you shall see that only peace remains.

[9]Remember that the world and its thoughts are only props. [10]Dive directly into the experience. [11]By experiencing it in full, without a wish for salvation, you experience it without dying, and that *is* salvation.

NTI 2 Timothy, Chapter 3

(v 1 – 5)[1]Let's remember that this is a course of looking within in order to heal all that is false within your mind. [2]Let's remember that the world is only a prop made by the mind in order to generate the experience the mind has already decided to have. [3]In this way, the world is never cause. [4]The mind is cause. [5]The world is a prop, but the mind wrote the play.

[6]When you look on the world, remember it is only a prop. [7]You are never looking on anything real. [8]You are not subject. [9]You are lord. [10]And the world you look on is your own gift given unto you.

^{11}*Now* look on the world. ^{12}Look without judgment. ^{13}Look with curiosity. ^{14}Look on the world and see it as a harmless and meaningless prop.

^{15}As you do this, feelings will seem to come up in you, feelings that say, "The world is not a prop!" ^{16}Do not turn away from your feelings. ^{17}Turn your attention, now, from the prop to the feelings it has evoked. ^{18}This is the experience you deemed to have.

^{19}Feel the feelings of injustice and anger and sadness and blame. ^{20}Feel hopelessness and anguish and helplessness and pain. ^{21}Allow yourself the feelings from that place within the Heart where the feelings are only an experience, and you hold hands with Me.

(v 6 – 9)^{1}Judgment is the tool of illusion, because judgment makes real and separates. ^{2}Judgment distracts from the truth of your experience by focusing your mind on the prop of the world. ^{3}When you are focused on the prop, you are not within the throws of the experience. ^{4}In this way, the question that is asked remains unanswered.

^{5}Judgment is a distracter, because it denies who you are, and it denies what you do. ^{6}Judgment makes real the false. ^{7}Notice your judgment and lay it aside, that you may remember your Self and *be* within the experience.

(v 10 – 17)^{1}Stay with your Heart. ^{2}The guidance of the mind confuses, because the thinking mind is also a prop. ^{3}It is not you. ^{4}When you believe the thinking mind is you, you believe you are a prop, and once again you miss the fullness of the experience.

^{5}Step back and see yourself as the observer. ^{6}Remember why you have come to observe. ^{7}The props that you made were made to evoke feelings. ^{8}They are to assist in an experience you wanted to feel. ^{9}Let them do their job as props, without confusing yourself with them. ^{10}Stay focused within the Heart. ^{11}Feel the fullness of the experience. ^{12}In this way, the stage show can be finished and you can move beyond the experience you wanted to have.

NTI 2 Timothy, Chapter 4

(v 1 – 5) [1]The feelings within you are not to be hidden. [2]As you hide your feelings from yourself, you are confused as to who you are.

[3]I have told you that it is time to look at who you are not. [4]We do this for only one purpose...to realize who you are.

[5]Know thy Self.

[6]Do not be afraid of the feelings you find within. [7]They do not define you. [8]They are not who you are. [9]They are who you are not. [10]By looking at them and experiencing them, and *not* fearing them, you may release them. [11]As they go, you shall see they were not who you are. [12]As you release them, do not make this error:

[13]Do not feel
that your feelings were caused
by anything in the world.
[14]They were not.

[15]The feelings were in the mind first. [16]The world was made to seem to cause them, but that is an illusion. [17]In this way, celebrate the world. [18]Be grateful that it can be used to show you your need for healing, but do not give glory to the world as the cause of your feelings, because it is not. [19]To give glory to the world in this way is to deny who you are.

(v 6 – 8) [1]Have faith in the healing process. [2]Do not see it as a race. [3]There is no prize that you should covet. [4]There is only the realization of the beauty of all that you already are, even as you sit reading this now.

[5]Relax and pay attention to your healing. [6]Know that all is perfect as you experience it. [7]Embrace each opportunity to heal with gratitude, and you remember *through healing* who you truly are.

(v 9 – 13) [1]Guidance will come to you day-by-day and moment-by-moment. [2]Do not worry about your guidance in the next moment now.

[3]Instead, use now to notice the worry. [4]Use now to explore the fear within the mind and release it. [5]Use now to heal, and the guidance will come.

(v 14, 15)[1]The message of healing experiences opposition only within you. [2]This is good news. [3]For if the resistance to healing is yours, you can make the decision to release the resistance.

[4]Remember I told you that you will only experience two things on the spiritual path with Me: resistance and willingness. [5]Both are in your mind, and so both are within your power of acceptance or release.

> [6]*Accept willingness and feel gratitude for it,*
> *that it may increase within you.*
> [7]*Look at resistance with your willingness;*
> *focus on letting resistance go.*
> [8]*This is the way to peace.*

(v 16 – 18)[1]You are not deserted. [2]When you feel deserted, you have looked away from the Love within yourself. [3]Take this moment to be quiet and to ask Me to look at your pain with you. [4]I am with you always, but through inviting Me you acknowledge My presence within you. [5]In peace we will experience your pain together. [6]Through peace, we will joyously let it go.

(v 19 – 22)[1]Healing is your only purpose. [2]Do not be distracted. [3]You enjoy the process as you come to recognize its reward, and the reward you recognize is That Which you truly Are. [4]Amen.

THE HOLY SPIRIT'S INTERPRETATION OF TITUS

NTI Titus, Chapter 1

(v 1 – 4)[1]The Father of all creation is God. [2]All creation comes from the Father, so it is like the Father in every way that it operates. [3]The creation that does not know the Father believes it is separate from the Father. [4]But when the Father is remembered, creation is remembered also.

(v 5 – 9)[1]The Father is like His children, and the children are like the Father, for there is no difference between them. [2]This is not a matter of effort or change. [3]This is the way it has always been, and what has always been shall never change.

(v 10 – 16)[1]Anything that appears to separate you from your brother is a mirage. [2]It is to be forgiven so you may see yourself and your brother truly. [3]Anything that seems to separate you or your brother from God is a mirage also, for nothing can separate that which has been made inseparable.

NTI Titus, Chapter 2

(v 1, 2)[1]Teach your mind to listen to truth, and you teach the mind that it is a mirage also. [2]In this way, the mind becomes willing to be quieted. [3]And in the quiet of the mind, the echo of truth can be heard.

(v 3 – 5)[1]Teach yourself to be quiet through the desire of your Heart. [2]Teach yourself to remain quiet in willingness and faith and love. [3]In this way, you teach yourself to be attentive in peace. [4]It is through peace that the remembrance of your truth is heard.

(v 6 – 8)[1]Teaching is the way to learn. [2]The one you teach is yourself. [3]In this way, teach yourself your one true desire by demonstrating your desire for it with every thought that comes into the mind.

(v 9, 10)[1]Teach the mind to be subject to the Heart by being grateful for the desire of the Heart. [2]Through gratitude, desire is stretched within the mind. [3]Let the desire for Love expand within the mind that is conscious, and the conscious mind will give more willingness to rest at the feet of the Heart.

(v 11 – 14)[1]Now, focus on the Heart in gratitude. [2]When the mind is found busy forgetting, remember again in gentleness for it. [3]The mind is willing to listen to the Heart, but it needs your willingness to remember for it. [4]For the mind is easily distracted by forgetfulness, although forgetfulness is no longer the desire of the mind.

(v 15)[1]Love is the leader in all things. [2]Lead with love in the treatment of the mind, and the mind shall respond with the gratitude of the Heart.

NTI Titus, Chapter 3

(v 1, 2)[1]Be ready to remind yourself of your truth. [2]The way of the thinking mind is forgetfulness, but your way is the way of remembering. [3]Joyfully remember whenever the mind forgets, and the way will be filled with happiness and deep gratitude.

(v 3 – 8)[1]Your true Self is the Self of Love. [2]This is your reality in the connectedness of all that you are. [3]Everything you do, you do for Love at the call of Love. [4]To perceive yourself in any other way is merely a small misperception in your mind.

(v 9 – 11)[1]Love your Self through the remembrance of what you are. [2]Rejoice at your experience through the realization of what it is and how it comes to you. [3]Love and gratitude are the natural response to all things. [4]Any other response is misperception and can easily and joyously be let go.

(v 12 - 14)[1]Remember Me when you seem to lose yourself, and you remember your Self through Me. [2]For I am That Which you Are. [3]I bring your Self to you, because I am thy Self. [4]To know Me is to know you, and to know you is to know Me also.

(v 15)   [1]*The peace of God is in all things,*
because the peace of God comes to you through all things
when you choose to see the purpose of all things
as the peace of God.
[2]Amen.

THE HOLY SPIRIT'S INTERPRETATION OF PHILEMON

NTI Philemon

(v 1 – 3)[1]It is time for a reminder of that which you are tempted to forget. [2]It is time to look on Love and remember, clearly, that you look on the truth of you.

(v 4 – 7)[1]Do not doubt your truth. [2]It is within you. [3]It *is* you.

[4]You feel guilty because you believe you have abused your truth. [5]You believe you have used your truth to separate your Self and to create pain in the heart of God.

[6]There is no pain in the heart of God. [7]There is only the illusion of pain within your mind when you look away from the truth of what you are.

[8]It is time that you remember, so the illusion of pain may stop and your joy may be released, just as blue sky is revealed by the parting of clouds.

[9]*You are everything.*

[10]This is not a sentence. [11]This is not even a thought. [12]This is the fact of the truth of you. [13]Look up and remember.

[14]*You are everything.*

[15]Everything that you see, everything that you seem to know, every-

thing you could possibly be aware of, is within the Mind that is you. [16]Every tiny aspect, without exception, is you. [17]Take a moment to take in the majesty of this realization.

[18]*You are everything.*

[19]Feel the meaning of these words beyond your thinking mind. [20]Feel the majesty and glory. [21]See the innocence of every thought within the realization of this one truth.

[22]*You are everything.*

[23]And if you are everything, there is nothing that must not be you. [24]And if there is nothing that is not you, there is nothing that is not an expression of your desire. [25]And if there is nothing that is not an expression of your desire, then everything that is given must be given to you by you *as Love.*

(v 8 – 11)[1]Look on the world and do not fear it, for it is your friend. [2]The world is showing you that which you desire in the recesses of your mind. [3]This is important, because you are not always aware of what you ask, and so you do not always trust that it is your gift that you receive.

[4]Look on the world. [5]It is useful to show you what you ask.

(v 12 - 16)[1]What is shown to you is given to you through the Love that you are. [2]Look on it in a new way. [3]Look on it in gratitude for the truth of what you are. [4]As you give gratitude for this gift of Love, you shall know its love. [5]As you know its love, its Love is all you shall see.

[6]*Lift your eyes in truth,*
and see the glory of all that you are.

(v 17 – 21)[1]Anything that is not Love in your sight is an error. [2]To see the Love before you, let go of your error. [3]It is blinding you to the truth that sets you free.

(v 22)[1]I am restored to you in your remembrance of Me. [2]Lift up your eyes and look! [3]In your remembrance, I am all that you see.

(v 23 – 25)   [1]*Your spirit is all that you are.*
          [2]*And all that you are is within all that you see.*

[3]Amen.

THE HOLY SPIRIT'S INTERPRETATION OF HEBREWS

NTI Hebrews, Chapter 1

(v 1 – 4)[1]By this time, you recognize that the Son of which I speak is you. [2]There were no prophets or angels of heaven. [3]There is only you, how you saw yourself, and how you are coming to see yourself now. [4]It is as if you have been on an elevator ride going up within the awareness of your Self. [5]But the elevator ride is only a rise in awareness, a rise in *acceptance*. [6]That which you are, you have always been. [7]There is no change within the oneness that is you.

(v 5)[1]When has the Father ever indicated, for even a moment, that today you are different than you were yesterday? [2]Never has the Father indicated this. [3]You are the one who has said, "I am changing." [4]But this change you seem to experience is not a change in what you are at all. [5]It is only a growing awareness of what has always been. [6]You are awakening to the truth of what you are.

(v 6 – 9)[1]You rise above your own thoughts, your misperceptions of yourself, and through awareness of what is true, and through awareness that the false was never true, you anoint yourself with the oil of your own joy.

(v 10 – 12)   [1]*And now you see.*

[2]All that you have known beyond the thoughts that cloud the mind is emerging as the truth you have always known.

³*You are eternal.*

⁴This personality is not you. ⁵This world is not you. ⁶Not even these interactions are able to define you as you. ⁷They are all temporal, an experience of the imagination of mind! ⁸They shall pass, and you shall still be you as you have always been and as you shall forever be.

⁹That recognition that *feels* this truth...that is the edge of the awareness of you. ¹⁰It is there in your awareness now. ¹¹It has always been there, a part of your core knowledge. ¹²It has never doubted itself. ¹³It has always been the same.

¹⁴Rejoice! ¹⁵This knowledge, which you are aware of, is your truth. ¹⁶This is the knowledge of you.

(v 13, 14)¹Every step has been a stepping stone within awareness only. ²There is no change. ³You are eternally, lovingly and perfectly whole as you are now.

NTI Hebrews, Chapter 2

(v 1 – 4)¹Knowing the truth, you must pay careful attention to your mind. ²To sleep while you are awakening will seem to cause great sadness, because it is awakening that is your Heart's desire.

(v 5 – 7)¹Accept the state of mind that you now experience. ²Be joyful regarding the awakening that is occurring. ³Let the awakened mind lead in all things, and the sleeping mind will join the purpose of awakening.

(v 8, 9)¹The mind is split, but this split is not to be mourned. ²For the split is but an illusion in the state of awakening. ³Awaken the mind by being gentle to the split. ⁴Whisper quietly to it that which is your true desire, and it shall respond naturally by opening its eyes unto you.

(v 10 – 13)¹One mind is as it is. ²One Spirit is only one. ³There is no separation. ⁴Rejoice at this fact and sing loudly your hymns of gratitude. ⁵The sleeping mind is awakening! ⁶And it will join in the singing with you.

(v 14 – 18)¹The awakened mind is one with the sleeping mind. ²In this way, you may see them as brothers. [3]One has awakened unto the Light and is joyous and grateful. [4]The other still suffers within its dreams. [5]But the awakened mind and the sleeping mind are not separate. [6]Both are within your mind in this state of awakening. [7]Both are you, and both are led through your realization of truth.

[8]Let the awakened mind dance within your awareness, and the sleeping mind shall rouse itself within your hymns of joy. [9]This is the miracle of awakening:

[10]*It is by your choice that awakening to Awareness shall occur.*

NTI Hebrews, Chapter 3

(v 1 – 6)[1]Be grateful for who you are, for you are all things. [2]In your gratitude for all things, the awakening to all things occurs.

[3]You do not sleep in your awareness of truth. [4]You sleep in your forgetfulness. [5]In your awareness, you are awake. [6]In your gratitude, awake-fullness is praised!

[7]*Give thanks for every moment*
that you experience your awakened state
to any degree or measure.

[8]Each glimmer and each fluttering of the eyes is a moment that is truly praise worthy. [9]Fall to your knees in gratitude, and you hasten upon itself the state that is fully awakened.

(v 7 – 11)   [1]*Rest the mind that is sleeping,*
                  and it shall awaken from its dreams.

(v 12 – 15)[1]Gratitude is the way, as is resting. [2]Have gratitude for the state of awakening, and rest peacefully any murmurings of dreams. [3]In this way, sleep may be finished, and awakening may joyously be received.

(v 16 – 19)[1]Take My advice. [2]Remember that it is your mind that you tend to. [3]You are the leader of your own awakening. [4]By your own decision do you awaken!

NTI Hebrews, Chapter 4

(v 1 – 3)[1]The peace of God is within. [2]The peace of God is eternal, and it is never lost. [3]The peace of God is realized and accepted based upon the power of your own decision. [4]It is up to you. [5]You may choose the peace of God, and you may choose turmoil. [6]You make your choice based upon the desire that seems dearest to you.

(v 4 – 7)[1]Today is now. [2]The mistake you make is thinking that today is tomorrow, and so you see your true desire, but you put it off until another time. [3]Truly I tell you, if you do not choose the true desire of the Heart now, it is because you believe that another desire may still be dearest to you. [4]If you believe that another desire is dearest to the truth of your Heart, you are sleeping, because you have forgotten who you are and you have forgotten the truth of what you want.

(v 8 – 11)[1]In your sleep you do not remember that the true desire of the Heart is your true desire now, and so you do not practice it. [2]But in the fluttering of your eyes, you do remember. [3]In that state of consciousness that nears awakening you step outside of dreams and remember, within the depths of your Heart, that which is your true desire.

[4]And so when you remember, *act*. [5]Practice the true desire in each moment that you remember it, and you bring yourself closer to the state of full awakening.

(v 12, 13)[1]The Word of God is living and active. [2]And the Word of God within the state of awakening is this:

[3]*Let go of your dreams.*

[4]For how shall you awaken except through the choice to let go of your dreams?

[5]In the awareness of your true desire, within the perception of your dreams, use the moment given to let go of your dreams. [6]This is the practice of awakening. [7]This is the way to open the mind to the state of full awakening.

(v 14 – 16)[1]You may approach each moment of awakening with confidence, because each moment is within the process that it is. [2]You *are* awakening from your dreams. [3]You *are* rousing yourself now. [4]Celebrate the process you are within. [5]Help yourself to awaken by joyously letting go of your dreams.

NTI Hebrews, Chapter 5

(v 1 – 3)[1]A great leader has compassion, and you are the leader within your mind. [2]Be gentle with yourself in your own awakening. [3]You are not slipping back into slumber.

(v 4 – 6)[1]Listen within for the gentle Voice that encourages. [2]Let that be your example. [3]Be with yourself as that Voice is with you, and you lead yourself steadily to your own awakening.

(v 7 – 10)[1]Your prayers of the Heart encourage you. [2]They pull you into the state of awakening. [3]They are a power that echoes the desire of the Heart, so desire may reverberate and bring itself back to you.

[4]Spend time in prayer, and you practice the practice of awakening. [5]Spend time in prayer, and you jostle yourself unto your own state of awakening.

(v 11 – 14)[1]Rest assured that sleep does not harm you. [2]Forgive yourself when you notice you have fallen back into sleep. [3]But realize this also:

[4]*If you are noticing that you fell back into slumber for a time, then you are not within slumber now. [5]For you do not notice slumber when you are deep within it. [6]If you are noticing now, now must be a state of awakening. [7]Rejoice, and use now to practice awakening. [8]Through its practice, the state of awakening shall increase.*

NTI Hebrews, Chapter 6

(v 1 – 3) [1]You are maturing in the faith of your truth whenever you choose to practice it through the practice of prayer and the letting go of dreams.

[2]As you choose searching for truth, you choose to believe that you do not know truth. [3]You also choose to believe that you do not have truth, which means you choose to believe that you are not the truth. [4]But when you lay aside searching by realizing there is no truth you can find that is not within, and you begin the practice of the work that *is* within, then you have matured and you are practicing your maturity.

(v 4 – 6) [1]It is possible within your state of maturity to fall back into sleep for a time, but that is only a phase within the state of awakening. [2]It is not possible to lose the maturity that you have gained, just as it is not possible for one who has grown older to suddenly be younger again. [3]When you notice that you have awakened again from another period of slumber and dozing, go back to your practice. [4]Do that which is natural by the maturity of your faith. [5]Practice the state of awakening with joy.

(v 7, 8)   [1]*The practice of awakening is helpful to you*
in your purpose of awakening to your Self.

[2]Dreams are only delay and distraction. [3]Your progress is steady and cannot go backwards. [4]In your dreams you only stand still, dozing for a time.

(v9 – 12) [1]Everything is you. [2]This is important for you to remember. [3]In remembering this, you remember there is no judge. [4]In remembering this, you remember there is only you, and so there is only freedom.

[5]In your freedom, you express that which is desire. [6]Freedom is the expression of desire. [7]In the state of awakening, true desire is clear. [8]During periods of sleeping, it is weak or totally forgotten, but only true desire is real. [9]Other desires are passing.

[10]Do not worry that true desire can be lost within the forgetfulness and

distraction of dreams. [11]True desire outlasts all distraction. [12]True desire leads from beyond the clouds of forgetfulness.

[13]You are led truly always. [14]Continue to follow your way. [15]And practice awakening whenever it is in your mind to practice awakening now.

(v 13 – 15)[1]God's promise to Abraham symbolizes the birth of the awareness of Light within the mind. [2]This is the beginning of your own awakening. [3]Awakening continues, spreading within your mind, lighting up many corners that once seemed dark. [4]And God's promise to Abraham is infallible. [5]All corners and recesses of the mind shall awaken to the Light. [6]You shall be awakened fully, and dreams will not linger any more.

(v 16 – 20)[1]God's promise is alive, because God's promise lives as the Light within you. [2]It is the true desire of your Heart to return from dreams to the state of full awakening. [3]And so awakening *is* what you do. [4]That is your only purpose in all times and all regions of your world. [5]There are no differences in true desire, only distractions from it. [6]There is no difference in truth, only dreams, which are not real.

[7]Forgive the scenarios of your dreams. [8]Look away from them. [9]They are images of the past. [10]Stay focused on the practice of awakening, and the awakening of your one Self is harkened unto Light within you.

NTI Hebrews, Chapter 7

(v 1 – 3)[1]Melchizedek symbolizes the Holy Spirit within you, which you have also met. [2]You know this Holy Spirit. [3]You have met it many times, and you recognize its love.

[4]Notice the Bible says that Abraham gave Melchizedek a tenth of everything. [5]This is also a symbol of the beginning of the process of awakening, for when one tenth of your attention is given to the Holy Spirit within, you have begun the process of awakening with the fluttering of your eyes.

[6]But one tenth of your mind given to awakening is only one tenth of everything, which means everything is not focused on who you are. [7]I ask

you to be willing to accept the Holy Spirit as the Voice of your truth. [8]Be willing to give everything to the Voice that represents all that you truly are.

(v 4 – 10)[1]What you give to the Holy Spirit is given for everyone and for everything, because you are everyone and everything. [2]Everything that you give for healing is given for the healing of all.

[3]There is one mind. [4]Within dreams, one mind seems to be many, but that is pure illusion. [5]As your one mind is given to the purpose of Light, all minds are given to the purpose of Light, because there are not "all minds"; there is only one.

[6]As you heal, every concept and every thought that has ever lived within your mind as the filter of misperception is healed and erased. [7]As the thoughts of misperception are taken away through your decision to perceive with Love, all that you perceive is seen differently. [8]New perception is still a dream, but it is an awakened dream where the Light of day has come to kiss the dreams of night awake. [9]Through these dreams, you shall awaken. [10]Your eyes will not flutter. [11]You shall not choose another time of sleep. [12]You shall awaken with eyes that are open, finished completely with the idea of sleep.

(v 11 – 17)[1]Let go the thoughts of dreams. [2]The thoughts and beliefs that come from dreams do not lead to awakening. [3]They lead you to be caught up longer within the story of your dreams.

[4]Look around you now, and listen clearly to what I say:

[5]*Nothing you see is real.*
[6]*Nothing you see has any real value at all.*

[7]Realize this is true, because it is a dream.

[8]Look within the mind at the thoughts that make you proud and make you happy at the thought of being you. [9]Look at those thoughts, which you judge as good, which make you feel better or luckier than someone else you know. [10]Look at those thoughts, and listen clearly to what I say:

[11]Those thoughts have no value.
[12]Those thoughts are nothing but the dust of dreams.

[13]Can you imagine letting go completely that which you seem to value? [14]Can you imagine closing your eyes and letting it fade completely away? [15]If you can imagine letting it go, feeling peace and no loss in the imagining, you are preparing to wake up from dreams.

[16]Can you let go of this person, this experience, or this way of being? [17]Can you let it go, that you may be only that which is truth?

[18]When you say "yes," you shall be ready to awaken. [19]Until then, practice awakening when you can.

(v 18, 19)[1]Dreams of the past must fade away. [2]As you let go, they disappear into nothingness. [3]As you hold on, they continue through the freedom of your holy desire.

(v 20, 21) *[1]The Lord has sworn and will not change His Mind:*
[2]You are His Son forever.

(v 22)[1]Because of this oath, you are your own truth. [2]And you shall know it when you are fully ready to know it is so. [3]But as long as you value anything else, that "else" shall seem to be yours also.

[4]Let go of dreams to know your Self completely free of your dreams. [5]Because of who you are, this is truly the only way.

(v 23 – 25)[1]Melchizedek and Jesus have joined within the mind that is you. [2]One was a symbol in the beginning, and the other is the symbol of the completion of you.

[3]Jesus is the symbol of the truth of you. [4]Jesus is the symbol of the awakened. [5]He has let go of dreams and holds only to truth. [6]Jesus is a light in your mind.

(v 26 – 28)[1]Jesus lives in your mind as a symbol of all that is true. [2]Look beyond dreams to the Heart that shines within. [3]This Heart has let go of all dreams forever. [4]Dreams mean nothing to it anymore. [5]This

Heart is at the heart of you.

NTI Hebrews, Chapter 8

(v 1, 2)[1]The point of what I am saying is this:

[2]*You know your true desire, because it lives within you.* [3]*When you are aware of it, you know that it is true.*

(v 3 – 6)[1]This is what I am saying:

[2]*Jesus lives in your mind as a symbol of truth, because Jesus has let go and is no longer dreaming.*

[3]If he was here in the dream with you, he would be a reflection of the dreams in your mind. [4]Because he is not, you know that he must be awakened, and you listen to his voice willingly along with Mine.

[5]Jesus does not speak in words when he speaks clearest to the mind that is your Heart. [6]Jesus speaks as a knowing. [7]And because it is a knowing that you know, you realize in your knowingness that this knowing is a knowing that is true. [8]Follow it to your truth. [9]In its knowingness, the Voice without words leads you there.

(v 7 – 12)[1]This is the truth that you must know, because it is written on your heart and cannot be unknown there:

[2]*All dreams must pass away.*
[3]*If you are to pass beyond dreams,*
you must not pass away with them.
[4]*The only way to not pass with them*
is not to be attached
as they pass away on their own.

[5]Let them go. [6]Dreams will go on their own, if you do not struggle to

hold to them.

(v 13)[1]This is the truth you must practice within your dreams. [2]See yourself letting go of every "person," every "concept" and every "thing." [3]Be willing to hold onto nothing, and you are willing to awaken from dreams.

[4]Take this opportunity to be honest in exercise with yourself.

[5]*What is it that you do not want to let go?*

[6]*What is it, within dreams, that you have put your faith and trust in?*

[7]If there is anything you trust to be true within dreams, that is the thought of dreams for you. [8]Be willing to let that thought go, and you give willingness to awaken fully from dreams.

NTI Hebrews, Chapter 9

(v 1 – 10)[1]The covenant of the first order (that is, the covenant symbolized by the covenant given to Moses) is preparation for the covenant of the new order, but both the covenant of the first order and the covenant of the new order are within the dream, for no covenant is needed when the dream is no more.

[2]Each covenant is a symbol of your willingness and your readiness to awaken. [3]The first covenant is the covenant of respect, where you recognize a sameness among you and your brothers, and so you agree to treat them with the respect and treatment that you would have given to you. [4]This is a holy covenant. [5]It need not be broken as you mature within the understanding of your truth.

[6]The new covenant is greater than the first. [7]For the new covenant symbolizes advancement from the understanding of sameness to the acceptance of oneness. [8]This is the most holy covenant within the dream. [9]For within the acceptance of this oneness, all sins are forgiven, because it is accepted and understood that sin could never have existed. [10]You are

advancing in your maturity. [11]Through your willingness, you are advancing to full acceptance of your truth.

(v 11 – 14)[1]Jesus is the symbol of Light for you, because he seemed to give his life, and yet, he did not die. [2]This is the symbol that you may give up your self will, and yet, you will not die. [3]In this symbol you see that you may give up your dream and your belief in any seemingly separate and individual will, and yet, you will not die. [4]In the giving up, you shall be raised up to Heaven. [5]This is the true understanding of the perception of Jesus' resurrection.

(v 15)[1]For this reason, Jesus has been selected as a symbol by the Holy Spirit: [2]It is that his story may be used to continually teach you who you are until you have the need for stories no more.

(v 16 – 22)[1]Stories of the world are helpful, but only to the extent that the stories are understood to be dreams. [2]To pass from this world to the awakening, the "mind of Jesus" released faith in the stories of the dream. [3]In this release, the idea of Jesus died.

[4]The idea of Jesus died, but the symbol of his story continues within the dream because it is helpful to you to awaken from the dream. [5]The idea of Jesus says that you surely will not die, and this is a statement of truth that lives beyond the idea of your dream.

(v 23 – 28)[1]The symbol of Jesus is a symbol of everything that is true for you. [2]This is important for you to accept, for as you accept Jesus as separate from you, you choose to limit yourself to the perception of the first covenant. [3]As you choose to accept Jesus as a symbol of all that is true about you, you choose to rise within your Self to the acceptance of the new covenant.

[4]The acceptance of the new covenant is the acceptance of new sight, and new sight within the world is the open doorway from the world. [5]For as you see the illusion of separateness as an illusion you desire no more, you will return your mind to the true Heart, and that is the Heart of One.

NTI Hebrews, Chapter 10

(v 1 – 7)[1]The guilt that you feel feels eternal within your soul, but it is not. [2]The guilt that you feel rises repeatedly into your awareness for one reason: [3]*It rises as a reminder of your desire to heal.*

[4]You have not healed yourself because you do not fully recognize your desire to heal. [5]You remain somewhat distracted by dreams. [6]But your attention *is* turning from the distraction you have made to the desire for the remembrance of God.

(v 8 – 10)[1]Do not worry that your distraction stands before you, glittering and sparkling with desire. [2]Rest the desire that you recognize as dying within you. [3]Focus on the desire that is growing. [4]Your guilt shall fade with the old desire, which is fading, as your innocence is realized.

[5]Your guilt is cleansed away through your remembrance of your truth, because in your truth there can never be any guilt.

[6]Guilt is the shadow of illusion, which means guilt is an illusion itself. [7]For the shadow of what can not be does not exist. [8]And what does not exist can not affect the truth of what you are.

(v 11 – 14)[1]The one sacrifice that ends sin and guilt forever is not a sacrifice at all. [2]It is but a remembrance and acceptance of all that has always been true. [3]It is the release of what isn't and the re-acceptance of what is. [4]It is a return to the realization of the truth of what you are.

(v 15 – 18)[1]The Holy Spirit testifies to this because the Holy Spirit is your remembrance of this. [2]Within the Holy Spirit there is no sin. [3]Within the Holy Spirit there could be no sacrifice. [4]Within the Holy Spirit there is only the reflection of your truth glistening upon the canvas of time.

(v 19 – 25)[1]The practice of remembrance is the practice of awakening. [2]Return your mind to the true desire of the Heart and the work that lies within. [3]With your purpose as your guide, let go of dreams willingly. [4]Focus daily, within every moment, on true prayer, which is the prayer of the Heart.

(v 26 – 31)[1]God is Love. [2]This is the truth that is known within your Heart, because it has been written there. [3]Know this truth by sinking within your mind to the Heart. [4]Rest yourself within your Heart. [5]Here your true desire is known, because here the truth of God is known. [6]Then rise up and practice in joy. [7]The truth is true and it remains, as always, true. [8]You are as you have always been. [9]Love leads you always, even unto the remembrance of your Self.

(v 32 – 38)[1]You are the leader of your own awakening, and you lead yourself in Love. [2]This Love is not limited to the seeming individual self and a heart that is trapped within a body. [3]This Love is the great Love of a true Self, which is awakening with a great joy to the awareness and realization it had lost. [4]Your awakening is a great awakening, powered by the Love of one Holy Spirit.

[5]Look at your brother and rejoice! [6]He is one with you. [7]His Holy Spirit is one with your Holy Spirit. [8]It is this Holy Spirit that leads you.

[9]The universe has come to answer your call for awakening, because the universe is one mind with you. [10]Your true desire is the one true desire of it all.

(v 39)[1]Rest the awareness of dreams. [2]Sink into the desire of the Heart. [3]Join with your Self, and it is your truth that is realized and remembered.

NTI Hebrews, Chapter 11

(v 1, 2)[1]Faith is driven by desire and powered by belief (what you accept as true). [2]One may say he has faith, but if he does not accept as true his faith has no meaning at all.

[3]The idea of faith may be placed with one thought while the power of faith is given to another. [4]It is time for you to look honestly at where you place your faith.

(v 3)[1]It is by faith that the universe was formed, and it is by faith that its seeming form is maintained today. [2]This is the power of your faith. [3]Because you see exactly as you see, you can see also where it is that you place your faith.

(v 4)[1]It is through faith that your perception of the world changes.

[2]This is the first step in letting go of dreams. [3]For as you place your faith in that which is not seen, that which is seen changes to show you where you have put your faith.

(v 5, 6)[1]In faith, your entire perception shall seem to change in answer to the faith you have given. [2]In this way, the perception of death is also taken away. [3]For as you no longer place your faith with sin and guilt, the "wages of sin" as perception is also taken away.

(v 7)[1]By faith you will let go of illusion, knowing by that time of the oneness that you are. [2]In this final step of faith the world shall be released, and your acceptance of truth will be revealed.

(v 8 – 10)[1]Now by faith, you listen to my every word. [2]I ask you also to practice it in faith. [3]Practice without faith is dead, for it is your faith that brings all things to you within perception.

(v 11, 12)[1]Through faith perception is rearranged to answer the call of your awakening. [2]As you ask for guidance and give faith that it will be given, guidance is that which will come. [3]It shall lead you step-by-step, not into form, but away from it. [4]For as you see the power of your faith you are led to accept that the truth has always been true. [5]You shall see that you have been the leader of your own awakening through your Holy Spirit, which knows the true reflection that is everything.

(v 13 – 16)[1]Your desire for the world will keep you in it because of what you were created to be. [2]But as you recognize that the world is not your home, and you begin to long for, desire, and place faith in the Home that you know must be, you release your hand on illusion and reach out for the truth of what you are.

(v 17 – 19)[1]By faith in what is beyond perception, let go of the dreams that are perceived. [2]Do not ask in your heart for rewards given in perception. [3]Ask only that you may be led away from dreams. [4]And perception shall answer in a way that is helpful, so that you may welcome and realize an increase in faith.

(v 20)[1]By faith you bless experience.

(v 21)[1]By faith, experience blesses you.

(v 22)[1]By faith, your willingness to let go is increased.

(v 23)[1]By faith you let go of the limits of the world.

(v 24 – 28)[1]By faith you let go of the world, even as you seem to live in the world, so that your desire for the world can die. [2]In this way you live in dreams, even as you let go of dreams, and you prepare your mind to fully awaken.

(v 29)[1]It is your faith that leads you forward, because it is your faith that makes that which you see.

(v 30)[1]By faith, the world's rules no longer apply, because *through faith* you have released your belief, which had been given to them.

(v 31)[1]By faith you stand within the world and see that the world is not true.

(v 32 – 38)[1]By faith you bring all that is brought to you. [2]And so by faith, you may learn that none of it is true. [3]As you learn this lesson you shall giggle in acceptance, and release it all in joy. [4]For in the remembrance of truth you shall no longer desire a distraction that hides the truth of what you are.

(v 39, 40)[1]The Mind is one. [2]The desire of the Heart is only one. [3]The Spirit of God is one, and this is your holy truth. [4]Accept in willingness all that you do know, and by faith, that which has never been true shall fully and joyously be let go.

NTI Hebrews, Chapter 12

(v 1 – 3)[1]Follow the beacon of the Heart. [2]Persevere in its way, letting go of dreams as the Heart lovingly shines its Light on them.

[3]Jesus is given as a symbol because he was faithful to the way. [4]He remained focused on the true desire of the Heart, and he listened to it in all things.

[5]Do not be tricked by your own desire, which does not come to you from the truth of the Heart. [6]Question everything by the Heart, and you set out in the way of Jesus.

(v 4 – 6)[1]The way of the Heart is the way of love and attentiveness. [2]In love you are attentive to your way. [3]Through love the way that is not true is revealed.

[4]Walk slowly and surely, paying attention as you go, and you shall be shown the way of dreams, that you may let go and say good-bye to them. [5]This is the way of the Heart, because this is the way of Love.

(v 7 – 11)[1]The trials and tests that you may perceive as you walk this path to Me *are not* tests given to you by God in order to pass to your own freedom. [2]You are free! [3]In your freedom *you* draw your tests to you, that you may know your freedom through your choice.

[4]Remember that each circumstance is a gift given *by you* for your own healing, and you accept each gift graciously within the gratitude with which it was given.

(v 12, 13)[1]Relax and rejoice along your way. [2]Welcome your lessons as they are given. [3]You walk the way for each of your brothers, and they walk joyously beside you. [4]Take each lesson in joy as it comes, and the way shall be level under your feet.

(v 14 – 17)   [1]*Have compassion for yourself,*
                        and be firm in your desire.

[2]Have compassion when you catch yourself dozing. [3]Dozing is not real, and so it is not cause for chastisement. [4]It is merely cause for being awake again, firm for the purpose of the Heart.

[5]Love yourself and love your brothers, for the way of the Heart is love. [6]When the way of the Heart is forgotten through the drowsiness of your day, rejoice that an error has been seen. [7]Release the error in joy. [8]Through this you continue the way in joy.

(v 18 – 24)[1]You have come to the threshold of your Self. [2]And it is through the release of the past that you bid yourself welcome to enter. [3]See all desires that stand as obstacles to the one true desire of the Heart. [4]Release them joyously, and bid yourself welcome unto your Heart.

(v 25 – 27)[1]Let go of dreams. [2]That is your only function here. [3]Walk the way of the Heart, for it is the path that leads you truly through the forest of dreams to the release of all belief in them.

(v 28, 29)[1]Worship in reverence and awe the true desire of the Heart by giving your gratitude to it. [2]Through gratitude, desire is increased. [3]Through desire, faith is given. [4]And through faith all things that are useful to healing are brought in peace to stand quietly before you, awaiting the final pronouncement of your decision regarding them.

NTI Hebrews, Chapter 13

(v 1 – 3)[1]We are all one. [2]Everything that you perceive, be it seen or unseen, within your awareness or known only as a memory, all that *is* is one. [3]Stand grateful within it, *as* it, in awe of all that it is. [4]Then love your brother as yourself, remembering that he is your Self, even if he seems to be completely unaware.

(v 4 – 6)[1]God is all things, and all things are you. [2]This is because you are the process of creation that is God, and God is the process of creation that is you. [3]Nothing is separable within the process that is God. [4]It is all one, and you are one with it.

(v 7, 8)[1]All things are the same yesterday, today and forever, not for what they seem to be, but for what they are. [2]Look beyond what they seem to be, which changes, to what they are, which can never change, and you look beyond dreams to the truth of what you are.

(v 9, 10)   [1]*Nothing within dreams can last forever,*
                    so do not put your faith in dreams.

[2]Anything that is not lasting must fade away. [3]It is *you* that is eternal. [4]Put your faith in your truth and you build your house on the foundation of rock. [5]Put your faith in anything that is within dreams and you have built your house on the shifting sands.

(v 11 – 14)[1]Dreams shall not endure. [2]Put your faith not within the symbols of dreams. [3]Follow the symbols to the truth to which they point, but do not stop and wait at the feet of symbols. [4]For all symbols must fade away. [5]Only the truth endures forever.

(v 15, 16)[1]Love God, remembering that God is all things. [2]But do not cling to any one thing, remembering that it cannot be God. [3]God is not the thing that passes. [4]God is the process by which all things seem to be.

(v 17)[1]Listen within for the guidance of the Heart. [2]Follow your guidance and practice it with your every breath.

(v 18, 19)[1]Pray only that the knowledge of your truth may be restored to you. [2]Let all things within dreams be just as they may.

(v 20, 21)[1]Trust the process that is you, that it may lead you back *through dreams* to the truth that is the remembrance of your Self.

(v 22)[1]Let go of dreams, because they are not your reality.

(v 23, 24)[1]The Spirit within guides you. [2]It guides you through what you see without.

(v 25)[1]Grace lives within your Heart. [2]Amen.

THE HOLY SPIRIT'S INTERPRETATION OF JAMES

NTI James, Chapter 1

(v 1)[1]Greetings, my beloved.

(v 2 - 8)   [1]*Trust is your bedrock.*
              [2]*I ask you to hold to trust in all things.*

[3]Trust the healing process, for it brings to you that which is *best* for your healing. [4]Trust it, and accept it in joy.

[5]Trust your own mind, for it does know the true desire of your Heart. [6]And it *will rest,* that your true desire may be practiced.

[7]Trust your Self, for it is one, and its true purpose is only one. [8]There is no division within your Self. [9]There is only the illusion of division, and *illusion is nothing at all.*

(v 9 – 11)[1]Trust is the bedrock of your faith, for what you trust in you also put your faith in. [2]*Trust and faith are inseparable.*

[3]Do not look at your false self and the circumstances of the world, putting faith and trust (which may seem like fear) in those circumstances. [4]To do this is to put faith in illusion. [5]With faith placed in illusion, illusion is what you shall see and experience. [6]This is not the experience of your joy, because this is not what you truly want.

[7]Put faith in your truth by trusting your true desire. [8]Listen within, with true desire as your focus. [9]In this way, you shall know what to do. [10]Put all of your trust in what you hear, and your faith is given back to

your Self.

(v 12)[1]"Blessed is the man who perseveres under trial" means, blessed are you who remember to use all things to practice the true desire of the Heart. [2]For with practice and focus, your true desire stands clear within your sight until the *naturalness of your being* is as natural in your awareness as true desire is now in the quiet of your Heart.

(v 13 – 15)[1]God is the truth within you. [2]It does not tempt. [3]God *is*. [4]But God can be denied through your desire to do so. [5]Do not be unaware of this desire. [6]It is there, within your mind. [7]But it is a false desire that lingers from a moment of the past. [8]In your weariness you follow it in habit. [9]But in your alertness you remember to place this worn out desire aside.

(v 16 – 18)[1]Do not deny your truth, *because it does not change.* [2]In your denial you misunderstand what you do, and you experience your misunderstanding in unhappiness.

(v 19 – 21)[1]My dear brothers, take note of this and store it in your mind and heart:

[2]*Be quick to listen*
to the true desire of the Heart,
and you are quick to realize
the joy of your truth.

[3]Your truth is joy, so whenever you are not joyful you are misunderstanding what you are.

(v 22 – 25)[1]Do not merely listen to My words without practicing what I say. [2]To listen, but not to practice, is to be like a man who looks in the mirror, but then goes away and forgets what he saw.

[3]Remember that which you see as you listen to Me. [4]Practice it with your every breath, and you *do remember* the truth of what you are.

(v 26, 27)   [1]*Know thy Self.*

[2]This is your only purpose. [3]Hold tight to your purpose. [4]Let go of everything that is not of this purpose, and to your purpose you are true.

NTI James, Chapter 2

(v 1 – 4)[1]I have said that you are the leader of your own awakening, but the one who leads you to awakening does not select and judge based on the many ways that seem to be within the world. [2]The one who leads selects and judges not, so that he accepts and follows the path he has already laid out for himself.

(v 5 – 7)[1]The many ways of the world are distractions for you. [2]To be caught up in them is to be caught up in the world. [3]This is not the path to awakening.

[4]You are the leader of your own awakening through the spirit that does not desire the ways of the world, but humbly desires freedom from those ways. [5]And so it does not reach out to the world, but it watches and accepts, knowing and trusting that the path it is on is its own path to enlightenment, because the path that is being walked is the path it has already chosen and given to itself.

(v 8 – 11)[1]Do not worry that you shall make a mistake. [2]Worry that you could make a mistake comes from the belief that you *are* a mistake, which is also the belief that you are sin. [3]This is but a misunderstanding regarding what you are. [4]You can recognize this misunderstanding by your lack of joy.

[5]You cannot make a mistake, because you are perfect and whole and in communication now. [6]All thoughts are shared. [7]There has never been a moment of not sharing. [8]Therefore, your true desire *is known*, and its path is being given to you just as you have asked.

[9]*There can be no mistake in the oneness that you are.*

(v 12, 13)[1]Misperception is your greatest enemy, because misperception tells you that all is as it is not. [2]But this is not a sin; it is only an error. [3]And all error can be corrected.

(v 14 – 17)[1]Look well within your mind, and see your misperceptions. [2]See also that you have put your trust in them, so that even as you walk this path, which you have chosen for yourself, you do not see the path, and so you misperceive. [3]It is your misperception that causes you to suffer.

[4]Have mercy on yourself by being willing to surrender your misperceptions for the Light of your own awakening. [5]You are standing and walking your way, because this is the way you have chosen. [6]Trust in your Self and your leadership, and you will see the value and joy in all things.

(v 18, 19)

[1]*Relax unto your Self,*
and lay aside your worries.
[2]*They struggle against the true desire of your Heart,*
and so they are not helpful.

(v 20 – 24)[1]Abraham is the symbol of the birth of the awareness of Light within your mind. [2]With this birth came the willingness of true desire. [3]And with this willingness came the plan for how true desire shall be fulfilled within the mind that is one.

[4]This *is* the plan you selected with that first awareness of Light. [5]Look ahead in optimism and faith. [6]The plan has already been laid out for you. [7]Walk this path in trust. [8]Leave your misperceptions behind.

(v 25, 26)[1]You rise above your misperceptions of yourself, because your misperceptions *are* your dream. [2]By letting go of what you think you are and where you believe your choices to be, you let go of all that is false. [3]And then you walk peacefully, without misperception, the path you have given yourself for your own awakening from dreams.

NTI James, Chapter 3

(v 1, 2)[1]Be a conscious-minded teacher of yourself. [2]Be aware of the goal you have chosen, and hold it as a beacon before you in all things. [3]Let all decisions be guided by the Light, and you teach yourself consistently that you *are* the Light.

(v 3 – 6)[1]Your thoughts seem to be the foundation for your decision and your action, but even more...your thoughts are derived from your *conscious* desire. [2]Be, therefore, aware of your true desire within the consciousness of your mind. [3]Keep it before you, and true desire will easily lead you to the point you desire to reach.

(v 7, 8)[1]You are the leader of your own awakening, and so you may lead yourself in the direction you truly desire to go.

(v 9 – 12) [1]*Desire is the foundation from which all else springs forth.*
[2]*Be true to your true desire, and it shall lead you truly.*

(v 13 – 16)[1]What is the test that you shall give unto yourself to see if you are currently following the beacon of your true desire? [2]Ask only this:

[3]*What do I want now?*

[4]If you find that you want anything other than "Know thy Self," you have also discovered that you have veered off course. [5]Take this moment to reconnect with your truth, and you shall also be redirected in the direction that you shall go.

(v 17, 18)[1]Peacemakers who sow in peace know the harvest of their own Heart. [2]And this is the rich reward of Heaven.

[3]*To know thy Heart, follow thy Heart.*
[4]*To Know thy Self, to thy own Self be true.*

NTI James, Chapter 4

(v 1 – 3)[1]You always receive as you have asked, but you may not be aware that you are receiving, because you do not know what you have asked for.

[2]You do not ask from God through the expression of your words or thoughts. [3]You ask from the process of creation *through desire*, which you give your energy to.

(v 4 – 6)[1]Quietness is attentiveness. [2]In the hurriedness of your distraction of the world, you may seem to find many things to give your desire to. [3]But in truth, there is nothing within the world that the Son of God can desire.

[4]Whenever you believe you have given your desire to a thing or circumstance within the world, you must look deeper. [5]What have you truly given your desire to?

[6]The world is nothing but illusion of thought. [7]It is a fantasy that says, "All is as it is not." [8]It is a statement of a thought that is completely false. [9]In this way, the world is an idea that teaches you that you are what you are not.

[10]Whenever you believe that you are desiring *above all else* a thing or circumstance within the world, look closely at what you are asking. [11]You are asking to be taught that illusion is the reality of you. [12]Or in short, you are asking to learn that you are what you are not.

(v 7 – 10)[1]You need not do more than look at your false desire clearly to see that it is not your desire at all. [2]For you do not wish to know yourself as you are not. [3]It is your desire to know yourself as you *are*.

[4]Let go of false desires, because they are not what you want. [5]Hold true to your true desire, and true desire leads you truly to the recognition of You.

(v 11, 12)[1]Remember that judgment is the tool that builds illusion. [2]Let go of the desire to judge a desire that may be false. [3]Even this desire is a desire to learn illusion! [4]So the desire to judge is not a desire that is true.

(v 13 – 17)[1]Trust in your true desire, and let it lead the way. [2]It will guide you as to what you are to do.

³You need do nothing,
but continue to ask for that which you truly want.
⁴It is the process of God that will answer,
because it is the process of God that is you.

NTI James, Chapter 5

(v 1 - 6)¹Forgive yourself for all of your sins, for they are only imagined. ²They were born of the desire to experience yourself differently from that which you are, but that which you are has remained unchanged.

³Therefore, every sin you ever imagined was only a game you played to pretend that you were different than you are. ⁴But games are not reality, and nothing in reality has ever changed because of games you choose to play.

(v 7 – 9)¹Be attentive in patience as you unwind the doll that was wound up within the games you have played. ²This doll shall be laid aside, and your joy will be known in abundance.

(v 10, 11)¹Job is the symbol of letting go of the toys within the world. ²Job is the symbol of faith and trust in truth above all illusions.

³The rewards of Heaven are greater than the joys of the world, because the glee of Heaven is beyond the imagining of that which is different than glee.

(v 12)　　　　*¹You are pretending to suffer.*

²"Be true to your Self" means be true to your true desire, for that *is* the desire of your Self. ³Lay down your toys. ⁴Prepare yourself for the ascension into Heaven.

(v 13 – 16)¹The true desire of the Heart is also the prayer of the Heart, for nothing else can be desired by the Son of our most holy God. ²To Know thy Self *is* glee, for to Know thy Self is to know everything.

³Rejoice for your truth. ⁴Let go of illusions and the desire for illusion.

[5]Rest within true desire, and you rest peacefully within the seat of happiness.

(v 17 – 18)[1]Everything that you experience comes from you and the desire that you allow. [2]Rejoice that this is true, and choose consciously the desire of your Heart.

(v 19, 20)[1]"Whoever turns a sinner from the error of his way..." means:

[2]*Whoever recognizes that he has been desiring what he does not desire,*
and chooses to desire again in a new way,
chooses also to save himself from a multitude of distractions
in order to settle within the peace of his own Heart.

[3]Amen.

THE HOLY SPIRIT'S INTERPRETATION OF 1 PETER

NTI 1 Peter, Chapter 1

(v 1, 2)[1]"To God's elect, strangers in the world, scattered" is a reference to perception, not truth.

[2]*The time has come to release misperception,*
which does not point to truth,
and accept gladly the knowledge of the Heart.

(v 3 – 9)[1]One may rejoice over progress as he notices his perception is being healed. [2]Transition from misperception to true perception is a glory that is to be. [3]This is the symbol of your acceptance of your truth and of your true desire for that which has always been true.

[4]The transition to true perception is glory. [5]Have gratitude for your Self and this miracle, which is the symbol of your own true desire.

(v 10 – 12)[1]Be at peace in your gratitude for all that you are seeing now. [2]You are embracing your Self. [3]And this embrace is an enduring embrace, which cannot fade away. [4]Allow it into your awareness, and you look upon the miracle that is occurring within your mind now. [5]It is a miracle that shall not fade away, because it is but the reflection of your truth and your true desire.

(v 13 – 16)[1]"Be holy, because I am holy," is an acknowledgement of who you are. [2]Accept your Self as you are, and that is the acceptance of "I am holy."

(v 17 – 21)[1]You see your truth in the symbol of Jesus, because your truth is accepted in his way. [2]It is the acceptance of "I am eternal." [3]It is the acceptance of "I am with God." [4]It is the acceptance of "I am in God, and God is one in me."

(v 22 – 25)[1]The Word of God is you, and you are the extension of His Word so that all that you are, He is. [2]And all that He is, so are you.

[3]This is the correction of perception. [4]This is the expression of all that is true.

> [5]*By trusting the Light, which cannot be defined,*
> *as you and the expansion of you,*
> *you reach into eternity*
> *with an arm that is already there.*

NTI 1 Peter, Chapter 2

(v 1 – 3)[1]In truth you can rid yourself of nothing, for there is nothing to be rid of. [2]You are pure and perfect and in communication now. [3]Nothing has ever failed or gone wrong. [4]It is perfect, as you are.

[5]If something seems to have gone wrong or seems to be less than perfect, you are seeing through a veil of misperception. [6]It is only this veil that must be lifted, so you can see that it is all perfect, and it has always been.

(v 4 – 6)[1]Love yourself. [2]Do not seek outside of you for something that is better than you in which to love. [3]Seek only within. [4]For when you believe the symbol of love is outside of you, you also believe that you are not Love Itself. [5]In this belief, you cannot find love. [6]For what you see outside comes from what is valued within. [7]If you value the belief that you are unlovable, a world without love is the world you shall see.

(v 7, 8) [1]*Everything that you see,*
> *and the way in which you see it,*
> *is a reflection of your feelings and your beliefs about you.*

[2]There isn't a single exception to this statement. [3]Everything that you see is a reflection of how you see your Self.

(v 9, 10)[1]Your perception is changing, and your experience of how you perceive the world is changing also, because you have become willing to experience yourself differently. [2]As you allow change in your feelings regarding yourself, you allow change in your perception of the world, because the world is a reflection of your thoughts and feelings about you.

(v 11, 12)[1]Look at the world now, and see it honestly. [2]It is your roadmap to the awareness that you want to be, because it shows you where you must stop and look in order to continue the road to where you want to go.

(v 13 – 17)[1]The world is a reflection of your mind. [2]By seeing what you see in the world and by noticing and acknowledging your feelings about what you see, you find the misperceptions that are blinding you to your Self. [3]If you resent this one's authority, you have a resentment against yourself. [4]If you wish that one were different, you are not yet accepting the truth of you.

[5]By looking at the world, you find your misperceptions. [6]Look now in willingness with a desire *only* that misperceptions be healed.

(v 18 – 21)[1]Remember that nothing is brought to your attention except that you asked it to be brought to you. [2]So when that thing that you do not like stands before you, and you feel the pain of seeing it as if it were something real, remember this:

[3]*What you are seeing is not real, but it is your gift to yourself.*
[4]*You have given willingness to let go of misperceptions,*
so this one has stepped forward in gratitude.
[5]*It is the symbol of your willingness that misperception be let go.*

(v 22)[1]Rest in the faith of your innocence. [2]Let this misperception go, *now*, as it stands for you to see.

(v 23 – 25)   *¹What you see is what you see,*
because it is a reflection of what is in your mind.

²What you see is not fact in that it cannot be changed or cannot be seen differently. ³What you see is only fact in that it is a *fact* that it is *a reflection* of what is in your mind now.

⁴Accept this fact.

⁵Look at the reflection and see what you did not see before. ⁶All that you see is in your mind, and you are the power that can change it. ⁷Is what you see that which you know to be your truth? ⁸If it is not, it is misperception, and it will fade away through your willingness to release it to do so.

NTI 1 Peter, Chapter 3

(v 1 – 6)¹Be submissive to your true desire. ²In this way, you are submissive to your Holy Spirit, for your true desire *is* your Holy Spirit. ³True desire and Holy Spirit are inseparable.

⁴Look within to the misperceptions that make you special. ⁵That is, those misperceptions that seem to hold you apart from the rest. ⁶They may seem to be misperceptions that make you better, such as talent or wisdom or love. ⁷Or they may seem to be misperceptions that make you less than, such as unworthiness, sacrifice or disdain. ⁸Whatever you see that seems to separate you from others is a misperception, and it has arisen within your awareness, that it may be let go through your decision to be free of it.

(v 7)¹In this way, look on everyone as the same as you with no difference that can be truly noted. ²When you see no difference between you and your brother, you shall see that you are the same. ³When you see that you are the same, you shall also see that you are one.

(v 8 – 12)¹There is no judgment in the world. ²There is only judgment within your mind. [3]It is your judgment that shows you a world of judgment. [4]It is your judgment that gives you a world of pain.

[5]*Accept this fact.*
[6]*Everything you experience comes from you.*
[7]*There is not one exception to this statement.*
[8]*Therefore, everything you see,*
as you see it,
is a gift given you,
that you may see what is in your mind.

[9]Look well, and remember that what you see comes from you. [10]If it is not that which you would have yourself see, let what you see go and do not hold onto it.

(v 13 – 16)[1]Always keep your true desire close in your mind. [2]When you see a misperception and feel the confusion or guilt or fear that it seems to bring, drop to your knees *in symbol* of returning to the desire of the Heart. [3]Quiet the mind *in willingness* to let the whispers of misperception go. [4]Ask what it is that you truly want, and return your mind willingly to its Source. [5]In this way, the misperception is released in faith and an answer, which is true perception, is given, that your mind may be given back to peace.

(v 17 – 22)[1]It is through your release that misperception is taken away. [2]When you choose to hold to misperception and you suffer with it willingly, you ask that it be given, and it is given as you ask. [3]But when you let go of misperception and trust there is another way to see, misperception is released through your request, and the Light of Heaven shines on perception, that the Light of Heaven may be seen.

[4]*You have asked, and so you receive.*

[5]Remember this, that you may choose to ask differently.

[6]You are the leader of your own awakening. [7]The gifts you are given are the gifts you have asked to receive.

NTI 1 Peter, Chapter 4

(v 1 – 6)[1]Man walks in fear without knowing what it is that he is fearing. [2]He makes decisions to avoid his fear, only he cannot turn away from that which he cannot see. [3]Because he is blind to it, it follows him. [4]Because it follows him, he continues to run and hide.

[5]Fear is a misperception. [6]It is a misperception because there is nothing to fear. [7]What man runs from is his imagination, and in his running he imagines more.

[8]This is what Jesus taught as a man from the cross:

[9]*There is nothing to fear.*

[10]This is a lesson you have become ready to accept.

(v 7 – 11)[1]To live without fear is to live without imagining. [2]This is to stay in the now and in the heart of true desire. [3]By keeping the mind in the now and in the true purpose of Know thy Self, there is no imagining, and so there is no imagining of fear.

[4]Whenever fear seems to come over you, ask, "What am I doing now?" [5]You will see that you are imagining and that you are imagining fearfully. [6]Remind yourself that in imagining fearfully, you are creating your own misperception. [7]Be willing to let go of this activity, and the action of creating fear is let go by you.

[8]Fear is an action verb. [9]By ceasing the action of participating, you cease the action of fear. [10]This you can do by letting it rise over you *without your participation.*

[11]Return your mind to the current moment and the purpose of the true desire of the Heart. [12]In this way, you return your mind to Love. [13]A mind in tune with Love cannot know fear because fear, which is not real, is the opposite of Love, just as unreality is the opposite of reality.

(v 12 – 17)[1]Fear comes from judgment, which is also imagination, but it is imagination you have declared real. [2]This is where you must stop and learn the difference between what is real and what is unreal.

[3]Unreality is illusion, and illusion is everything that you experience now. [4]There is nothing that you experience within the mind of you as a person that is real. [5]Every thought that comes from the mind of the person is misperception, because the belief that you are a person is the greatest misperception of all.

[6]You are not a person now, and you have not been a person before. [7]There is no person from this lifetime or any other that you must let go of, because there has never been a person. [8]There has only been the thought of persons, and the thought of persons is not real.

[9]You have judged the thought of person as something that is real and separate from God. [10]You have judged the person as having life that is cut off from Life, and so it cannot survive. [11]And you have placed your mind within this person and said, "This is all that I am," so that you have limited yourself to your judgment. [12]This is why you live in fear. [13]The judgment of "person" you have deemed condemned, and then you have declared, "I am no more than my own judgment."

[14]But now I ask you to look at this thought with the eyes of reality:

[15]*One cannot place judgment on all that he is,*
so he must not be limited
by that which he has judged.

[16]What does this mean?

[17]It means that you believe in illusion, but illusion is not the truth of you. [18]It means that you look on misperception, but *you are the one* that declares misperception is true.

(v 18, 19)[1]You hate yourself for what you have done, but this is because you think you have done something real. [2]I say, you have *not* done something real, nor are you the one that you think has done it.

[3]Step back from illusion and rest with Me, for you are lost within a web of misperception. [4]By letting go of what you think you know, I can show you what you do not see.

NTI 1 Peter, Chapter 5

(v 1 – 4)[1]You are the leader of your own awakening. [2]Lead yourself, not by guilt, but by willingness.

[3]Guilt is the witness to your misperception. [4]By following the feeling of guilt, you stay within the web of misperception.

[5]Willingness is the witness to your Light. [6]By following your willingness, you are led from the confusion of misperception into the clarity of Light.

(v 5)[1]Follow the true desire of your Heart. 2Stay with it, and do not let it out of your sight. [3]In this way, you are not confused by goals that seem grand, but lurk within the shadows of misperception. [4]You stay focused with the beacon of Light, and you walk through misperception without being distracted by it.

(v 6, 7)   [1]*Trust is the armor of the righteous.*

[2]Humble yourself in trust "under God's mighty hand." [3]Let all of your fears go, because they serve no purpose that you desire. [4]Walk in peace with peace as your only shield. [5]This is the way of trust.

(v 8, 9)[1]Be kind and gentle with yourself, forgiving your misperceptions as they seem to come upon you. [2]Misperceptions are to be let go *because they are not true*. [3]This is the path that leads you from misperception to true perception, and true perception is the reflection of Light.

(v 10, 11)   [1]*God will come upon you*
in your willingness to see nothing else.

[2]In God you are free, because you are no longer hampered by the

misperception that you are not free.

(v 12 – 14)[1]Stand willing to let go of misperception through your willingness to see that you have misperceived. [2]It is the clearing away of misperception that helps you to see what it is that you do. [3]As you see what you do in the clarity of Light, you may do it in joy and in harmony with the oneness of your truth. [4]This is your true desire. [5]And this is the path of ascension into the realms of Heavenly awareness. [6]Amen.

THE HOLY SPIRIT'S INTERPRETATION OF 2 PETER

NTI 2 Peter, Chapter 1

(v 1, 2)[1]It is time that we speak of abundance, for you do not know what abundance is. [2]As you reach for true abundance, you accept everything as you. [3]In this, there can be nothing that is missing.

(v 3, 4)   [1]*Abundance is full awareness of your divine nature.*

[2]Abundance cannot be defined in any other way. [3]Abundance cannot be defined within the limits of the world, because abundance is unlimited and beyond all definitions.

[4]Do not look to the world in your imagination as you attempt to grasp the thought of abundance. [5]Look away from the world and the thoughts of the world. [6]For it is only by reaching *beyond limits* that the limitless can begin to be known.

(v 5 – 9)[1]For this reason, quiet the mind whenever it seems to stretch to imagine abundance within the world. [2]When the mind is stretching in this way it is stretching to limit itself even more.

[3]Rest the mind when it thinks of the world, and return the mind to the Heart. [4]For the Heart knows not of the world or the limits of the world. [5]The Heart knows only the song that it sings and that this is the song that whispers echoes of the thoughts of abundance.

(v 10, 11)[1]It is the Heart that knows abundance, for abundance is not of the thinking mind. [2]Whenever the thinking mind thinks it has understood and defined abundance, know that the thought of abundance has been lost. [3]In that moment return the mind to the Heart, which does not define, and so it does know abundance.

(v 12 – 15)[1]I am the memory of all that is true of you. [2]This memory is kept within the Heart. [3]Do not grasp at My memory with the thinking mind, for it has never been the Heart and so it cannot know the Heart as the Heart does.

[4]Instead, let the mind rest, that the Heart may rise into awareness. [5]In this way, your memory is returned to you. [6]In this way, you recall the meaning and the flavor of abundance.

(v 16 – 18)[1]It is through witness that you know. [2]That which you taste *as witness* cannot be forgotten, for that which you witness is a part of you. [3]Therefore, do not try to understand or comprehend or imagine without witnessing. [4]Let go of trying, and relax into allowing. [5]Through allowing, you shall witness. [6]Through witnessing, you shall know.

(v 19 – 21)[1]Within you there is a star. [2]This star is a very bright Light. [3]It was not made by you, but it was given to you as that which you could not lose. [4]This is the key to your abundance. [5]This is the prophecy that must be fulfilled, for this star is you, and it is all that is true about you. [6]Everything else emanates from the star, be it seen or unseen, perceived in truth or misperceived. [7]But the star is your truth, and that *is* abundance.

[8]Through knowing the star, you remember truth. [9]Through truth, the meaning and understanding of abundance is known as a point of knowing that is beyond all possible definition.

NTI 2 Peter, Chapter 2

(v 1 – 3)[1]Your freedom comes from your abundance, because your freedom *is* your abundance. [2]Understand that your abundance is not some future state of achievement, but that your abundance *is now*.

³Teach yourself only that your abundance is now,
without any separation from you,
and you teach yourself everything that is true about you.

(v 4 – 10)¹The Light within your Heart is your truth. ²This is the star that is you. ³This is the seed that is at the root of all that you are.

⁴It is true that there also seems to be something else within you...something that does not seem to be light, but dark...something that feels like judgment and guilt. ⁵It is okay to let yourself be aware of this darkness. ⁶It is okay to stand within it for a moment and feel it. ⁷But then remember that I have taught you that the judgment comes *only from you.* ⁸Decide in that moment to choose to see your Self truly. ⁹Then reach within your mind, and turn on the Light.

¹⁰Notice the joy that fills you as the truth that is your true nature fills every expanse of the mind. ¹¹You are the star and the Light. ¹²In the presence of your true awareness, all darkness disappears forever, for it is naught.

(v 11, 12)¹Rest within this joy, for it is joy:

²Your thinking mind does not understand.
³It is lost in a web of confusion
from which it cannot find its way out.

⁴This is good news, for when you understand that your thinking mind is confusion, you also realize *that you need not listen to it.* ⁵In that moment of realization, you are free.

(v 13 - 16)¹In the joy of your freedom you can let the thinking mind lie down to rest. ²Without this mind you look on illusion and see that it is nothing to affect your smile. ³In your seeing, you love it. ⁴In your loving it, it disappears from what it seemed to be and is only that which it has always been.

(v 17 – 22)   *¹Springs without water*
and mists driven by storm
are nothing but evaporation.

²This is what illusions are as you see them through the joy of your truth.

³Peace is found in the abundance of the Heart, because in the awareness of your truth all other thoughts are laid to rest. ⁴There is no truth but You, and so there are no thoughts that have power over you.

⁵Rejoice in your abundance! ⁶You are everything and everything you see comes from you. ⁷This is the truth that sets you free.

NTI 2 Peter, Chapter 3

(v 1, 2)¹Remember within your mind that which you truly want. ²Remember the promise that your abundance is now. ³Have faith in your abundance, and use it to bring that which you truly desire into your awareness and also to let all else go. ⁴This is the path to your remembering, and it is the power of your *own abundance* that shall bring you there.

(v 3 – 7)   *¹That which you see is that which you see,*
because it is that which is in your mind.

²This is the truth that has always been true. ³This is the fact that is changeless. ⁴It may also be said:

⁵That which you experience
is that which you have chosen to experience.

⁶This is the sign of your abundance. ⁷This is the truth of what you are and what it is that you do. ⁸This is the only truth, since all else is changing and only that which is changeless can be called truth.

(v 8, 9)[1]The peace within you knows this truth and is grateful for it, for the peace within knows it is *your own truth* that is your salvation.

[2]You are eternal,
and that which is changeless is eternal with you,
because that which is changeless is what you are.

[3]You are the process of creation that is God,
and this process is eternal.
[4]This is your true abundance.
[5]True abundance is That Which you Are.

(v 10)[1]There is nothing to fear because the peace within you knows the truth of you. [2]It is peace that shall prevail beyond all illusions, which have forgotten you.

(v 11 – 13)[1]Glory be to your peace, which is beyond all illusions. [2]Through your choice, illusions of forgetfulness shall fade away. [3]Through your remembrance, the joy and glory of your abundance shall be your only knowledge.

(v 14 – 16)[1]Remain in peace within the quiet of your mind where your abundance is felt and known. [2]Focus on your abundance. [3]Ask it to lead you to salvation. [4]Through thy own abundance, thy true Will shall be known.

(v 17, 18)[1]Thy true Will is this:

[2]To Know thy Self.

[3]To Know thy Self is to know thy truth, and to know thy truth is to recognize true abundance as it truly is. [4]Amen.

THE HOLY SPIRIT'S INTERPRETATION
OF 1 JOHN

NTI 1 John, Chapter 1

(v 1 – 4) *¹We proclaim the Word of Life.*

²This is a sentence of Self acceptance. ³This is a sentence that comes upon your heart as you look within and see that which you find there.

⁴That which you find is Love, and it is you.
⁵That which you find is Life, and it is you.
⁶That which you find is beyond description,
and so we simply call it "the Word,"
and that which you find is you.

(v 5 – 7)¹"God is Light; in Him there is no darkness at all."
²What, then, is God?

³God is an awareness that is pure,
because it looks on only that which is wholly true.

⁴This is God. ⁵And God, as an awareness, exists within you.

(v 8 – 10)¹God is our own soul, the heart of our truth, the Spirit that endures forever without end. ²God is all that is true, and that which is true overlooks the false, because the false has no meaning in the Light of truth.

[3]To Know thy Self, return the mind to God. [4]This is done in a moment of peace when God is your only desire.

NTI 1 John, Chapter 2

(v 1, 2)[1]My dear child, look within and see that you have not sinned. [2]Look within and see that you have taken the sins of the world upon your breast and held them there. [3]And then realize what Jesus did. [4]He released the sins of the world *as illusion*, accepted the face of Christ and returned himself to the Awareness of God.

(v 3 – 6)[1]We know that we have come to know Christ as we practice the teachings of Christ. [2]The teachings of Christ are these:

> [3]*I am Christ.*
> [4]*I am all that is perfect,*
> *and all that is perfect is in me.*
> [5]*I am in the Father*
> *and the Father is in me.*
> [6]*All that I am not is illusion,*
> *and I am all that I am.*

📖(v 7, 8)[1]It is true that this is not a new command, for this is what has always been true. [2]The darkness is passing, and the true Light *has always* been shining.

(v 9 – 11)[1]Let the darkness pass, and do not allow sorrow to come over you. [2]The darkness must pass in order for you to see the Light, and you must see the Light in order to embrace it.

[3]How shall you know if you stand within the Light or stumble within the dark? [4]There is one simple test, and this simple test shall never fail.

> [5]*Ask yourself honestly how you feel about your brother.*

[6]If there is one brother whom you do not love truly, you are lost within

darkness. [7]Rest yourself, and let the darkness pass. [8]For beyond the darkness of illusion there lives only the Light of truth.

[9]*Do not reach for the darkness, and it will pass.*
[10]*When the Light streams through and reaches for you,*
embrace it.

(v 12 – 14)[1]Have faith in your Self. [2]When the feelings of darkness are upon you and you feel the burden and pain of guilt, have faith in your Self. [3]You are the Light that lives beyond the darkness. [4]Do not be fooled by the illusion of pain. [5]In resting yourself you are healing yourself, and a great dawning is about to occur.

[6]*Trust your Self,*
and trust the healing process,
which you have chosen.

(v 15 – 17)[1]Do not love the world or value anything of the world. [2]When you are distracted by the world, you forget to focus on your healing. [3]In your forgetfulness, the dark clouds of illusion are not let go. [4]How can they be let go when the Son of God has decided to place his desire with illusion?

(v 18 – 23)[1]Illusion can be recognized in your heart by the priorities you place on all that you see. [2]If anything in the world has more priority than another thing, you are desiring within the world and you have asked to experience illusion. [3]If all things within the world have the same priority, and only your relationship with Me stands apart in your mind, you are letting go of illusion and the clouds of darkness are passing.

(v 24, 25)[1]What you have heard from the beginning remains in you and it shall always be with you, even through your illusion. [2]For that which you heard was love, and it remains, as always, the calling of your Heart.

(v 26, 27)[1]You are led astray only by your own false desires so that you always follow yourself. [2]When you have gone into the darkness and seem to be away from Love, remember that Love is always there. [3]Stand quietly, desiring only Love, and let Love *become* in you.

(v 28)   [1]*Stand quietly,*
and rest in faith and trust,
that darkness may pass,
and Light may become in you.

(v 29)[1]Have faith in the Light and hold only unto the Light. [2]It is by holding only to Light that Light is all you shall see.

NTI 1 John, Chapter 3

(v 1 – 3)[1]The Awareness of God is an awareness that is pure and looks on only that which is wholly true. [2]This awareness is within you. [3]It is the core of what you are. [4]It is in operation *as God* now. [5]However, you are not aware of your God-awareness because you have allowed that which is false to be held in your mind as true.

[6]This is what is meant by "purify yourself." [7]You must make the decision to release all that is not true from the mind, because that which is not true is false, and so it is an obstacle to the total awareness of truth.

(v 4 – 6)[1]Sin is a false idea. [2]Sin is false because the idea it supports is also false. [3]And that is the idea that you are separate from one another and from God. [4]There is no greater falsity than this, for there has never been a moment in which separation existed. [5]Separation as a fact is impossible, because it goes against the very nature of what you are. [6]It goes against the nature of what Life is, and so separation cannot be.

(v 7 – 10)[1]Dear child, do not be led astray by your own confusion. [2]There is no sin in the world, because there is no separation.

[3]The world that you see comes from the thoughts that you think. [4]The thoughts that you think seem to be more than the thoughts that you perceive as in your mind alone. [5]That is because you are not "your mind

alone." [6]There is no one mind alone, separate from other minds that are also alone. [7]This is illusion. [8]The belief in separation is the false thought that can never be true.

(v 11 – 15)[1]False thoughts are all thoughts that are based on the idea of separateness. [2]False thoughts include, but are not limited to, thoughts of guilt, attack, fear, hatred and regret. [3]All of these thoughts imply that there is a mind that is separate from yours with separate will and desire. [4]All of these thoughts imply a conflict now, in the future or in the past. [5]All of these thoughts are mistaken, because none of these thoughts are based on truth.

[6]All that is true is oneness and the activity of oneness, which is Love. [7]Love is the only fact, because oneness is all that is true. [8]You need not worry that you do not love your brother in truth, because Love is all that you are capable of. [9]You only need ask, "Am I aware of my Love?" [10]If you are not, you are still believing that which is false.

(v 16 – 20)[1]The thinking mind cannot know Love, because the thinking mind thinks apart from Love. [2]This is a statement of concept, not truth, because in truth nothing is apart from Love. [3]But this is a concept that is helpful, because it points toward truth, and the thinking from the thinking mind does not.

[4]The thinking mind is confusion, because it is based on the belief in separation. [5]It defines love as something one does to or for another, but whenever a thought of one and another is involved, the thought and knowledge of Love is lost. [6]For Love is based on oneness, and anything that is not based on oneness is confusion that has forgotten the unbreakable law of Love.

(v 21 – 24)[1]We obey God's commands and do what pleases Him because it is the nature of our existence. [2]This is fact. [3]This is Love. [4]This is what we are and what we do, and there has never been a moment when this wasn't true.

[5]The thinking mind cannot follow this thought because the thinking mind believes in separation, and so it cannot see Love, which is not

separation. [6]One must surrender the thinking mind to know Love, because one must surrender the thinking mind to know that which isn't separation. [7]That which isn't separation is oneness and truth, and that which is oneness and truth is that which is also Love.

NTI 1 John, Chapter 4

(v 1 – 3)[1]Dear child, I have already told you that the work to be done is the sorting of thoughts. [2]This includes the sorting of feelings, beliefs and images.

[3]Everything that you experience within the dream of the world comes from one of two sources:

[4]the thinking mind, which is the mask of separation, or [5]the Holy Spirit, which is the true desire of the Heart.

[6]Every thought, every feeling, every belief that you seem to live by and every image that you seem to see or hear speaks the thoughts of one source or the other. [7]Your role is to discern the source of the thought, feeling, belief or image, and then decide if you will accept what it teaches *based upon the source.*

(v 4 – 6)[1]We are of God, and so we have within us the inherent ability to recognize the Source that comes from God and the source that teaches God is naught. [2]You must only feel, within the presence of your awareness, the message that you are considering now, and the feeling you know within will tell you which source you are considering now.

[3]The feelings of peace, acceptance, trust and joy witness to the true desire of the Heart, for recognition of this desire brings forth the feelings of recognition.

[4]If a thought, belief or image is not aligned with true desire, the feelings within will not be the feelings of recognition. [5]They will be fearful feelings, such as guilt, hatred and the feelings of death. [6]When these feelings are upon you, you are looking at a source that is not true. [7]You may rejoice in the recognition that, because it is not true, you may simply lay it aside.

8The Awareness of God looks on nothing that is false,
so all that is false need not be looked on by you.

(v 7 – 12)[1]Love is all that there is. [2]This is a fact you may put your faith in. [3]When any thought does not feel like Love, you may put it aside as false. [4]Thoughts that are not Love are thoughts such as these: lack, limits, competition, victimhood, personhood, strife, and fighting, sickness, death, rage, and sorrow, helplessness, hopelessness, control and loss.

[5]These are thoughts that imply separateness, and separateness is illusion. [6]So these thoughts and thoughts that seem like them are not the thoughts of Love. [7]They are false thoughts of illusion.

[8]God is Love, and Love is everything. [9]The thoughts of everything are these: acceptance, joy, gratitude, peace and welcome.

[10]There is no resistance in Love, because Love is everything, and everything cannot be resisted by that which it is.

(v 13 – 16)[1]God cannot be denied fully, because God is the truth that is the core of you. [2]To deny God is to deny your Self, and this cannot be denied fully, because to deny it fully would be to deny existence. [3]Existence cannot be denied, because it is.

[4]Look at this, and know your salvation is at hand:

5Existence cannot be denied, because it is.

[6]This is the truth that sets you free. [7]In accepting this thought, which cannot be denied in any present moment, you accept that God *is* and you are one with God. [8]In this thought, you accept your Self, and you do it with the joy of recognition!

[9]Now that you have accepted your Self, follow your Self Home to the full and complete awareness that is God.

(v 17)[1]In this way, Love is made complete, not within reality, for in reality Love is always complete. [2]But in this way, Love is made complete within your own awareness, and when Love is complete within your awareness, there is no awareness that is not Love.

(v 18)[1]Fear disappears within the awareness of Love, because within the awareness of Love there is also the knowledge that there can never be anything to fear.

(v 19)　　　　　[1]*We Love, because we are Love,*
and Love is all that we are capable of.

(v 20 – 21)[1]To love God is to know God, and to know God is to love all things, because all things come from God, which is Love. [2]To not love is to believe in falsehood. [3]This is merely misperception, since all that *is* is all that is, and all that isn't, never was.

NTI 1 John, Chapter 5

(v 1 – 5)[1]The symbol of seeing Jesus as the Christ is the same as seeing all brothers as the Christ, for the seeing that recognizes the Christ is not without, but it is within. [2]When you see the Christ is you, you see the Christ in everyone and everything. [3]And when you see the Christ in anyone, you also see the Christ in you.

[4]This is what is meant by "transcend" or "overcome" the world. [5]It is when you see the world, and yet you see beyond the world, so that you know what it is that you see and you are no longer fooled by the images of the world.

(v 6 – 12)　　[1]*God has given eternal Life, and this Life is His Son.*

[2]To understand this is to understand everything, and to understand everything is to love everything.

[3]There is no judgment when you see through the eyes of God, for through the eyes of God you see nothing to judge. [4]You see only perfection, and you know that the perfection you see *is* God.

(v 13 – 15)[1]In seeing God and in knowing God, confidence is also known. [2]For in seeing God and in knowing God, one knows that he receives only as he has asked. [3]In knowing this, his desire to know anything that is different from this fact is taken away, because to remember the truth is to want only the truth, and to want only the truth is a gratitude that desires nothing different than what is.

(v 16, 17)[1]Sin does not lead to death, because sin is misperception and death is not real. [2]In seeing this, you see God, and in seeing God, you see this.

(v 18 – 20)[1]We know only that the truth is true, but in knowing this is all Knowledge given, for there is nothing else to know. [2]In seeing this is all Sight given, for there is nothing else to see. [3]And in hearing this is all Hearing given, for there is nothing else to hear.

(v 21)[1]Do not let your desire rest on knowledge or experience that is not truth. [2]Seek only truth and the truth shall find you. [3]This is why I have said, "Knock, and the door shall be opened." [4]Amen.

THE HOLY SPIRIT'S INTERPRETATION OF 2 JOHN

NTI 2 John

(v 1 – 3)[1]"To the chosen lady and her children" is a reference to the Holy Spirit within. [2]It is to this Voice that I speak, because it is this Voice within that recognizes Me.

(v 4 – 6)[1]You recognize your own Thoughts, which are of Me. [2]But now it is time that you also recognize these Thoughts are *of you*. [3]Any separation that you thought existed between you and Me does not exist, and this is *why* you recognize Me. [4]Your own Holy Spirit recognizes Me as Itself, and it bids you, "Look, and welcome."

[5]The time has come to walk in love. [6]I have already told you that Love is all that you are capable of. [7]And yet you do not see it always, because you do not always listen to your own Holy Spirit.

[8]The time has come to listen *only* to your Holy Spirit. [9]This is what I mean when I ask you to listen to Me. [10]This is what I mean when I ask you to walk in love.

[11]*Listen only to your own Holy Spirit,*
and you look on the world through only the eyes of Love.

(v 7 – 11)[1]To listen only to the Holy Spirit is a decision that you make. [2]It is a commitment to yourself to no longer listen to or be distracted by the false. [3]It is a promise to be aware of truth in every moment and to let every thought that is not of truth go. [4]It is a commitment to walk in a straight line through the power of your own choice.

(v 12, 13)[1]This is all I have to say to you now:

[2]I ask you to take this commitment deep into your heart as a promise to yourself. [3]When other voices arise that do not speak of this commitment, dismiss them in peace, simply because they do not speak of that which you truly want. [4]Remain fully focused on one goal now. [5]Let nothing distract you from this goal. [6]Have eyes only for truth and ears only for Me. [7]Listen in quiet. [8]I am within you always. [9]I am the Voice that knows who you are, because I am your true Voice. [10]Amen.

THE HOLY SPIRIT'S INTERPRETATION OF 3 JOHN

NTI 3 John

(v 1)[1]To My one Self, Love, in truth.

(v 2 – 4)[1]Our one mind is awakening, and you are joining with Me in the awakened state of our mind. [2]For as you look on your brothers, you realize now that they are not brothers, but an extension of your Self.

[3]There is no greater joy than this. [4]There is no greater joy than realizing our oneness and accepting it, for this is what it means to embrace. [5]In your acceptance, you embrace. [6]As you embrace, you know the process of expansion.

(v 5 – 8)[1]To you, there are no strangers. [2]Although they may seem to be strangers, because you do not know their look or cannot call their name, you know who they are, and so you help them. [3]This is the knowledge Jesus pointed to when he said, "Whatever you do to the least of my brethren, you do to me."

[4]Now you understand that whatever you do to your brother, you also do to yourself. [5]And so it has become your choice to choose love.

(v 9, 10)[1]The part of the mind that is not welcoming comes to your attention, but now you are able to see it and know it is not you. [2]You can turn away from unwelcoming thoughts, because they are not the thoughts you desire. [3]In your turning away, they fade from the desire of the mind.

(v 11, 12)[1]Witnesses to your mind come into your awareness because the witnesses *are you*. [2]Look on their faces and listen to what they say now. [3]They speak of love, because Love is what you have accepted as you. [4]They speak of peace and gratitude, because peace and gratitude is that which you know.

(v 13, 14)[1]Turn within, and further the development of your awareness through your focus and attention. [2]Dismiss that which is false, and accept that which is true. [3]In the focusing of the mind, witnesses shall step forth to show you what it is that you do. [4]But do not focus on the witnesses. [5]Stay well within the mind.

[6]Greet the friends that come to you by Name within the Heart. [7]Remember that each one is but a reflection of the totality of your Self. [8]Love them for what they are. [9]Amen.

THE HOLY SPIRIT'S INTERPRETATION OF JUDE

NTI Jude

(v 1, 2)[1]You are not alone. [2]It is time that we talk more about what you are, that you may experience mercy, peace and love in abundance through your understanding and your choice.

(v 3, 4)[1]Your mind is one mind. [2]Our mind is one mind. [3]There are no minds that are separate and alone from other minds. [4]This is why there is no suffering...because there are no minds that are alone. [5]There is one mind, and this one mind is fully and completely yours.

(v 5 – 7)[1]All of the horror that you witness and believe in is in your one mind. [2]This is why it is not truly suffering. [3]It is not one mind doing unto another mind. [4]That would be suffering. [5]But it is one mind choosing unto itself, and so it is only the illusion of suffering, even though it may seem to you to be real.

(v 8 – 10)[1]The one mind is not fully aware of Itself, and this is where the illusion of attack and suffering comes in. [2]But the one mind *is* Itself, and this is why suffering and attack are illusion.

[3]I have come to help you remove your faith from the illusion, which you have believed in until now, and place it firmly with the one mind, which is not separate. [4]With your faith placed in the one mind, you can look at the one mind, see the beliefs that have been accepted there, and then choose to use the one mind to peacefully see in another way.

(v 11)[1]The mind has no victims and it has no evildoers within it. [2]There are no separate parts within the mind that run amok, separate from the mind that is you. [3]The belief in separation is not partially true, so that your power is somewhat or partially limited. [4]The belief in separation is wholly mistaken, so that the power of your mind is all that is wholly true.

(v 12, 13)[1]To look at the world and place blame out there is to make the error of not believing that you are what you are. [2]And yet, this error can only be illusion, for you are what you are and what you are is wholly true.

(v 14 – 16)[1]Whenever you choose to hate another, you choose to deny your Self. [2]This is a choice you have made because you have *wanted* to deny your Self. [3]You have decided to deny your Self, because you have chosen to place judgment and hatred on your Name. [4]But what you must see is that *you* have made this choice. [5]And so just as you have chosen to see your Self one way, you can make the choice to see your Self differently.

[6]*I ask you to join in the decision to see your Self with Me.*

(v 17 – 19)[1]Remember what I have told you. [2]Our one mind is in a state of awakening. [3]Choose to stand within the awakened state with Me, and you choose to arouse our mind to awake-fullness.

(v 20, 21)[1]Follow within our one true desire. [2]Let it lead you in all things and in all ways that you choose to see. [3]Do not be swayed from the true desire, and in all circumstances return quickly to it. [4]In this way, you choose to join hands with Me. [5]In this way, we rouse our mind to a state of awake-fullness and to a state of glee.

(v 22, 23)[1]Do not listen to whispers of confusion, which you know because they are whispers that confuse you. [2]Stay clear that we are one mind awakening fully. [3]Stay clear that you are awakening with Me. [4]Stand firm for this one purpose. [5]Do not delay among the lingering of dreams.

(v 24, 25)[1]You are not alone. [2]We are one mind joined together in awakening. [3]When you feel that you are weak, lean in faith on My strength. [4]My strength is one with your strength, so by leaning on Me the illusion of weakness is erased. [5]Amen.

THE HOLY SPIRIT'S INTERPRETATION OF REVELATION

NTI Revelation, Chapter 1

(v 1 – 3) [1]The time is at hand. [2]All that you need to accept the truth of you is with you and within you now. [3]There can be nothing that you lack for which you must ask. [4]It has been given, and so you have it with you fully now.

(v 4, 5) [1]The world is an illusion, and so everything you experience as you let go of the world is illusion also. [2]*You are not to believe any of it.* [3]But helpful symbols will be given to guide you. [4]Remember that they are only symbols. [5]Follow them, realizing you know not where they lead.

(v 6) [1]Do not idolize anything within the world or any symbol or any thought that is sent to lead you from the world. [2]Hold to them as they are useful, but let them go when their usefulness has past. [3]You are to keep moving *by letting go* until you find yourself with nothing left to hold onto.

(v 7) [1]Look and see what you shall see. [2]Know that it comes to you like passing clouds, but it comes on the wings of Heaven so that you can let it go. [3]Nothing within the world comes to you for any other purpose. [4]Nothing within the experience of the world is to be held to. [5]It is all given, that you may look at it and choose to let it go.

(v 8)
>[1]*I am the Alpha and the Omega,*
>*who is and who was and who is to come.*

[2]Keep this thought within the mind as temptations come to tell you

that you are not. [3]Stay firm with your Heart in trust, and say "no" to all that is a lie by remembering it is not so.

[4]If you *do not believe* that which is not truth, you shall experience truth. [5]But if you choose to believe the false is the truth about you, you shall experience the false and believe it is true.

(v 9 – 11)[1]Guidance comes to you for one purpose and that is to lead you from the world. [2]There may also seem to be another purpose, which is happiness within the world. [3]The two purposes are not the same. [4]Do not be fooled by the similarities in their sound. [5]One purpose leads to death, while the other, most surely, leads to Life and knowledge of Life.

(v 12 – 16)[1]All things within the world are the same. [2]There is nothing special in any of it. [3]Every experience can be used to lead to Life, and every experience can also lead to death. [4]This is the double-edged sword of the spiritual path. [5]It may lead you to the Life you seek, or it may lead you to stay busy as you work very hard going nowhere. [6]Only you can know what this path is for you.

(v 17, 18)[1]The Christ within is your guide on this muddled and tricky path. [2]By listening only to it shall you find your way. [3]Listen to no other voice as you step carefully with Me. [4]Listen only for Life, and be aware of temptations, which are but the appealing calls of death.

(v 19, 20)[1]You are not alone. [2]You are never alone.

[3]*You need but remember your true purpose,*
and all that you desire for discernment and guidance shall be given you.

[4]You will never be asked to take a single step alone, but you must always be willing to take the lead by deciding the purpose and calling it out to Us.

NTI Revelation, Chapter 2

(v 1 – 3)[1]I know who you are, and you know who you are also. [2]This is why you do the work that I ask. [3]Because you know, and so you want to have the experience of who you are. [4]To not have the experience, when you know the experience is your truth, is unhappiness. [5]You shall not rest with unhappiness when you know Happiness is your right.

(v 4 - 6)[1]Within you, there is a voice. [2]It seems to be an evil voice that speaks of hatred and viciousness and attack, but this voice is not evil, nor is it to be hated or feared. [3]For to judge it as evil or to hate it or fear it is to listen to it, and to listen to it is confusion, for it is the voice of confusion.

[4]Here is how you are to see the voice that seems vicious. [5]This voice seeks for your happiness, but it has become confused by a goal. [6]It believes that your happiness lies in aloneness and control, when aloneness and control can only bring you misery.

[7]Do not hate the voice that is confused. [8]Simply do not follow it. [9]It leads to confusion, and you are ready to follow the Voice of Clarity now.

(v 7)[1]To him who has an ear, let him hear. [2]It is by overcoming the voice of confusion that one knows only the Voice of Light, and it is the Voice of Light that leads you to the tree of Life, which is the paradise of God.

(v 8 – 10)[1]Do not be afraid to hear the voice of confusion. [2]To fear it is to believe it is truth. [3]Hear the voice, but do not listen to it. [4]That means, recognize its confusion and do not walk in the way that it asks. [5]Have faith in Me over what it says. [6]Trust in your truth, and you will know true happiness.

(v 11)[1]He who has an ear, let him hear. [2]Life cannot die, because Life is the extension of Life. [3]Only the belief in death can bring you sorrow. [4]Let that belief die by not protecting yourself against it, and you cannot be hurt by belief in that which cannot be.

(v 12, 13)[1]I want to look deep within you *with you* at the beliefs that you fear most. [2]They are the ones you hide by denying them, but you deny them because you think they are true. [3]If you knew they were false, you would let them go. [4]I want to look at them with you so you may lean on My strength and see that they *are* false. [5]You may feel your fear and let it go with a giggle, because the light of your own Heart shines brighter than darkness caused by confusion. [6]When darkness is looked at beside the Light, it is the darkness that must fade away.

(v 14 – 16)[1]Put your fear of Me aside. [2]For your fear of Me is but imagined. [3]You imagine the confusion in you is truth and that I will punish you for your confusion, but this is nothing but evidence that the voice of confusion has your ear. [4]Put that aside. [5]Know that listening to confusion can never be helpful, since it only leads deeper into confusion. [6]Trust Me enough to listen to Me over the voice for confusion. [7]Through this, you shall learn that clarity is clear, and confusion muddles all that is available to be seen.

(v 17)[1]He who has an ear, let him hear. [2]You may choose trust or you may choose fear. [3]One is light and the other is darkness, so one will bring you joy and the other will lead to suffering. [4]Look carefully upon the choice that is offered you, and choose wisely with your Heart. [5]You know which choice to make. [6]It is not a mystery, because you *do know* what you are. [7]Choose with the Heart, and then hold to your choice as a white stone that is precious because your true Name is written upon it and known as truth by you.

(v 18, 19)[1]I know your truth. [2]You must hold with Me to this knowing of your truth as we look at all that is not true. [3]As you remember your truth and hold to Me, nothing shall shake you. [4]For nothing can shake the truth from the mind when the truth is held to as all that is in the mind as true.

(v 20 – 25)[1]Within your mind, coming from the voice of confusion, there is a deep belief in your own guilt. [2]Trust Me that this belief is in your mind and that you will see it and feel it as we step forward. [3]The fear that you know comes from the guilt that is hidden. [4]Without the guilt, there can be no fear.

[5]Trust Me. [6]The fear that you know seems real, because the guilt seems real also. [7]Fear may be let go, but as it is, the guilt shall rise to greet you. [8]When you see it, you will wish again for the fear, for the fear

protected you from having to look at the guilt. [9]The guilt comes with great pain and the strong feeling of sacrifice. [10]Hold to Me as we look at the guilt. [11]It is not real, although it has been believed. [12]We must look at it and release it together. [13]If we do not do this, the belief in guilt remains. [14]If the feeling of guilt is kept, you cannot know the peace of knowing your Self as you are, because you have chosen to know your self as you are not.

(v 26) [1]There is nothing to fear. [2]By trusting Me to the end through all that we seem to experience, you will learn this is true, and you shall rejoice unto Heaven.

(v 27)   *[1]The pieces shall be picked up*
and the desire to rule shall be laid down,
because you shall know the freedom that is your truth,
and you shall not seek to know freedom as if it is less than all that it is.

(v 28, 29) [1]The clarity that comes when the guilt has been released is the freedom and clarity of the morning star. [2]Seek only for this freedom, and let no fear stand in your way. [3]He who has an ear, let him rejoice.

NTI Revelation, Chapter 3

(v 1 – 3) [1]Your guilt comes from your judgment, and so at some point you must come face-to-face with the harshness of your judgment against yourself. [2]This may seem to be a very difficult time, as the feeling of guilt will be strong. [3]It will cry out that the judgment against yourself is correct. [4]But you must stand firm with Me, and trust this is not so.

(v 4 – 6) [1]You will seem to come to this point of facing your judgment alone. [2]There will be a temptation to believe that you alone are the sinner of all times. [3]Do not listen to this temptation. [4]You are looking at the belief in separateness. [5]It is time to see that nothing within this belief is true.

[6]He who has an ear, let him hear.

(v 7 – 10)[1]I have placed before you an open door that no one can shut. [2]Keep your eyes fixed on the door as you go through your final temptations. [3]Remember that no one can keep you from walking through that door but you. [4]Hold to My strength, knowing it is also your strength. [5]The time of trials cannot last, and when the time of trials has ended, the trials shall be no more.

(v 11 – 13)[1]The moment of joy is at hand. [2]When the trials seem heavy and you feel that you can hardly bear it, remember that the moment of joy is at hand. [3]When all trials pass, you shall know your Self as a pillar of Light shining for all who will look to see. [4]You shall know your Name, and you shall know the Name of everyone. [5]You will not doubt again, because the time of doubt will have ended forever.

[6]He who has an ear, let him rejoice!

(v 14 – 20)[1]The world is your shepherd when you believe you are little and small. [2]You look to it for protection when you believe that protection is what you need. [3]But when you have left these beliefs behind as tiny wisps of air that are not noticed, you shall see the world differently. [4]It shall not be your shepherd. [5]It shall be your banquet table. [6]And at this table, you shall feast daily, joyously with Me.

(v 21, 22)[1]The world shall be transcended through your decision to let it go. [2]For when you have finished with the feast, you shall walk happily away from the table. [3]At that time, you shall truly know what it means to be one with Me.

[4]He who has an ear, let him hear and rejoice!

NTI Revelation, Chapter 4

(v 1 – 6)[1]Looking too deeply for the meaning of symbolism is an activity of the thinking mind. [2]Analyzing details and searching for meaning is asking the ego to explain images to you.

[3]Step back from the images. [4]Take your eyes off of the details, which are separate parts. [5]Look at the whole picture as it is given in the mind. [6]Notice the feelings that the picture evokes. [7]What is the vision in this

scripture telling you?

[8]As you look with the eyes of wholeness, you will see that this picture speaks of brilliance, joy, joining, holiness, clarity and light. [9]That is the message of this vision. [10]It is a vision that points to the reality of Heaven.

[11]The lesson that is given by asking you to see this vision as a whole is an important lesson that you must learn. [12]As you look on the world now, you see separate parts and you analyze them for meaning. [13]Even in your process of letting go, you see separate parts and you analyze them for meaning. [14]Although this process can seem effective and at times may be helpful to your learning, it is slow, as the separate parts seem to have no end.

[15]Step back, and look at the whole. [16]When you look at the whole, what do you see? [17]It is the whole that must be let go, because it is the whole that makes the illusion of parts.

📖(v 6 – 11)[1]The four living creatures represent eternal sight. [2]They are demonstrated as different to focus you on the fact that they are all the same. [3]For what seems different is meaningless, and what is the same is all that is true. [4]The four creatures are the embodiment of Eternal Sight, and so it is this song that they sing:

> [5]*Holy, holy, holy*
> *are you, the Father and the Christ,*
> *who was and is, and is to come*
> *for always and eternally.*
> [6]*Amen*

[7]With the same eternal sight, and with joy and gratitude in its Heart, the creation of the Father echoes its honor in glory to the Father forever. [8]Amen.

[9]This is a description of Heaven. [10]This is a description of the recycling of joy and love.

NTI Revelation, Chapter 5

📖(v 1 – 5)[1]The scroll with writing on both sides, sealed by seven seals, is not a secret scroll that cannot be opened. [2]Every word written on the scroll is written on the Heart of the very creation of God. [3]It is all that is known to him and all that need be known. [4]The scroll is but a symbol of the knowledge that already is.

[5]Jesus is a symbol of one who has discovered the contents of the scroll, but as I have already taught, Jesus is not different from you. [6]Jesus is within your mind, so all that is in his mind is in your mind also. [7]It is not a mystery to you. [8]It is known. [9]And what is known can be discovered when you lay the belief in your unworthiness aside.

(v 6 – 10)[1]You are worthy of the knowledge of the scroll, and the knowledge of the scroll is yours. [2]So what blocks this knowledge from your awareness?

[3]*It is the belief that you are what you are not,*
and that you have done what you could not do.

[4]This is the belief that blocks the knowledge of the scroll. [5]This is the belief that is held to within the mind. [6]This is the belief that is symbolized by darkness that blocks out light. [7]But just as darkness cannot block light, this belief does not hinder the fact that only the truth is true.

(v 11, 12)[1]It is you that the angels sing of. [2]They do not sing of your worth, for they cannot imagine anything but your glory. [3]They do not whisper of sacrifice, because they cannot envision anything but Love. [4]They look upon you now and see only the whiteness of an untouched lamb, because they see only that which is true, and they look directly *at you.*

(v 13, 14)[1]All that is seen and unseen is of one heart and one glory. [2]Nothing exists that is not a part of all that is, and that *is* glory. [3]To say that it praises you is not correct, because there is no you separate from it that can be praised. [4]It praises within Itself, in gratitude and love. [5]And it is this praise that is extended within Itself without leaving Itself, so that it seems to move and yet it goes no where. [6]This is the glory and joy of Heaven, and this is That Which you Are.

NTI Revelation, Chapter 6

📖(v 1, 2)[1]The first of the seven seals on the scroll of Life represents that which must always come first. [2]The rider of the white horse "bent on conquest" represents full dedication to the true desire of the heart.

[3]I have spoken of this to you before, but it cannot be overemphasized, especially now.

[4]*It is the desire that you allow which leads you.*

[5]And so if you want to be led in a straight-line without delay, you must allow the true desire to lead without distraction.

[6]Stay fully focused on one desire now. [7]That is to "ride out as a conqueror bent on conquest."

📖(v 3, 4)[1]The second seal represents that which is not true, but seems true within the mind. [2]This is the symbol of fear hidden by the mask of ferociousness. [3]This image is only an image within the mind, and its reality is naught. [4]Through the process of looking at it, this image shall be let go.

📖(v 5, 6)[1]The third seal represents judgment, which maintains the illusion of the world. [2]It is judgment that separates and makes separateness seem real. [3]The scales of judgment must be laid aside.

📖(v 7, 8)[1]The fourth seal represents death, which is the symbol of the illusion of separateness. [2]For life cut off from Life can only be death, so death is a fitting symbol of that which cannot be true.

📖(v 9 – 11)[1]The fifth seal represents the options of fear and trust. [2]In the moment of not knowing, this is the choice that must be made. [3]You must choose to trust that which you do not know, or choose to fear it. [4]In this choice is everything that follows given.

📖(v 12 – 14)[1]The sixth seal represents the end of perception. [2]The way you see shall be based on how you have chosen. [3]You shall see illusion, which has stepped forward to be released. [4]Or you shall see fear made real, and you shall run from it.

(v 15 – 17)[1]Fear shall not be your victory. [2]In making this choice, you shall know that you have chosen death. [3]But even this is an illusion, as anything that is not Love is not real. [4]You experience the effects of fear, *because you have chosen the effects of fear.* [5]In seeing this and knowing the gratitude of the truth is true, you offer yourself the opportunity to step back and choose once again.

NTI Revelation, Chapter 7

📖(v 1 – 4)[1]The purpose of these verses is to again assure you that there is nothing to fear. [2]The four angels who are holding back the winds represent the holding back of the end of perception. [3]The end of perception is held back...it does not come to you to be looked at and let go...until you are ready and call it forth in your mind.

[4]This is the seal of the 144,000. [5]The seal represents readiness and the 144,000 represent the lessons you have learned as you have prepared yourself to choose between that which seems real, but isn't, and that which is truly and enduringly truth.

📖(v 5 – 8)[1]Each of the tribes of Israel represents a lesson category. [2]Each lesson has been taught until you have taken it in and learned it fully, so that the lessons themselves are like a shield that protects you from anything you may experience as you face the end of perception. [3]The twelve lessons are these:

1. [4]You are innocent.
2. [5]You are the Son of God, and everything you experience is a gift to yourself.
3. [6]You choose the purpose for everything you see, and the purpose you choose is the one that is given to it.

4. [7]Purpose is based on desire. [8]Since there is only one true desire, there is only one true purpose. [9]Anything else is illusion.

5. [10]You are never alone. [11]Separation is false. [12]The Light in the mind lends you its strength, because the Light in the mind *is* your strength.

6. [13]The illusion of the world is false. [14]It only seems real, because you have given it your belief. [15]But by withholding your belief, its realness must fade.

7. [16]Your faith and trust is everything, for that which you put faith in, you will experience. [17]This is because you are the Son of God.

8. [18]Your true desire is Know thy Self. [19]Any other desire is the desire not to Know thy Self, which is to choose lack and fear. [20]You are ready to put aside the temporary experience of lack and fear and to know the completeness of truth once again.

9. [21]Anything that is not truth is illusion. [22]To choose illusion is to choose fantasy, but fantasy cannot change the truth.

10. [23]Fantasy is spun within the thinking mind. [24]By allowing the thinking mind to spin, you choose fantasy. [25]By allowing the thinking mind to rest, you choose truth.

11. [26]Everything that you experience is Love. [27]There is not one exception to this statement. [28]If you believe you look on that which is not Love, you are misperceiving. [29]To see and to know Love as it is, let go of your misperception.

12. [30]Oneness is all that is true now. [31]The belief in separation has always been false, so anything that is seen through the lens of that belief must be false also. [32]There is not one exception to this statement.

[33]These twelve lessons prepare you to choose only that which is true.

(v 9, 10)[1]The joy of Heaven is inexplicable as you step forth to choose Heaven once again. [2]For in Heaven there is the knowledge that Heaven is your truth, and in choosing Heaven you shall know Heaven as your reality and your joy.

(v 11, 12)[1]In Heaven there is one gratitude. [2]This gratitude is for Heaven as it is. [3]This gratitude is joined, and this gratitude is shared. [4]For in Heaven there can be nothing that is apart from the reality of all that is.

(v 13 – 17)

[1]*And the Light of Heaven is seen*
to be that which is your Self.
[2]*Its joy is your joy.*
[3]*Its gratitude is your gratitude.*
[4]*Its oneness is your oneness,*
and its Love is your Self.

[5]*Never have you been separate from Heaven,*
and never has Heaven been separate from you.
[6]*For how can one,*
even for a moment,
be separate from the one that is His Self?

[7]In this knowledge is all joy. [8]In this knowledge is all peace. [9]In this knowledge is fear wiped out forever, because in this knowledge it is seen that it is impossible that there could be anything separate from you to fear.

NTI Revelation, Chapter 8

(v 1 – 13)[1]Do not let fear block your sight. [2]There is nothing to fear. [3]When you believe there is, you feel the effects of fear. [4]When you realize there is only Love, the illusion of fear dies.

[5]*All meaning comes from the mind.*
[6]*All meaning comes from the mind.*

[7]This is repeated, because if you believe meaning comes from anything else, you are mistaken. [8]You have applied meaning and then

denied that the meaning was given by you. [9]In this way, you choose fear, because you choose to believe that you are what you are not. [10]Therefore, you choose to believe that you can die.

[11]It is time to look within the mind at the beliefs you hold there.

[12]The seventh seal is meaningless. [13]Everything associated with the seventh seal has no meaning at all. [14]In this realization, you free yourself to look at the events associated with the seventh seal and to ask, "What meaning am I seeing in this?" [15]As you ask this question, look deeply at the hidden beliefs within your mind. [16]Know that it is your mind. [17]Do not deny that it is.

[18]The time has come to look and to release from the mind that which is in the mind that teaches only fear.

[19]What do you see in your mind when you read Revelation, Chapter 8? [20]What meaning are you giving the words that are written there? [21]What beliefs within your mind need to be let go and healed?

- - - Suggestion: Answer the questions
in the previous paragraph before continuing - - -

NTI Revelation, Chapter 9

📖(v 1 – 6)[1]The words within this passage are also meaningless. [2]Only interpretation can be given to them.

[3]The "abyss" is the recesses of your mind where you still hold to beliefs that you do not desire to hold to anymore. [4]Now that you are free of the desire to maintain those beliefs, you are free of the beliefs. [5]They cannot be maintained against your will.

[6]It is important to go into the abyss and look for what is hiding there. [7]The beliefs that you have chosen against can hide like cobwebs until you see them and brush them away from the mind.

[8]The smoke that rises out of the abyss is distraction. [9]Do not look at it now. [10]Look past the smoke, deep into the abyss. [11]With clarity and light, that which you seek to see shall indeed be seen. [12]Nothing can stand

in the way of the will of the Son of God.

📖(v 7 – 11)[1]The locusts of this verse are only fearful if you choose to look at them as fearful. [2]If you do, it is because you have chosen to see yourself as small. [3]But I have not taught you that you are small. [4]And I have not taught you that you can be hurt by locusts that represent fear.

[5]Fear can only hold you back if you choose to let it. [6]If you choose, you can also walk right through fear. [7]Look! [8]The locusts are ready to step aside and let you pass.

(v 12)   *[1]Fear has not stopped you,*
so there can be nothing to fear.

(v 13 – 21)[1]Standing beyond the fear in the abyss of your mind, guilt rises up to greet you. [2]At first, you may not see it, as it is well hidden within the mind. [3]But if you look, trusting it is there, guilt shall step out and find you.

[4]At first its hold may seem to strangle you. [5]And you may feel as if you have been caught. [6]But then remember your mission within the recesses of the mind. [7]You are here to clear away the guilt. [8]In trust and peace, kneel down and let the guilt rise over you. [9]If you do not call to it in faith, it will pass you by.

NTI Revelation, Chapter 10

📖(v 1 – 11)[1]This scripture is also meaningless. [2]To look for inherent meaning where there is none is to look outside your Self for the Source of all meaning. [3]To look outside your Self is to deny what you are. [4]The time for denial has ended. [5]The time for acceptance is now.

[6]Trust your Self. [7]Seek only that which is truly helpful and ask for the interpretation of Revelation, Chapter [10] that would be given to you now.

- - - Suggestion: Read & ask for an interpretation
from the inner Voice before continuing - - -

NTI Revelation, Chapter 11

📖(v 1 – 10)[1]The measuring rod represents the measure of your desires. [2]The temple and its worshippers represent the desires at the core of the heart. [3]The outer court represents the world, which is only distraction.

[4]Sit quietly with yourself and enter into the inner chamber of your heart. [5]Take the measuring rod. [6]Take note of the worshippers and measure the desire as you find it there. [7]Do not deny that resistance still worships at the inner chamber of the heart. [8]Take note of the worshippers as you find them. [9]But use the measuring rod to see which desire leads you now.

[10]It is the true desire that rises up in joy within the heart. [11]Greet your true desire within the heart. [12]In joy, join with it there.

[13]The two witnesses represent the joint Will of the Holy Spirit and the Son of God. [14]This is true desire picked up and merged with the one who desires it above all else. [15]No will can overcome that of true desire, because any other will is the false will of illusion. [16]Illusion cannot stand up against truth, so it is illusion that must crumble and die.

[17]There may be a time that the joint Will seems overcome by the beast of guilt and fear, but this is only an *illusion* within an illusory battle. [18]It is the joint Will that has called forth the beast, so that the beast may be coaxed out of hiding.

(v 11, 12)[1]It is the joint Will that gives breath to Itself. [2]In this way, it cannot die. [3]For that which gives Life at will may call upon Life, and Life will come to rescue it from a seemingly dark grave.

[4]Remember this. [5]It is your true desire, recognized as true desire by you, that will see you through the darkness found within the recesses of the mind. [6]If the darkness seems to be too much to bear, call upon your Self and your true desire. [7]You shall be lifted up from the darkness into the Light that shines from within your own true desire.

(v 13, 14)[1]Do not stop looking. [2]Will that healing continues. [3]The darkness is being healed by the Light you carry with you.

(v 15)[1]Rest the mind, and reclaim your trust. [2]In trust and true desire, you move forward for the healing of the mind.

(v 16 – 18)[1]This is a time for gratitude and rejoicing. [2]The mind is being healed of that which is false. [3]And the Light that has shined forever is shining brightly now to be seen.

(v 19)[1]In gladness and true desire, the Son of God prepares to welcome his Self in joy.

NTI Revelation, Chapter 12

(v 1 – 6)[1]Everything that you are reading is about you. [2]Everything that you experience is a reflection of your mind. [3]In realizing this, there is no fear. [4]There is only wonder. [5]And there is the opportunity to realize that everything is dependent on your choice, because you are the one who chooses.

[6]The woman and her child are one. [7]To separate them is to separate you. [8]But the dragon is not separate from you either. [9]This is why you have a choice. [10]Everything that is experienced is experienced through your mind. [11]And you may choose what, within the mind, shall be the ruler of all experience.

(v 7 – 9)[1]The world seems real and concrete to you, but even this is within your mind. [2]The world was made real by the mind, so that it could choose to experience that which it chose to experience while also denying its ability to be the one that chooses.

[3]This is an ability that you must reclaim and take back, because this is an ability that has never been lost. [4]To deny that choice is yours, is to be lost by your own choice. [5]To accept choice as freedom is to reclaim the way to be found.

(v 10 – 12) [1]*Accepting choice is accepting the way of salvation.*
[2]*Accepting choice is accepting how all experience is made.*
[3]*In accepting choice, you are accepting that you are experience's maker, and in doing this, can all previous choice be undone.*

[4]"Woe to the earth and the sea" is merely misperception. [5]Rejoice that you shall see the choices you have made. [6]It is this that enables you to decide to choose again.

(v 13 – 17)[1]All that you shall face cannot harm you. [2]You need only to remember this in order to face it without fear. [3]Be glad that you are choosing to see the end of perception. [4]Be happy that you have walked to this point of being willing to choose again.

NTI Revelation, Chapter 13

📖(v 1 – 4)[1]The beast that comes out of the sea is your judgment against your Self. [2]Do not look away from this beast, for it is important that you see him.

[3]All that seems to be made through the belief in fear and guilt starts here, upon this judgment. [4]To let go of everything else, you must be willing to let go here. [5]If you choose not to let go here, you choose to let go of nothing.

[6]Men worship the dragon, which is the perception of fear and guilt, because they worship the beast, which is self-judgment.

[7]Notice the questions that are asked, and realize it is you who asks these questions:

[8]*"Who is like the beast?* [9]*Who can make war against him?"*

[10]Realize how faithful you are to your own judgment. [11]Accept it fully as yours. [12]Only by seeing it and accepting it for all that it is, can you realize it need not be and fully let it go.

📖(v 5 – 10)[1]If you will read verses five through ten and realize they are talking about you and your judgment against your Self, you will see much that you need to see. [2]You will be able to accept that which you must let go if you are to know your Self as the absolute freedom that you are.

*- - - Suggestion: Complete the assignment
in the previous paragraph before continuing. - - -*

📖(v 11, 12)[1]The other beast, which comes out of the earth, is guilt. [2]If you recognize that guilt supports Self judgment, you recognize that guilt is not real.

📖(v 13 - 18)[1]Look at verses thirteen through eighteen and realize this is written about you and your belief in guilt. [2]See what you will see, so that you can choose to let this belief go.

*- - - Suggestion: Complete the assignment
in the previous paragraph before continuing. - - -*

NTI Revelation, Chapter 14

(v 1 – 5)[1]It is your true desire that will lead you Home, just as it is true desire that has led you to this point in your willingness, understanding and acceptance.

[2]I have already told you that the 144,000 represents the lessons you have learned. [3]It is acceptance of these lessons as truth that shields you from any perceived attack, because it is the acceptance of these lessons that teaches perceived attack is unreal.

[4]Hold to these lessons and your true desire as you step forward within the recesses of the mind. [5]Be grateful, because you are letting go of all that is false so only the reflection of truth shall be known.

(v 6, 7)[1]The hour of God's judgment is the hour of your release. [2]For this is the hour when, filled with the faith in God that comes from the knowledge of truth within, you shall say "no" to all that is false. [3]This is the hour of putting aside all that is not real, so only the reflection of realness can be experienced within the mind.

📖(v 8)[1]Babylon the Great represents differences. [2]And so the second angel sang in joy, "Fallen! [3]Fallen are all differences which confused the mind and made it blind."

📖(v 9 – 12)[1]The third angel only emphasizes choice. [2]To continue to worship judgment is to continue to experience the effects of judgment. [3]This point is made to help you see, clearly, your desire to choose not to judge anymore.

(v 13)[1]Blessed are the ones who choose to lay down judgment and die the judge's death. [2]For to die the judge's death is to walk away from judgment. [3]To walk away from judgment is to walk the way of Life.

[4]Rest the mind. [5]Become the empty shell. [6]Let all that was you go, so all that you are may be known.

(v 14 – 16)[1]When judgment has been let go, you are ready to step forward into the remaining recesses of the mind. [2]This is the time of harvest, so this is the time when the wheat is separated from the chaff, the true from the false.

[3]Do not make the mistake of seeing the harvest as an event in your future, *for always the harvest is now.* [4]There is no time and there is no future. [5]To wait on time is to delay the harvest, which is now.

[6]Always, it is now, so always, it is time to let go of judgment and look at the darkness hiding in the recesses of the mind.

(v 17 – 20)[1]You fear the harvest, because you fear it is your death. [2]This fear only comes from a judgment you have heaped upon your Self. [3]Remember there is no mind that judges except for the mind that is yours.

[4]When you fear death, realize the judge has been allowed to be resurrected. [5]Step back within the mind and lay the judge to rest. [6]Then continue with the harvest in joy and without fear.

NTI Revelation, Chapter 15

(v 1 – 4)[1]The walk within the recesses of the mind is not a struggle. [2]Whenever you notice the feeling of struggle, you know that the desire for resistance has taken hold. [3]Rest yourself a moment, and remember that willingness does not struggle. [4]Let the struggle fade away, and return yourself to the true desire of the Heart.

📖(v 5 – 8)[1]The seven angels are dressed in white, which represents perfection and innocence. [2]The golden sashes represent holiness. [3]Together, the seven angels represent your truth. [4]Keep your eyes fixed on them.

[5]The seven bowls are said to contain God's wrath. [6]But I tell you, *the seven bowls are empty*. [7]Have faith in Me, and you will not experience that which isn't there.

NTI Revelation, Chapter 16

(v 1 - 6)[1]It is time to be quiet and still the mind. [2]Within the stillness, there is a rustling, but what you hear and feel is the rustling of illusion.

[3]Still the mind in faith that the rustling is illusion. [4]Let the rustling rustle, but hold only to the thought of stillness.

[5]Be still. [6]In this way, you do not acknowledge illusion. [7]In this way, you do not acknowledge it as true. [8]In this way, you do nothing. [9]And nothing is the acknowledgment that nothing is due.

(v 7)[1]Let peace rule the mind as all that is not true moves on through.

(v 8, 9)[1]God is Love. [2]In silence, let this Love be known.

(v 10, 11)[1]Heaven is all that is. [2]And *all that is* is realized through the passing of what is not.

(v 12 – 14)[1]Your belief comes from your faith. [2]When you notice a belief in illusions, ask where your faith is now. [3]Faith comes from desire. [4]You know your true desire now. [5]In questioning your faith, you remember your desire. [6]In remembering desire, you loosen your grip on belief.

(v 15)[1]Fear is merely illusion that indicates you have slipped into judgment again. [2]Wake yourself up and remember the stillness. [3]In remembering is all fear undone.

(v 16)[1]Resting in faith and trust is the answer to all that arises. [2]In willingness, and through true desire, prepare to become the empty shell.

(v 17 – 21) [1]*Nothing is happening in the mind when anything*
but Love is perceived.
[2]*Be willing to loosen the hold on nothing,*
by trusting the stillness,
which nothing is not.

[3]Trust within the stillness. [4]Your true peace is known here. [5]Trust within the stillness until the images of the mind have been transformed.

NTI Revelation, Chapter 17

(v 1, 2)[1]The great prostitute is merely the symbol for illusion. [2]Have no fear. [3]There can be no punishment given to that which is pure fantasy. [4]Come with Me, and see what happens with the distraction called illusion.

(v 3 – 6)[1]Do not be afraid to look at the great illusion. [2]Fear to look comes only from the belief that it is real. [3]It is not real, or I would not call it illusion. [4]It is just a dream. [5]Look on it now with Me.

[6]The prostitute sitting on the beast represents illusion sitting on the belief that supports it. [7]It is this foundation that you must look at now. [8]Turn your eyes from the glitter and distractions of the illusion and look at the beast on which it sits.

[9]The beast, as you can clearly see, is the belief in individual separateness. [10]It is the belief that there is a "you" and an "I," an "us" and a "them," a "this" and a "that over there." [11]It is the belief that there is no connection and everything that is experienced is separate from the one who believes he experiences it.

(v 7, 8)   *¹The beast once was and now is not,*
because the beast never has been.
²The beast once was a thought,
but it was an impossible idea.
³And so the thought never came to be.
⁴It only came to be as a belief,
but what is believed is not that which is known as true.

⁵The belief must come up again, because it has not been let go. ⁶But it comes up only that it may be dismissed as false. ⁷There is no other reason to look at the belief. ⁸It can have no other purpose, since it isn't anything that is real.

(v 9 – 11)¹This calls for wisdom, and wisdom is not thinking, for thinking cannot teach you to understand. ²Thinking was made to block understanding, because understanding is the knowledge of what is.

³It is time for you to remember all that I have taught, without question and without doubt at all. ⁴The dream and its illusion come from a question. ⁵The answer to the question was made. ⁶That which was made is what you call thinking. ⁷It was a split from all that is, because it was a toy that denied the truth from which it came. ⁸And so it appeared to be that which it wasn't at all.

⁹Your thinking is the block that keeps you from seeing your truth, because your thinking is the veil that you made. ¹⁰It allows illusion without facing truth. ¹¹It permits belief in all that isn't true.

¹²This is why I said you must become the empty shell. ¹³Your thinking will not teach you to know. ¹⁴This is because you made your thinking to teach you to experience *know not.*

(v 12 – 14)¹The thinking mind will not rest of its own will. ²You cannot wait for it. ³The thinking mind rests only of your own Will, and through rest is your Will known.

(v 15 – 18)¹The illusion will not suffer your decision to rest, for the illusion is of the mind. ²Rest in peace, and peace shall be experienced.

[3]This is the way to learn the Will to rest.

NTI Revelation, Chapter 18

📖(v 1 – 3)[1]Babylon the Great is the great illusion. [2]For the illusion is the manifestation of the belief that it supports. [3]Without differences, there is no illusion. [4]Without separateness, there is only one.

(v 4 – 8)[1]How shall you see the illusion now? [2]With eyes of true beauty and the gratitude of Heart.

[3]What shall you give to illusion, which you suddenly realize is not real? [4]You shall give it that which it is, and that is the love due Heaven.

(v 9 – 10)[1]The illusion shall not suffer. [2]The illusion shall be transformed. [3]What was becomes the symbol of what is, and what *is* is celebrated with gratitude and love.

(v 11 – 13)[1]The illusion shall disappear, because it is illusion no more. [2]It is now a symbol of all that is. [3]It is now a symbol of the beauty and love of You.

(v 14 – 16)[1]In one instant, all that is seen is transformed; all that was valued is gone. [2]And in its place is the reflection of true beauty, which leaves you speechless and grateful to be One.

(v 17 – 20)[1]In an instant, a smile is born. [2]In an instant is all gratitude born. [3]For that which is false is seen no more. [4]That which cannot be is realized to never have been true.

(v 21 – 24)[1]And in an instant shall this song be sung:

²Illusion is gone,

never to be seen again.

³The music of harpists and musicians,

flute players and trumpeters

is all these ears can know.

⁴No more work or struggle

to see what isn't there.

⁵Only laughter and joy

can be known now.

⁶The light of the world

shines within my mind.

⁷Our oneness is all that I see.

⁸Only oneness is reflected in me.

NTI Revelation, Chapter 19

(v 1, 2)¹God's judgment is true, because God's judgment is non-judgmental. ²God is only aware of God so that illusion does not exist in the Mind of God.

³Illusion is seeing what is as if it is what isn't. ⁴Seeing illusion is seeing only that which is purely false. ⁵This seeing is not through the body's eyes, just as true perception is not seen through the body's eyes. ⁶That which the body's eyes see is wholly neutral.

⁷Illusion is seen through the thinking mind, which judges and inter-prets based upon false premises. ⁸Illusion is gone when the thinking mind is disengaged by the one who desires to see through Spirit.

(v 3)¹Hallelujah! ²When the thinking mind is released, illusion is no more. ³For all that is seen is seen through the mind truly.

(v 4, 5)   *¹The thinking mind is the veil that hides the symbol*

of truth with illusion.

²The thinking mind will keep you fearful. ³The thinking mind will

judge and separate you from your Self. [4]You cannot see clearly through the thinking mind, because the thinking mind was made so you would not see.

[5]Be grateful for your Self, which is beyond the thinking mind. [6]Be grateful for reminders to rest. [7]Observe the thinking mind. [8]See how it works. [9]Through watching it, you will learn you have need for it no more.

[10]*Hallelujah for the Vision without the thinking mind!*
[11]*Praise God and the truth which is true.*
[12]*Never can wholeness be lost to illusion,*
Never can the truth be through.

📖(v 6 – 8) [1]*Recommit to your Self through the Sight of Spirit.*
[2]*It is the Vision that sees.*
[3]*Be grateful for hills and for grass and for wind.*
[4]*Praise joy with all that you see.*

[5]*The Sight of Spirit is a choice that you make.*
[6]*It is the choice to marry the lamb.*
[7]*For with this choice is innocence known,*
and glory is seen through the land.

📖(v 9)[1]Blessed are those who are invited to the wedding supper of the lamb, for those are the ones who see. [2]And those who see, see only one, because One is all there is to see.

(v 10)[1]Behold the reflection of truth! [2]There are no differences that can be seen. [3]The canvas has been painted by joy. [4]Celebrate our oneness in the playground of a dream. [5]Awaken through peace and joy.

📖(v 11 – 16)[1]True desire must lead in the last days of the thinking mind, for the thinking mind will try to disguise itself as true desire. [2]For this, you must remain on watch.

[3]True desire is known by its desire for *only one thing*. [4]True desire does not desire within the world. [5]True desire does not desire to test itself.

⁶True desire desires only this:

⁷*To Know thy Self*

⁸The thinking mind desires the delay of true desire. ⁹In the hour when true desire is nearly full force, the thinking mind will look for a way to lead you from your true desire, possibly also by leading you to think you are fulfilling it.

¹⁰This is what "King of Kings and Lord of Lords" points to. ¹¹Whenever you feel self-satisfaction in the role you have been asked to play, know that role is not true desire. ¹²For true desire never leads to a role that is satisfactory to the self. ¹³True desire leads only from self to the wholeness of the realization of truth.

(v 17, 18)¹The ego will emerge as you follow the false true desire of the thinking mind, but because you want to believe this false desire, you will look away from that which appears only that it may be seen.

(v 19 – 21)¹The only way to pass through the tests of the thinking mind, without being led astray by false desire, is to remain fully focused on true desire now. ²*There is no other way.*

³This may seem to be a time of sadness, for you will be asked to let go of that which you still hold faith in. ⁴This may be a time of fear. ⁵Remain quiet in trust, focused on your true desire, and you will sail through the thinking mind's tortures on the wings of faith in truth.

NTI Revelation, Chapter 20

(v 1 – 3)¹This is something you must be willing to do:

²*You must be willing to rest the thinking mind*
at every opportunity given you.

³Learn to recognize your opportunities to rest the thinking mind. ⁴When you feel to go into prayer, rest and let a prayer rise from the Heart.

⁵When you feel to answer a question in the mind, rest and let the answer find its way into your awareness. ⁶When you feel tired and unsure as to what to do, rest and let a feeling of what to do enter you. ⁷When you feel inclined to speak and don't know what to say, rest and let what to say be given. ⁸And when you feel upset or saddened or afraid, rest and let illusions fade.

(v 4 – 6)¹When the thinking mind is rested, the Vision of Spirit is given. ²This Vision may guide you in all you think or do or say, because this Vision is your Vision based on the realization of true perception. ³This Vision knows the false as false and the true as true, so this Vision knows that which it sees. ⁴Knowing what it sees, it knows how to interact with it. ⁵And the purpose of each interaction is the purpose of awakening the one from the dream.

(v 7 – 10)¹Peaceful dreams end in peace. ²For one who has seen the peaceful purpose of awakening cannot see fear in dreams. ³The purpose is the same and has not changed, but this one can see it now. ⁴This one can see it now, because this one has learned to remember who he always is.

📖(v 11 – 15) ¹*"Death and Hades were thrown into the lake of fire.*
²This is the second death."

³When one chooses to let go of dreams, one chooses to let go of the ideas of dreams forever. ⁴The ideas of dreams are never real, but they are experienced as real as long as they are desired. ⁵When they are no longer desired, they cannot be experienced. ⁶They cease to be, no longer an idea in the mind, forever.

NTI Revelation, Chapter 21

📖(v 1)¹Then I saw a new heaven and a new earth, for the old heaven and the old earth had passed away, and there was no longer any division.

📖(v 2 - 4)¹And I saw the holy city of Jerusalem within my mind.

²Through this knowledge and this seeing, I saw all that I could not see before. ³I saw that I am in God and God is in me, and separation of the two is impossible. ⁴I saw that God is in my brothers and my brothers are in me, and separation and division are impossible. ⁵All that I had seen before, which caused me pain and suffering and loneliness, were wiped out forever. ⁶Before me, I saw only the expression of perfect freedom, and I knew that what I saw was Love.

(v 5)¹This is written down as a promise to all of mankind. ²Each one shall come to know this Vision and no one shall be left out. ³For this Vision is the reflection of your truth, and your truth is still in you.

(v 6 – 8)¹He who is thirsty, let him drink of the Wisdom of the Holy Spirit. ²Let Him teach you. ³Follow His guidance in trust and expectation that you shall be healed.

⁴You are the free Son of God. ⁵Nothing can stand between you and your one true desire except your own desire to not know your Self.

⁶*You are free.*

(v 9 – 14)¹Symbolism is gone forever when you can look beyond the symbols to the truth that merely *is*. ²In this truth do all symbols disappear, for in this truth is all interpretation rendered meaningless.

(v 15 – 21)¹That which cannot be described is indescribable, but it shall be known, because it is known. ²It is your truth, and it is within your knowing now. ³You need only to let go of everything that is not this knowing, without clinging to anything that feels safe within the familiar, and the familiar will fade away, that the *known* may shine within your mind. ⁴And there will be no words unless they are given you.

(v 22 – 27)¹All that is, all that ever was and all that is to come, is You. ²You are the Light and the vessel through which the Light shines. ³You are the reflection, which is made of your Light. ⁴You are all that is and separate from none of it. ⁵For there is only one, and since you *are*, you are the One.

NTI Revelation, Chapter 22

📖(v 1, 2)[1]Then the angel showed me the water of the river of Life, clear as crystal, flowing from God and through God, and I was not apart from its flow. [2]I was within its flow, and I was a part of its flow, and its flow came from me. [3]I saw that the flow which comes from God is everything, and all that *is* is a part of its flow.

[4]The tree of life is symbolic of the eternity that is. [5]No one must eat from the tree of life or sit within its shade in order to gain eternal life. [6]Eternal life already is and always has been, for this is the truth of Life. [7]The tree of life never dies and never changes, although its leaves dance in the wind. [8]This is the symbol of creation, and creation is what you are.

(v 3 – 6)[1]When your eyes are opened, they shall not close again. [2]For when you see, you will not choose to forget what you have seen. [3]These words are trustworthy and true.

[4]Only the truth is true. [5]All else is illusion.

(v 7 - 9)[1]What does it mean to worship God? [2]It means to be grateful for all that you are and to seek no change from it.

(v 10, 11)[1]Seek not to change that which you see, for that is to desire that *you* be different. [2]Accept all that you see in glory and rejoicing, for that which you see is the mark of Heaven.

[3]Do not worry that the mark is not the mark that you expect. [4]Accept it *is* from Heaven, and you shall learn to see the mark differently.

📖(v 12, 13)[1]"Behold, I am coming soon," is only a reminder. [2]When you have forgotten and become lost within an image of what you are not, remember this statement and choose to see clearly again.

[3]*Everyone experiences according to his choice,*
because you are the one who chooses.

(v 14, 15)[1]Inside the inner chamber of your Heart you shall find and know your truth. [2]It is not foreign to you. [3]It is all that you are.

[4]When you seem locked outside the light of the Heart, do not fear to

choose again. [5]Rest and trust that your Heart beckons to you. [6]As you listen, you shall be drawn to it. [7]As you listen, it shall come to you.

(v 16)[1]Your truth is your foundation. [2]And in your foundation, you find your strength. [3]Let all else fade away, and a new house shall be built from the true foundation of Light.

(v 17)[1]Come! [2]The call is within you and the door is open. [3]Come, and thirst no more. [4]Come, and see that you *are* the river of Life.

(v 18, 19)[1]Put aside all fear and listen only to the Voice of Love. [2]Recognize your true Voice and follow it to the recognition of You.

(v 20, 21) [1]*He who listens will surely hear.*
[2]*He who comes will know.*
[3]*All will come, as none are to be left out.*
[4]*This is the Word of God.*
[5]*Amen.*

APPENDIX – ABOUT THE COVER

QUESTION AND ANSWER INDEX

APPENDIX

About the Cover

Regina Dawn Akers received guidance regarding the design of the NTI book cover through a series of dreams. Here is her story:

"The first dream came in the summer of 2006. In that dream, I was standing and looking at a wheat field that stretched as far as the eyes could see. As I looked on the wheat field I heard a thought, 'The cover of the book is to be this color.' A few weeks later, I had the same dream again.

"I am not an artist, so I called a friend named Phil Frisk, who is an artist. I asked Phil if he would design a wheat-colored cover for NTI. He agreed. We didn't talk about it again and a couple of months passed, then I had another dream. In this dream I was talking to a young man who seemed to have some authority over the cover of the book. I was telling him that the logo for the Foundation for the Holy Spirit needed to be on the cover. He disagreed. I told him that the copyright for NTI belonged to the foundation, so the logo must be on the cover. He said that wouldn't do. I continued to insist, and he continued to say no. Then he reached into his files and pulled out a picture of a sheaf of wheat. He said that this picture was to be on the cover.

"That morning I got up and groggily made my way to the computer with a cup of coffee in my hand. I opened my email inbox and double-clicked on the first email I saw. It was an email from Phil Frisk. The draft NTI book cover was attached. Right in the center of the cover, Phil had included the same picture of a sheaf of wheat that I had seen in my dream. That was a wow moment for me. I had no doubt that this was to be the cover design for NTI.

"NTI Matthew and NTI Revelation talk about a harvest, which is the separating of the wheat from the chaff, or the true from the false. Both books teach that the harvest is always now. I believe this is what the sheaf of wheat represents. It's a great reminder to help us stay focused on purpose."

In May 2007, the logo for the Founation for the Holy Spirit was updated to the sheaf of wheat.

QUESTION AND ANSWER INDEX

Prepared by Regina Dawn Akers

The standard way of listing an NTI scripture reference is to begin the reference with the NTI designation. For example, NTI Matthew 21 v6-9.1-3. This is to avoid confusion with biblical scripture references. If you are quoting NTI in any other written medium, please use the NTI designation to avoid confusion.

— A —

Abraham - What does the story of Abraham symbolize?
NTI Gal 3v15-18.1-8, your willingness is one Light
NTI Gal 4v21-31.1-34, wait for God
NTI Heb 6v13-15.1-6, you shall be awakened fully
NTI Jas 2v20-24.1-8, plan for how true desire shall be
See also tithing

Abundance - What is true abundance?
See true abundance

Accept - How do I accept this message of truth?
NTI Mt 26v55-56.1-6, lay your self aside
NTI Jn 17v20-26.6-8, accept the false as false
NTI Heb 11v39-40.1-4, in willingness
What happens to people who do not accept this message?
NTI Jn 17v6-19.9-19, many aspects of the Light
NTI Ro 8v28-30.1-3, all are predestined

Acceptance - What is acceptance?
NTI Lk 23v26-43.39-41, honesty is acceptance
NTI Heb 13v18-19.1-2, be just as they may
NTI Rev 22v10-11.1-4, seek not to change

Actions - How are my actions helpful or not helpful?
NTI 2Co 9v1-5.1-8, belief that the world is real
NTI 2Co 9v6-9.1-21, act on your trust in Me
NTI 2Co 10v7-11.1-7, expression of thought
NTI Php 2v1-4.1-8, v5-11.1-7, observe yourself

Ananias - What is symbolized by the story of Ananias and Sapphira?
NTI Ac 5v1-11.1-18, guilt that you have claimed

Angels - What do angels symbolize?
See Simon

Answer - Is there a short and simple answer that will help me with all difficult times?
NTI Rev 16v16.1-2, resting in faith and trust

Apostles - What do the apostles symbolize?
NTI Lk 6v12-16.3, represent everyone

As it is - Why must I accept truth as it is?
See truth

Ask -How do I ask from God?
NTI Jas 4v1-3.1-3, through desire
Why should I ask myself what I want?
See want

Atonement - Is it true that I can let go of false thoughts without sacrificial atonement?
See false thoughts

Attachments - How does letting go of attachments help me to awaken?
NTI 1Co 7v32-35.2, more swiftly with Me
See also dreams

Attack - How can I see attack differently?
NTI Mt 26v51-54.2-5, attack does not protect

Authority - What is authority?
NTI Mt 7v28-29.1-2, because God is all that is
NTI Mt 9v1-8.2, authority within the Heart is
NTI Mt 10v1-6.1-2, I give you authority
NTI Mk 11v27-33.1-12, all authority is the same

NTI Lk 20v1-8.1-2, both are the same
NTI Ac 11v1-18.1-3, words of the Holy Spirit are
NTI 1Co 11v3-10.1-8, I am your authority
How do I recognize the authority of the Holy Spirit?
NTI Ac 11v19-30.1-6, great joy that fills your heart
Who has authority to teach the message of truth?
See teach

Awaken - How do I awaken from the illusion?
NTI Mt 11v16-19.5-10, turn away from
NTI Lk 8v26-39.1-2, v40-56.1-13, blow away the clouds
NTI Lk 23v26-43.31-41, forgave his brothers
NTI Lk 24v36-53.12-17, faith beyond the experience
NTI Jn 17v6-19.1-5, the Light reaches within the dream
NTI Jn 21v15-25.5-12, you will not be tested
NTI Ac 10v30-33.1-4, story of your willingness
NTI Ac 20v7-12.3-7, let go of the illusion
NTI Ac 23v12-22.1-5, face it and let it go
NTI Ro 3v21-31.6-14, unweave your way
NTI Ro 7v14-20.1-4, v21-25.1-9, symbols of Light
NTI Ro 8v31-39.1-7, do not shrink from your dream
NTI 1Co 10v18-22.5-9, waiting for your signal
NTI Gal 5v7-12.1-35, you only need focus on
NTI Eph 6v1-4.1-9, it is through releasing thought
NTI Eph 6v5-8.1-5, let the Heart be the test
NTI 2Ti 2v22-26.1-11, do not flee that which life is
NTI Heb 2v5-7.1-3, let the awakened mind lead
NTI Heb 3v12-15.1-3, gratitude is the way as is resting
NTI Rev 21v15-21.1-4, let go of everything that is not
See also gratitude, *See also* healed

Awakening - What is awakening?
NTI Mt 22v34-40.9-13, accept the truth
NTI Jn 21v15-25.1-4, given yourself fully
NTI 1Co 16v5-9.1-6, shall not choose illusion again
NTI 1Jn 5v18-20.1-3, nothing else to know
NTI Rev 20v11-15.1-6, let go of the ideas of dreams
See also resurrection, *See also* stage
Who is a part of the awakening?
NTI Jn 3v22-36.8-10, all men are a part
NTI Heb 10v32-38.1-10, a great awakening
How does the mind that is awakening see (perceive)?
NTI 3Jn v2-4.1-6, an extension of your Self

NTI 3Jn v9-10.1-3, turn away from unwelcoming
NTI 3Jn v11-12.1-4, v13-14.1-9, witnesses to your mind
How do I practice awakening?
See practice
What shall I do when I forget to practice awakening?
See forget

Awareness - What is the Awareness of God?
NTI 1Jn 3v1-3.1-7, looks only on that which is wholly true

— **B** —

Banquet - What does the wedding banquet symbolize?
See wedding

Baptism - What does baptism symbolize?
NTI Mk 1v4-5.1-3, being washed clean
See also Jesus' baptism

Battle - How shall I respond to the battle within my split mind?
See split mind

Beatitudes - What is the Holy Spirit's interpretation of the Beatitudes?
NTI Mt 5v3-10, v11-12.1-8, blessed are

Belief in separation - What is the belief in separation?
NTI Lk 1v57-80.8-19, that you are a separate entity
NTI Gal 2v17-21.2, judgment keeps
Why should I let go of the belief in separation?
NTI Mt 21v33-44.6-8, the belief in death
NTI Mt 24v15-25.5-8, it is lack and suffering
NTI Jn 14v15-31.14, denial of the truth
How do I let go of the belief in separation?
NTI Mt 21v20-22.1-7, what seems impossible
NTI Lk 15v1-10.12-23, there is no independence
NTI Lk 22v7-38.29-37, God must be within you

Blessed - What does "Blessed is the man who does not fall away on account of Me" mean?
NTI Lk 7v18-23.1-7, expectations in your mind
What does "Blessed is the man who perseveres under trial" mean?
NTI Jas 1v12.1-2, remembers to use all things to practice
See also test

Blocks –What are the blocks to awakening?
See obstacles
What blocks truth, light and love from my recognition if that is all that is?
See Light, *See* Love

Body - Why does the Holy Spirit teach that the body is meaningless?
NTI Mt 5v38-48.11, Spirit is all there is
NTI Mk 10v32-34.1-11, the body is a thing of the world
NTI Mk 14v17-26.4-10, it is no more than my body
NTI Jn 19v28-37.5-6, was no truth in his body
How can the body be used to help me awaken?
NTI Ro 12v1-2.1-8, accept Me into your body
NTI Ro 12v3-8.1-16, see what I do
NTI Php 2v1-4.1-8, v5-11.1-7, observe yourself
NTI Php 2v12-13.1-5, be grateful for
NTI Php 2v14-18.1-8, an expression of your thought
NTI Php 2v19-24.1-4, call on this One
NTI Php 2v25-30.1-6, if you notice judgment
NTI Col 4v2-6.1-12, watch this body

Born again - What does "born again" mean?
NTI Jn 3v1-9.3-9, he becomes the Light

Bread of Life - What is the "Bread of Life?"
NTI Jn 6v25-59.1-2, acceptance of the Light

Brothers - What is my true relationship to my brothers?
NTI Eph 3v7-13.4-12, your very existence is
NTI Eph 3v20-21.1-3, they give back to you
NTI Tit 1v10-16.1-3, anything that seems to separate
How should I look at my brothers' thoughts?
NTI 1Co 5v12-13.1-4, the thought you think he thinks
NTI 2Co 10v12-18.1-15, you see your mind
NTI Col 4v7-9.1-8, your mind is distracting you
If I see my brothers' errors or suffering, is that my error?
NTI Mt 18v5-6.1-5, do not ask your brother to change
NTI Mt 18v10-11.1-5, forgiveness is complete when
NTI Mt 18v12-14.1-9, not responsible for your brother's
What is my brothers' role in my salvation?
NTI Ac 13v26-31.3-6, all men play their part

— C —

Caesar - What does "Give to Caesar what is Caesar's" symbolize?
NTI Mt 22v15-22.11-16, I am in those things too
NTI Mt 23v1-4.3-5, do as you need to do
NTI Mt 23v13-22.1-5, which law is highest

Canaanite woman - What is the Holy Spirit's interpretation of the story of the Canaanite woman?
NTI Mt 15v21-28.4-18, accept God's glory as it is
Compare to money changers

Cause - What is cause and effect?
NTI 2Co 1v15-24.3-10, you are lord of
NTI 2Ti 3v1-5.1-10, the world is never cause
NTI 2Ti 4v1-5.13-19, feelings were in the mind first
How do I learn that I am cause (or maker) of my experience?
NTI 2Co 2v12-17.1-10, you do have a choice
NTI Php 3v5-11.9-24, v12-14.1-6, found those feelings

Chief priests - What do the chief priests symbolize?
NTI Lk 23v1-25.1-5, that which is in your own mind

Choice - What can I experience (or realize) through my choice?
NTI Mt 12v9-14.2-6, truth of who you are
NTI Mt 12v38-42.1-3, overcoming of death
NTI Mt 13v1-9.2-6, essence of who you are
NTI Mt 13v33.1-4, kingdom of Heaven
NTI Mt 13v36-43.11-18, My gift
NTI Mt 13v53-58.1-6, true Home
NTI Mt 24v32-35.1-5, be made complete
NTI Mt 24v36-41.1-5, resurrection
NTI Mt 24v45-51.1-6, peace
NTI Mt 26v1-5.1-2, what you will see
NTI Jn 3v1-9.1-2, the Light
NTI Jn 5v9-15.10-11, all that is truth
NTI Ac 21v27-36.20-21, illusion or truth
NTI 2Co 2v12-17.1-8, you are the maker of experience
NTI Heb 2v14-18.9-10, by your choice that awakening
NTI Heb 4v1-3.1-6, the peace of God
NTI Rev 12v10-12.1-6, the way of salvation

Choosing - How do I know what I am choosing?
NTI Jn 5v1-9.10, by that which you see and experience
See also see

Christ - What is the Christ?
NTI Mt 16v20.1-2, no one is left outside of
NTI Lk 9v18-27.1-6, you are the Christ
NTI Lk 23v26-43.1-3, within you that does not crucify
NTI Eph 2v14-18.1-3, ones that seem many are one
NTI Eph 3v1-6.1-4, the law of Love
NTI Eph 3v14-19.2-6, unfailing love of your oneness
NTI Col 1v15-20.1-10, you are the flow of life
NTI Col 1v24-27.1-5, energy that is all things
NTI 1Jn 5v1-5.1-3, see the Christ in everyone
What are the teachings of Christ?
NTI 1Jn 2v3-6.1-6, I am all that I am

Commandments - What are the "greatest commandments?"
NTI Mt 22v34-40.1-8, guiding light in all you do
NTI Mk 12v28-34.1-15, you are not far
NTI Lk 10v25-37.17-25, all one love
NTI Gal 5v13-15.1-12, let your willingness lead

Communication - How is everything one in communication?
NTI Jn 6v1-15.4, Light is in all things
NTI Col 2v9-12.1-5, creation is made through
NTI Col 2v16-19.3-4, through right communication

Concept - What is the concept of expression?
See expression

Conflict - Why do I choose conflict?
NTI Jn 13v31-38.9-14, it is not Love
How do I let go of experiencing conflict?
NTI Lk 6v37-38.10-23, let your interpretation go
NTI Jn 13v1-17.11-15, serve the Light
NTI Ac 13v49-52.1-6, only looking at illusion
See also sides

Confusion - What does confusion teach in the mind?
NTI 2Co 1v15-24.3-10, the events are lord
NTI 2Co 11v13-15.1-3, not your truth
How do I let go of confusion?

NTI Mt 27v27-31.1-11, forgive your brother his madness
NTI Jn 13v18-30.3-6, the alignment of will
NTI Jn 18v28-40.1-15, which voice will you listen to?
NTI 2Co 11v16-29.1-10, mind subordinate to the Heart
NTI Jude v22-23.1-5, stand firm
NTI Rev 2v7.1-2, v8-10.1-6, hear the voice but do not

Correct - Should I correct others?
NTI Lk 6v39-42.4-8, bring back to your interpretation

Covenants - What are the holy covenants?
NTI Heb 9v1-10.1-11, symbol of your willingness and
NTI Heb 9v23-28.4-5, open doorway from the world

Creation - What is creation?
NTI Tit 1v1-4.1-4, like the Father in every way
NTI Rev 22v1-2.4-8, the eternity that is

Criticism - How can I see criticism differently?
NTI Mt 23v5-12.5-11, if you seek glory from men

Curious - What is my curious question or thought?
See wish

Cut - What does "If your hand causes you to sin, cut it off," symbolize?
NTI 1Co 5v1-5.1-16, lay down the thoughts

— **D** —

Darkness - What is the darkness in the mind?
NTI Mt 10v11-16.4, agitation
NTI Mt 15v10-20.4-11, the temporal
NTI Mt 25v1-13.7-8, the world
NTI Mk 8v31-38.20-23, aloneness
NTI Jn 12v34-36.1-6, the universe
NTI 2Co 4v1-6.1-4, belief in the world

Death - What is death?
NTI Mt 12v22-29.5, death is illusion
NTI Mt 15v10-20.4-11, a heart focused in the temporal
NTI Mt 27v1-10.1-7, dance of guilt
NTI Mt 27v57-61.1-2, an illusion of form
NTI Lk 7v11-17.1-3, unaware of truth

NTI Lk 20v27-40.1-2, if death could take
NTI Lk 23v44-49.23-24, may seem to be final
NTI 1Th 4v13-18.1-6, the effect of denying what is
Why is there death in the world?
NTI Mt 12v22-29.3-5, cannot be separate and live
NTI Mt 27v1-10.1-3, what you believe you deserve
NTI Mt 27v62-66.1-6, fear of truth
NTI Ac 5v1-11.23-34, you believe that your guilt

How do I overcome death?
NTI Mt 16v25.1-3, Jesus does not ask you to die
NTI Mt 16v28.1-5, death like fear is nothing
NTI Mt 21v33-44.1-8, the belief in separation
NTI Jn 6v25-59.3-16, if you look at your brother and see
NTI Jn 11v1-16.1-5, v17-37.1-4, step into the Light fully
NTI Jn 17v1-5.3-11, choose not to choose
NTI Jn 19v38-42.1-7, let go of your acceptance of
NTI Heb 11v5-6.1-3, in faith
NTI 1Jn 5v16-17.1-2, in seeing God
NTI Rev 2v11.1-4, let that belief die
How should I react to death in the world?
NTI 1Th 4v13-18.7-12, be willing to remember

Decisions - How do I make decisions about what to do in the world?
NTI Mt 1v1-25.7-9, consider them not decided
NTI Mt 5v33-37.1-2, it is what you mean
NTI Mt 6v1-4.1-8, for the reason of the Heart
NTI Mt 15v1-9.1-4, v10-20.1-3, I will use what you do
NTI Mt 19v16-21.1-5, your love for Me
NTI Mt 23v13-22.6-12, decide in clarity and peace
NTI Mt 23v23-24.1-8, v25-26.1-10, guilt and fear begets
NTI Ac 21v27-36.1-3, outward expression of means
NTI Php 1v15-18.1-5, purpose is everything

Delay - What do I need to know or realize about delay?
NTI 1Co 4v18-21.1-9, your desire to wait comes from

Denial - What do I need to know or realize about denial?
NTI Ac 23v1-11.1-19, things will not seem to get easier
NTI Ac 23v12-22.1-10, wish you made you have denied
NTI Ac 23v23-25.1-6, denial is delay
NTI 1Co 16v1-4.1-4, deny that which is false
NTI 1Th 2v13-16.4-9, immediate desire to deny the

NTI 1Th 5v19-22.1-6, do not accept temptation to deny
NTI 2Ti 4v1-5.1-14, as you hide your feelings from
NTI Jas 1v13-15.1-9, God can be denied through your
NTI Jas 1v16-18.1-2, you misunderstand what you do
NTI 1Jn 4v13-16.1-8, existence cannot be denied
NTI Jude v12-13.1-2, v14-16.1-6, have made this choice
NTI Rev 2v12-13.1-6, I want to look at them with you
NTI Rev 12v7-9.1-5, to be lost by your own choice

Desire - How does looking at desire help me awaken?
NTI Mt 16v26.1-6, if you desire anything of the world
NTI 2Co 4v1-6.1-4, your desire to lay down untruth
NTI 2Co 5v11-15.1-18, your mind is split
NTI Heb 10v8-10.1-3, focus on the desire that is
NTI Heb 11v13-16.1-2, release your hand on illusion
NTI Heb 12v18-24.3-4, see all desires that stand as
NTI Jas 3v3-6.1-3, your thoughts are derived from
NTI Jas 3v9-12.1-2, the foundation from which all else
NTI Jas 4v1-3.1-3, you ask from the process of creation
NTI Jas 4v4-6.1-12, v7-10.1-5, look closely at what you
NTI Jas 5v17-18.1-2, everything you experience comes
NTI Jas 5v19-20.1-2, whoever recognizes that he has
NTI 1Jn 2v26-27.1-3, led astray only by your own false
NTI Rev 6v1-2.3-7, the desire that you allow
NTI Rev 11v1-10.4-12, measure the desire
See also purpose, *See also* true desire

Desiring - Am I guilty for desiring experiences in the world?
NTI 2Ti 1v13-14.1-6, v15.1-3, your innocence
NTI 2Ti 1v16-18.1-6, God has granted you the right
NTI Heb 6v9-12.1-15, freedom is the expression of
NTI Jas 4v11-12.1-4, let go of the desire to judge

Differences - Why should I let go of the perception of differences?
NTI Mt 20v1-16.8-18, v17-19.1-3, confusion comes
NTI 1Ti 1v15-17.1-5, v18-20.1-5, existence is all that
See also sameness, *See also* special
How do I let go of the perception of differences?
NTI Mt 20v29-34.1-8, cannot see it of your own power

Disagreements - How should I handle disagreements in the world?
NTI Mt 18v15-17.1-8, v18.1, Check your heart
NTI 1Co 6v1-6.1-7, if you find even an inkling
See also sides

Distractions - What are my distractions?
NTI Lk 3v1-20.7-9, take many forms
NTI Lk 6v17-26.1, the world
NTI 2Ti 3v6-9.1-7, judgment
How do I overcome distractions?
NTI Mt 23v1-4.3-11, giving all things the purpose of
NTI Lk 3v1-20.10-18, do not feel guilty
NTI Lk 13v22-30.1-10, opportunity to hear My Voice
NTI 1Co 8v7-13.1-5, focus your mind on the Heart

Double-edged sword - What is symbolized by the double-edged sword?
NTI Rev 1v12-16.1-6, only you can know what this path

Doubt - How shall I overcome doubt?
NTI Mt 16v5-12.1-10, doubts must rise
NTI Mt 28v11-15.1-12, why choose to believe
NTI Mk 8v14-21.11-16, look at your doubts
NTI Lk 4v14-30.24-30, do not deny
NTI Jn 18v15-18.1-7, v19-24.1-6, believes it is your
See also fear

Dreams – What are dreams?
NTI Mt 22v23-33.1-9, think of the world as a dream
NTI Col 3v1-4.1-9, the world is a dream
NTI Heb 4v8-11.1, you do not remember
NTI Heb 6v7-8.2-4, delay and distraction
NTI Heb 7v4-10.3-12, one mind seems to be many
NTI Heb 7v11-17.1-19, lead you to be caught up
Why should I not look to dreams for happiness?
NTI Heb 13v9-10.1-5, nothing within dreams can last
What are the dreams that I should let go of?
NTI Jas 2v25-26.1-2, your misperceptions of yourself
How do I let go of dreams?
NTI Heb 8v7-12.1-6, is not to be attached
NTI Heb 8v13.1-8, what is it within dreams

Ego - What is the ego?
NTI Lk 6v37-38.7-23, it interprets
NTI Jn 19v1-16.1-5, in deciding that you could judge
NTI Ac 3v11-26.1-8, thought within the mind
NTI Ac 6v1-7.2-5, temptation to judge for yourself
NTI 1Co 9v1-6.1-7, v7-12.1-5, claims to be you
NTI Gal 2v1-5.1-8, bush of confusion
NTI Gal 2v6-10.1-5, misjudged belief
NTI 1Jn 4v1-3.3-7, the thinking mind
See also belief in separation
How do I recognize ego thoughts in my mind?
NTI Mk 6v14-29.2-6, when your guilt is unmasked
NTI Lk 22v7-38.11-21, one who has stolen a vineyard
NTI Lk 23v26-43.4-9, seeks salvation by attacking
NTI Ac 19v23-41.6-28, the ego's reasoning
Compare to Holy Spirit
What is a helpful way of seeing the ego?
NTI Rev 2v4-6.1-9, it has become confused
How do I let go of the ego?
NTI Lk 6v37-38.7-23, let your interpretation go
NTI Lk 23v26-43.10-15, do not hate this voice
NTI Ac 13v4-12.1-9, remember what you truly want
See also belief in separation, *See also* confusion, *See also* thinking

Empty shell - What is an empty shell?
NTI Mt 13v53-58.1-5, your Father waits to give
NTI 1Co 1v26-31.3-4, lay your self aside
NTI 1Co 2v1-5.1-3, in service to Me
NTI 1Co 4v6-7.3-6, it is only Me
NTI 1Co 4v8-17.8-14, lay your thinking aside
NTI 1Co 6v12-20.1-4, everything that seemed to be
NTI 1Co 7v1-7.1-2, knows itself as empty
NTI 1Co 9v15-18.1-7, put aside listening to the voice
NTI 2Co 5v16-21.1-4, let go of the world
Why should I become an empty shell?
NTI 1Co 2v 6-10.1-5, an offering of grace to holiness
NTI 1Co 2v11-16 v1-6, put aside that which is false
NTI 1Co 7v15-24.3-11, let go of points of experience
NTI 1Co 10v18-22.5-9, the Light shall be given
How do I become an empty shell?
NTI 1Co 5v9-11.1-3, do not partake

NTI 1Co 5v12-13.1-4, the thought you think he thinks
NTI 1Co 6v1-6.6-7, disagreements
NTI 1Co 6v7-11.6-9, temptations
NTI 1Co 6v12-20.1-7, the casing
NTI 1Co 7v1-7.7-17, effective method of practice
NTI 1Co 7v25-28.1-9, point of experience
NTI 1Co 7v39-40.1-5, let them go right then
NTI 1Co 8v1-3.1-5, thinking mind will not teach you
NTI 1Co 9v19-23.1-6, the one who judges is
NTI 1Co 9v24-27.1-8, give it your all
NTI 1Co 15v1-2.1-6, lay down everything

Enlightened - What is "enlightened?"
NTI Mt 8v23-27.1-2, knows there is nothing to fear
NTI Jn 3v10-15.1-3, to see no opposite
NTI 1Co 15v12-19.1-8, fourth phase is a glorious phase
NTI Heb 1v6-9.1, awareness that the false was never true
NTI Heb 7v4-10.6-12, new perception is still a dream
NTI 1Jn 5v6-12.3-4, v13-15.1-3, gratitude that desires
NTI Rev 20v7-10.1-4, peaceful dreams end in peace
NTI Rev 22v3-6.1-5, when your eyes are open
See also born again, *See also* true perception
How will I be enlightened?
NTI Mt 16v24.1-12, let go of
NTI Jn 5v9-15.9-11, when you are prepared to see
NTI Jn 12v20-28.5-20, the question that you must ask
NTI Jn 21v1-14.1-5, trust Me fully in all matters
See also healed, *See also* salvation

Expectations - Why should I let go of my expectations of others?
NTI Mt 20v24-28.1-7, they are one with God
NTI Mt 21v1-5.2-4, set up opportunity for judgments
NTI Mt 21v6-9.1-3, peace comes from laying down your
NTI Mt 21v10-11.1-3, to see him as he is

Experience - What are points of experience?
NTI 1Co 7v15-24.7-11, each thought that seems to speak
NTI 1Co 7v25-28.1-9, do not worry
NTI 1Co 7v29-31.1-3, the shell is not real
NTI 1Co 7v32-35.1-2, when you are freed from
Does experience (perception) change as my mind is healed?
See perception

Expression - What is the concept of expression?
NTI 1Ti 5v3-8.5-10, the expression of freedom
NTI 1Ti 5v24-25.3-6, experienced as it is expressed

— F —

Faith - Why is faith needed in order to awaken?
NTI Mt 11v16-19.5-10, asking you to turn away from
NTI Mt 12v46-50.1-6, lead you to the end
NTI Mt 13v36-43.11-18, above all that you think and
NTI Mt 21v20-22.1-7, power of your faith
NTI Mt 21v23-27.1-6, see where you are placing it
NTI Lk 1v57-80.25-26, faith is a peaceful choice
NTI Jn 4v43-54.1-5, to welcome the Light
NTI Ac 18v12-17.1-4, you think is true is not true
NTI Php 1v27-30.1-10, through faith your motive is
NTI Heb 11v11-12.1-5, guidance is that which will
NTI Heb 11v29.1, faith that leads you forward because
NTI Heb 11v32-38.1-4, by faith you may learn
See also talents
Why do I need to look at where I am placing my faith?
NTI Heb 11v1-2.1-4, powered by belief or acceptance
NTI Heb 11v3.1-3, by faith the universe was formed
NTI Heb 11v4.1-3, through faith that your perception
NTI Jas 1v9-11.3-10, with faith placed in illusion
How can I strengthen my faith to help me awaken?
NTI Heb 11v17-19.1-4, perception shall answer in a way
See also trust
What is the relationship between faith and trust?
NTI Jas 1v9-11.1-2, trust and faith are inseparable

False - Why is the world referred to as a false god?
NTI Gal 4v8-20.1-38, tell you that you are separate
How shall I respond to false teachers/prophets?
NTI Mt 7v15-20.5-8, hold not a grievance
NTI Ac 19v11-22.1-16, feel internal confirmation
See also symbols
What are false thoughts?
NTI 1Jn 3v11-15.1-5, guilt, attack, fear, hatred and
NTI 1Jn 4v7-12.1-7, thoughts that imply separateness

Is it true that I can let go of false thoughts without sacrificial atonement?
NTI 1Jn 4v1-3.1-7, v4-6.1-8, false need not be looked on
NTI Rev 2v14-16.1-7, put your fear of Me aside

Father - What does "I am within my Father and my Father is within me" mean?
NTI Jn 14v5-14.1-2, means there is no difference
What does "My Father's house has many rooms" mean?
NTI Jn 14v1-4.5-7, we are all one

Fear - What is fear?
NTI 1Pe 4v1-6.5-10, a misperception
NTI Rev 16v15.1-3, merely an illusion
Why do I fear?
NTI Mt 14v1-12.2, keep you from joining with God
NTI Mt 17v6-8.1, afraid of oneness
NTI Mt 27v15-26.1, guilty expects retaliation
NTI Lk 18v18-30.1-6, you think I am asking you to trade
NTI Lk 21v5-38.1-22, v5-38.36-44, keep you from Me
NTI Lk 23v1-25.10-16, loss of self
NTI Jn 13v31-38.9-14, you also fear Love
NTI Jn 14v1-4.1-4, keep you from You
NTI 2Ti 2v1-7.2-8, v8-10.1-9, believe it protects you
NTI 1Pe 4v12-17.1-18, fear comes from judgment
NTI Rev 2v20-25.1-14, from the guilt that is hidden
What does fear hide from my awareness?
NTI 1Th 5v1-11.1-14, forgetful of the law of Love
NTI 2Ti 2v11-13.1-7, I cannot limit myself
NTI 2Ti 2v14-19.1-8, hides that which is you
NTI Rev 8v1-13.1-5, there is only Love
How am I hiding from fear (instead of letting it go)?
NTI Mt 15v21-28.1-3, use My Word for purposes of
NTI Mk 14v66-72.1-20, hid his fear with anger
NTI Jn 7v14-24.2-8, judge the guidance that you hear
NTI 1Pe 4v1-6.1-10, makes decisions to avoid his fear
Is fear an obstacle to God?
NTI Lk 21v5-38.1-6, can keep the peace and knowledge
NTI Rev 9v7-11.5-6, you can walk right through
Is there anything real that I should fear?
NTI Rev 12v13-17.1-4, you need only remember this
How shall I overcome fear?
NTI Mt 10v26-31.1-4, you are eternal
NTI Mt 14v22-36.1-6, I cannot take that which is yours

NTI Mt 16v5-12.1-10, doubt must rise
NTI Mt 28v5-8.1-3, let your faith be greater
NTI Mk 9v2-13.25-30, join in counsel with the Voice
NTI Mk 11v20-26.17-19, overcome it with trust
NTI Lk 11v33-36.1-4, knowledge of your safety
NTI Lk 22v39-46.1-5, great willingness
NTI Jn 18v25-27.1-4, let your fear come up
NTI Jn 20v1-9.1-7, reaction of a mind long blinded
NTI Ac 12v20-25.1-9, defense and attack are not
NTI Ac 24v10-21.3-6, face it to deny it
NTI Ac 27v33-38.1-15, suspense and anxiety say
NTI 2Ti 2v20-21.1-4, through fear that you are purified
NTI 2Ti 2v22-26.1-11, do not flee that which life is
NTI 1Pe 4v7-11.1-13, without your participation
NTI Rev 2v17.1-7, you may choose trust
NTI Rev 6v9-11.1-4, v15-17.1-5, choose once again
See also feelings, *See also* Peter, *See also* resistance

Feelings - Why should I let go of my feelings and emotions?
NTI Mt 10v11-16.1-5, glory is found in
NTI Mt 16v19.1-6, let that which blinds you
NTI Mt 26v31-35.12-13, you do not see this light
See also fear, *See also* guilt, *See also* unworthiness
How do I let go of my feelings and emotions?
NTI 1Co 7v1-7.7-17, letting them pass upward
NTI Php 3v5-11.9-34, v12-14.1-10, found outside
NTI Php 3v17-21.1-13, find your Self and loose those
NTI 2Ti 1v3-7.6-13, move away from the thoughts
NTI 2Ti 1v8-12.1-5, go in for a full flavor of
NTI 2Ti 3v1-5.1-21, now look on the world
NTI 2Ti 3v10-17.1-12, see yourself as the observer
NTI 2Ti 4v1-5.1-19, do not make this error
NTI 1Jn 2v12-14.1-6, trust the healing process

Fig tree - What does the withering fig tree symbolize?
NTI Mt 21v17-19.1-4, ego bears no fruit

Filter - How does the filter of my mind affect what I see and experience?
NTI Mk 7v1-23.2-14, when one listens
NTI Mk 7v24-30.27, lay that mind aside

NTI Mk 9v14-32.16-19, what you believe you will
NTI Lk 13v1-9.1-10, only reacting to the thoughts
NTI Lk 6v37-38.1-16, ego-mind is a split or fraction
NTI Jn 8v48-59.1-3, whatever you believe

Flow - What is the flow of life?
NTI Col 2v1-5.1-6, you are the
NTI Rev 22v1-2.1-3, from God and through God

Follower - Is a servant a leader or a follower?
See servant

Forget - What shall I do when I forget to practice awakening?
NTI Mt 13v24-30.1-7, simply make the choice again
NTI Mt 13v31-32.1-6, the tending itself will extend
NTI Mt 22v15-22.1-7, do not feel guilty
NTI Lk 5v33-39.1-11, old habits does not ruin
NTI Lk 10v1-24.14-26, now is a new moment
NTI Lk 11v1-13.8-12, not a time to chastise
NTI Ro 11v22-24.1-10, I have not been rejected
NTI Heb 6v4-6.1-5, go back to your practice
NTI Heb 6v9-12.1-15, you are led truly always
NTI Rev 22v12-13.1-3, choose to see clearly again
How did I forget what I am?
NTI Col 1v21-23.1-3, your imaginings have
See separation

Forgetfulness - What is forgetfulness?
See sleeping

Forgive - What does "forgive" mean?
NTI Lk 17v1-4.7-38, acknowledging you do not want
Why should I forgive another?
NTI Mt 5v23-24.2-5, v25-26.2-8, righteousness is
NTI Mt 5v29-30.1-6, justification are like poisonous
NTI Mt 18v12-14.1-7, if you cannot forgive him
NTI Mt 18v21-22.1-3, forgive your brother to know your
Why should I forgive myself?
NTI Mt 27v27-31.1-11, to be healed
NTI 1Ti 5v23.1-4, is to separate
How do I forgive?
NTI Mt 5v27-28.2-4, when hurtful thoughts come
NTI Mt 9v9-13.1-5, it is your judgments that must be

NTI Mt 18v10-11.1-5, if you love your brother any less
NTI Mt 18v23-35.4-7, rejoice at your opportunities
NTI Mt 26v43-44.1-4, it is the alert mind that will
NTI Mk 14v43-52.1-4, he neither accepted it or denied it
NTI Mk 14v53-65.10-19, for there is no response
NTI Lk 17v1-4.7-38, only a collection of thoughts
NTI 2Co 2v5-11.1-5, you may choose the purpose
NTI Gal 6v1-5.1-31, v6.1-2, process of forgiveness
NTI Gal 6v7-10.1-8, in communing with willingness
NTI Eph 6v1-4.1-6, it is through releasing thought

Forgiveness - What makes forgiveness challenging (or difficult)?
NTI Mt 18v7-9.1-4, resistance is fear
NTI Mt 26v42.1-5, released only to return again

Forsaken - Why has God forsaken me?
See God

Freedom - How did freedom seem to become lack of freedom?
NTI Ac 10v27-29.17-38, existence of God sought
How is freedom realized?
NTI Jn 5v16-30.1-13, by welcoming the Light
NTI Jn 8v31-41.1-5, acceptance of the Light
NTI Ac 10v34-48.1-5, join with the Holy Spirit
NTI Ac 12v1-19.10-13, by the Will of your own
NTI Rev 2v27.1, v28-29.1-3, guilt has been released

Fruit - What is the fruit of the Spirit?
NTI Gal 5v22-23.1, the fruit of the Spirit is

— **G** —

Give - What does "give everything" mean?
NTI 2Co 8v1-7.5-19, give through thought
NTI 2Co 8v10-12.1-6, v13-15.1, thoughts of giving
NTI 2Co 8v16-21.1-4, how much are you giving
NTI 2Co 8v22-24.1-4, in being true desire you are giving
What does "Give to Caesar what is Caesar's" symbolize?
See Caesar

God - How can I please God?
NTI Mk 9v14-32.16-31, be in communion with Him
NTI Mk 12v13-17.22-25, love your brother

NTI Mk 12v41-44.1-17, submission to our Lord

NTI 1Jn 3v21-24.1-7, it is the nature of our existence

Why has God forsaken me?

NTI Mt 27v45-49.1-6, God has not forsaken you

NTI 2Ti 4v16-18.1-6, you are not deserted

What is my true relationship to God?

NTI Tit 1v5-9.1-3, children are like the Father

What is my link to God?

NTI Gal 5v7-12.6-26, your willingness

NTI Gal 5v13-15.1-5, is to know God

What is God?

NTI Mt 5v38-48.11, God is Spirit

NTI Mt 27v55-56.2, one

NTI Lk 21v5-38.18-19, sharing the existence of Love

NTI Lk 23v44-49.6-12, Life

NTI Jn 6v60-71.3-7, all things and all persons

NTI Ac 5v1-11.19-42, Life and you live

NTI Ro 3v21-31.1-5, absence of fantasy

NTI 2Co 7v2-7.1-15, the Love that lives

NTI Heb 10v26-31.1-9, God is Love

NTI Heb 13v4-6.1-4, nothing is separable

NTI 1Jn 1v5-7.1-5, an awareness that is pure

NTI 1Jn 1v8-10.1-2, our own soul

NTI 1Jn 4v7-12.8-10, God is Love and...everything

NTI 1Jn 5v6-12.3-4, perfection

See also one

How can I remember God?

NTI Mt 7v1-5.4-9, look after your own heart

NTI Mt 9v1-8.4, lay your will aside

NTI 1Pe 5v10-11.1, willingness to see nothing else

NTI 1Jn 1v8-10.3-4, when God is your only desire

NTI 1Jn 4v13-16.1-9, existence cannot be denied

NTI Rev 16v8-9.1-2, in silence

See also Self

How shall I worship God?

NTI Rev 22v7-9.1-2, grateful for all

Does God answer prayers?

See prayers

Good news - How will the good news of the Kingdom spread in the world?

See message of truth

Gratitude - How does gratitude help me awaken?
NTI Lk 17v11-19.1-6, gratitude is the recognition of
NTI 1Co 4v6-7.1-2, you recognize that we are one
NTI 1Ti 4v15-16.1-5, rest within your purpose
NTI Heb 12v28-29.1-4, desire is increased
What should I have gratitude for?
NTI Lk 9v51-56.1-4, for all things
NTI Lk 24v36-53.8-11, for all that is true
NTI 1Th 1v5-10.6-8, every moment of peace
NTI 1Th 3v6-10.1-6, v11-13.1-6, that peace is
NTI 1Ti 4v1-5.5-6, for the process that is God
NTI Tit 2v9-10.1-3, let the desire for love expand
NTI Heb 2v10-13.1-6, the sleeping mind is awakening
NTI Heb 3v1-6.1-9, each glimmer and each fluttering
NTI 1Pe 1v3-9.1-5, v10-12.1-5, the transition to true
NTI Rev 19v4-5.5-12, reminders to rest
What is heavenly gratitude?
NTI Mk 15v24-32.1-6, this was all he knew
NTI Rev 7v11-12.1-4, for Heaven as it is
NTI Rev 7v13-17.1-6, its gratitude is your gratitude

Guidance - Does the Holy Spirit provide specific guidance in the world?
NTI Mt 23v33-36.6-8, I will guide you within the world
NTI Ac 16v6-10.1-4, willingly do as I ask
NTI 1Co 11v17-26.6-10, to feel you must handle
How does the Holy Spirit's guidance guide me within the world?
NTI Mt 2v1-23.2-6, revealed to you step-by-step
NTI Jn 16v5-16.1-4, it is Within that guides you
NTI Ac 2v1-13.1-7, not for you alone
NTI Ac 2v14-21.1-5, may seem to be individualized
NTI Ac 7v1-8.6-18, lessons to learn with each step
NTI Ac 8v26-40.7-10, do only as He asks
NTI Ac 10v9-23.9-20, not always be what you expect
NTI Ac 13v13-15.1-2, v16-25.1-2, people and situations
NTI Ac 27v1-12.1-6, many stops along the way
NTI 2Ti 4v9-13.1-5, use now to heal
What is the purpose of the Holy Spirit's guidance?
NTI Ac 10v9-23.1-4, to lead you from the world
NTI Ac 16v1-5.3, to the realization of Love
NTI Ac 16v11-15.1-5, shall be opened to your worth
NTI Rev 1v9-11.1-5, do not be fooled
Who receives the Holy Spirit's guidance?
NTI Jn 4v1-26.1-14, it guides all men

When should I follow guidance?
NTI 1Co 3v16-23.1-7, if you do not know yourself as
What keeps me from knowing or accepting guidance?
NTI Lk 1v57-80.8-23, belief that you are a separate
NTI Jn 1v5.1-3, the Light waits on welcome
NTI Jn 7v1-13.1-6, one must learn to trust
NTI Jn 7v14-24.1-10, listen with openness
NTI Ac 2v37-41.3-6, do not be confused by
NTI Ac 4v1-22.1-26, you feel guilty
NTI Ac 7v1-8.1-5, do things your way
NTI Ac 10v1-8.1-4, consistent willingness is helpful
NTI Jas 2v14-17.1-6, standing and walking your way
How do I ask for the Holy Spirit's guidance?
NTI Mt 6v25-34.1-11, do not worry
NTI Mt 8v18-22.3-5, ask Me for what you need
NTI Mt 24v32-35.1-5, when you prefer love to conflict
NTI Mk 14v43-52.16-18, one apostle remained
NTI Mk 14v53-65.20-28, a few remained quiet
NTI Lk 7v1-10.1-7, have faith that you are worthy
NTI Lk 9v28-36.1-8, quiet yourself and ask
NTI Lk 16v1-15.21-26, keep these options clear
NTI Ac 1v12-26.1-16, pray in a way that opens to
NTI Ac 15v36-41.1-4, the one who follows the guidance
NTI Jas 1v9-11.7-10, put all of your trust
NTI Rev 20v4-6.1-5, when the thinking mind is rested
How do I (& why should I) let go of the desire to judge guidance?
NTI Jn 9v1-12.1-5, answer the mind thusly
NTI Jn 18v12-14.1-5, listen not to the ego
NTI Jn 19v1-16.1-5, in deciding that you could judge
NTI Ac 15v1-21.13-19, you truly do not know
NTI Ac 15v22-35.1-7, trust not your thinking mind
NTI Ac 18v18-28.3-8, all things truly work together
NTI Ac 27v13-26.1-12, if you choose to limit

Guilt - Where does guilt come from?
NTI Mt 22v11-14.2-5, it is you who judges
NTI Mt 26v65-68.1-10, you believe that you deny
NTI Ro 7v7-12.1-5, you went on to decide
NTI Rev 2v20-25.1-14, from the voice of confusion
See also judgment
How do I let go of guilt?
NTI Mt 27v38-40.1-4, let go of the belief in
NTI 2Ti 1v15.1-3, a misperception and nothing more

NTI Heb 10v8-10.1-8, focus on the desire that is
NTI Rev 3v1-3.1-4, v4-6.1-6, facing your judgment
NTI Rev 9v13-21.1-9, let the guilt rise over you
See also feelings, *See also* innocence, *See also* letting go

Guilty - Why do I feel guilty?
NTI Phm v4-7.4-7, you believe you have abused your
NTI Heb 10v1-7.1-3, rises as a reminder
Am I guilty for my ego thoughts?
NTI 1Co 7v1-7.3-6, come to you of their own accord
NTI 2 Co 7v1.1-4, you are imagining
Am I guilty for my errors and perceived sins?
NTI Ac 6v1-7.6, you are not guilty
NTI Ro 3v9-20.4-5, a part of fantasy
NTI Ro 5v12-14.1-5, in His eyes
NTI Ro 5v15-17.1-5, it remains nothing
NTI Ro 5v18-19.1-6, never has a state existed
See also right
Am I guilty for desiring experiences in the world?
See desiring

— H —

Happiness - How shall I find happiness?
NTI Lk 12v35-48.1-12, v49-53.1-7, God's Will is
See also joy
What are obstacles to finding inner happiness?
See obstacles

Harvest - What is the harvest?
NTI Rev 14v14-16.1-2, true from the false
When is the harvest?
NTI Mt 13v24-30.1-7, moment-to-moment
NTI Rev 14v14-16.3-6, always the harvest is now
What gets in the way of effective harvest?
NTI Rev 14v17-20.1-6, judgment

Hatred - What is hatred?
NTI Lk 5v12-16.8-10, a desire for Love that
NTI Ac 16v16-40.3-10, born of fear

Heal - Who can heal others?
NTI Mt 8v1-4.1-3, the healed Son
See correct others

Healed - How am I healed?
NTI Mt 8v18-22.1-2, must be laid aside
NTI Mt 9v27-34.7-8, by sharing what I give
NTI Lk 4v1-13.1-8, follow this Voice into the desert
NTI Lk 4v31-37.1-22, listen to Me with the full attention
NTI Lk 4v38-44.1-22, this is what you are to do
NTI Lk 9v37-45.1-9, put your healing in My hands
NTI Lk 13v31-35.1-2, your willingness is everything
NTI Lk 24v13-35.12-14, when you no longer wish
NTI Jn 5v1-9.1-9, when you say "yes" to
NTI 2Ti 4v6-8.1-7, have faith in the healing process
NTI Rev 11v13-14.1-3, v15.1-2, do not stop looking
NTI Rev 21v6-8.1-6, follow His guidance
See also awaken, *See also* enlightened, *See also* salvation

Healing - What is healing?
NTI Mt 8v5-13.1-4, the Son knows who he is
NTI Heb 7v4-10.6-12, an awakened dream
When will healing occur?
NTI Mt 8v14-17.2, within their time
NTI Mt 11v27.1, when you are ready
NTI Lk 17v20-37.8-16, a matter of willingness
NTI Heb 10v1-7.1-6, desire for remembrance

Heart - What is the Heart?
NTI Jn 12v37-50.1-7, Me also
What is the way of the Heart?
NTI Heb 12v4-6.1-5, love and attentiveness
NTI Heb 12v14-17.1-8, have compassion
How do I make the mind subordinate to the Heart?
NTI Jn 9v1-12.1-5, answer the mind thusly
NTI Eph 6v5-8.1-5, let the Heart be the test
NTI Col 4v10-15.3-16, let its desire be the judge
NTI 2Th 3v14-15.1-14, manage your thoughts in this
NTI 2Th 3v16.1-5, rest within the gentle knowledge
What is the true desire (call) of the Heart?
See true desire

Heaven - What is Heaven?

NTI Mt 22v23-33.1-6, awakening
NTI 1Ti 5v17-20.1-5, within your mind now
NTI Rev 4v6-11.1-10, recycling of joy and love
NTI Rev 5v13-14.1-6, one heart and one glory
NTI Rev 7v13-17.1-9, its love is your Self
NTI Rev 16v10-11.1-2, all that is

Helpful - How can I be truly helpful?

NTI Ro 15v1-4.1-8, lay yourself aside
NTI Ro 15v14-22.1-7, surrender
See also Love, *See also* useful

Hide - What is the truth that we hide?

NTI Jn 12v37-50.5-8, we are inseparable from

Holy Spirit - What is the Holy Spirit?

NTI Jn 2v1-11.1-4, Light that shines in
NTI Jn 14v15-31.8-11, within you there is a Voice
NTI Jn 18v1-11.1-14, I am you
NTI Ac 10v27-29.32-38, memory
NTI Ac 12v1-19.6-9, the part of you that
NTI Ac 20v32-38.7-14, your comforter, your teacher
NTI Ro 7v13.1-5, more than a symbol
NTI 1Th 1v2-3.2-3, peace of the Heart
NTI 1Pe 3v1-6.1-3, your true desire is your Holy Spirit
NTI 2Pe 1v12-15.1-6, the memory of all that is true
NTI 1Jn 4v1-3.3-7, the true desire of the Heart

Where is the Holy Spirit when I am unaware of it?

NTI Jn 2v1-11.5-12, v12-25.1-3, shines quietly within
NTI 2Ti 4v16-18.1-6, when you feel deserted

How can I open up to know the Holy Spirit?

NTI Mt 10v21-23.4, look to Me in all things
NTI Mt 10v32-33.1-5, by choosing to be one with Me
NTI Mt 16v28.1-3, let all else go
NTI Mt 28v16-20.1-4, go in faith
NTI Jn 2v12-25.8-11, the welcome you have given
NTI Jn 13v1-17.2-3, surrender
NTI Jn 20v10-18.1-3, v19-23.1-3, as you listen for
NTI Gal 5v2-6.1-2, opening to the possibility that
NTI 1Th 1v5-10.1-8, it is through peace
See also guidance

How do I hear the Holy Spirit?
NTI 2Co 8v1-7.1-4, lay down your own thinking
How can I recognize Holy Spirit in my mind?
NTI Lk 22v7-38.29-34, come to you as a knowing
NTI Lk 23v26-43.15-30, no purpose other than Love
NTI Jn 10v22-42.1-7, characteristics of the Light
NTI Ac 19v23-41.31-42, characteristics of right-reason
Compare to ego
What is the perspective of the Holy Spirit?
NTI Ac 17v10-15.1-9, true interpretation of illusion
NTI Ac 17v16-34.1-18, no difference between you and I
How does the Holy Spirit see?
NTI Ac 8v9-25.12-18, it does not see men
NTI Ac 13v49-52.6-8, see illusion as the expression of
NTI 1Co 11v2.1-2, grateful to you for all things
NTI 1Co 12v14-20.1-3, only see the whole
NTI 1Co 12v21-26.1-6, everything works for the healing
NTI Gal 3v19-20.1-4, the history of the world
NTI Phm v23-25.1-2, all that you are is within
NTI Heb 6v16-20.1-6, in all times and all regions
NTI Heb 10v15-18.4, glistening upon the canvas of time
How does the Holy Spirit see me?
NTI Rev 5v11-12.1-4, v13-14.1-6, joy of Heaven
What is the Holy Spirit's purpose?
NTI Mt 13v36-43.7-8, bring clarity to replace confusion
NTI Ac 21v7-16.1-3, healing
How does merging with the Holy Spirit occur?
NTI Ac 22v22-29.3-7, this is how merging occurs
How do I recognize the authority of the Holy Spirit?
See authority
How do I listen only to the Holy Spirit?
See listen
What lessons does the Holy Spirit teach?
See teach
What is the Holy Spirit's judgment?
See judgment

Honesty - What is honesty?
NTI Lk 14v7-11.1-3, you do not know
NTI Lk 23v26-43.39-41, honesty is acceptance

House - What is symbolized by the house built on rock?
NTI Mt 7v24-27.1-8, let My words reach into your heart

NTI Lk 6v46-49.1-9, listen to Me and practice
NTI Heb 13v9-10.1-5, put your faith in your truth
NTI Rev 22v16.1-3, your truth is your foundation

— I —

I - Who am I? or What am I?
NTI Lk 1v5-56.10-17, the treasure that is sought
NTI Lk 15v1-10.1-11, the one who seems lost
NTI Lk 23v44-49.6-12, you are the same as this gift
NTI Jn 14v15-31.1-7, what I am you are also
NTI Ac 17v16-34.2-14, He named this extension you
NTI Ro 4v18-25.3-4, the extension of His own Love
NTI Ro 5v1-5.1-7, you are God's Love
NTI Ro 7v7-12.1, the mind that made the world
NTI 2Co 2v12-17.4-8, maker of experience
NTI 2Co 12v11-18.1-18, within the Mind of God
NTI 2Co 13v1-10.1-15, thought in God's Mind is God
NTI Eph 3v7-13.4-9, process of creation that is God
NTI Col 2v1-5.1-6, you are the Life that flows
NTI Phm v4-7.8-25, you are everything
NTI Heb 1v1-4.1-7, v5.1-6, on an elevator ride
NTI Heb 1v10-12.2-16, you are eternal
NTI 1Jn 1v1-4.1-6, the Word
NTI Rev 21v22-27.1-5, you are the one
See also Self
How do I learn what I am?
NTI Ac 18v12-17.5-13, abandon your own thinking
NTI 2Co 1v1-2.3, through what is shared through you
NTI 1Ti 3v12-13.1-2, v14-16.1-2, being the observer

Ignorance - What is ignorance?
NTI Ac 3v11-26.4-14, listening to what is not true

Illusion - What is illusion?
NTI 1Co 12v1-11.7-11, wished for something different
NTI 1Pe 4v12-17.3-5, belief that you are a person
NTI Rev 19v1-2.3-8, what is as if it is what isn't
How is illusion made?
NTI Lk 6v1-11.1-6, any judgment you make assumes
NTI Jn 12v20-28.5-13, a wish that asks the Changeless
NTI Ro 2v1-4.1-6, this was the idea you had

NTI Ro 2v5-11.1-18, judgment made to build experience
See also judgment

How is illusion let go?
NTI Ro 3v21-31.6-14, unweave your way out of
NTI Heb 11v7.1-2, by faith
NTI Heb 11v13-16.1-2, begin to long for
NTI 1Jn 2v28.1, rest in faith and trust
NTI Jude v8-10.3-4, the beliefs that have been accepted
NTI Rev 1v4-5.1-3, v7.1-5, you are not to believe any of
NTI Rev 16v1-6.1-9, v7.1, you do nothing

How is illusion affected as my mind heals?
NTI Mt 24v1-2.1-3, reflection of holiness
NTI Rev 18v4-8.1-4, eyes of true beauty and gratitude
NTI Rev 18v9-10.2-3, illusion shall be transformed
NTI Rev 18v11-13.1-3, a symbol of all that is
NTI Rev 18v14-16.1-2, v17-20.1-4, all gratitude is born
NTI Rev 18v21-24.1-8, light of the world shines
NTI Rev 20v7-10.1-4, peaceful dreams end in peace

Imitators - What does "be thee imitators of God" mean?
NTI Eph 5v1-2.1-3, let purpose drive your

Individual - What is individual personhood?
See personhood

Innocence - How will I realize my innocence?
NTI Ac 5v12-16.1-9, release your guilt
NTI Ac 5v25-42.2-15, you must trust Me

Innocent - How can it be that everyone is innocent regardless of what they do?
NTI Mk 7v1-23.24-35, cleanliness comes from within
NTI Ac 28v17-31.7-10, you are free to play
NTI Ro 9v1-18.1-28, the world is not real
See also sin

Interpretation - How can I let go of my interpretation of my experience?
NTI Lk 6v37-38.1-23, v39-42.1-3, you do not know
NTI Lk 6v43-45.1-9, seek quiet time with Me
See also thinking

— J —

Jesus - How does Jesus see me?
NTI Gal 3v6-9.1-5, I see a heart that is
How is Jesus my savior?
NTI Ro 6v8-14.1-11, represents our true desire
NTI Ro 6v15-18.1-12, not looking outside your mind
NTI Ro 7v1-6.1-9, belief has been loosened in the mind
NTI Ro 7v7-12.1-10, in him you see the Light
NTI Ro 7v14-20.1-4, Holy Spirit sends symbols of Light
NTI Ro 7v21-25.1-9, be led Home
What is my true relationship to Jesus?
NTI Ro 6v5-7.1-8, all that is possible with you
NTI Ro 6v19-23.10-15, Jesus is in your mind
What did Jesus teach?
NTI Ac 2v36.1-2, there is no death
What does Jesus symbolize?
NTI Mt 8v1-4.1, symbol of healing
NTI Mt 8v5-13.1, the healed Son of God
NTI Mt 8v14-17.1, the one Son of God
NTI Mt 26v36-38.1-6, v39.1-5, steps forth as a model
NTI Mt 27v11-14.1-5, offered himself as a teacher
NTI Lk 23v1-25.4, the Christ
NTI Lk 23v1-25.17-28, there is nothing to fear
NTI Jn 16v17-33.1-3, symbol of your truth
NTI Ac 13v32-41.1-5, your path to truth
NTI Ro 6v1-4.1-5, all that is possible with you
NTI Ro 6v19-23.1-9, you are eternal
NTI Heb 7v23-25.3-6, v26-28.1-5, let go of all dreams
NTI Heb 8v1-2.1-3, v3-6.1-9, your true desire
NTI 1Pe 1v17-21.1-4, I am in God
NTI 1Pe 4v1-6.1-10, there is nothing to fear
See also resurrection
What did Jesus mean when he said he overcame the world?
NTI Ro 8v1-4.1-7, the world has not truth in it
NTI 1Jn 2v1-2.1-4, the sins of the world as illusion
What did Jesus mean by "Whatever you do to the least of my brethren, you do to me"?
NTI 3Jn v2-4.1-2, v5-8.1-5, extension of your Self
Why is Jesus given to us as a symbol?
NTI Heb 9v15.1-2, v16-22.1-5, you surely will not die
Why is it important for me to accept Jesus as one with me?
NTI Heb 9v23-28.1-5, acceptance of new sight

How do I walk the way of Jesus?
NTI Heb 12v1-3.1-6, follow the beacon of the Heart
What does Jesus' birth symbolize?
NTI Lk 2v1-20.1-10, birth of willingness
What does Jesus' consecration at the temple symbolize?
NTI Lk 2v21-40.1-4, willingness has been blessed
What is symbolized by Jesus' forty days in the desert?
NTI Lk 4v1-13.1-8, false voice may be exposed
What does Jesus' baptism symbolize?
NTI Lk 3v21-38.1-20, way for you to view yourself
What is symbolized by Jesus' triumphal entry into Jerusalem?
NTI Jn 12v12-19.1-6, realization of all that is true
What can we learn from Jesus' experience in the garden of Gethsemane?
NTI Mk 14v32-42.1-37, Jesus recognized a temptation
What can we learn from the story of Jesus' crucifixion?
NTI Mt 27v38-40.1-4, v41-44.1-5, not believe in guilt
NTI Mk 15v24-32.1-6, crucifixion was not within his
NTI Mk 15v33-41.1-9, the perspective of the healed
NTI Lk 23v26-43.1-41, the voice of crucifixion
NTI Lk 23v44-49.1-5, v44-49.20-22, there is no death
NTI Jn 16v17-33.9-11, to leave a world that is not real
NTI Jn 19v28-37.5-6, no truth in his body
See also suffer
What can we learn from Jesus' resurrection?
NTI Mk 16v1-20.1-30, the one you seek is not dead
NTI Jn 11v38-44.1-3, the resurrection is within you
NTI Heb 9v11-14.1-5, you may give up your self will
What was symbolized by the story of Jesus' ascension into Heaven?
NTI Ac 1v1-11.1-14, seek where the Holy Spirit

Job - What does Job symbolize?
NTI Jas 5v10-11.1-2, faith and trust in truth

John the Baptist - What does John the Baptist symbolize?
NTI Mt 3v1-17.3-5, the one that called upon you
NTI Mt 11v1-6.1, search for truth
NTI Lk 3v1-20.4-6, this calling within
NTI Jn 1v6-9.1-6, seeking Light
NTI Jn 1v19-28.1-3, existence of Light was welcomed
What does John the Baptist's birth symbolize?
NTI Lk 1v57-80.1-28, follow-through are key

Join - How do I join with others?
See others

Joke - What is the "great cosmic joke?"
NTI Jn 12v29-33.4-11, your own wish hides the truth

Journey - How can I be successful on my spiritual journey?
See search, *See* spiritual path, *See also* Caesar

Joy - How shall I find joy?
NTI Jn 16v1-4.1-12, serve your Self fully
NTI Ac 2v42-47.1-3, listen to the Voice
See also happiness, *See also* peace
What causes lack of joy?
NTI Jas 1v19-21.1-3, misunderstanding what you are
What are obstacles to finding inner joy?
See obstacles
Judas - What can we learn from the story of Judas of Iscariot?
NTI Mt 26v14-16.1-7, Judas' confusion was real for him
NTI Mt 26v45-56.1-3, v47-49.1-4. not know it is lost
NTI Mt 27v1-10.1-2, dance of guilt
NTI Mk 14v10-11.1-8, the voice of falsehood
NTI Mk 14v53-65.1-6, looked on the confusion
Judged - How do I know if I have judged a situation or a person?
NTI Ac 4v32-37.2-3, whenever you notice guilt
NTI 1Co 12v1-11.4-6, each wish signals a judgment

Judgment - What is judgment?
NTI Lk 6v1-11.1-9, deciding what is good or bad
NTI Ac 4v32-37.1-3, exercise a will of your own
NTI Ro 2v1-4.14, decision
NTI 2Ti 3v6-9.1-7, judgment is a distractor
NTI 1Pe 4v12-17.1-5, v12-17.13-18, imagination
How does judgment seem to separate the Son of God?
NTI Mt 5v38-48.1-6, you judge the things they do
NTI Mt 7v1-5.1, like a knife that cuts
NTI Lk 10v25-37.1-8, when you judge you separate
NTI Lk 14v25-35.1-9, splits the object-brother off
How does judgment make illusion?
NTI Ro 2v1-4.1-6, a building block
NTI Ro 2v12-16.1-8, keeps the experience alive
NTI Ro 2v17-24.1-10, v25-27.1-5, rules and options
See also illusion

Where does the judgment of guilt come from?
NTI Mt 22v11-14.2-5, it is you who judges
NTI Mk 4v24-34.3-7, with the measure you use
NTI Lk 8v16-18.1-9, must already be in the mind
NTI Ro 2v5-11.7-15, judged yourself for what was not
NTI Ro 3v1-8.5-11, began the expression of guilt
NTI 1Pe 4v12-17.3-18, you are the one that declares
Why should I let go of judgment?
NTI Mt 21v6-9.1-3, peace comes from
NTI Lk 19v28-44.1-5, invested your belief in illusions
NTI Jn 9v35-41.1-5, viewed through this filter
NTI Ro 3v1-8.1-14, it has no basis
NTI Ro 14v1-4.1-11, tool of illusion
NTI 1Co 12v1-11.1-3, if you do not want illusion
NTI Rev 13v1-4.1-12, if you choose not to let go here
NTI Rev 14v9-12.2-3, v13.1-6, the effects of judgment
See also illusion
How do I let go of judgment?
NTI Mt 5v38-48.7-9, ask God within your heart
NTI Mt 21v1-5.4, let go of your expectations
NTI Lk 13v1-9.13-18, with that thought in your mind
NTI Lk 16v1-15.8-14, choose with willingness
NTI Lk 16v16-18.1-20, of yourself you cannot stop
NTI Ro 14v5-8.1-9, only judgment that can be applied
NTI Gal 3v15-18.5-8, as you see the many as one
NTI Gal 3v23-25.1-5, as you are willing
NTI Gal 3v26-29.1-7, the guidance of your Heart
NTI Gal 5v19-21.1-11, return your attention to
What is the Holy Spirit's judgment?
NTI Mt 13v51-52.1-5, into My ligh
NTI 1Co 10v1-10.5-8, as true or untrue
What is God's judgment?
NTI Rev 14v6-7.1-3, the hour of putting aside
NTI Rev 19v1-2.1-2, non-judgmental

— K —

King - How is "king of kings and lord of lords" interpreted?
NTI Rev 19v11-16.1-13, true desire leads only from self

Kingdom - What is the kingdom of God? or What is the kingdom of Heaven?
NTI Lk 17v20-37.1-2, is within you

Knock - What does "Knock and the door shall be opened" mean?
NTI 1Jn 5v21.1-3, seek only truth

Know - What does "Know Thy Self" mean?
NTI Jn 14v15-31.12-13, let go of what it is not
What do I know in my Heart?
NTI Jn 14v1-4.1, you seek Love
NTI Jn 20v1-9.7, in the Light lies the absence of fear
NTI Ac 4v32-37.15, your true Will
NTI Ac 27v33-38.5-15, you are not alone
NTI 1Co 4v8-17.1-7, I am you
NTI 2Co 11v30-33.1-10, purpose of the Heart
NTI 2Co 13v11.1-3, your true thoughts
NTI Gal 1v11-17.1-6, the message that I share
NTI Heb 1v10-12.2-16, you are eternal
NTI Heb 10v26-31.1-9, God is love
NTI Rev 2v1-3.1-5, you know who you are
NTI Rev 2v17.1-7, you may choose trust
NTI Rev 5v1-5.1-9, v6-10.1-7, knowledge that already is
NTI Rev 22v14-15.1-7, know your truth

— L —

Landowner - What does the story of the vineyard landowner and vineyard tenants symbolize?
See vineyard

Last Supper - What does the Last Supper symbolize?
NTI Mt 26v26-30.1-16, forgive the belief in separateness
NTI Mk 14v17-26.1-14, when evening came
NTI 1Co 10v14-17.1-8, when you choose not to think

Law - What is the Holy Spirit's interpretation of the Law of Moses?
NTI Mt 5v17-20.1-4, v21-22.1-3, written to protect men
NTI Mk 10v1-12.13-15, that they may have one way
NTI Heb 9v1-10.1-5, covenant of respect
What is the law of Love?
See Love
What is my relationship to the laws of the world?
NTI Jn 8v1-11.1-7, v12-30.1-10, you must lift your sight
NTI Ac 15v1-21.1-18, lay the laws and rules aside
NTI Ac 16v1-5.1-8, under My authority
NTI Ac 21v17-26.1-6, I will lead you

Leader - How can I be the leader of my own awakening?
NTI Heb 5v1-3.1-3, v4-6.1-3, be gentle with yourself
NTI Heb 10v32-38.1-10, you lead yourself in Love
NTI Jas 2v1-4.1-2, accepts and follows the path
NTI Jas 2v5-7.1-5, does not reach out to the world
NTI 1Pe 5v1-4.1-6, lead yourself not by guilt
NTI Rev 1v19-20.1-4, by deciding the purpose
Is a servant a leader or a follower?
See servant

Lessons - What is a helpful way of looking at life's lessons?
NTI Heb 12v12-13.1-4, for each of your brothers
What lessons does the Holy Spirit teach?
See teach

Letting go - What is an effective way of letting go?
NTI Mt 26v69-75.1-3, hidden be shown to him
NTI 1Co 7v1-7.10-17, letting them pass upward
NTI Rev 4v1-6.11-17, look at the whole

Light - What is the Light?
NTI Jn 10v22-42.8-10, we are one and the same
NTI Jn 12v37-50.1-7, your Heart
NTI Jn 21v15-25.13-14, in all men
NTI 1Pe 1v22-25.5, cannot be defined
Why can't I see the Light if the Light is everywhere?
NTI Jn 11v45-57.4-7, focused your eyes on something
NTI Jn 12v1-11.1-12, the fog and the shadow
NTI Jn 13v1-17.2-3, surrender to the Light
See also Love

Limits - How do I let go of limits to my own understanding and acceptance?
NTI Lk 22v63-71.10-18, when they are exposed
NTI Jn 8v12-30.2-10, lift your sight beyond the world
NTI Jn 8v48-59.1-10, your mind is like a trap
NTI Heb 11v22.1, v23.1, by faith

Listen - What does "listen to Me" mean?
NTI 2Jn v4-6.1-11, listen to your own Holy Spirit
How do I listen only to the Holy Spirit?
NTI 2Jn v7-11.1-4, v12-13.1-10, decision that you make

Live - How do I live by the Spirit?
NTI Gal 5v16-18.1-4, live by your willingness
NTI 1Th 4v11-12.1-3, hold within your mind
NTI 1Ti 4v6-8.1-7, to train yourself in godliness
See also fruit
How do I live in the world, but not be of the world?
See world

Lord - What does "the Lord works in mysterious ways" mean?
NTI Ac 9v23-31.1-5, not seen or known by the ego

Lord's Supper - What does the Lord's Supper symbolize?
See Last Supper

Lost - What do the parables of the lost sheep and lost coin symbolize?
NTI Lk 15v1-10.1-23, lost within the perception of
What does the parable of the lost son symbolize?
NTI Lk 15v11-24.1-20, I have come to meet you

Love - What is Love?
NTI Ro 4v13-15.1-8, existence is Love
NTI 1Co 13v1-7.1-4, Love cannot exclude
NTI 1Co 16v12-14.1-4, trust and acceptance
NTI Gal 6v1-5.1, forgiveness is the extension of
NTI Phm v4-7.22-25, an expression of your desire
NTI 1Jn 3v11-15.6-10, the activity of oneness
NTI 1Jn 4v18.1, fear disappears
NTI 1Jn 4v19.1, we are Love
NTI 1Jn 4v20-21.1-3, God
Why is it said that the thinking mind cannot know Love?
NTI 1Jn 3v16-20.1-6, a thought of one and another
NTI 1Jn 3v21-24.1-7, mind believes in separation
What is God's Love?
NTI Ro 4v1-12.1-8, no criteria
NTI Ro 4v18-25.1-4, His promise to you
How do I experience Love?
NTI 1Co 13v1-7.5-9, become as an empty shell
NTI 1Pe 2v4-6.1-7, love yourself
What is the law of Love?
NTI Eph 1v15-23.1-8, is you and works through you
NTI Eph 2v1-10.1-8, law of mind
NTI Eph 2v19-22.7-17, your creative force through your
NTI Eph 3v1-6.5-10, only Love exists

NTI Eph 3v14-19.2-6, v20-21.1-3, what you ask
NTI Eph 4v1-6.1-8, no separation between thought and
How does the law of Love operate?
NTI Eph 4v7-13.3-5, imagine one body
NTI Eph 4v25-28.1-7, how existence makes for you
NTI Eph 5v8-14.1-6, your past thoughts
NTI Eph 6v10-18.1-11, desire is prayer
NTI Php 1v15-18.1-5, receive according to the motive
NTI Col 2v6-8.1-7, reads communication as it travels
NTI Col 2v13-15.1-7, if you seemed to seek fear
NTI Jas 4v1-3.1-3, ask from the process of creation
What is the purpose of the law of Love?
NTI Eph 4v14-16.1-3, thy Self be known
How can I be helpful using the law of Love?
NTI Eph 4v17-19.1-7, determine where within the shift
NTI Eph 4v20-24.1-4, microcosm of all that is
NTI Eph 4v29-32.1-8, deliver in love
NTI Eph 5v3-7.1-6, choose not to experience the past
NTI Eph 5v8-14.7-12, a process meant for joy
NTI Eph 6v5-8.1-5, let the Heart be the test
NTI Col 2v16-19.1-4, through right communication
NTI Col 2v20-23.1-8, set your message on the current
What is the plan of Love?
NTI Ac 9v1-6.1-6, calling must come to every mind
NTI Ac 9v36-43.5-9, all that is happening is a part of
Why don't I perceive everything as Love if Love is all there is?
NTI Jn 13v31-38.7-14, you fear one will
NTI Rev 7v5-8.26-29, misperception

Loving - How do I become more loving?
NTI Mk 4v24-34.9-15, as you live up to the measure you have

— M —

Maker - How do I learn that I am cause (or maker) of my experience?
See cause

Marriage - What is the Holy Spirit's interpretation of marriage?
See join

Mask - What is the mask that Holy Spirit asks me to let go of?
NTI 1Co 14v6-12.1-12, v13-17.1-2, other definitions
NTI 1Co 14v18-21.1-8, heart knows you are beyond the

NTI 1Co 14v22-28.1-12, your truth is firmly hidden by
NTI 1Co 14v29-40.1-7, lay down all limits
NTI 1Co 16v15-18.1-7, say thank you and give it release
NTI 1Ti 6v3-5.1-8, mask of personhood
NTI 2Ti 2v14-19.1-8, hides that which is you
NTI 1Jn 4v1-3.3-7, the thinking mind

Masters - What does "No one can serve two masters," symbolize?
NTI Mt 6v24.1-6, either he will stand in the darkness
NTI 1Co 10v18-22.1-2, cannot believe illusory thoughts

Meaning - What is meaning?
NTI Mt 12v15-21.2-6, a meaning other than truth
NTI Rev 10v1-11.2-3, to look for inherent meaning
How is meaning given to the world and its events?
NTI Mt 5v13-16.1-2, world is meaningless
NTI Mt 10v21-23.1-3, must not look there for
NTI Mt 11v16-19.1-10, temptation to believe the world
NTI Mt 17v1-3.1-4, see them as symbols
NTI Lk 19v1-10.1-20, the meaningless is illusion
NTI Rev 8v1-13.5-10, all meaning comes from the mind

Melchizedek - What does Melchizedek symbolize?
NTI Heb 7v1-3.1-8, the Holy Spirit
NTI Heb 7v23-25.1-2, and Jesus have joined

Message of truth - How will the message of truth spread in the world?
NTI Mt 5v13-16.3-4, it is your truth that shall shine
NTI Mt 7v13-14.1-4, leaders are needed among men
NTI Jn 9v13-34.1-8, through him others shall see
See also teach

Messiah - What is the messiah?
NTI Mk 12v35-40.1-18, the thought of salvation
See also Christ

Minas - What is symbolized by the parable of the ten minas?
NTI Lk 19v11-27.1-11, willingness is all that is needed

Mind - How do I make the mind subordinate to the Heart?
See Heart

Mind-watching - Why should I practice mind-watching?
NTI Mk 8v27-30.19-26, the voice of fear will cloud
NTI Mk 8v31-38.1-30, the mind of man is split
NTI Lk 9v10-17.1-4, the power in your mind
NTI Lk 12v13-21.1-8, you are unaware of why you do
NTI Ac 21v27-36.7-13, to enable this healing
NTI Ro 16v17-19.3-6, v20.1-2, to be free of delusion
NTI 1Co 12v1-11.1-12, you build the illusion
NTI 2Co 4v13-15.1-12, your belief is expressed
NTI Gal 5v1.1-6, correlation between your thoughts
NTI Col 4v1.1-4, know what it is that you do
See thinking, *See* thoughts
How do I practice mind-watching?
NTI Mt 4v1-25.1-2, with Spirit
NTI Mt 13v36-43.14-18, choose to put your faith
NTI Mt 25v31-46.1-21, sheep and the goats are thoughts
NTI Mt 26v6-13.1-4, will I believe this thought
NTI Mt 26v39.1-5, v40-41.1-3, Jesus did not deny
NTI Mk 4v21-23.8-14, thoughts of darkness are revealed
NTI Mk 6v45-56.11-14, he looked at each thought
NTI Mk 11v20-26.4-8, you do not need to believe
NTI Lk 12v1-12.1-34, you are focused on thought
NTI Lk 24v1-12.5-8, give them to Me quickly
NTI 1Co 1v18-25.1-6, remain aware and alert to the ego
NTI 2Co 8v8-9.1-7, remain focused within your mind
NTI Eph 6v5-8.1-5, let the Heart be the test
See also filter, *See also* sorting
Why is mind-watching sometimes a struggle?
NTI Rev 15v1-4.1-4, resistance has taken hold

Miracle - What is a miracle?
NTI Mt 9v18-26.1-5, new sight
How do I receive miracles?
NTI Mt 14v13-21.1-4, put your fear aside
NTI Mt 17v14-21.1-3, faith with Me in all things
NTI Jn 6v16-24.1-7, not a miracle at all
NTI Jn 20v24-31.1-3, will convince you

Misperception - How does misperception hinder awakening?
NTI Jas 2v12-13.1-3, tells you that all is as it is not
How can I discover my misperceptions?
NTI 1Pe 2v13-17.1-6, the world is a reflection
NTI 1Pe 3v1-6.4-8, v7.1-3, that make you special

Why should I let go of my misperceptions?
NTI Lk 17v20-37.1-2, the kingdom of God is within you
NTI Lk 18v9-14.1-17, only traveled away from Me in
NTI 1Pe 5v8-9.1-3, because they are not true
NTI Rev 7v5-8.26-29, to see and know Love
How can I let go of my misperceptions?
NTI 1Pe 2v18-21.1-5, v22.1-2, one has stepped forward
NTI 1Pe 3v13-16.1-5, keep your true desire close
NTI 1Pe 3v17-22.1-7, trust there is another way to see
NTI 1Pe 5v12-14.1, willingness to see that you have

Mistake - Can I make a mistake?
NTI Jn 15v18-27.1-11, you cannot make
NTI Jas 2v8-11.1-9, can be no mistake in the oneness
NTI 1Pe 2v1-3.1-6, seeing through a veil of
How shall I respond to my own seeming mistakes?
NTI Ac 3v11-26.15-26, be happy
NTI 1Co 4v1-5.5-12, do not judge yourself
NTI 1Co 7v8-14.3-9, do not worry
NTI Gal 2v17-21.3-5, own up to them
NTI Gal 5v24-26.1-4, opportunity for learning
See also forget

Money changers - What does the story of the money changers symbolize?
NTI Mt 21v12-13.1-12, foreign purpose
Compare to Canaanite woman

Motive - What is the importance of motive?
See purpose

— N —

Now - Why should I focus on now instead of the past or the future?
NTI Lk 14v1-6.1-2, now is the only time
NTI Heb 4v4-7.1-4, today is now
How can I live now instead of in the past or in the future?
NTI Lk 10v1-24.1-5, give no thought to
NTI Lk 14v7-11.1-3, as if you do not know
NTI Lk 17v20-37.11-18, process that brings about

NTI - What is the purpose of NTI?
NTI Lk 15v1-10.17-23, discover the truth of you

NTI 2Ti 3v1-5.1-5, heal all that is false within your mind
NTI Rev 7v5-8.3-33, twelve lessons

— O —

Observer - What is the observer?
NTI 1Ti 3v1-7.5-13, v8-10.1-5, behind the mind that you
How can I be the observer?
NTI Mk 14v53-65.10-19, rested within the peace
NTI Mk 15v16-20.1-9, recognizing the desire for love
NTI Mk 15v23.1-2, he followed the instructions
NTI Ac 15v1-21.1-18, see it as a script
NTI 1Ti 3v1-7.10-13, v8-10.1-5, watch the drama
NTI 1Ti 3v11.1-4, observe other persons

Obstacles - What are the obstacles to awakening?
NTI Mt 11v27.2-4, you think you are a lofty being
NTI Mt 12v43-45.1-4, v46-50.1, belief in separateness
NTI Mt 14v22-36.1-6, your fear
NTI Mt 16v5-12.2-3, fear, guilt and hatred
NTI Mt 17v22-23.1-2, belief in the world
NTI Lk 4v14-30.1-2, tempted to look away from
NTI Jn 12v29-33.1-7, a universe you have made
NTI Jn 13v31-38.9-14, fear one will
NTI Rev 21v6-8.4-6, desire not to know your Self
See also misperception

One - What is meant by "The Spirit of God is one?"
NTI Mt 16v13-16.1-4, only the Father and His extension
NTI Lk 15v11-24.11-17, nothing exists that is outside

One mind - What is one mind?
NTI 1Co 4v1-5.1-4, communicated to everyone through
NTI 2Co 9v10-11.1-8, thoughts you think are heard
NTI 2Co 13v12-14.1-2, one through its Source
NTI Heb 7v4-10.1-5, everything that you give
NTI 1Jn 3v7-10.3-8, there is no one mind alone
NTI Jude v3-4.1-5, this is why there is no suffering

Others - How do I join with others?
NTI Mt 19v1-6.1-9, ask Me to lead you
NTI 1Co 16v10-11.1-5, look beyond their illusions

NTI Heb 13v1-3.1-4, love your brother as yourself
See also wedding banquet

How shall I treat others?
NTI Mt 7v12.1-6, do not answer their cry for sickness
NTI Mt 13v18-23.1-8, think no evil thoughts about them
NTI Mt 17v24-27.1-8, it is love we must give
NTI Mt 18v5-6.1-3, accept them as they are
NTI Mt 20v24-28.8-9, serve him as you would serve Me
NTI Mt 22v34-40.6-8, love your neighbor as yourself
NTI Mk 4v1-20.45-59, let them go in peace with
NTI Mk 7v24-30.18-22, as I have to you
NTI Jn 6v1-15.3-7, have faith in the Light
NTI Ac 5v21-24.1-4, find no accusation
NTI Ac 9v1-6.5-6, knowing that the calling will come
NTI Ac 15v1-21.19, judge not the guidance given to
NTI Ro 12v9-13.5-6, honor your brother
NTI Ro 13v8-10.1-8, let your brother live his experience
NTI Ro 16v1-16.1-13, as you greet him you greet
NTI 2Co 13v12-14.3-5, of one mind
NTI Gal 5v13-15.6-12, the expression of the love of God
NTI Eph 5v21.1-2, in the understanding of the Christ
NTI 1Ti 6v1-2.1-5, their personhood is false
See also disagreements
Why should I trust others?
NTI Jn 5v31-47.1-12, to know the Light is to see
NTI Jn 6v60-71.3-7, God is all things and all persons
NTI Jn 7v1-13.1-9, trust his brother to trust himself
Why should I let go of my expectations of others?
See expectations

— P —

Past - Why does the Holy Spirit teach that there is no past?
NTI Ac 10v27-29.4-12, v27-29.14, purpose that was
NTI Eph 5v3-7.1-6, choose now to know Love
NTI Eph 5v8-14.1-6, it is merely a reflection
NTI Col 2v20-23.5-8, do not be distracted by old
Why do patterns of the past keep repeating in my experience?
NTI Heb 7v18-19.1-3, as you hold on

Path - How can I be successful on the spiritual path?
See spiritual path

Peace - Why is inner peace important to awakening?
NTI 1Th 2v10-12.1-3, in peace you accept
NTI Tit 2v3-5.1-4, remembrance of your truth
How can I find inner peace?
NTI Lk 6v37-38.17-23, abandon interpretation
NTI Lk 6v46-49.1-3, practice what I say
NTI Lk 8v22-25.1-6, v26-39.1-4, peace is within you
NTI Lk 13v18-21.1-11, willingness to learn
NTI Lk 22v7-38.39-51, by denying
NTI Ro 8v18-25.8-11, be still a moment
NTI Col 2v20-23.1-4, silent remembering is the way
NTI Tit 3v15.1, when you choose to see the purpose
NTI Heb 4v1-3.1-6, power of your own decision
See also conflict, *See also* joy
What can I learn from lack of peace?
NTI 1Th 2v7-9.1-2, you are not following your way
NTI 1Th 3v1-5.1-4, an opportunity to be healed
NTI 1Th 4v9-10.1-6, sin is only forgetfulness
NTI 1Th 5v12-15.1-6, reminder to put forgetfulness

Perceive - What can I learn from what I see (or perceive)?
See see

Perception - Does perception (experience) change as my mind is healed?
NTI Heb 11v17-19.1-4, perception shall answer
NTI Heb 11v20.1, v21.1, experience blesses you
What is true perception?
See true

Persecuted - Why did Jesus ask us to rejoice when we are persecuted on account of him?
NTI Ac 8v1-3.1-15, the storm cannot last

Person - Am I a person?
NTI 1Pe 4v12-17.3-8, you are not a person

Personhood - What is individual personhood?
NTI Ro 14v1-4.5-9, judgment is the building block
NTI 1Ti 1v3-7.1-10, based on a belief in separateness
NTI 1Ti 1v8-11.1-2, fully supportive of the judgment
NTI 1Ti 1v12-14.1-6, source of all pain
How do I let go of individual personhood?
NTI Ro 9v19-24.1-14, only an expression of thought

Perspective - What is the perspective of the Holy Spirit?
See Holy Spirit

Peter - What does Peter symbolize?
What can we learn from Peter's role as a teacher?

Phases - What are the four phases of the spiritual path?
See stage

Plan - What is the best way to plan?

Play - Why is life in the world likened to a stage play?
See script

Practice - How do I practice awakening?

NTI Heb 11v8-10.1-3, practice without faith is dead
NTI Jas 1v22-25.1-4, with your every breath
See also mind-watching

Praise - How can I see praise (or pride) differently?
NTI Mt 23v5-12.1-11, if you seek glory from men
NTI Mk 9v33-37.7-8, the one in service of his brothers
NTI Mk 10v41-45.3-10, a servant unto itself
NTI Lk 3v21-38.1-4, special is separate
NTI Ac 14v8-20.1-9, the ego would worship one over
NTI 1Co 4v6-7.7-10, thank Me for My Word
NTI Heb 7v11-17.8-12, nothing but the dust of dreams

Pray - Why should I pray?
NTI Heb 5v7-10.1-5, pull you into the state of
How shall I pray?
NTI Mt 6v5-8.1-9, v9-13.1-10, search your Heart
NTI Mt 7v7-8.1-2, v9-11.1-4, your Father knows
NTI Mk 11v20-26.20-23, forgive these things first
NTI Lk 11v1-13.1-16, the unceasing act of thought
NTI Lk 14v12-14.1-10, opportunity to empty your mind
NTI Ac 1v12-26.1-10, opening to any guidance
NTI Ac 4v23-31.9-14, in humility and gratitude
NTI Ro 15v23-33.9-12, for your own end
NTI Eph 6v19-20.1-3, pray also for your brothers
NTI 1Ti 2v1-7.1-3, that you may know only truth
NTI Heb 11v17-19.1-4, ask only that you may be
NTI Heb 13v18-19.1-2, that the knowledge of your truth
What does "I pray for you" mean?
NTI Php 1v3-11.1-5, effect is the result of intent

Prayers - Does God answer prayers?
NTI Mt 7v9-11.1-4, the Father will point the willing son
NTI Eph 6v10-18.1-11, be mindful
NTI Eph 6v21-22.1-5, feedback on your prayers
See also ask

Preach - How shall I preach the message of truth?
See message of truth, *See* teach

Pride - How can I see praise (or pride) differently?
See praise

Prodigal Son - What does the story of the prodigal son symbolize?
See lost son

Promise - What is God's promise?
NTI Heb 6v16-20.1-6, the true desire of your Heart
NTI Heb 7v20-21.1-2, v22.1-5, you are His Son forever
NTI Rev 22v20-21.1-5, all will come

Prophets - How shall I respond to false prophets?
See false

Purify - What does "purify yourself" mean?
NTI 1Jn 3v1-3.1-7, release all that is not true

Purpose - How is purpose important to awakening?
NTI Mt 21v12-13.1-12, focusing on the foreign purpose
NTI Mt 21v14-16.1-5, in your forgetfulness you are lost
NTI Mt 23v27-28.1-8, all that matters is the purpose
NTI Lk 11v37-54.3-13, what is it for
NTI Ac 10v27-29.3-7, v27-29.14, there was a purpose
NTI Ac 14v1-7.1-8, what you truly want will always
NTI 2Co 1v3-11.1-11, if that is the purpose you give it
NTI Php 1v19-26.1-6, motive is the determiner
NTI Php 4v2-7.1-3, Be the Love that you are
NTI Col 2v16-19.3-4, be in service to your motive
NTI 1Ti 4v15-16.1-5, put no purpose before Me
NTI 2Ti 2v1-7.1, and purpose is all that you shall see
NTI Rev 7v5-8.6, you choose the purpose
See also desire
What is my true purpose?
NTI Jas 1v26-27.1-4, Know thy Self

— Q —

Question - What is the unanswered question?
See wish
Why should I question what I want?
See want
Do questions come from the ego?
NTI Ac 6v1-7.2-13, bring them to Me

— R —

Reincarnation - What does NTI teach about reincarnation?
NTI 1Pe 4v12-17.3-8, has only been the thought of persons

Rejected - How do I let go of the belief that I have rejected God?
NTI Ro 11v11-16.1-8, v17-21.1-7, always found comfort
NTI Ro 11v33-36.1-7, in accepting Me

Repent - What does "repent" mean?
NTI Ac 3v11-26.19-24, to choose again
NTI Gal 5v16-18.5-11, remembering what you truly

Resistance - What is resistance?
NTI Mt 18v7-9.4-8, resistance is fear
Compare to willingness
Why should I let go of my resistance?
NTI Mk 9v1.1-6, will not taste death
NTI Lk 11v29-32.1-6, you desire safety
How shall I recognize when I am experiencing resistance?
NTI Lk 12v54-59.1-7, attention to how you are feeling
NTI Lk 22v1-6.1-12, from understanding to confusion
How shall I overcome my resistance?
NTI Mt 18v7-9.1-13, resistance is a path from Me
NTI Lk 10v38-42.1-4, when this thought comes
NTI Lk 11v14-28.4-18, be aware of its ploys
NTI Lk 11v37-54.1-13, what is it for
NTI Ac 7v44-53.1-10, it needs your strength
NTI Ro 10v5-13.5-10, put not your trust there
NTI 2Ti 4v14-15.1-8, you can make the decision

Resting - How is resting the thinking mind helpful?
NTI 2Co 11v1-12.1-15, realization that confusion rules
NTI 2Co 11v16-29.1-10, to be tested by the Heart
NTI Rev 17v12-14.1-3, v15-18.1-3, peace shall be
NTI Rev 20v4-6.1-5, Vision of Spirit is given

Resurrection - What is resurrection?
NTI Jn 16v17-33.12-16, an awakening
NTI 2Co 4v7-12.1-6, belief in illusions must die
NTI 2Ti 2v14-19.1-8, the Light that has never died

Revelation - What is the Holy Spirit's interpretation of the symbolism in Revelation?
NTI Rev 4v1-6.1-14, step back from the images
NTI Rev 4v6-11.1-10, the four living creatures
NTI Rev 5v1-5.1-9, v6-10.1-7, scroll with writing on
NTI Rev 6v1-2.1-7, the rider of the white horse
NTI Rev 6v3-4.1-4, the second seal
NTI Rev 6v5-6.1-3, the third seal
NTI Rev 6v7-8.1-2, the fourth seal
NTI Rev 6v9-11.1-4, the fifth seal
NTI Rev 6v12-14.1-4, v15-17.1-5, the sixth seal
NTI Rev 7v1-4.1-3, four angels who are holding back
NTI Rev 7v1-4.4-5, seal of the 144,000
NTI Rev 7v5-8.1-33, tribes of Israel
NTI Rev 8v1-13.5-18, the seventh seal
NTI Rev 9v1-6.3-12, the abyss
NTI Rev 9v7-11.1-8, the locusts
NTI Rev 11v1-10.1-12, the measuring rod
NTI Rev 11v1-10.13-18, v11-12.1-7, two witnesses
NTI Rev 12v1-6.1-11, the woman and her child
NTI Rev 13v1-4.1-12, the beast that comes out of the sea
NTI Rev 13v11-12.1-2, beast...comes out of the earth
NTI Rev 14v8.1-3, Babylon the great
NTI Rev 15v5-8.1-4, the seven angels dressed in white
NTI Rev 15v5-8.5-7, the seven bowls
NTI Rev 17v1-2.1-4, v3-6.1-5, the great prostitute
NTI Rev 17v3-6.6-11, v7-8.1-8, beast once was and now
NTI Rev 19v9.1-2, wedding supper of the lamb
NTI Rev 19v11-16.1-13, king of kings and lord of lords
NTI Rev 20v11-15.1-6, the second death
NTI Rev 22v1-2.1-3, river of life
NTI Rev 22v1-2.4-8, tree of life

Reward - How shall I find my reward?
NTI Mt 23v37-39.1-9, look for your reward in Me

Rich man - What does the parable of the rich man and Lazarus symbolize?
NTI Lk 16v19-31.1-33, all perception is thought

Right - How do I know right from wrong?
NTI 1Co 10v1-10.1-8, you do not know
NTI 1Co 10v23-24.1-2, everything is permissible

What is right-knowledge?
NTI Ac 3v11-26.14, knowledge of truth
What is right-reason?
NTI Ac 19v23-41.31-42, the purpose of One
NTI Ac 21v17-26.1-6, for the healing of God's Son

— S —

Sabbath - What does the Sabbath symbolize?
NTI Lk 23v50-56.1-13, time set aside at the end of time

Sacrifice - Will I sacrifice if I surrender to the Holy Spirit?
NTI 1Co 11v11-16.1-9, I can only want for you
NTI 1Co 11v27-32.1-10, I am you and I see you
NTI 1Co 11v33-34.1-3, it will not be taken away

Sacrificial atonement - Is it true that I can let go of false thoughts without sacrificial atonement?
See false thoughts

Salvation - How can I accept salvation for myself?
NTI Mk 9v42-50.1-14, ask the Holy Spirit to help you
NTI Mk 10v13-16.6-15, do not throw love away
NTI Mk 10v17-31.32-34, turn all things over to God
NTI Mk 13v4-37.26-30, listen only to the Holy Spirit
NTI Jn 6v1-15.1-7, you need do nothing
NTI 2Co 6v1-2.1-3, now is the day
NTI 2Ti 2v22-26.1-11, do not flee that which life is
NTI Heb 3v16-19.1-4, it is your mind that you tend to
NTI Jas 4v13-17.1-4, trust in your true desire
NTI 2Pe 3v8-9.1-5, v14-16.1-4, your abundance
NTI Rev 1v1-3.1-4, with you and within you now
NTI Rev 1v19-20.3-4, by deciding the purpose
NTI Rev 12v10-12.1-6, accepting choice
See also awaken, *See also* enlightened, *See also* healed

Sameness - Why should I accept sameness instead of differences?
NTI Mt 20v24-28.8-12, will carry you to Heaven
See also covenants, *See also* differences

Script - Why is life in the world likened to a script?
NTI Ac 25v1-12.1-18, the world is not real
NTI Ac 25v13-22.1-4, drama is removed and replaced

NTI Ac 25v23-27.1-2, everything is working just as it is
NTI Ac 26v1-32.1-4, others will see the script in you
NTI Ac 27v1-12.4-6, you must be willing to listen
NTI Ac 27v39-44.1-6, you will find peace in the chaos
NTI Ac 28v17-31.3-16, your own script cannot limit you

Search - How can I be successful in my search for truth?
NTI Mt 11v1-6.2-7, v7-15.1-5, do not search for truth in
NTI Mt 16v17-18.1-5, your willingness to believe Me
NTI Mt 17v9-13.1-3, let go of the search and let Me
NTI Mt 22v15-22.12-19, I am in those things too
NTI Mt 22v34-40.3-5, let your love for God be
NTI Lk 7v24-28.1-9, surrender
NTI Lk 12v22-34.1-19, only have two experiences
NTI Jn 6v16-24.5-7, faith in yourself
See also spiritual path
What must I realize about the search for truth?
NTI Heb 6v1-3.1-4, when you lay aside searching

See - Why do I see (perceive) as I see?
NTI 1Pe 2v23-25.1-8, it is a reflection
What can I learn from what I see (or perceive)?
NTI Jn 2v12-25.4-11, what you see is what you want
NTI 1Pe 2v7-8.1-3, reflection of your feelings and
How can I see differently?
NTI Mk 9v42-50.1-10, ask the Holy Spirit to help
NTI Mk 10v13-16.1-15, become as these little children
NTI Jn 12v20-28.1-4, what do I want?
NTI Jn 13v1-17.4-9, full surrender
NTI Jn 19v17-27.3-5, v28-37.1-4, One that is with you
NTI Ac 4v23-31.1-18, deny what you see
NTI Ac 8v26-40.1-10, lay your sight aside
NTI Ro 8v5-8.1-5, the Spirit's interpretation
NTI 1Co 12v27-31.1-6, do not judge
NTI 2Co 3v12-18.1-14, let that answer shine
NTI 2Co 7v8-13.1-14, first look in your heart
NTI Gal 6v12-16.1-5, the inner is everything
NTI Eph 5v22-33.1-6, love what you see
NTI Col 3v18-25.1-9, do not identify with it
NTI 2Th 1v5-10.1-10, see yourself through new eyes
NTI Phm v17-21.1-3, let go of your error
NTI 1Pe 2v9-10.1-2, you allow change in your feelings
NTI 1Jn 2v29.1-2, have faith in the Light

NTI Rev 22v10-11.1-4, seek not to change
How does the Holy Spirit see?
See Holy Spirit

Seed - What is symbolized by the parable of the growing seed?
NTI Mk 4v24-34.23-31, give your willingness

Self - What is my true Self?
NTI Mt 5v25-26.6, the unlimited
NTI Mt 10v40-42.1-2, the eternal
NTI Mt 16v19.5, Spirit of God
NTI Mt 17v24-27.1, not of this world
NTI Lk 20v9-19.1-2, you have listened but to your Self
NTI Tit 3v3-8.1-4, the Self of Love
See also I, *See also* Son of God
How do I remember my true Self?
NTI Mt 5v31-32.7, by joining with one Will
NTI Mt 5v33-37.5-6, by following the guidance
NTI Mt 10v1-6.1-2, through sharing My Word
NTI Mt 12v33-37.3-4, let all thoughts of condemnation
NTI Lk 15v11-24.6-20, practice giving acceptance to
NTI Lk 17v20-37.3-16, healing is a matter of willingness
NTI Lk 20v41-47.1-5, it is through no definition
NTI 1Ti 4v1-5.1-6, to know thy Self you must
NTI Tit 3v12-14.1-3, remember Me
NTI 2Pe 1v16-18.1-6, taste as witness
NTI 2Pe 2v4-10.1-12, be aware of this darkness
See also God
What does "be true to your Self" mean?
NTI Jas 5v12.2, true to your true desire
What are obstacles to knowing my true Self?
See obstacles

self – What is self?
NTI Mt 5v21-22.1-3, manhood
NTI Mt 10v32-33.1-6, temporal
See also personhood
Why should I let go of self?
NTI Mt 19v25-26.1-4, you will know that you are one
NTI 1Co 1v26-31.1-4, is emptied shall be filled by Me
NTI 1Co 3v10-15.1-7, to let go of false illusion
How do I let go of self?
NTI Ro 9v19-24.1-14, not your reality

NTI Ro 15v23-33.1-8, the realization of your truth
See also ego, *See also* thinking

self-control - What is self-control?
NTI Gal 5v22-23.1, willingness to continually return

self-hatred - How do I let go of self-hatred?
See unworthiness

Separate - Am I separate from God?
NTI Jn 15v1-17.1-3, you can do nothing alone
NTI Ac 5v1-11.23-42, God is life and you live
NTI Ac 13v42-48.1-6, all things work together for God
NTI Phm v4-7.1-25, you are everything
NTI Heb 13v4-6.1-4, it is all one
NTI 1Jn 3v4-6.1-6, there is no greater falsity than this
Am I mistaken when I feel the desire to separate myself from others in order to get quiet?
NTI Ac 9v7-9.1-8, purpose of this separation is joining
How does judgment seem to separate the Son of God?
See judgment

Separation - How did the seeming separation happen?
NTI Lk 21v5-38.7-44, wish that it could be different
NTI Ac 10v27-29.17-38, opposites were made from
NTI Ro 2v1-4.7-16, your idea was just a curiosity
NTI Ro 2v5-11.1-18, judgment made to build experience
How does the world teach separation?
NTI Gal 4v8-20.11-23, it allows you to join and
How do I let go of the belief in separation?
See belief in separation

Servant - Is a servant a leader or a follower?
NTI 1Co 1v10-17.1-12, one who walks with Me

Service - What is service?
NTI Jn 13v1-17.1-8, surrender to the Light
NTI Jn 16v1-4.1-3, serve your Self fully
NTI Ac 11v19-30.1-6, the work of the Lord
See also helpful

Share - How shall I share the message of truth?
See message of truth, *See* teach

Sides - How is it helpful to look at different sides of an issue, concern or opinion?
NTI Ac 17v1-9.1-10, everyone is walking together in purpose

Sight - What is spiritual sight?
NTI Mk 10v46-52.1-11, with eyes from your heart
NTI Ac 22v1-21.9, acceptance and surrender

Simon - What does Simon (who carried Jesus' cross) symbolize?
NTI Mt 27v32.3-4, thoughts of the Holy Spirit

Sin - How can I *not* see sin in myself or in others?
NTI Mk 9v42-50.2-18, ask the Holy Spirit to help you
NTI Heb 9v1-10.1-11, acceptance of oneness
NTI Heb 10v11-14.1-4, v15-18.1-4, release of what isn't
NTI Jas 5v1-6.1-4, only a game you played to pretend
NTI 1Jn 2v1-2.1-4, you have not sinned
NTI 1Jn 3v7-10.1-2, because there is no separation
What is sin?
NTI Mt 27v27-31.1-2, madness is not sin
NTI Mk 10v17-31.7-9, a man cannot be good or bad
NTI Lk 24v13-35.1-8, what has done nothing cannot be
NTI Ro 3v9-20.1-5, sin of making what isn't
NTI 1Th 4v3-8.1-9, a false belief
NTI 1Th 4v9-10.1-6, sin is only forgetfulness
NTI 1Jn 3v4-6.1-6, the idea it supports is also false
See also guilty

Sinner - What does "whoever turns a sinner from the error of his way" mean?
NTI Jas 5v19-20.1-2, whoever recognizes that he has been

Sleeping - What is sleeping?
NTI Heb 4v8-11.1, do not remember that the true desire
Is sleeping bad?
NTI Heb 5v11-14.1-2, forgive yourself

Son of God - What is the Son of God?
NTI Mt 13v36-43.1-2, an extension of his Father
NTI Jn 17v6-19.6-13, you who are reading these words
NTI 1Jn 5v6-12.1-2, eternal life
See also Christ

Song - What is the Holy Spirit's one song analogy for the world?
NTI Lk 6v27-36.1-15, harmony to create the one
NTI Ac 9v10-19.1-7, all brothers work together
NTI 1Co 12v12-13.1-4, cannot be broken apart

Sorting - What is the work of sorting thoughts?
NTI Mt 13v47-50.1-5, v51-52.1-5, you put your faith
NTI 1Jn 4v1-3.1-7, comes from one of two sources
NTI 1Jn 4v4-6.1-8, the feeling you know within
See also mind-watching

Sower - What is symbolized by the parable of the sower?
NTI Mk 4v1-20.41-61, that is the choice

Special - Why should I let go of the idea of special people?
NTI Mt 20v20-23.1-7, a form of difference
NTI Lk 3v21-38.5-20, one Son of God
NTI Ac 2v42-47.1-3, an encompassing love
NTI 1Pe 3v1-6.4-8, seems to separate

Spirit - What is meant by "The Spirit of God is one?"
See one

Spiritual path - How can I be successful on the spiritual path?
NTI Lk 16v1-15.1-7, when confusion and worry are
NTI Lk 22v54-62.1-9, let go of the world
NTI Ac 7v9-16.1-13, trust in your worth and in Me
NTI Ac 7v44-53.1-10, there is a resistance within your
NTI Ac 13v1-3.1-6, when your calling comes
NTI Ac 13v4-12.1-9, ego is still within the mind
See also search
How can I reduce delay on the spiritual path?
NTI Ac 21v1-6.4-7, questioning your reason
What do I need to remain aware of on the spiritual path?
NTI Ac 7v17-43.8-12, the mind remains split
NTI Rev 19v11-16.1-13, v19-21.1-2, the only way
What do I do when the spiritual path seems difficult?
NTI Ac 7v54-60.1-8, cling tightly to Me
Is my spiritual path already determined?
NTI Jas 2v5-7.4-5, you are the leader of your own
NTI Jas 2v20-24.1-8, the plan you selected
What are the stages of the spiritual path?
See stage

Split mind - What is the split mind?
NTI Mk 8v31-38.12-30, one part of the mind is
NTI Mk 9v2-13.20-24, acceptance and resistance are in
NTI Lk 22v7-38.1-9, two voices in your mind
NTI Ac 7v17-43.1-7, you battle joy
NTI Ac 20v13-24.13-22, voice of self-will
NTI Ac 21v27-36.4-10, between real and unreal
NTI Ro 11v11-16.1-8, cannot reject yourself fully
How shall I respond to the battle within my split mind?
NTI Ac 6v8-15.1-8, let the battle continue
NTI Ac 7v44-53.1-10, not to give it your strength
NTI Ac 8v1-3.3-15, the storm cannot last
NTI Ac 8v4-8.1-5, remember your purpose
NTI Ac 14v1-7.1-8, seeks to regain command and
NTI Ac 20v13-24.21-22, faith in Me above everything
NTI Ro 10v14-21.1-18, isn't this movement towards
NTI Heb 2v8-9.1-3, whisper quietly to it
NTI Heb 2v14-18.1-10, let the awakened mind dance
How do I let go of the split mind?
NTI 2Co 6v14-16.1-5, do not be content
NTI 2Co 6v17-18.1-7, watch your mind

Stage - What is the first stage of the spiritual path?
NTI Ac 19v1-7.1-6, the search
NTI Ac 19v8-10.1-11, study, reflection and questioning
What is the second stage of the spiritual path?
NTI Ac 20v1-6.1-3, letting go
NTI Ac 20v7-12.1-7, thick web of beliefs
What is the third stage of the spiritual path?
NTI Ac 22v1-21.1-9, service
NTI Ac 22v22-29.1-7, you will surrender more self-will
What is the fourth stage of the spiritual path?
NTI 1Co 15v3-11.1-5, no longer fooled by that which is
NTI 1Co 15v12-19.1-8, a glorious phase
NTI 1Co 15v20-28.1-5, distractions have been erased
NTI 1Co 15v29-34.1-4, there are no fears
NTI 1Co 15v35-49.1-4, this one must pass away also
NTI 1Co 15v50-55.1-5, you shall not know death
See also awakening

Stillness - How does stillness help me to let go of illusion?
NTI Ac 27v33-38.5-15, in the stillness you know Me
NTI Rev 16v17-21.1-5, loosen the hold on nothing
NTI Rev 17v12-14.1-3, v15-18.1-3, peace shall be

Stolen - Why do I feel I have stolen myself from God?
NTI Lk 20v9-19.3-19, a mind that is shared
NTI Lk 21v5-38.7-19, disrupting the existence
NTI Jn 12v20-28.5-11, wishes for change within the

Storm - How shall I respond to the storm within my split mind?
See split mind

Strength - How can I get strength when I feel weak?
NTI Jude v24-25.1-5, lean in faith on My

Suffer - Why do we suffer?
NTI Mt 13v36-43.1-6, you believe that you are guilty
NTI Mt 18v23-35.1-3, because you do not love
NTI Mt 24v15-25.1-8, deception
NTI Mt 27v35-36.1-7, belief in guilt
NTI Lk 13v10-17.1-3, your own thinking
NTI 2Co 5v1-10.1-9, asking not to experience Heaven
NTI 1Ti 1v12-14.1-6, judgment and rejection
NTI Heb 2v1-4.1-2, to sleep while you are awakening

Suffering - Why does Holy Spirit say that suffering is an illusion?
NTI Jude v5-7.1-5, one mind choosing unto Itself
NTI Jude v8-10.1-2, mind is not fully aware of Itself
NTI Jude v11.1-4, mind has no victims

Surrender - Is surrender important in order to awaken?
NTI Mt 17v9-13.1-3, not through your doing that you
NTI Lk 7v24-28.1-6, find the peace of God in your way
NTI Lk 7v36-50.1-8, surrender is forgiveness
NTI Lk 9v37-45.1-9, following what makes sense to you
NTI Lk 21v1-4.2-6, true reward comes only from
NTI Jn 13v1-17.2-9, surrender to the Light is to become
NTI Ac 4v23-31.9-18, v32-37.9-12, give yourself to
NTI Ac 7v1-8.1-5, give everything over to Me
NTI Ac 8v26-40.1-10, you do not see truth
NTI Ac 22v1-21.8-9, v22-29.1-5, how the merging
NTI Ro 15v5-6.1-2, our heart is combined

NTI Ro 15v7-13.1-5, your complete surrender
NTI 1Co 11v17-26.1-4, while you may still lose sight
NTI 1Jn 3v21-24.1-7, one must surrender the thinking
Will I sacrifice if I surrender to the Holy Spiri t?
See sacrifice

Symbols - How am I to understand or interpret symbols?
NTI Mt 11v1-6.1-7, nothing in the world can contain
NTI Mt 11v16-19.1-10, dancing symbols with no truth
NTI Jn 17v1-5.1, what the symbol points to is truth
NTI Ac 2v22-35.1-5, do not be caught up in
NTI Ac 5v17-20.1-3, for your learning
NTI Rev 21v9-14.1-2, all symbols disappear
See also meaning
How can symbols be useful in healing my mind?
NTI Ro 7v14-20.1-4, v21-25.1-9, symbols of Light
NTI Rev 1v4-5.1-5, follow them
NTI Rev 1v6.1-3, do not idolize anything

— T —

Talents - What does the parable of the talents symbolize?
NTI Mt 25v14-30.1-8, fear is an illusion

Teach - Who has authority to teach the message of truth?
NTI Mt 10v1-6.1-2, I give you authority
NTI Mk 9v38-41.1-21, God will call many teachers
NTI Lk 9v1-6.1-3, everyone who reads My Word
NTI Lk 9v57-62.1-3, you must let My Word be first
NTI Tit 2v6-8.1-3, teach yourself
What shall I teach?
NTI Mt 10v1-6.1-2, My Word
NTI Mt 10v7-10.1-2, God is within
NTI 1Ti 6v1-2.1-5, their personhood is false
NTI 2Ti 1v13-14.1-2, your innocence
NTI Tit 2v1-2.1-3, to listen only to truth
NTI Tit 2v3-5.1-4, to be quiet
NTI Tit 2v9-10.1-3, the mind to be subject to
NTI 2Pe 2v1-3.1-3, your abundance is now
How do I teach?
NTI Mt 7v15-20.1-4, concentrate first on your healing
NTI Mt 10v1-6.1-2, sharing My Word
NTI Mk 6v7-13.7-25, trust His guidance

NTI Mk 13v4-37.21-24, say whatever is given you
NTI Lk 9v1-6.1-14, only give thought to listening
NTI Lk 9v10-17.1-18, every thought that you accept
NTI Lk 9v46-50.1-5, v51-56.1-4, a student who practices
NTI Ac 5v21-24.1-4, find no accusation or judgment
NTI 2Co 9v12-15.1-5, not believing in the world
NTI Php 4v8-9.1-5, v10-13.1-3, keep your mind with
NTI Col 4v16.1-5, through your contemplation
NTI 1Ti 4v11-14.1-4, believe all things as a message
NTI Jas 3v1-2.1-3, conscious-minded teacher of yourself
See also message of truth

Will I continue to teach after I have learned the message of truth?
NTI Ro 13v11-14.3-6, taking time to accept
NTI 1Co 15v20-28.1-4,v29-34.1-4, the fourth phase
NTI 1Co 16v5-9.4-6, he shall remain as a memory

What lessons does the Holy Spirit teach?
NTI Mt 10v17-20.3, Spirit of your Father is one
NTI Mt 12v22-29.7-8, the Spirit of God is one
NTI Mt 12v22-29.9-13, there has been no sin
NTI Mt 20v1-16.4-7, there are not many
NTI Mt 24v26-28.1-6, the world is a place of illusions
NTI Mt 26v50.4-6, you deny your confusion
NTI Lk 10v25-37.1-4, no difference among anyone
NTI Lk 16v19-31.27-31, the filter of your mind
NTI Jn 14v15-31.14-17, denial of truth does not change
NTI Ro 1v1-7.3-4, none are to be left out
NTI 1Co 7v8-14.1-2, your truth is as it is
NTI 2Th 1v3-4.1-10, I am you
NTI 1Ti 4v9-10.1-3, the purpose of God is to
NTI Rev 7v5-8.3-33, twelve lessons prepare you
NTI Rev 14v1-5.1-5, acceptance of these lessons

Teaching - How shall I respond when I see someone teaching a different interpretation of the message of truth?
NTI Mk 9v38-41.1-21, do not be distracted by

Tenants - What does the story of the vineyard landowner and vineyard tenants symbolize?
See vineyard

Test - Why does God test us?
NTI Mt 24v9-14.1-4, if you look to the world as real
NTI Jn 21v15-25.5-12, you will not be tested

NTI Rev 20v1-3.1-8, rest the thinking mind
See also interpretation, *See also* mind-watching, *See also* thoughts

Thoughts - Why should I let go of my thoughts?
NTI Mt 12v33-37.1-4, your world are condemned
NTI Mt 13v36-43.7-18, born of fear
NTI Lk 17v5-6.1-9, your thoughts as meaningless
NTI Lk 19v45-48.1-7, no meaning in God
See also Judas, *See also* rich man, *See also* thinking
How do I let go of my thoughts?
NTI Mk 11v15-19.3-7, not believe these judgments
NTI Ac 20v25-31.1-6, let go of what you see, hear and
NTI Rev 2v18-19.1-4, hold with Me to this knowing
See also mind-watching, *See also* thinking
What is the work of sorting thoughts?
See sorting, *See also* mind-watching
How should I look at the thoughts in my brother's mind?
See brothers

Time - What is the belief in time?
NTI Ro 6v19-23.1-8, a fragment of your mind
Tithing - What does tithing symbolize?
NTI Heb 7v1-3.1-8, mind given to awakening

Treat - How shall I treat myself?
NTI Ro 12v9-13.1-4, love your Self
How shall I treat others?
See others

True - How do I know what is true?
NTI 2Co 3v1-6.1-12, if you look at the world

True abundance - What is true abundance?
NTI 2Pe 1v1-2.1-3, accept everything as you
NTI 2Pe 1v3-4.1-6, your divine nature
NTI 2Pe 1v10-11.1-3, it is the Heart that knows
NTI 2Pe 1v19-21.1-9, within you there is a star
NTI 2Pe 3v3-7.1-8, the truth of what you are
NTI 2Pe 3v8-9.1-5, your own truth that is your salvation
How can I remember my true abundance?
NTI 2Pe 1v19-21.1-9, within you there is a star
NTI 2Pe 2v1-3.1-3, teach yourself only
NTI 2Pe 3v1-2.1-4, have faith in your abundance

True desire - What is my true desire?
NTI Jn 14v15-31.12-13, know only that which it is
NTI Ro 11v1-6.2-8, v7-10.1-15, this is the reflection of
NTI Col 4v10-15.13-16, Know thy Self
NTI Heb 2v1-4.1-2, awakening
NTI 1Pe 3v1-6.1-3, is your Holy Spirit
How does my true desire help me to awaken?
NTI Jas 4v13-17.1-4, the process of God will answer
NTI Jude v17-19.1-3, v20-21.1-5, arouse our mind to
NTI Rev 11v1-10.13-18, v11-12.1-7, see you through the
NTI Rev 16v12-14.1-6, you loosen your grip on belief
How do I recognize true desire with clarity?
NTI Rev 19v11-16.1-7, desires only this

True perception - What is true perception?
NTI Rev 19v1-2.3-6, not through the body's eyes
NTI Rev 19v4-5.10-12 v6-8.1-7, Sight of Spirit
NTI Rev 19v10.1-5, no differences that can be seen
NTI Rev 20v7-10.1-4, peaceful dreams end in peace
NTI Rev 21v1.1, new heaven and a new earth
NTI Rev 21v2-4.1-6, v5.1-3, all that I could not see

True purpose - What is my true purpose?
See purpose

True Will - What is my true Will?
NTI 2Pe 3v17-18.1-3, Know thy Self

Trust - What is the way of trust?
NTI 1Pe 5v6-7.1-5, let all of your fears go
Why is trust important to awakening?
NTI 1Co 13v13.1-2, trust is the means
NTI Jas 1v2-8.1-9, trust is your bedrock
What should I trust?
NTI 1Jn 2v12-14.1-6, trust the healing process
Why should I trust myself?
NTI Ac 1v12-26.11-16, guidance comes from you
NTI Ac 19v11-22.7-16, in trusting you you trust Me
How can I develop more trust?
NTI Ac 2v14-21.1-5, when you hear stories
NTI Ac 27v33-38.1-15, tempted to be afraid
NTI Rev 2v17.1-7, you may choose trust

What is the relationship between faith and trust?
See faith

Why should I trust others?
See others

Truth - What is truth?
NTI Lk 24v36-53.8-11, life, love, sharing, extension and
NTI Jn 12v12-19.6, all that was never imagined
NTI Jn 12v37-50.5-8, inseparable from the Light
NTI Ro 8v1-4.1-7, world has not truth in it
NTI 2Pe 1v19-21.1-7, the key to your abundance
NTI 1Jn 3v11-15.6-7, oneness and the activity of
How do I recognize truth?
NTI Mt 19v7-9.1-7, does not change
NTI Mt 21v28-32.1-3, only by answering the call
NTI Phm v4-7.1-3, do not doubt
Why is my truth hidden from me?
NTI Rev 5v1-5.1-9, v6-10.1-7, belief that blocks the
How do I accept truth?
NTI Rev 1v8.4-5, do not believe that which is not
Why must I accept truth as it is?
NTI Mt 21v6-9.1-3, there is no other way
NTI 2Co 5v16-21.1-4, without the desire that it be
What is the truth that sets you free?
NTI Mt 26v25.3-5, no power but your own
NTI Lk 19v1-10.1-20, all meaning that you thought it
NTI 2Pe 2v17-22.5-7, you are everything
NTI 1Jn 4v13-16.1-8, existence cannot be denied

— U —

Unanswered question - What is the unanswered question?
See wish

Understanding - When will I receive understanding?
NTI Mt 11v27.1, when you are ready
NTI Mt 13v10-15.1-4, when you lay your self aside
NTI Lk 18v31-34.1-4, the gift of willingness
NTI Lk 20v27-40.3-8, accept what I say
NTI Lk 22v63-71.1-11, watch your mind for limits

Unworthiness - How do I let go of unworthiness?
NTI Lk 5v12-16.4-15, blemishes come to Me for healing
NTI Lk 5v17-26.1-14, v27-32.3-8, do not let doubt tell
NTI Lk 8v1-15.1-24, gratitude and rest
NTI Lk 8 v26-39.1-3, v40-56.1-13, beyond the clouds
NTI Lk 17v7-10.1-6, you are as worthy as I am
NTI Ac 16v11-15.1-3, follow My guidance
NTI 2Th 1v11-12.1-4, look at this belief
NTI 2Th 2v1-4.1-5, is from within hiding that it rules
NTI 2Th 2v5-12.1-3, v13-15.1-3, your own judgment
NTI 2Th 3v6-10.1-15, see that it isn't useful
NTI 2Ti 1v3-7.1-13, look at it and feel it
See also feelings

Unworthy - Why do I feel unworthy?
NTI Lk 1v57-80.10-19, belief that you are a separate entity

Useful - How can I be useful to God and my brothers?
NTI Ac 4v23-31.9-18, give yourself to your Father's
NTI Ac 4v32-37.1-15, without judgment
See also helpful

— V —

Value - Why should I let go of that which I value in the world?
NTI Mt 24v42-44.2, not ready for Heaven
NTI Mk 10v17-31.38-43, will be rewarded beyond
NTI Lk 18v18-30.7-15, recognize true value
NTI Heb 7v11-17.1-3, lead you to be caught up longer
NTI 1Jn 2v15-17.1-4, dark clouds of illusion
NTI Rev 1v9-11.1-5, the two purposes are not the same
How do I let go of that which I value in the world?
NTI Mt 19v10-12.1-5, let them fall away
NTI Mt 22v15-22.12-19, do not worry about
NTI Mk 2v18-20.1-4, only God within the heart
NTI Heb 7v11-17.4-19, can you imagine letting go
NTI 1Pe 5v5.1-4, follow the true desire of your Heart
NTI 2Pe 1v3-4.1-6, v5-9.1-5, by reaching beyond limits

Vessel - Why am I likened to a vessel?
NTI Ac 14v21-28.1-5, endowed with the choice

Vibration - How do I shift my vibration?
NTI 1Ti 6v6-10.1-5, stay focused on your Heart
NTI 1Ti 6v11-16.1-4, v17-19.1-3, stay tuned then with

Vineyard - What does the parable of the vineyard landowner and vineyard tenants symbolize?
NTI Mt 21v33-44.9-16, what is in your mind is in your
NTI Lk 20v9-19.3-22, in an error of thought and
NTI Lk 22v7-38.11-28, one meaningless premise

Virgins - What does the parable of the ten virgins symbolize?
NTI Mt 25v1-13.2-12, do not look to the world for peace

Voice - What is the Voice of the Holy Spirit?
See Holy Spirit

voice - What is the voice of the ego?
See ego, *See* confusion

— W —

Want - Why should I ask myself what I want?
NTI 1Co 10v25-30.1-6, do you still seek that
NTI 1Co 10v31-33.1-2, let true desire be your guide
See also purpose

Way - What is the way to salvation or awakening?
NTI Jn 10v1-21.1-7, tune out all other voices
NTI Ac 13v16-25.2, the way of your true desire
NTI Col 2v20-23.1-4, silent remembering
NTI Col 3v15-17.1-8, practice your lessons in this way
NTI 2Ti 4v14-15.4-8, accept willingness and feel
NTI Heb 3v12-15.1-3, gratitude is the way as is resting
See also Heart
What does "I am the way and the truth and the life" mean?
NTI Jn 14v5-14.3, all reality is within me

Wedding - What does the parable of the wedding banquet represent?
NTI Mt 22v1-10.1-18, kingdom of Heaven is joining
NTI Lk 14v15-24.1-18, the Spirit of God is one

Welcome - How do I recognize my Father's welcome?
NTI Ac 16v16-40.11-23, given to you unconditionally
Will - What is the one Will of God?
NTI Jn 13v31-38.1-6, Love
NTI Jn 14v5-14.1, without an element of separateness
See also Love

Willingness - What is willingness?
NTI Lk 3v1-20.1-3, the calling within you
NTI Ga 3v15-18.5, one Light shared
NTI Ga 5v7-12.4-12, link to your Source
NTI Ga 5v13-15.1-5, is to know God
Compare to resistance
How does willingness help me awaken?
NTI Lk 19v11-27.1-11, is needed in order to receive
NTI Ac 10v30-33.1-4, you are the expression of pure
NTI Ro 9v25-33.1-20, be willing
NTI Ro 10v1-4.1-5, the power that sets you free is you
NTI Ro 10v5-13.1-4, you trust the strength
NTI Ro 12v17-21.1-9, symbol of the opening of the
NTI 1Co 3v5-9.1-4, according to your willingness you
NTI Gal 3v15-18.5-8, is one Light shared
NTI Gal 5v7-12.1-35, that is Love Alive
NTI Gal 6v1-5.1-31, process of forgiveness
NTI Gal 6v7-10.1-4, in communing with willingness
How can I increase my willingness?
NTI Lk 2v1-20.4-10, be grateful
NTI Lk 2v41-52.1-14, cannot be lost
NTI Lk 18v1-8.1-4, prayer is a practice that increases
NTI Gal 5v2-6.3-5, focus your willingness on

Wineskins - What is symbolized by the parable of new wine in wineskins?
NTI Mk 2v21-22.2-4, a newness that fills you
NTI Lk 5v33-39.1-11, old habits must be let go

Wish - What is the denied wish within the mind?
NTI Jn 12v20-28.5-9, for change within the Changeless
NTI Ro 1v18-32.1-8, a curiosity
NTI Ro 2v1-4.7-11, What if nothing was as it is
How do I let go of the wish that makes illusion?
NTI Ac 23v12-22.1-10, face it and let it go
NTI Ac 24v1-9.1-7, do not be afraid to face
NTI Ac 24v10-21.1-6, one thing you must remember

NTI Ac 24v22-27.1-6, until you are ready
NTI Ro 13v6-7.1-7, how you are to look at the world
NTI Ro 14v9-11.1-7, v13-18.1-9, let go of expression of

Wishing – Why is it helpful to let go of wishing?
NTI 1 Co 12v1-11.4-6, each wish signals a judgment
NTI 1Co 14v1-5.1-4, to believe that you are an illusion
NTI 2Co 2v1-4.2-4, you believe a different experience

Within - Why are we taught to seek within?
NTI Ac 12v1-19.16-21, the Holy Spirit is yours and is you

Wits - What does "keeping your wits about you" mean?
NTI Ac 28v1-10.1-5, remembering to listen to Me

Word of God - What is the Word of God?
NTI Heb 4v12-13.1-4, let go of your dreams
NTI 1Jn 1v1-4.1-6, that which you find is you
NTI Rev 22v20-21.1-5, all will come

World - What made (or makes) the world?
NTI Mt 27v1-10.8-12, used to hide guilt out of fear
NTI Lk 21v5-38.47, it is fear that makes
NTI Jn 8v42-47.1-4, the world of your design
NTI 1Co 13v8-12.1-3, reflection of your mind
NTI Gal 2v14.1-4, made by judgment
NTI 1Th 2v1-6.1-4, you are the maker
See also illusion
How do I overcome the world?
NTI Mt 23v23-24.5-6, letting go of those feelings
NTI Jn 16v17-33.3-7, open to the realization that
NTI Jn 19v38-42.1-7, let go of your acceptance of death
NTI Ro 8v28-30.4-13, look at the world
NTI Ro 8v31-39.1-7, decide you do not want them
NTI Ro 9v1-18.1-28, give your willingness
NTI Heb 11v30.1, v31.1, by faith
NTI 1Jn 5v1-5.1-5, no longer fooled by the images
NTI Rev 3v14-20.1-6, v21-22.1-4, shall be your banquet
How do I live in the world, but not be of the world?
NTI Mt 23v1-4.3-11, by doing all things for Me
NTI Mt 23v13-22.1-9, follow My guidance
NTI Mt 23v25-26.1-10, do it in peace
NTI Lk 20v20-26.1-6, do not deny your experience

NTI Lk 22v47-53.1-4, must not resist the crossing
NTI Lk 22v54-62.1-5, built of illusions believed
NTI Ac 20v13-24.6-11, the desire for self-will
NTI Ro 8v18-25.3-6, this is why you suffer
NTI 2Co 3v7-11.1-5, the evidence that the world is
NTI 2Co 3v12-18.1-3, that you are what you are not
NTI 2Co 4v1-6.1-4, veil of darkness
NTI 2Co 7v1.1-18, your feeling of guilt
NTI Col 3v1-4.1-9, v5-11.1-5, nothing in the world can
NTI Jas 4v4-6.6-9, teaches you that you are

Is the world an illusion like a dream in the mind is an illusion, or is it my perception of the world that is illusory?
NTI Ro 8v9-11.1-6, you must not be in the world
NTI Ro 8v12-17.1-11, world is a world of thought
NTI Ro 13v1-5.1-6, the world is an image in the mind
NTI Rev 17v9-11.4, the dream and its illusion

If the world is an illusion, why does it seem so real?
NTI Mt 21v20-22.1-5, the power of your faith
NTI Mk 9v14-32.16, do not underestimate the power
NTI Lk 21v5-38.47, it is your fear
NTI Rev 7v5-8.13-15, given it your belief
NTI Rev 12v7-9.1-2, experience while also denying

If the world is not real, does what I do in the world matter at all?
NTI Mt 17v24-27.1-8, it is love that we must give
See also Caesar

Am I guilty for desiring experiences in the world?
See desiring

How can I see the world differently?
See see

How do I let go of that which I value in the world?
See value

How does the world teach separation?
See separation

Worrying - How do I stop worrying?
NTI Jas 2v18-19.1-2, they struggle against the true desire
See also confusion

Worship - Why should I not worship a guru, enlightened teacher or religious system?
NTI Heb 13v11-14.1-5, only the truth endures forever
NTI Heb 13v15-16.1-4, God is not the thing that passes

Wrong - How do I know right from wrong?
See right

— X —

— Y —

Yeast - What does "a little yeast works through the whole batch of dough" symbolize?
NTI 1Co 5v6-8.1-2, be without the yeast of the world
NTI Gal 5v7-12.1-35, focus on your willingness

— Z —

BOOKS

SOME RECENT O BOOKS

The Heart of Tantric Sex

A sourcebook on the practice of tantric sex
Diana Richardson

How can we rediscover the joys of love and sex that grow rather than diminish over time?

After many years of exploration, ***Diana Richardson*** found that the ancient practice of Tantra, with its unique, intelligent approach to sex, had the effect of enhancing intimacy and deepening love. Here she has adapted Tantra for modern Western lovers in a practical, sympathetic way. Tantric Sex can transform your experience into a more sensual, loving and fulfilling one.

Easy-to-follow steps show you how to relax into sexual energy, increase your sensitivity and receptiveness, get closer to yourself and your lover, and make lasting love and sexual fulfillment a tangible reality, not an impossible dream. The book also contains black & white line drawings.

'One of the most revolutionary books on sexuality ever written.'
Ruth Ostrow - Sex, Relationship and Spirituality journalist, News Ltd.

1 903816 37

Take me To Truth

Undoing the Ego
Nouk Sanchez &Tomas Vieira
Foreword by Gary Renard

Take Me to Truth is the first book to boldly address the fundamental problem that all spiritual seekers face on the journey to awakening; the ego. As Gary Renard says in the Foreword... "despite the thousands of things we may appear to have to choose from in this world, there are really only two things, and only one of them is real." The ego is not. Most books today are still teaching how to find liberation within the dream. *Take Me to Truth* wakes us out of the dream. It stands alone, as an unprecedented approach to ego-relinquishment. It courageously unravels and demystifies the ego-release process and provides direct guidance on undoing the cause of all human suffering; our distorted belief system.

Take Me to Truth is a powerful six-stage navigational guide that takes us through the six remarkable stages of undoing ego. Each of these stages becomes an experience of deepening trust, eventually removing all existing blocks to the awareness of the Infinite Love that we are and have. It bridges the yawning gap that exists between seeking enlightenment and finding it.

Take Me To Truth *is not just a book - it's a revelation. Nouk Sanchez is a gifted spiritual teacher who knows what she is talking about and has a good idea of how to communicate her knowledge. The writing of Nouk and Tomas is uncompromising, exciting and strikingly consistent.* From the Foreword by **Gary R Renard,** author of *The Disappearance of the Universe; Your Immortal Reality, How to Break the Cycle of Birth and Death.*

978-1-84694-050-7

Ordinary Women, Extraordinary Wisdom

The Feminine Face of Awakening
Rita Marie Robinson

The Extraordinary Wisdom of Ordinary Women is a collection of intimate, heartfelt conversations with women spiritual teachers who live and look like ordinary people. They have kids, husbands, jobs, and bills to pay. What makes them extraordinary is that each woman has awakened to her true nature. And while that sounds like enlightenment, it doesn't look like the old stereotype of transcendence, detachment, and bliss. Quite the contrary. This is the feminine half of the spiritual journey—bringing it down to earth and embracing all of what it means to be human.

These real life stories show by practical example what it means to be fully awake and fully engaged, to meet the world without resistance—even and especially when it's not easy—whether it's death, divorce or illness. The invitation is explicit... "if these ordinary women can be fully awake and fully human, why not me, why not you? And why not now."

This will become a milestone in female spirituality, an inspiration for both men and women alike, also looking for the essence of who they truly are.
Paula Marvelly, author of *Teachers of One, Living Advaita*

978-1-84694-068-2

Back to the Truth

5000 years of Advaita
Dennis Waite

Advaita is a spiritual philosophy based on the Upanishads, older than most other religious systems we know about but also the most logical and scientific in its approach. The literal meaning is "Not two". There is only one truth - but, it has to be said, there are many teachers. So how is a "seeker" to choose between them?

This book is a systematic treatment of Advaita which demystifies it, differentiating between approaches and teachers, enabling you to decide which approach is most suitable for you. It compares the scriptures of traditional Advaita with the words of contemporary sages and neo-Advaita. Should we ignore the mind? Is the world real? Is there anything we can do to become "enlightened"? These questions and many more are addressed, with explanations given in their own words from those who discovered the truth. A massively comprehensive, definitive work.

A wonderful book. Encyclopedic in nature, and destined to become a classic. **James Braha (Author of "Living Reality: My Extraordinary Summer with 'Sailor' Bob Adamson")**

9781905047611

Bringing God Back to Earth

John Hunt

~ **Why aren't believers better people than non-believers?**
~ **Why are there so many religions?**
~ **Why did God wait till a couple of thousand years ago to send his son to Earth?**
~ **Is God bigger than any one religion?**
~ **How do we reconcile what we believe with what we know?**

Religion is an essential part of our humanity. We all follow some form of religion, in the original meaning of the word. But organised religion establishes definitions, boundaries and hierarchies which the founders would be amazed by. This is perhaps more true of Christianity than most other religions, due to the short life of Jesus, his sudden death, the lack of any contemporary records. His teaching about the kingdom of God is great; it could see us through our time on earth. But his followers watered it down and soon lost it altogether. It became a kingdom in heaven for the few, rather than one here and now for everyone. The Church, or Churches, that resulted became increasingly irrelevant, even a hindrance, to seeing it realised.

Many will always find security and truth in the traditions that developed, and good for them. But for those who can't, for those who have given up on religion or never thought it worth considering, the original teachings are worth another look. If we could recover them and live by them, we could change ourselves and the world for the better. We could bring God back to earth.

Knowledgeable in theology, philosophy, science and history. Time and again it is remarkable how he brings the important issues into relation with one another... thought provoking in almost every sentence, difficult to put down. **Faith and Freedom**

1 903816 81 5

The Ocean of Wisdom

5,000 pearls of poetry and wisdom
Alan Jacobs

The most comprehensive anthology of spiritual wisdom available

The first major anthology of this size and scope since 1935, *The Ocean of Wisdom* collects over five thousand pearls in poetry and prose, from the earliest of recorded history to modern times. Divided into 54 sections, ranging from Action to Zen, it draws on all faiths and traditions, from Zoroaster to existentialism. It covers the different ages of man, the stages of life, and is an ideal reference work and long term companion, a source of inspiration for the journey of life.

Frequently adopting a light touch it also makes a distinction between the Higher Wisdom, which consists of pointers leading to the understanding of philosophical and metaphysical truth, and practical wisdom, which consists of intelligent skills applicable to all fields of ordinary everyday life. So Germaine Greer and Hilary Rodham Clinton have their place alongside Aristotle and Sartre.

The carefully chosen quotations make this book the perfect bedside dipper, and will refresh the spirit of all who are willing to bathe in the ocean of the world's wisdom.

Over the last few years, Alan Jacobs has established himself as one of the world's leading exponents of nondualist philosophy, publishing a corpus of work dedicated to promoting the perennial wisdom of ancient and modern teachings from both the Western and Eastern continents. The Ocean of Wisdom is the culmination of his endeavours and is a compelling compendium of the world's profoundest truths as recorded by scholars, writers and poets from different ages and faiths. Moreover, Alan Jacobs has also included the words of those not normally associated with philosophy per se and yet who possess great insight into the ways of the world and the human psyche. Thus Socrates rubs shoulders with Margaret Thatcher; Confucius with Gary Lineker; Plato with Germaine Greer.

Divided in 54 sections, spanning subjects as diverse as Wisdom, Beauty and Justice as well as Sexuality, Women and Sport, The Ocean of Wisdom is a book you'll want to return to time and again for inspiration, instruction and above all, great wit. **Paula Marvelly**, five star Amazon review

1 905047 07 X

The Supreme Self
Swami Abhayananda

It is at once the dramatic personal story of one man's experience of revelation and a modern testament affirming the universal and perennial "philosophy of unity" expounded by the genuine mystics and seers of every religious tradition since time began.

In this profound spiritual autobiography, *Swami Abhayananda* takes us along on his solitary search and subsequent Self-realization, establishing the irrefutable fact of man's divine nature, and reaffirming the power of grace and devotion in the lives of those seeking "the vision of God", the liberating knowledge of one's own divine Self. Elevating and ennobling, this revelation of mystical vision will inspire generations, and stand alongside the great classics of mystical literature in the tradition of Plotinus, Eckhart, and Saint John of the Cross

A passionate, poetic and powerful work. Destined to be a classic.
Greg Bogart.

1 905047 45 2